STANLEY CAVELL
PHILOSOPHY'S RECOUNTING
OF THE ORDINARY

Stanley Cavell:
Philosophy's Recounting
of the Ordinary

STEPHEN MULHALL

CLARENDON PRESS · OXFORD

Oxford University Press, Great Clarendon Street, Oxford OX2 6DP
Oxford New York
Athens Auckland Bangkok Bogotá Buenos Aires Calcutta
Cape Town Chennai Dar es Salaam Delhi Florence Hong Kong Istanbul
Karachi Kuala Lumpur Madrid Melbourne Mexico City Mumbai
Nairobi Paris São Paulo Singapore Taipei Tokyo Toronto Warsaw
and associated companies in
Berlin Ibadan

Oxford is a registered trade mark of Oxford University Press

Published in the United States by
Oxford University Press Inc., New York

First published 1994
First issued as paperback 1998

British Library Cataloguing in Publication Data
Data available

Library of Congress Cataloging in Publication Data
Mulhall, Stephen, 1962- .
Stanley Cavell : philosophy's recounting of the ordinary / Stephen Mulhall.
Includes bibliographical references.
1. Cavell, Stanley, 1926- . 2. Philosophy, Modern—20th century.
3. Literature—Philosophy. 4. Psychoanalysis and
philosophy. 5. Motion pictures—Philosophy. I. Title.
B945.C274M85 1994 191—dc20 93-8410
ISBN 0-19-824074-0
ISBN 0-19-823850-9 (Pbk.)

Printed in Great Britain
on acid-free paper by
Bookcraft (Bath) Ltd,
Midsomer Norton, Somerset

For Cathleen, Shelagh,
Patrick, and Clare—
at last.

FOREWORD

An Audience for Cavell's Philosophy

If the chapters which follow do not make it clear why I believe that Cavell's philosophy deserves a wider and more appreciative audience than it has hitherto attained, then nothing I can say in introducing them will compensate for that failure. What does require some prefatory explanation, however, is why I believe that providing an exegetical account of his work is either a necessary or an appropriate means of bringing about that happy eventuality. That I feel it necessary implies an unwillingness or an inability to allow Cavell's words to earn or establish an audience by their own efforts—as if I doubted their capacity to attract others in the way that they have attracted me. That I feel it appropriate suggests a failure to comprehend the almost comic mismatch (of purpose, of style, of achievement) between Cavell's mannerly, idiosyncratic, intensely personal, and endlessly reflexive prose and the level, distanced tones of the exegete.

With respect to the second worry, I can only assure the reader that no one appreciates the risks that are being run more intensely than I do, and that they would not have been run at all had I not reached the conclusion that constitutes my response to the first worry. For it seems to me that there are strong reasons both external and internal to Cavell's own project that at present militate against the possibility of its receiving a just assessment on its philosophical merits; and the sole justification of this book's existence is the contribution it can make towards overturning the external obstacles and illuminating the true import of the internal ones. Its purpose, in other words, is not to attempt to do what can and must only be done by Cavell's own prose, but to clear the space that is required for it to do so.

The external obstacles are not difficult to identify: they relate to the directions in which Cavell's philosophical endeavours have driven him, and the precise nature of their initiating and governing methodological impulse. Cavell's work grows out of the tradition of ordinary language philosophy; and although it began by focusing on issues in aesthetics, ethics, politics, and philosophical methodology, the specific conclusions it generated led him to explore themes in literary criticism and literary theory, film studies, psychoanalysis, and the writings of Emerson and Thoreau. The overarching concern of this diverse body of work is scepticism: on Cavell's understanding of its nature, the sceptical impulse is to be understood not only as that with which and against which modern philosophy distinctively struggles, but also as a central presence in other projects, disciplines, and bodies of work (the Shakespearean corpus, Romanticism, psychoanalysis, and American Transcendental-ism). In other words, the later expansion of Cavell's range of reference indicates neither a diffusion of interests nor a search for illustrations of philosophical conclusions independently established, but an enactment of his distinctive understanding of the nature of modern philosophy and its location within a wider cultural framework.

However, recognition of the importance of Cavell's work has been relatively slow in coming; so it roughly coincided with the expansion of its scope. As a result, prevailing conceptions of his project tend to ignore his earlier, more orthodox contributions to philosophy, relating it primarily to other fields and assessing its significance there in ways which do not acknowledge its philosophical roots. The existing range of responses to Cavell's work (as manifest in the secondary literature) is thus limited in more than size. On the one hand, both those who have eagerly taken up his insights on literary topics and those who find them peculiarly galling have lacked the resources or the inclination to engage with their philosophical roots in any real depth, and so have often lacked a sense of their true import.[1] And on the other, philosophers have been presented with a double reason for drawing the conclusion that Cavell's work is impertinent to their concerns: first, because it appears to be focussed upon literature, film, and psychoanalysis rather than philosophy; and second, because in so far as it has a philosophical tone, it is derived from that of Austin and Wittgenstein, whose voices are barely audible in the exchanges which make up the present of analytical Anglo-American philosophy.

A key motivation behind the writing of this book is therefore to overcome the undeserved but deleterious consequences of the belated discovery and the unfashionable tone of Cavell's philosophy. By provid-ing a detailed and full-length study of the structure and development of his writings from a philosophical perspective, I aim to demonstrate the power and fertility of Cavell's particular inflexion of the Wittgenstein-

---

[1] Cf. the array of articles collected in *IIS* and R. Fleming and M. Payne (eds.), *The Senses of Stanley Cavell* (Lewisburg, Pa., 1989), or the limited focus of M. Fischer, *Stanley Cavell and Literary Skepticism* (Chicago, 1989).

ian tradition, the primarily philosophical impulse that governs every aspect of his intellectual project, and the internal logic behind the chronological trajectory and the interdisciplinary array of his intellectual interests. In so doing, of course, I attempt to make the strongest case possible on his behalf; but I do so in order to open up his work to genuine and informed critical response rather than to close off the possibility of a substantial intellectual critique. Indeed, in the final chapters—in which I discuss Cavell's own place in the wider cultural framework of modernity by locating its perfectionist liberal impulse against both secular and religious competitors—I hope to contribute to just such a critique; but a pre-condition for the worth of such a response is that it be based upon an accurate conception of its target.

So much for external obstacles; but what of the internal obstacles mentioned earlier? Here, my use of the concept of internality is meant to capture a sense that the difficulties Cavell's writings have faced in establishing an audience for themselves within the Anglo-American philosophical community are ones which the nature of the project they subserve makes unavoidable—indeed, that they are sometimes ones which they deliberately create and maintain. In the first place, as we have already seen, Cavell identifies himself with the tradition of ordinary language philosophy as established by Austin and Wittgenstein; but he understands as well as anyone that this tradition's relation with orthodox analytical philosophy is essentially subversive, a relation in which the guiding assumptions of that mainstream's self-understanding are placed under radical questioning, and so one which those in the mainstream are likely to mishear or repress. As Cavell himself puts it:

my ... obligation has seemed more specifically to be that of keeping lines open to the events within American academic philosophical life that we can call the reception of ordinary language philosophy (... represented here primarily by some work of J. L. Austin's) together with that of Wittgenstein's *Investigations*, as if certain paths for philosophy, opened by those events, are always in danger of falling into obscurity. (*CR*, p. xiv)

At the same time, however, Cavell also identifies himself with the task of linking the Anglo-American and the Continental traditions in philosophy: their separation is by now well documented, but is experienced by Cavell as a splitting of the two halves of his (philosophical) mind—an experience to which the possessor of an *American* philosophical mind, one whose history is formed from the immigration and intermingling of both traditions, is perhaps particularly open—and so as something to be overcome.

When I first read ... Emerson['s] ... saying 'broad noon shall be my England of
the senses and the understanding; the night shall be my Germany of mystic
philosophy and dreams', I felt I had at once a determination of the goal of my
private life, the putting together of day and night, of body and soul; and a
determination of a task of philosophy, the placing in the same daily cycle of
England and of Germany, a task I felt the perspective of America made both
possible and necessary. Something like the healing of the rift between the
English and the German traditions of philosophy—or failing that, the witnessing
of it—has also been a motive of my writing from its earliest to its latest
installments. (*SW* 149)

Putting together these two self-identifications, it should be obvious that
Cavell's philosophical writing will necessarily be doubly liable to the
accusation that it is not philosophical at all. However, it invites that
accusation not (or not merely) in order to offend or scandalize Anglo-
American philosophers but in order to allow them to question their
own conception of the subject, to put their present understanding of
philosophy to the test. And so it must invite such a dismissal whilst not
in fact offering any grounds on which it might be justified: in other
words, according to Cavell's understanding of the matter, whilst his
writing is designed to place the self-understanding of mainstream
analytical philosophy in question, it is also designed to maintain its
links with that mainstream. His Wittgensteinian and Continental
questioning must—if it is to retain the title 'philosophical'—itself be
recognizable by those questioned as pertinent to the concerns and presuppositions of their approach: after all, talk of keeping lines open and
of realigning two traditions implies the possibility of two-way traffic.
Whether or not Cavell's work succeeds in achieving this delicate
balance, in striking a tone of radical yet undismissible criticism, can
only be seen in the sequel; but, once again, a correct evaluation of
its success presupposes an accurate conception of what it is aiming to
accomplish.

If it is important to see that Cavell's philosophical writing involves
an attempt to acknowledge the competing demands of three interacting
conceptions of philosophy, it is also vital to note that he takes his self-
appointed task—that of producing philosophy in the late twentieth
century—to involve him inextricably in the particular problematic of
modernism. What he takes that problematic to be is spelt out in his
early writings primarily (but not exclusively) with respect to recent
developments in certain artistic traditions, particularly painting and
music. 'The essential fact of (what I refer to as) the modern lies in the

relation between the present practice of an enterprise and the history of that enterprise, in the fact that this relation has become problematic' (*MWM*, p. xix).

The difficulty of this relation between the present and the past takes the form of an inability to rely upon or take for granted the defining or governing conventions bequeathed by the past of one's practice. This has been an obvious and central recent development in the fields of painting, music, and literature; and it has very precise characteristics. First, it places the present of the enterprise in as much doubt or uncertainty as its past: for if one can no longer rely upon the validity of inherited conventions, it is not clear how one is to engage in the enterprise any longer. Second, in so far as one does so engage, the question of that enterprise's continued existence and so of its nature will be at the heart of one's endeavour: in other words, any practice in the condition of modernism becomes its own subject, as if its immediate task is to establish and maintain its own existence. And third, it is vital to see that the relation of the present and the past of such a practice remains a question for those engaged in it; to be unable to rely upon past conventions would not be a problem if as a result of this perception one were willing or able entirely to dismiss their significance or relevance. Such dismissals are, of course, possible, but they result in work that Cavell categorizes as modernizing rather than modernist; those bent merely on newness do not have the past as a problem, do not see the need to make one's present effort become a part of the present history of the enterprise to which one has committed one's mind.

Appreciating that this is the condition in which Cavell understands philosophy to be should help to account for several important but puzzling (and so potentially off-putting) aspects of his own writing. It explains, for example, the fact that the question of the nature of philosophy is so central and pervasive a presence in his work; and why both these remarks and the seemingly autobiographical accounts of his personal experience of the motivation towards philosophy (for example, a sense of its periodic oscillations between inescapability and irrelevance, of its capacity to go dead for its practitioners) are for him no less philosophical than remarks about art or politics or morality. It explains why Cavell is so concerned with the question of the authority of philosophy, and so of his own philosophy; his continually reiterated anxieties about his own right to contribute to this enterprise, to regard those contributions as anything other than expressions of a personal point of view, are tied up with his perception that philosophers cannot authorize their own remarks by reference to an agreed-upon set of conventions or standards. It also begins to explain a feature of his writing which has become increasingly prominent over time, a feature one might call its 'lack of momentum'—a sense that there is no necessity to continue beyond the end of any given sentence, that each sentence is being tested not only for its contribution to a larger project but for its right to be deemed 'philosophical', for its right to claim to be a contribution to the present of an enterprise with such a tangled and problematic history. These often-noted features of Cavell's prose are therefore not to be seen as purely idiosyncratic stylistic tics, but as manifestations of his conception of the cultural situation in which philosophy finds itself.

Introducing the concept of modernism is also important if we are to gain some initial perspective upon the criticism that is most commonly levelled at Cavell's writing and cited as a ground for refusing to attend to the work it is attempting to do—its self-indulgence. The prevalence of this criticism and the virulence with which it is pressed home have been mapped elsewhere;[2] and this is clearly the point at which Cavell's work causes most offence. His use of elaborate parentheses, fine-grained distinctions and qualifications, and ornate rhetorical strategies (the opening paragraph of *The Claim of Reason*, which consists of two sentences, one of which is two hundred words long, seems to be the most favoured example) has suggested a simultaneous obsession with style and self that leads many intelligent philosophers to stop reading. In part, of course, such mannerliness is an expression of Cavell's interest (identified earlier) in questioning the boundary between philosophy and literature; his claim is not that there is no such boundary but that we do not understand what it is, and his prose is an enactment of his desire to explore what might be at stake in this question. However, if we keep in mind the condition of modernism as Cavell identifies it, another set of reasons for these features of his prose emerges. For an inevitable consequence of a practice's inability to take for granted its inherited conventions means that both practitioners and audience have no agreed, objective standards by reference to which to determine either the real value of a given work of art or whether it is a work of art at all.

---

[2] See Fischer, *Stanley Cavell and Literary Skepticism*, 144 n. 6.

... we can no longer be sure that any artist is sincere—we haven't convention or technique or appeal to go on any longer: *anyone* could fake it. And this means that modern art, if and where it exists, *forces* the issue of sincerity, depriving the artist and his audience of every measure except absolute attention to one's experience and absolute honesty in expressing it ... and of course it runs its own risks of failure, as art within established traditions does. (*MWM* 211)

In other words, the possibility and the experience of fraudulence will be endemic to the experience of the product of any practice in the condition of modernism. If, in the absence of agreed conventions that determine whether or not something counts as a work of art (even if only a bad one), a work is produced which claims to be art—to exemplify the present of the relevant tradition or practice—it must validate that claim purely from its own resources; or, to put it the other way around, the perceiver must decide whether or not the object itself deserves the title of a work of art purely on the basis of her encounter with the object itself. The fact that it is accepted by the public as art is not proof of its genuineness; the artist herself may not know; and any given critic may be shown up as an incompetent or an impostor. So each individual is left facing each individual object, not knowing whether she may have missed its tone or neglected an allusion, or whether the object had not established its tone or had buried its allusion too deep. Often it is not clear who is on trial, the object or the viewer; so all the viewer can do is trust the object, spend time with its difficulties despite the fact that this investment may be betrayed, because only thus can its full impact be properly assessed.

If we apply these remarks to Cavell's own philosophical practice, then several points stand out. First, it will seem the very reverse of surprising that his writing should elicit accusations of fraudulence and self-indulgence: indeed, their prevalence in fact confirms Cavell's own hypothesis about the situation in which he finds himself—namely, that it is one in which the issue of sincerity (and so of insincerity) must be forced. Second, acknowledging this last point does not amount to undermining the power of such accusations: the fact that the condition of a practice is such that its practitioners run the risk of fraudulence and self-indulgence does not transform their failure to avoid such a fate into a success. None the less (and third), these points should give Cavell's critics pause: for they imply a very different understanding of the nature and import of those critical judgements than might be held by those making them. More precisely, they imply that such judgements have no authority for or over any other potential reader—that they are at best the honest expression of the critic's own experience of Cavell's prose rather than the articulation of an impersonal, disciplinary condemnation of it; and when this is realized, the possibility arises that their personal impression was derived too hastily, that it was the result of insufficient attention to the prose and their experience of it, that it might in fact amount to a judgement upon their own failures of trust and sincerity rather than an assessment of Cavell's professional or personal inadequacies. In short, seen against the background of modernism, those making such critical judgements have an obligation at least to reconsider the true nature of their position—to ask whether Cavell's text has betrayed them or they it.

Once again, that question can only be given an answer by returning to those texts to make a personal assessment; but even if that assessment goes Cavell's way—even if a given reader's conclusion is that Cavell has avoided the traps of fraudulence and betrayal of trust—it may be worth spelling out exactly what Cavell himself takes success in this situation to amount to. It is something that he outlines at some length with respect to the practice of contemporary music:

Convention as a whole is now looked upon not as a firm inheritance from the past but as a continuing improvisation in the face of problems we no longer understand. Nothing we now have to say, no *personal* utterance, has its meaning conveyed in the conventions and formulas we now share. In a time of slogans, sponsored messages, ideologies, psychological warfare, mass projects, where words have lost touch with their sources or objects, and in a phonographic culture where music is for dreaming, or for kissing, or for taking a shower, or for having your teeth drilled, our choices seem to be those of silence, or nihilism (the denial of shared meaning altogether), or statements so personal as to form the possibility of communication without the support of convention—perhaps to become the source of new convention. And then, of course, they are most likely to fail even to seem to communicate. (*MWM* 201–2)

Transposing these remarks to the context of philosophy, I think we can say that Cavell's aim is to create a set of texts, to establish and maintain a texture of prose, that can earn the title of philosophy from its readers. Produced in a cultural context in which the conventions determining what does and does not count as a work of philosophy can no longer be taken for granted—in which Cavell thinks of himself as struggling to inherit three linked but disparate paradigms of the philosophical enterprise, to remain true to their underlying spirit by questioning rather than merely replicating their most basic assumptions—his writings aspire to establish a new set of conventions for philosophy, a new mode of recognizably philosophical endeavour. Just as a Caro steel sculpture aims to convince its viewers that this too—an installation of discontinuous, unworked pieces of coloured metal lacking a base or plinth—is sculpture, so the goal of Cavell's prose is to elicit from its readers the startled acknowledgement that this too—this mannerly prose, with its foregrounding of rhetoric and self and its reflexive obsession with its own status—is a way of doing philosophy. Not the only way, of course; but a way that has as much right to invoke the term 'philosophy', with all its historical and cultural baggage, as anything else available in the academic and non-academic world.

If it is important to note that Cavell's practice is an attempt to construct a viable set of conventions within which useful philosophical work can be done, it is also worth emphasizing how he imagines that process of construction coming about. For these new conventions are established by articulating and elaborating what might seem at first to be essentially private and personal insights but which offer the hope of grounding a community (at least a community of two). This vision of an uncoerced community, a coexistence of self and society, is one that will emerge in the following chapters as the result of a line of argument which does not at all depend upon accepting Cavell's characterization or location of the modernist problematic in philosophy. It may, however, help the reader not only to have advance notice of this shaping theme, but also to appreciate two significant consequences of it. First, the person engaged in constructing the new conventions can only do so by foregrounding himself or herself; lacking the support of existing impersonal convention, communication (and so the possibility of establishing new conventions) requires the articulation of inherently personal statements. And second, acceptance of those statements as the possible ground for new conventions and so a new community is also an ineluctably personal matter: if no agreed-upon conventions can determine whether or not a new set of conventions counts as a mode of doing philosophy, each individual reader must rely solely upon the conviction (or lack of it) that Cavell's prose, in all its idiosyncratic rigour, can elicit, and no such reader can rely upon any other reader's agreement. In this sense, as Cavell specifies with respect to Wittgenstein's writings, a modernist work is, logically speaking, esoteric:

That is, such works seek to split their audience into insiders and outsiders (and split each member of it); hence they create the particular unpleasantness of cults (at best as a specific against the particular unpleasantness of indifference or intellectual promiscuousness, combatting partialness by partiality); hence demand for their sincere reception the shock of conversion. If I say that the basis of the present publication is that Wittgenstein's thought is still to be received, I mean to suggest that his work, and of course not his alone, is essentially and always *to be* received, as thoughts must be that would refuse professionalization. (*CR*, pp. xvi–xvii)

It seems to me just a fact about the reception of Cavell's work thus far that it divides its audience in exactly the way specified above—into those who have experienced conversion and those who see only the enthusiasm of a cult where the rigorous application of professional standards ought to be. What those on the outside should realize is that the enthusiasm of those on the inside derives in part from their belief that Cavell's texts do live up to (a recognizable variant or revised set of) professional standards; to demonstrate the grounds for this belief is one of this book's main purposes. But those on the inside should realize that the attitude of those on the outside is one that they too can (and perhaps must) sometimes adopt—that the oscillation between inevitability and irrelevance to which Cavell often alludes when discussing philosophical motivation generally is one which he deliberately works to elicit within each of his readers. Once more, the deepest reasons for this desire to create an internal split in each member of his audience will emerge only towards the end of this book; but it is important to be clear from the outset that to deny or repress that split is to fail to allow Cavell's prose to do the work it is designed to do.

To conclude: it might be best to think of this Foreword as an attempt to make initially plausible the possibility that many of the obstacles in the way of establishing an audience for Cavell's philosophy—of recognizing it as philosophy at all—are not only internal to the nature of his particular project (and therefore unavoidable but not necessarily insuperable) but are also central topics within it and so fundamental to Cavell's self-understanding. In other words, and to a degree that is both exhilarating and threatening, his readers are likely to find that the difficulties they most often encounter in gaining access to Cavell's thought are something that he has already identified and explored within it. This not only implies that experiencing those difficulties should be regarded more as a reason for going further into that thought than for staying outside it; it also demonstrates that, even at this seemingly external level, Cavell's work is capable of revealing that what might seem like purely personal and contingent matters are in fact the topics of a potentially fruitful interpersonal philosophical debate—to find, in other words, that our understanding of the divisions between the personal and the philosophical, and between the personal and the social, is less reliable than we might have thought. Since these questions are precisely the ones to which most attention is devoted in this book, I hope that this Foreword will be enough to persuade those who have experienced acute difficulties of this sort with Cavell's work to suspend their disbelief at least until the book's end—at which point the option of re-encountering Cavell's own prose may have come to seem a more attractive one.

ACKNOWLEDGEMENTS

Several institutions and individuals were instrumental in the successful completion of this study. A first draft was written during the last years of my tenure of a Prize Fellowship at All Souls College, Oxford; and I find it difficult to imagine that embarking on a project of this size would have seemed feasible without the time for thought and research, as well as the scholarly and secretarial resources, that the College provides for its Fellows. Here, once again, I would like to thank Deborah McGovern, the Visiting Fellows' Secretary, for her guidance and patience. That first draft was brought to its present state in the first months after my arrival at the University of Essex; and the intellectual environment provided by my new colleagues made my task easier and more stimulating. In particular, I would like to thank Jay Bernstein, for reading through and offering detailed comments on the whole manuscript, and Karen Shields and Barbara Crawshaw, who worked miracles in producing readable text from my confused and confusing files, style sheets, and floppy disks. Many other people made particularly important contributions along the way. Adam Swift placed a copy of *The Claim of Reason* in my hand when I visited him at Harvard in 1983, at a time when I hadn't even heard of Stanley Cavell; little did he know … Peter Hacker suppressed his considerable qualms about the project in order to offer me a set of penetrating comments on early drafts of the early chapters. Philip Wheatley formed the other half of a two-person reading group on Cavell's writings for several months at a pivotal stage of my project, and has been consistently supportive in many other ways. A version of material from Chapters 2 and 11 has appeared in the *Journal of Political Philosophy* (1993), under the title 'Perfectionism, Politics and the Social Contract: Rawls and Cavell on Justice'; I benefited greatly from the comments of its editor and two anonymous referees. In the final months of work on the text, I attended and delivered a paper at a conference on Cavell's philosophy held at the University of Warwick in March 1992; there I experienced the stimulating criticisms and the infectious enthusiasm of Gillian Rose and James Conant, and there I was fortunate enough to meet and talk to Stanley Cavell himself. Since that encounter, he has sent me unpublished material, answered my questions, and offered generous encouragement without at any time attempting to influence or alter the lines of my interpretation of his work. I hope that this book can stand as a partial acknowledgement of the illustriousness of his example. Finally, I would like to thank Alison Baker, who had much to put up with during the gestation of this project, and who did so with her usual grace and good humour.

CONTENTS

ABBREVIATIONS

Introduction

On Saying What We Mean

The opening, eponymous essay of Cavell's first published book *Must We Mean What We Say?* takes the form of a reply to some criticisms of the methods of ordinary language philosophy levelled by Benson Mates. These criticisms might now seem not to deserve the detailed attention Cavell devotes to them (the essay, first published in 1957, is some forty-three pages long), since philosophers are now more familiar both with the method they assail and with more sophisticated ways of assailing it. However, Cavell's particular way of marshalling and developing a response remains largely unfamiliar; and since he thereby sets out a version of or gloss upon the procedures of ordinary language philosophy that underpins everything else he has written—not just in the sense that his work exemplifies those procedures, but also in the sense that the question of their form and their foundations constitutes his main subject-matter—anyone interested in tracing out the general contours of Cavell's writings must begin by providing an interpretation of that essay, a gloss upon that gloss.

As both Mates and Cavell agree, philosophers who proceed by reference to ordinary language think it sufficient to terminate (or at least pertinent to the continuance of) a philosophical debate to point out that their interlocutor is employing words in a non-standard way—in short, misusing them. Pointing out this alleged misuse will typically involve either citing an *instance* of what is ordinarily said ('We say ... but we don't say ... '), or offering an *explication* of what is implied or meant when we utter sentences of the first type ('When we say ... we imply ...'; 'We don't say ... unless we mean ...'). The example which Mates and Cavell concentrate upon is a claim of the second sort made by Ryle, namely, 'When we say "The boy was responsible for (some action)", we imply that the action was an offence, one that ought not to have been done, one that was his fault'; together with an instance of the first sort offered by Austin, namely, 'We say "The gift was made voluntarily"', an instance which seems to conflict with Ryle's explication because we know that when we say 'The gift was made voluntarily' we do *not* imply that the action of making the gift was one which ought not to be done, or was someone's fault. The proximate cause of the dispute between Mates and Cavell is the difference in their reactions to such a conflict between practitioners of the same philosophical method.

Mates's response is clear: the disagreement between Ryle and Austin is symptomatic of the shallowness of their method. All that we have here is two professors of philosophy each claiming that the way he speaks is the right way to speak, and that what he intuits about the English language is true of it; it hardly seems to be a dispute which further discussion will settle. Moreover, not only do these professors fail to see that the only sensible way of *finding out* what is ordinarily said when is to make an empirical survey of the linguistic habits of a representative sample of English speakers; they also fail to make it clear *why* we should be at all concerned with what is ordinarily said when in the first place, why a philosophical investigation should respect such constraints when in search of answers to its problems. Cavell disagrees with both of Mates's criticisms, and spends the remainder of his essay attempting to explain why.

Speaking for Ourselves, Speaking for Others

For Cavell, the dispute between Ryle and Austin is an instance of one practitioner of a given method qualifying the claim of another on the basis of considerations which that other is bound to recognize as pertinent; and as such, it no more invalidates the method as a whole than one scientist's correction of a fellow scientist's hypothesis on the basis of scientifically pertinent considerations invalidates the practice of science. What Austin's counter-example shows is that Ryle, who was rightly suspicious of philosophers' attempts to apply the term 'voluntary' to any action which is not involuntary, wrongly specified the circumstances in which the application of that term is legitimate. Ryle took those circumstances to be ones in which there was something *morally* fishy about the action at issue, whereas Austin identifies them as ones in which the action is fishy in any one of a variety of ways. Both agree that a wide range of actions cannot intelligibly be described either as voluntary or as involuntary; this resistance to such modification, the fact that such actions cannot be said to go on in any special or specific way, is part of what makes them *normal* actions. Austin therefore agrees with Ryle that the question whether an action is voluntary or not only arises when that action is in some way unusual or extraordinary or untoward; but, as his example of the voluntarily made gift shows, that untowardness need not be a matter of moral fishiness. Giving one's milkman a Christmas gift of £5,000 is an unusual action, and so the question whether it was a voluntary one may intelligibly be raised; but it is not an action which is in any way *morally* awry—it is not something that one ought not to have done, something about which one is necessarily at fault.

In short, the disagreement between Ryle and Austin can quickly be settled in Austin's favour by invoking considerations (i.e. conflicting instances) which Ryle must see to be grounds for discarding his proposed explication of 'voluntary', since any such explication is itself based solely upon those sorts of consideration. However, even if there is no reason to believe that the dispute between the two professors is futile because irresoluble, this interpretation of that dispute so far leaves untouched the main thrust of Mates's criticism. For how can we claim to come to a conclusion about the respective merits of the opposing positions purely on the basis of our own intuitions about the right way to speak? Doesn't this merely reproduce the professors' original failure to back up their (possibly idiosyncratic) intuitions about linguistic rectitude with the hard evidence of a linguistic survey? Such a criticism assumes that neither Ryle nor Austin nor Cavell is entitled to produce instances of what is ordinarily said when in the absence of experimental studies confirming their occurrence in the language. But this assumption ignores the fact that the person producing the instance of what is said in English is himself a native speaker of English; and such speakers do not in general require *evidence* for what is said in the language—rather, they are the *source* of that evidence. To answer some kinds of specific questions (e.g. ones concerning the history of the language or a special form in the morphology of one of its dialects), such speakers may need to count noses; but in general, to tell what is and is not English the native speaker can rely on her own nose—after all, if she could not, there would be no corpus of utterances upon which the descriptive grammarian might base the construction of a grammar for the language. There is no reliance upon intuition or memory here; a normal person may forget or remember the meaning of certain words in her language, but she does not forget or remember *the language.* A native speaker is not someone who knows her language fairly well, in the sense in which a native English speaker might know German fairly well; and she stands in no need of empirical surveys in order to state what is ordinarily said when. 'All that is needed is the truth of the proposition that a natural language is what native speakers of that language speak' (*MWM 5*).

Cavell expands upon these remarks in the second essay of this collection in a way which helps to clarify their force. In 'The Availability of Wittgenstein's Later Philosophy', he points out that the knowledge upon which an ordinary language philosopher is drawing is no more mysterious, and no less firmly grounded, than that upon which the logician draws when deciding to transcribe 'Nobody is in the auditorium' differently from 'Peabody is in the auditorium'. It is obvious to her that we do not want the same sorts of inference to be drawn from the first as from the second; but how does she know that? However she knows it, that is how Austin knows that we only say of an action that it is voluntary when there seems to be something fishy about it. Possession of this capacity, this knowledge, is simply part of what it is to be a native speaker of the language.

But what kind of knowledge is this? The short answer Cavell offers is: self-knowledge.

If it is accepted that 'a language' (a natural language) is what the native speakers of a language speak, and that speaking a language is a matter of practical mastery, then such questions as 'What should we say if . . .?' or 'In what circumstances would we call . . .?' asked of someone who has mastered the language (for example, oneself) is a request for the person to say something about himself, describe what he does. So the different methods [of eliciting answers to such questions] are methods of acquiring self-knowledge . . . (*MWM 66*)

This answer may, however, seem not only short but also a little quick. For even if we accept that the ability to speak (of which the ability to give answers to such questions is an aspect) is a species of practical mastery, we may balk at describing the knowledge thereby deployed as a species of *self*-knowledge; for the latter term usually applies to such phenomena as a person's awareness of her character, an acquaintance with the state of her particular heart and soul. The worry may become clearer if we take an analogous case: if we asked a carpenter what she would do when constructing a table from mature pine wood, she would deploy her practical mastery of her craft in answering; but we would naturally think of this not as her telling us something about herself (i.e. not as her telling us what *she*—as opposed to anyone else—does) but as her telling us something about her craft (i.e. telling us what she—and any other carpenter—*does*). In short, it seems to be a matter of invoking knowledge rather than self-knowledge, something objective or impersonal rather than personal.

This worry touches on an issue that is at the heart of Cavell's understanding of the method of ordinary language philosophy; for the claim that the knowledge this method draws upon is a species of self-knowledge, something essentially personal, is the first manifestation of a theme that comes to dominate the later development of his thought. In those later contexts, as we shall see, Cavell elaborates and defends his position in a very detailed way, but he does not do so in this early essay. Accordingly, it may appear best simply to acknowledge the force of this objection at this point and defer the question of its true import until later. None the less, given the centrality of this theme to Cavell's overall project, it seems to me to be worth while to attempt to provide at least the outline of a defence that might be mounted on his behalf even at this point. Regardless of the outcome of this attempt, however, it ought to be borne in mind that the very provocativeness of Cavell's reading of this aspect of ordinary language philosophy indicates the degree to which his appropriation of this philosophical method is by no means a simple reiteration of orthodox understandings of it.

To begin our defence with some speculation: a closer examination of the carpentry analogy that was used to illustrate the difficulty Cavell faces can in fact give us an initial reason for questioning its force. For in order to claim that the carpenter's responses are essentially impersonal, one must be assuming that the capacity they manifest is essentially impersonal—detachable from the person of the carpenter; one must, in other words, think of her expertise as expressible in a body of theoretical rules which anyone may in principle grasp and deploy—so that the authority of our carpenter's words and deeds rests not upon anything specific to her but upon what she knows. But such a picture is at the very least controversial: is the authority of a master carpenter solely based on her possession of expertise expressible in an abstract set of principles, or is it also (and perhaps more fundamentally) based on her capacity to exercise right judgement from case to case in a manner that cannot be captured by or reduced to routines? The manner in which such practical skills are traditionally taught—by a process of apprenticeship in which the student absorbs the example of the master's practice in a wide variety of circumstances rather than studying textbooks—suggests that the latter picture is more realistic, i.e. that the practice rests in the last analysis on the specific responses of particular people rather than on a body of abstract principles. In other words, if we understand such practical abilities as a matter of 'know-how' rather than 'knowledge of', the claim that when the master carpenter exercises her practical mastery she displays an aspect of her self—that the authority of her testimony and practice is as much dependent upon who she is as upon something (independently specifiable and universally accessible) that she knows—may seem less implausible. So, even if invoking 'know-how' does not bring Cavell's concerns fully into the ordinary ambit of the concept of self-knowledge, it does offer a way of understanding practical abilities that makes it at least difficult to avoid making reference to the concept of the self.

However, the claim that a native speaker's practical mastery of *words* displays an impersonal knowledge of language rather than knowledge of self may seem to be immune to any version of the counter-argument just deployed with respect to carpentry. For that counter-argument involves the idea of an expert or master of the craft—a person specially endowed with a talent which may not be possessed to an equal degree by her apprentices, which certainly is not possessed by most people, and which therefore makes plausible the idea that her expertise may not be expressible or transmissible in impersonal form; and the idea of such an unequal distribution of talent is not easily transferable to the domain of language, in which everyone seems to be on an equal footing with everyone else—at least with respect to acquiring and deploying the capacity to make the types of claim upon which ordinary language philosophy is built. It does not take a 'master speaker' to see that 'Peabody is in the auditorium' and 'Nobody is in the auditorium' have a different logical structure, or to see that an action need not be *morally* awry if the question of whether it was voluntary is to be raised; access to such insights is simply part of what it is to be a competent speaker, and most human beings are capable of acquiring that competence. Cavell would not deny this disanalogy; but he would argue that it does not license the idea that linguistic competence is essentially impersonal in the sense to which he objects. For even if we accept that the capacity to become competent speakers is universally distributed rather than unique or rare (and so impersonal in one sense), it does not follow that the basis or ground of that competence is essentially impersonal—that it is a system of precisely defined and wholly transparent linguistic principles, a body of objective linguistic expertise which ultimately authorizes any claim one might make concerning what is said when. It is this notion of impersonality that Cavell wishes to oppose when he talks of linguistic competence as a species of self-knowledge; for on his view, it misrepresents the way in which the capacity for speech is ultimately based on the speaker's self-reliance. He spells out his reasons for rejecting the impersonal model more fully in an excursive chapter of *The Claim of Reason*,[1] in which he argues that to think of the capacity to speak as based on abstract rules or principles is to make words both less flexible and less inflexible than they really are.

Less flexible, because the notion of an underlying justificatory rule or principle governing the use of a word would be unable to accommodate the *way* in which words allow of being projected into a wide range of new contexts. To take just one example: we learn to 'feed the cat' and to 'feed the lions', and then, when someone talks of feeding the meter or feeding the film into the camera or feeding our pride, we understand them; we accept the projection of this word into those new contexts. When introduced so bluntly, such projections may seem surprising, but according to Cavell they are not dismissible as merely optional or metaphorical extensions of a word's range of employment: rather, he argues that tolerating such projections is of the essence of words. It is, of course, true that we were not forced to project this particular word in this particular way: we could have used other words for these new contexts, either by projecting another established word or by inventing a new one. However, if we adopted the first of those two strategies, we would thereby lose a way of speaking which allowed us to make certain discriminations: if, for example, we talked of 'putting' film in the camera and 'putting' money in the meter as we do of putting a lens on the camera or a dial on the meter, our way of speaking would fail to distinguish between putting a flow of material into a machine and putting a part made of some new material on a machine. We would also begin to deprive ourselves of certain of our concepts: for the idea that pride can be fed is no more metaphorical than the idea that it can grow—someone ignorant of either connection (e.g. someone who did not appreciate that emotions can be nourished or starved, tamed or allowed to grow wild, stunted in some environments and helped to flourish in others) would be ignorant of something essential to our concept of the emotions. And such a strategy would of course commit us to an extension of the legitimate range of that other word, thus leaving us exactly where we started: for if we talked instead of 'putting money in the meter', we would have projected a connection between that new context and the old ones relating to such phrases as 'put the

---

[1] *CR*, ch. 7, 'An Excursus on Wittgenstein's Vision of Language'.

cup on the saucer', 'put your hands over your head', and 'put out the light, and then put out the light'.

The second strategy, taking the option of inventing a new word for new contexts, would not be any more successful. For in so doing, we would lose a way of making or registering new connections (if we talked of 'foding the meter', it could not capture our sense of the connections between living beings and machines or emotions), open up a question about the legitimate projections of this new word (could we or would we fod a 'Speak your Weight' machine?), and would at the limit deprive all words of any meaning (for every context differs in some respect from every other, and will accordingly require a different word, so that no word would be employed more than once, i.e. no word would have a use, a meaning). So, such projections of the word 'feed' as the ones mentioned do indeed uncover or display aspects of its meaning, and exemplify an essential feature of linguistic meaning in general; but it is difficult to believe that any rule formulation which might be hypothesized to underlie the initial range of our uses of that word could also have allowed in advance for these (and further) projections of it.

Similarly, no such rule could accommodate the ways in which what counts as a legitimate projection is deeply controlled. For although words must allow of projection, not just any projection will be acceptable. We can feed a lion, but we cannot feed a lion by placing a bushel of carrots in its cage; and its failure to eat them cannot count as a refusal to do so. The words 'feed' and 'refusal' are intolerant of being projected into such contexts, because certain key connections which exist between these words and other words in their normal contexts do not transfer to the new one—to talk of the lion 'refusing' to eat the carrots would imply a connection between that creature's behaviour and the behaviour of other creatures in other contexts which we count as 'refusing to mate' or 'refusing to obey'. Once again, these limits are not arbitrary or optional: if someone does not perceive that when the lion fails to eat the carrots it is not refusing to eat them—if she does not perceive that such a projection is illegitimate— she would lack a full grasp of the meaning of the word 'refuse'. But the precise shape and extent of such limits in every new context is not (and could not possibly be) capturable in advance in an algorithmic rule-formulation.

Cavell summarizes his vision of language, and of human life with language, as follows:

I am trying to bring out, and keep in balance, two fundamental facts about human forms of life, and about the concepts formed in those forms: that any form of life and every concept integral to it has an indefinite number or instances and directions of projection; and that this variation is not arbitrary. *Both* the 'outer' variance and the 'inner' constancy are necessary if a concept is to accomplish its tasks—of meaning, understanding, communicating, etc., and in general, guiding us through the world, and relating thought and action and feeling to the world. (*CR* 185)

But if impersonal algorithms could not conceivably capture the simultaneous stability and tolerance of the meanings of words, then our capacity to understand those meanings—to accept and engage in the simultaneously flexible and inflexible practices of their projection—cannot be based upon a grasp of such algorithms. More specifically, it follows that the knowledge a native speaker draws upon when answering questions about what is said when cannot be thought of as a body of such principles, and her authority for making such pronouncements cannot be something that she derives from such principles. Anyone who thinks the reverse has in effect got things precisely the wrong way around: a native speaker's utterances are the corpus on the basis of which (descriptive and prescriptive) grammars and rule-books are constructed—they are not themselves based on such a body of rules. On Cavell's view, the error lies in picturing the native English speaker's relation to English on the model of her relation to German; absorbing the tenets of a grammar book may be essential if the English speaker is ever to learn German, but it is not how she acquired English. Adapting one of Wittgenstein's remarks about St Augustine (*PI* 32), we might say that the error amounts to picturing the acquisition of language as if children came into the world already possessed of a language, only not the one spoken by those around them; whereas in reality, they come possessed only of themselves, of their body of personal responses to their teachers and their world.

These formulations hark back to Cavell's earlier claim that native speakers do not have evidence for what is said in the language; they are the sources of that evidence, the last court of appeal for such claims. If we think of the putative underlying rules or principles (the speakers' supposed evidence for their claims) as a species of explication, then what must be understood is that explications are surviews or epitomes of instances; instances authorize explications rather than the other way around. And nothing authorizes instances other than the person whose utterances they are. Accordingly, when a native speaker tells her interlocutor what is said when, her authority is, in the last instance, herself; she offers her practice, her personal responses, as an example or paradigm. The sharp distinction between knowledge and self-knowledge, between practitioner and practice, which is essential if we are to regard linguistic understanding as essentially impersonal rather than personal, is thus unavailable in that context; to think otherwise is to fail to understand the nature of the practical ability that all of us, as native speakers, possess.

The point that the last few paragraphs have broached is clearly of vital importance, and we shall return to it in much more detail at later stages in this book. But we can think of it now as, in effect, an attempt on Cavell's part to take very seriously the fact that answers to questions about what is said when typically come in first-person form—'We say ... we don't say ...', rather than, for example, 'She says ... she doesn't say ...' or ' ... is said ... is not said'. Of equal significance, however, is the fact that this first-person form is a *plural* form: in stating what is ordinarily said when, we claim to be speaking for others as well as for ourselves. It follows that, in acquiring and displaying such knowledge about ourselves, we acquire and display knowledge of others; in this region of self-knowledge, to know one's own mind is to know other minds—which does not make such knowledge both subjective and objective, but rather both personal and interpersonal. Of course, it is this aspect of the ordinary language philosophers' procedure which motivates Mates's invocation of the linguistic survey; for how can we know what other people will say when without asking them?

Cavell's response to this is formulated with great care. First, he points out that, although it may be unclear how or why such knowledge is available to us, and so may be worth considering its source and nature more closely, it is at least clear *that* it is available. We simply *do* very often know what other native speakers will say when; this is just a datum about us as speakers, the datum upon which the procedures of ordinary language philosophy rely and in the absence of which they would not even have the preliminary plausibility needed to make them fitting targets of criticism and evaluation. Second, he suggests that it is not easy to imagine a generalized lack of such agreement with other native speakers; for although it is obviously possible that we should sometimes be wrong in stating what we (native speakers) say and do, it would be extraordinary if this were to be a common phenomenon:

My point about such statements, then, is that they are sensibly questioned only where there is some special reason for supposing what I say about what I (we) say to be wrong; only here is the request for evidence competent. If I am wrong about what he does (they do), that may be no great surprise; but if I am wrong about what I (we) do, that is liable, where it is not comic, to be tragic. (*MWM* 14)

Third, Cavell claims that the procedures of ordinary language philosophy do not *presuppose* universal agreement among native speakers but rather constitute a means of exploring or mapping the extent of that agreement. This follows from what one might call the essentially democratic nature of the speech community. For, of course, the authority possessed by any individual's specification of what we say when rests solely upon her competence as a native speaker, and this is an authority possessed to exactly the same degree by any other competent native speaker; so such specifications cannot presuppose but must rather attempt to elicit the agreement of others, and they may fail to do so. In other words, making claims about what we ordinarily say when may reveal that the most common concept is not used by us in the same way; the claim to community may simply be rejected by the people for whom we claimed to speak. What the procedures of ordinary language philosophy *do* bring out is what it would be like to discover such a breakdown of agreement: 'We, who can speak for one another, find that we cannot speak for them. In part, of course, we find this out in finding out that we cannot speak *to* them. If speaking *for* someone else seems a mysterious process, that may be because speaking *to* someone does not seem mysterious enough' (*MWM* 68).

In other words, the first-person plural form of claims about what is ordinarily said when makes manifest the fact that sharing a language, being able to speak to one another, is in part a matter of being able to speak for one another; communication hangs together with community. The extent and existence of that community cannot be guaranteed in advance, and any specific claim to community with other speakers may fail; but to deny the general capacity of a native speaker to speak for her community is to deny her the capacity for speech. These matters—the connections between a capacity for speech, a form of self-knowledge which is knowledge of others, and a set of methods for mapping out the scope of community—are ones which the procedures of ordinary language philosophy bring to light, and they clearly require elucidation; but the air of mystery surrounding them should be a spur to further enquiry rather than to a denial of their existence.

Bespeaking the World

So much for Cavell's response to Mates's first criticism concerning the need for linguistic surveys to establish what we ordinarily say when. What about the second of Mates's worries? Why should a philosopher engaged in extraordinarily difficult and unusually fundamental metaphysical enquiries be bound to observe the constraints of ordinary language that are given expression in instances and explications of the Austinian or Rylean sort? A short answer to this second question has already emerged: if the philosopher refuses to observe those constraints, he[2] exiles himself from the linguistic community and so gives us no reason to heed his pronouncements; his refusal to speak as a member of our community removes his authority to speak *for* that community. More specifically, if he claims that one can never know of the existence of external objects with certainty, and his use of such terms as 'object' or 'certain' or 'know' is not the ordinary one, then he does not come into conflict with our ordinary claims to know, for example, to know that there is a table in the next room.

However, as it stands, this response would be inadequate. On a general level, it fails to acknowledge that the sceptical philosopher regards himself as having made a *discovery* about our ordinary relation to objects; that sense of awful revelation could hardly have been generated if his use of the term 'object' throughout his investigation was deliberately technical or non-standard. It is rather that his investigation is precipitated by worries which seem to him to have immediate application to ordinary, everyday examples of objects; and it is the *results* of that investigation which force him to claim that our ordinary claims to know of the existence of objects are in some way flawed. (This general attitude to the sceptic is one which Cavell develops in some detail in later writings, and will be fleshed out more fully in that context.)

---

[2] As a general stylistic rule in this book, in contexts which require the use of a third-person singular pronoun to signify 'he or she', I employ 'she' rather than 'he'; and when a hypothetical individual's thoughts and deeds are being discussed for reasons which make that individual's gender irrelevant, I treat that individual as female. When, however, such a hypothetical individual is a sceptic, or more precisely is someone intended to represent the sceptical voice in philosophy (and elsewhere), I will treat that individual as male. This may at first appear to combine the costs of applying an unorthodox general stylistic rule with the costs of failing to adhere to it without exception; but it would be better thought of as the construction of a more complex rule whose 'kink' highlights an issue that will turn out to be absolutely fundamental to an adequate grasp of Cavell's conception of scepticism. I hope that this word of explanation will suffice to allay irritation until the import of that issue can be properly elucidated.

On a more specific level, such a swift dismissal of Mates's worry would involve ignoring or repressing the genuinely puzzling nature of the ordinary language philosophers' claims about what we say when. For when Mates objects to the claim that 'When we ask whether an action was voluntary, we imply that there is something fishy about it' (a statement Cavell labels 'S'), he does so on the grounds that this implication is no part of the ordinary meaning of the term 'voluntary'. His objection to such explications of what we mean by what we say is not so much that this is just part of the ordinary meaning of our terms and so can be ignored; it is rather that it is an *erroneous* explication of that ordinary meaning. No such implication will be found in the entry in a dictionary against 'voluntary'; and it is neither deductively nor inductively derivable from it. It may be true that we would not normally use the term 'voluntary' except in circumstances where questions about an action's fishiness had arisen; but that is merely a matter of the (presumably) conventional relation between a statement and the contexts of its utterance, and the occasions upon which we use an utterance cannot be considered part of its meaning or logic. Such implications are simply part of the pragmatics of an utterance rather than of its semantics, and so should not be offered as an explication of what we must *mean* by what we say.

Cavell acknowledges the point that 'voluntary' does not *mean* 'fishy' (i.e. that the connection between 'voluntary' and 'fishy' is not analytic), and that the existence of such an implication is not a matter of deductive or inductive logic; but he argues that Mates's relegation of those implications to the category of 'pragmatics' merely masks the fact that the constraints they impose upon native speakers can no more be avoided or flouted than can the constraints Mates is happy to agree are imposed by the 'semantics' of an utterance. Cavell takes the case of someone asking me whether I dress the way I do voluntarily, and considers the implication of the question, namely, that there is something peculiar about the way I dress: 'Call this implication of the utterance "pragmatic"; the fact remains that he wouldn't (couldn't) say what he did without implying what he did: he MUST MEAN that my clothes are peculiar. I am less interested now in the "mean" than I am in the "must"' (*MWM* 9).

The relegation of such implications to pragmatics cannot lessen the element of *necessity* in the relation between a given utterance and its pragmatic implications. Matters falling under Mates's heading of pragmatics may differ in some ways from those falling under that of semantics, but they all function as necessary constraints upon what a native speaker says and does.

> ... something *does* follow from the fact that a term is used in its usual way; it entitles you (or, using the term, you entitle others) to make certain inferences, draw certain conclusions. (This is part of what you say when you say that you are talking about the *logic* of ordinary language.) *Learning what these implications are is part of learning the language*; no less a part than learning its syntax, or learning what it is to which terms apply: they are an essential part of what we communicate when we talk. (*MWM* 11–12)

Even granted the element of necessity that Cavell identifies here, however, how are we to account for its presence? Whence the hardness of the (logical?) 'must' in claims about what we must mean by what we say? An answer to this question begins to emerge if we acknowledge that saying something is one kind of doing, that is, that when we talk about talking, we are talking about a species of action.

> When we say how an action is done (how to act) what we say may report or describe the way we in fact do it ... but it may also lay out a way of doing or saying something which is to be *followed* ... Statements which describe a language (or a game or an institution) are rules (are binding) if you want to speak that language (play that game, accept that institution); or rather, *when* you are speaking that language, playing that game etc. *If it is TRUE to say '"I know it" is not used unless you have great confidence in it', then, when you are speaking English, it is WRONG (a misuse) to say 'I know it' unless you have great confidence in it.* (*MWM* 15–16)

The crucial point here is that actions can—in various specific ways—go wrong, that they can be performed incorrectly; and our successful performance of them depends upon our adopting and following the ways in which the action in question is done, upon the ways which are normative for it. This element of normativity thus operates at two levels: first, in that there must be specifications of what counts as performing the action well and what counts as performing it badly; and second, in that there must be specifications of what one must do if one is to count as performing that action *at all*. Cavell illustrates the latter element of normativity by reference to someone being told that, in chess, one *must* move the Queen in straight paths: 'if I say truly and appropriately, "You must ..." then in a perfectly good sense nothing you then do can prove me wrong. You CAN *push the little object called the Queen* in many ways, as you can *lift* it or *throw* it across the room; not all of these will be *moving the Queen*' (*MWM* 28). What the chess student has been told is one of the rules governing the game of chess; and if her actions are to count as playing that game, they *must* conform to those rules. The parallel with the case of voluntary action should be clear: you *must* mean (imply), in speaking English, that something about an action is fishy when you say 'The action is voluntary'; if you do not, then you have not stated that the action was voluntary.

Moreover, if it is impossible to avoid implying whatever is implied by our utterances, then it is equally impossible to avoid being implicated in and by what we say. If we say that an action is voluntary, then we imply that it is in some way fishy; and this licenses a listener to expect an explanation or specification of the respect in which that action is fishy. In other words, we must either live up to that expectation, or come up with a good reason for not doing so—a reason which acknowledges the general implication but which justifies its suspension or cancellation in this specific context. '... the "pragmatic implications" of our utterances are ... *meant*; they are an essential part of what we mean when we say something, of what it is to mean something. And what we mean (intend) to say, like what we mean (intend) to do, is something for which we are responsible' (*MWM* 32). Certain ways normative of performing speech-acts must be observed if one is to be speaking at all; but to engage in such actions is to create expectations (and perhaps to fail to live up to them), to take on obligations (and perhaps to fail to fulfil them), to be responsible for the implications of what one does (and perhaps to act irresponsibly). In this sense, to say something is to put oneself in some particular position or other with respect to one's interlocutors, and thus to leave open only certain ways of *re*positioning oneself, e.g. by pertinent excuses, clarifications, apologies, etc.—what Cavell in later writings calls 'elaboratives' (see *MWM* 26–30, and Chapter 2 of this book). A native speaker not only speaks *for* others, she speaks *to* others; and both roles come with a freight of rights and duties, costs and benefits.

In short, since saying is doing, any speaker of a language must conform to the constraints that are given expression in explications. But Cavell adds to this the obvious point that natural languages are *primarily* something employed or embodied in action, that they exist primarily in and through their use by native speakers. What this means is that the pragmatic element of an utterance's meaning is not something secondary to its semantic element, not something grafted on to the latter only as a result of the speaker's decision to use those words to say something—as if using words to say something is not of their essence, as if the words of a language might be detached from their modes of employment and still be regarded as meaningful. On the contrary, the semantics of an utterance are merely one aspect of what is meant in saying it.

> Since saying something is never *merely* saying something, but is saying something with a certain tune and at a proper cue and while executing the appropriate business, the sounded utterance is only a salience of what is going on when we talk (or the unsounded when we think); so a statement of 'what we say' will give us only a feature of what we need to remember. But a native speaker will normally know the rest; learning it was part of learning the language. (*MWM* 32–3)

One may wish to distinguish between the semantic and the pragmatic elements of an utterance's meaning for certain purposes, and concentrate upon the former; but that utterance has a semantics, just as it has a pragmatics, only because it can be used to say something. Semantic meaning is thus not logically prior to or independent of utterance-meaning, as if meaningful utterance were possible only because the words and phrases thus employed were already and independently possessed of a meaning; semantic meaning is rather one facet or salience of the meaning of speech-acts, and so exists only on the presupposition that something *counts* as making a meaningful utterance, as engaging in a speech-act. It follows that the meanings of the words used in an utterance are inseparably bound up with what is meant by saying them; and since the 'pragmatic' implications of our utterances are an essential part of what we mean when we say something, then they are an essential part of what our words mean. 'If "What *A* (an utterance) means" is to be understood in terms of (or even as directly related to) "What is (must be) meant in (by) saying *A*", then the meaning of *A* will not be given by its analytic or definitional equivalents, nor by its deductive implications. Intension is not a substitute for intention' (*MWM* 31).[3]

---

[3] As Cavell acknowledges in a footnote, there seem to be similarities between his conception of the relation between meaning and saying and that of Paul Grice; but it would be very unwise to conclude that a real affinity exists here. Cavell claims only that speaking is a form of acting, and that what words mean and what is meant by saying them are interwoven; and the conjunction of these claims leaves him a great distance away from the machinery of speech-act theories and intentional analyses of sentence-meaning. Moreover, Cavell's inclination to regard propositional or semantic meaning as an aspect of utterance-meaning, and to regard pragmatic constraints as logical ones, directly contradicts Grice's practice of separating the meanings of words and phrases from the conversational implicatures which constrain their employment, and of regarding only the

However, even if this vision of language as primarily embedded in the stream of life were to convince us that the pragmatic implications of utterances are an indispensable aspect of the logic of language (and so of words), it would leave untouched a final worry. For why should a discovery concerning what we must say when about a given action, situation, or object be the final arbiter on philosophical questions concerning the true nature of that action, situation, or object? Why, for example, is it assumed that we find out what involuntary and voluntary actions *are* in finding out when we should *say* of an action that it is involuntary or voluntary?

Cavell responds to this final and fundamental worry by turning the question on its head. He argues that anyone possessed of the idea that finding out what something is must involve investigation of the world is thinking of a restricted set of examples, such as investigating the contents of a bottle or the behaviour of an animal; in these contexts, language clearly cannot help us, but why should we restrict ourselves to such cases? When, for example, we employ a dictionary to discover that an 'umiak' is a type of Eskimo boat, do we find out what 'umiak' means or what an umiak is? The correct answer to that is surely 'both', in which case we seem to have discovered something about the world by rooting around in a dictionary:

If this seems surprising, perhaps it is because we forget that we learn language and learn the world *together*, that they become elaborated and distorted together, and in the same places. We may also be forgetting how elaborate a process the learning is. We tend to take what a native speaker does when he looks up a noun in a dictionary as the characteristic process of learning language ... but it is merely the end point in the process of learning the word. When we turned to the dictionary for 'umiak' we already knew everything about the word, as it were, but its combination: we knew what a noun is and how to name an object and how to look up a word and what boats are and what an Eskimo is. We were all prepared for that umiak. What seemed like finding the world in the dictionary was really a case of bringing the world to the dictionary ... Sometimes we need to bring the dictionary to the world. That will happen (say) when we run across a small boat in Alaska of a sort we have never seen and wonder—what? What it is, or what it is called? In either case the learning is a matter of aligning language and the world. (*MWM* 19–20)

Many things we might want to know about the world can only be

former as matters of 'logic' (cf. Grice's William James Lectures, and sect. 2 of his article 'The Causal Theory of Perception', both in his *Studies in the Way of Words* (Cambridge, Mass., 1989)). Cavell's later awareness of these divergences seems evident in the absence of any references to Grice's work in Cavell's other writings.

discovered by leaving our armchair and unearthing the facts; but any such empirical investigation presupposes a prior alignment of language and the world, because in its absence we would have no idea what to look for when we did investigate the facts. In order to be capable of discovering by empirical investigation whether the liquid in a particular bottle is water, we must first know what would constitute its being water, what would have to be the case for it to count as water—and that is a matter of knowing how and when to *say* of something put before us that it is water. In Wittgensteinian terms, the grammar of our language determines a logical space of possibilities, and the world determines which of those spaces are filled; we can investigate the latter only by looking to see what is the case, but we can investigate the former from our armchair by utilizing our knowledge of the criteria governing the application of the words of our natural language to the world. Since these criteria determine what it is for something to be an instance of water, an umiak, a boat, and so on, then an investigation of what we should say when teaches us as much about the world as it does about language.

If we look back at Cavell's earlier remarks concerning statements about voluntary actions, we can see that it is precisely this method of learning about the world that was already at work. When elucidating the necessary implications of such speech-acts, Cavell was in effect elucidating our criteria for *counting* a given utterance as a statement of the relevant sort: for the reason any statement that a given action was voluntary *must* carry the implication that something about it was fishy was that in the absence of such an implication we would not *call* the relevant utterance a statement that an action was voluntary. Here, we see once more that elucidating what we would say when about such speech-acts is a way of displaying the nature of those human actions. In just the same way, we can move from Austin's claim that 'We say "The boy made the gift voluntarily"' to the claim that one may make gifts voluntarily; for in reminding ourselves which actions we would call 'voluntary', we remind ourselves of the nature of voluntary actions.

What the umiak example shows is that the methods Cavell has employed in elucidating the nature of speech-acts and other sorts of human actions—the methods of ordinary language philosophy—can be applied irrespective of whether the focus of the investigation is an action, an object, or anything else in the world with which human beings align themselves by means of their language. The criteria which manifest this alignment are *elicited* by asking us what we should say

when, i.e. they *govern* our speech; but they do not have *application* only
to speech-acts, or even to non-linguistic human behaviour—they apply
to anything to which we apply language.

What do such answers [to questions about what we say when] look like? They
will be facts about what we call (how we conceive, what the concept is, what
counts as), for example, a piece of wax, the same piece of wax, seeing
something, not really seeing something, not seeing all of something, following,
finding, losing, returning, choosing, intending, wishing, pointing to something,
and so on. And we could say that what such answers are meant to provide us
with is not more knowledge of matters of fact, but the knowledge of what
would count as various 'matters of fact'. Is this empirical knowledge? Is it a
priori? It is knowledge of what Wittgenstein means by grammar—the knowledge
Kant calls 'transcendental'. (*MWM* 64)

At this point, a summary of Cavell's picture or vision of the procedures
of the ordinary language philosopher may be in order. Such a philosopher asks herself what we should say when; and in answering her own
questions, she draws upon a species of self-knowledge which is a
fundamental aspect of her competence as a native speaker of the
language, namely, her capacity to make manifest the criteria governing
her use of words. Such philosophizing is thus a matter of recalling,
exploring, and displaying criteria: it is to engage in what Wittgenstein
called a grammatical investigation. According to Cavell, criteria function
both vertically and horizontally, aligning a speaker with the world (by
specifying what will count as an instance of a particular matter of fact)
and with other people (by determining the extent to which she can
speak for and to them); but the nature, extent, and security of those
alignments are not determinable in advance of grammatical investigation. In short, ordinary language philosophizing is a matter of tapping
the resources of the self in a way which will allow the philosopher to
recall, explore, and display the nature, extent, and security of her
alignments with the world and with the human community.

As this summary suggests, Cavell's conception of ordinary language
philosophy is from the outset an intriguing and idiosyncratic blend of
elements from the work of Austin and Wittgenstein: beginning from a
classically Austinian emphasis upon 'what we say when', he ends up
placing great weight upon the essentially Wittgensteinian notions of
grammar and criteria. However, it is important to note that his elaborated version of ordinary language philosophy is not offered as a
definitive rebuttal of any and all of the worries one might have about

the comprehensibility or legitimacy of these philosophical methods. Of course, if Cavell succeeds in convincing us that his vision of those methods is more accurate or insightful than that of Mates, then he will have shown *Mates's* worries to be unfounded (because based upon a misunderstanding of the object of his criticisms). However, Cavell's depiction is not meant to dissipate or deny our sense that there is *something* mysterious or unclear about the powers and resources of ordinary language philosophizing; on the contrary, by getting us to see the true nature of those methods more clearly, he aims to locate the true sources of those worries more accurately. In the terms of his depiction, three such sources stand out: the sense in which the ordinary language philosopher is drawing upon a species of self-knowledge, the sense in which she can speak for others, and the sense in which her utterances can reveal the true nature of matters of fact.

What this depiction *also* makes clear, however, is that those three sources of worry share a common feature: they all presuppose the existence and availability of criteria. But this means that we can specify the source of our sense of mystery with greater precision: if we wish fully to comprehend the power and the legitimacy of the procedures of ordinary language philosophizing, we must achieve a grasp of the status and functioning of criteria. Criteria as such plainly exist, since in their absence ordinary language philosophy could not even get off the ground, let alone achieve the plausibility which makes it an obsessive target for critical fire; but in the absence of an account of how and why criteria are available for such potent employment, ordinary language philosophers will lack a full understanding of, and security within, their own methods and procedures. In this sense, for Cavell the concept of a 'criterion' opens and delimits the space of all his future work.

Given, however, that criteria are Janus-faced, the space they open up will have two equally significant axes—the alignment of a speaker and her world, and the alignment of a speaker with other speakers. A central portion of Cavell's later work can be roughly divided into writings which explore the first axis and those which explore the second—with the proviso that a constant preoccupation of both is the ways in which criteria constitute the *intersection* of those two axes. This rough division will accordingly function as a preliminary means of orienting this study of his work; and in Part I, I will examine the ways in which Cavell sees criteria as functioning to align speakers with one another in the domains of aesthetics, morality, and politics.

PART I
Patterns, Agreement, and Rationality

Aesthetics: Hume, Kant, and Criticism

I want to begin this investigation of the ways in which Cavell sees criteria as functioning to align human beings with one another by looking at his work in the field of aesthetics, and in particular at another essay in *Must We Mean What We Say?* 'Aesthetic Problems of Modern Philosophy' falls into two main parts—an analysis and attempted dissolution of two specific problems in the arena of aesthetics, and an examination of the nature of aesthetic judgement and debate in general; and it is the latter part with which I shall be most concerned. As we shall see, the task of summarizing and analysing such a short stretch of text can itself be accomplished within a correspondingly brief compass: but the determining importance of this material for the rest of Cavell's work (both within this first collection and in the future) demands that it be presented at the outset of our investigation and in a relatively self-contained way.

In these few pages, Cavell is interested in casting light upon the role of rationality in aesthetics by asking: Does the notorious lack of agreement over aesthetic judgements entail that such judgements lack rationality, or does it rather show the sort of rationality such judgements possess? He begins by summarizing Hume's conclusions about this issue, finding them to be lacking in credibility for several reasons, but also finding them to be symptomatic of more contemporary misconceptions by virtue of Hume's emphasis upon agreement as the standard of taste:

Hume's descendants, catching the assumption that agreement provides the vindication of judgement, but no longer able to hope for either, have found that aesthetic (and moral and political) judgements lack something: the arguments that support them are not conclusive in the way that arguments in logic are, nor rational in the way arguments in science are. Indeed they are not, and if they were there would be no such subject as art (or morality), and no such art as criticism. It does not follow, however, that such judgements are not conclusive and rational. (*MWM* 88)

To explain these remarks, Cavell turns to Kant, whose writings on aesthetics defend the specific assumption that judgements concerning the beautiful demand or impute or claim general validity (universal agreement), and that in making such judgements we go on claiming this agreement even when we know from experience that they will not receive it. According to Kant, this claim to universal agreement is not a sign of our blockheaded inability to learn from experience; rather, it 'so essentially belongs to a judgement by which we describe anything as *beautiful* that, if this were not thought in it, it would never come into our thoughts to use the expression at all, but everything which pleases without a concept would be counted as pleasant'.[1] Cavell defends Kant's claim here by offering us a reinterpretation of the examples which the latter employed in his own defence, examples intended to illustrate the essential differences between judgements concerning what is beautiful and judgements concerning what is pleasant.

If *A* claims that canary wine is pleasant, and *B* responds by saying that it tastes like canary droppings, *A* might go on to defend his claim, but it would be perfectly legitimate for him simply to say that *he* likes it, i.e. that it pleases *him* even if it doesn't please his interlocutor: for the matter is one of personal taste. However, if *A* claims that a pianist plays beautifully, and *B* responds by saying 'How can you say that? There was no line, no structure, no idea what the music was about. He's simply an impressive colorist', it would clearly be odd if *A* responded simply by saying 'Well, I liked it'. 'Of course, he *can*; but don't we feel that here that would be a feeble rejoinder, a *retreat* to personal taste? Because *B*'s reasons are obviously relevant to the evaluation of performance, and because they are *arguable*, in ways that anyone who knows about such things will know how to pursue' (*MWM* 91–2). The point here is that to call something beautiful is not merely a matter of personal taste; as Kant puts it, to say that something is beautiful *for me* would be laughable, precisely because it would be a misuse of the concept 'beautiful', an attempt to eradicate the differences between judgements of personal taste and judgements of beauty. For Cavell, those differences come out in the different sorts of reasons we offer for such judgements: as the example shows, aesthetic judgements are arguable, and arguable in certain ways; and someone who fails to support his judgement in those ways is not engaging in aesthetic judgement at all because he is failing to honour the obligations which making such judgements entails.

[1] I. Kant, *Critique of Judgement*, trans. J. C. Meredith (Oxford University Press: Oxford, 1952), sect. 8, p. 53.

Those of us who keep finding ourselves wanting to call such differences 'logical' are, I think, responding to a sense of necessity we feel in them, together with a sense that necessity is, partly, a matter of the *ways* a judgement is supported, the ways in which conviction in it is produced: it is only by virtue of these recurrent patterns of support that a remark will count as—will be— aesthetic, or a mere matter of taste, or moral, propagandistic, religious, magical, scientific, philosophical . . . (*MWM* 93)

Cavell in effect presents us with a way of elucidating the nature of aesthetic judgements that involves reminding us of the criteria which govern our practice of making those judgements. Just as an utterance does not count as a statement that an action is voluntary unless the speaker is implying that there is something fishy about it (in which case she is obliged to locate its fishiness and respond appropriately to those who contest her description of the action in competent ways), so an utterance does not count as the judgement that a musical performance is beautiful unless the speaker is claiming that others should agree with that judgement (in which case she is obliged to identify the features of the performance which justify her judgement and respond appropriately to those who contest her description of the performance in competent ways). Part of what it means to be capable of making aesthetic judge- ments is to be capable of entering the relevant sorts of support for one's judgement, of recognizing competently entered objections to it, and of making appropriate responses to those objections. In this respect, that which distinguishes aesthetic judgements from judgements of personal taste is anything but arbitrary.

This suggestion of Cavell's may seem to bypass the essence of the Humean's objections to claims that aesthetic judgements are rational, for it does not address the fact that aesthetic disputes and disagreements—even if conducted according to non-arbitrary proced- ures governed by shared criteria of relevance—may none the less be interminable, or terminate without agreement. It is this—the fact that anyone who can follow the argument need not accept the conclusion, even if she doesn't find anything definitely wrong with it—that leads Kant to claim that the imputed universality of aesthetic judgements does not spring from (the application of) a concept, that it cannot be thought of as objective universality; and it makes the Humean reject the idea that there is a logic to aesthetic judgement at all. Cavell's response to this point is cautious:

I do not know what the gains or disadvantages would be of unfastening the term 'logic' from that constant pattern of support or justification whose peculiarity is that it leads those competent at it to this kind of agreement, and extending it to patterns of justification having other purposes and peculiarities. All I am arguing for is the idea that *pattern* and *agreement* are distinct features of the notion of logic. (*MWM* 94)

One might put this in the following way. Cavell is not suggesting that logic or rationality is a matter of the existence of patterns (of support, objection, response) *rather than* of agreement (in conclusions); he is suggesting that logic or rationality might be more fruitfully thought of as a matter of agreement in *patterns* rather than an agreement in *conclusions*. Whether the particular patterns or procedures are such that those competent in following them are guaranteed to reach an agreed conclusion is part of what distinguishes one type or aspect of rationality from another; but what distinguishes rationality from irrationality in any domain is an agreement in—a commitment to—patterns or procedures of speaking and acting. Those competent in logic and science (whatever the other differences between the two enterprises) employ agreed procedures designed to produce agreed conclusions; but what makes such procedures rational ones may be the commitment to patterns of support and justification rather than the guaranteed agreement in conclusions which those patterns generate.

This suggestion clearly requires more exploration and elucidation before it will produce conviction; but one worry that emerges immediately is also one with which Cavell attempts to deal immediately. For an objection we might have to the idea that guaranteed agreement in conclusions is merely a peculiarity of one sort of pattern of reasoning is that it is hard to imagine what the point or purpose of a pattern of reasoning which fails to guarantee such agreement might be. What is the use of agreeing on how to run an argument if the procedures upon which we agree offer no guarantee of agreeing on the substance of that argument? Cavell's response to this worry has two parts. First, he is quick to point out that he is not denying the *possibility* of agreement in conclusions about aesthetic matters: if the agreed procedure lacked any possibility of generating agreement in conclusions—if, that is, one were to embark upon such arguments without even the *hope* of agreement emerging—then the status of the procedure as a rational one might well be impugned; but it is clearly false to say that agreement on conclusions on aesthetic matters is ruled out a priori. Second, he suggests that if we attain clarity on the type of agreement that *is* realizable in aesthetic debates, then the point of the procedures which permit us to realize it will also become clearer. This suggestion emerges when he discusses the role of the critic:

If we say that the *hope* of agreement motivates our engaging in these various patterns of support, then we must also say, what I have taken Kant to have seen, that even were agreement in fact to emerge, our judgements, so far as aesthetic, would remain as essentially subjective, in his sense, as they ever were. Otherwise art and the criticism of art would not have their special importance nor elicit their own forms of distrust and of gratitude. The problem of the critic, as of the artist, is not to discount his subjectivity but to include it; not to overcome it in agreement but to master it in exemplary ways. Then his work outlasts the fashions and arguments of a particular age. That is the beauty of it. (*MWM* 94)

In the domain of logic and science, agreement between practitioners over the rectitude of a well-supported conclusion is guaranteed because disagreement with any legitimately supported conclusion is evidence of one's incompetence in the practice; in other words, such agreement merely signifies that the conclusion is legitimately grounded. In the case of aesthetics, disagreement with a legitimately supported judgement is *not* a criterion of incompetence in the practice—competent practitioners must be able to recognize when a judgement is well supported, but they are not bound to adopt any and all well-supported aesthetic judgements. None the less, agreement on particular judgements made by particular persons is possible; so when it *is* achieved, it cannot simply signify that the judgements are legitimately supported. It also reveals that there is something that makes these individuals' expressions of aesthetic taste more valuable than another person's. What might this be?

Since such an individual's judgement must be supported by reasons, but cannot be thought of as merely the result of applying general a priori aesthetic principles to the particular case in hand (i.e. since, as Kant puts it, she is not merely subsuming this particular under a concept), then her capacity to elicit agreement with her judgement must depend upon a heightened capacity to support it with object-specific reasons—to anchor her judgement in the particular features of the concrete object to which she is responding. In other words, she must be better at locating and characterizing the features of the specific art work to which she is responding, and better at getting other people to perceive those features themselves. To excel in the way good critics excel will therefore involve a mastery of the practice of aesthetic debate with others—of knowing in any individual case when and how to enter

considerations in support of one's judgement, how to respond to competing judgements, how to tell when reasons and justifications have come
to an end and a stand must be taken on the bedrock of direct perception
from which any explanation and discussion must start, i.e. when to say
'This is simply what I see'.

Accordingly, one pre-condition of such mastery will be a capacity to
put the world of one's aesthetic responses to words—for if we are to
bring others to see what we see, we must be capable of identifying what
it is that we see, what it is about any particular object that leads us to
judge it in the way that we do. Amongst other things, this will demand
an absolute honesty in articulating our responses to the art work; but
this honesty is only one aspect of a more general capacity to understand
ourselves in our relation to these objects. In short, if the critic is to
achieve the agreement she seeks, she must rely upon a capacity for self-
knowledge and a capacity to give expression to that self-knowledge in
ways which will persuade people to try to share the subjective world of
her aesthetic responses which is thereby displayed. What bridges the
gap between the imputation of agreement and its realization in the
practice of aesthetic debate is thus the controlled deployment of
subjectivity. The hope of achieving agreement can be realized only if
the person making the judgement is prepared to make a public declaration of her individual response to the art work, to display to others the
weave of reactions, associations, and speculations elicited by that object
in words that will strike them as providing a framework in terms of
which they too can respond.

This means that agreement in the field of aesthetics signifies something completely different from agreement in logic or science. Guaranteed agreement exists only through the exclusion of subjectivity, by
leaving the individual practitioner no room to exercise her personal
judgement in evaluating the legitimacy of a conclusion. The *absence* of
guaranteed agreement means that when agreement is achieved it is
based upon subjectivity rather than upon its exclusion. The good critic
is someone who has not discounted her individuality but mastered it in
ways which other individuals find exemplary; by speaking for herself as
honestly and accurately as she can, she has discovered that she can
speak for others—she has articulated her subjective world, her inner
life, in a way which strikes others as the manifestation of something in/
of themselves. It is this discovery which the structure of the practice of
aesthetic debate makes possible; by committing myself to a set of
procedures which do not guarantee agreement, I give myself the

opportunity to explore the depth of the connection between my inner life and that of others, to assess the degree to which others inhabit my world—to reveal that in my subjectivity which is intersubjective.

Aesthetic debate is thus a way of constructing or discovering community through the articulation and development of individuality; it shows a way in which community can be founded upon the fuller expression, rather than the complete repression, of individuality. The possibility that we may find limits to that community is the price to be paid for the possibility of creating that community without sacrificing subjectivity. The fact that such a community of response and thought is not guaranteed shows something about the sort of community it is—one in which membership is freely willed, elicited rather than compelled from each individual. If this sort of community can result only from abandoning the guarantee of agreement, then it is hardly surprising that we sometimes choose abandonment; and with such a vision to prompt us, the risks involved in attempting to achieve it (humiliation, rebuff, the discovery of isolation) may seem well worth running.

Such is Cavell's understanding of the point of agreeing to a set of procedures for debate which do not guarantee an agreed conclusion to the debate. But of course, seen from this angle, the procedures of aesthetic discussion also provide him with a way of underlining certain key aspects of the procedures of ordinary language philosophy. As we saw in the previous chapter, those procedures also draw upon an aspect of self-knowledge, presupposing a willingness to present one's own personal responses as exemplary or paradigmatic for others, and thus to explore the degree to which the philosopher can speak for others by stating what we say when. In this sense, engaging in philosophy is also a way of exploring the extent of one's community with others by exploring an aspect of one's self.

Focussing upon such an abstract structural analogy at the level of procedures may, however, seem misleading, since it seems to mask important differences—differences in the aspects of the self deployed in the two practices, and differences in the purposes for which they are deployed. For whereas agreement upon criteria is the goal in pursuit of which the philosopher articulates her personal *linguistic* responses, the critic elaborates her personal *aesthetic* responses in order to produce agreement over the status of a particular object; the critic is not aiming to recall the grounds upon which things can rightly be judged to be 'beautiful' or to be 'works of art' in the absence of any concrete instances of such objects, but rather encouraging us to recognize the beauty of a particular thing. Since, however, eliciting such recognition centrally depends upon the critic's heightened or refined capacity to identify the features of the object that are determining her aesthetic responses and to convince us that those features ought to call forth a similar response in us, there is a clear sense in which her judgements must at least be intended to be exemplary for our practice of applying aesthetic concepts. In articulating and elaborating her personal judgement that a given object is a good or successful as opposed to a bad work of art, or indeed that an object—a row of bricks, a tangle of metal, a drip-painted canvas—is a work of art as opposed to something else entirely, the critic offers us an answer to the question what we should say when confronted with it. Cavell makes the point in the following way: 'Kant's "universal voice" is, with perhaps a slight change of accent, what we hear recorded in the philosopher's claims about "what we say": such claims are at least as close to what Kant calls aesthetical judgements as they are to ordinary empirical hypotheses' (*MWM* 94). Using terms introduced in the preceding chapter, we might say that the critic holds out her personal response as an instance of how the relevant aesthetic terms should be applied, as a paradigm of how those terms should be projected into this new context. And of course, on this characterization of the art of criticism, engaging in it can be seen as a way of contributing not only to a more adequate understanding of certain works of art, but also and simultaneously to a more adequate understanding of the grammar—that which governs the application and so determines the meaning—of aesthetic terms. In this respect, criticism becomes not simply analogous to but rather a mode of the practice of ordinary language philosophy—one distinctive but recognizable way of engaging in that activity.

This is why Cavell regards his essays on Beckett, Shakespeare, poetry, and music in *Must We Mean What We Say?* as internal to the philosophical work it accomplishes. Sometimes, it is true, there is an immediate thematic link between one of his more obviously philosophical essays and the specific literary texts he chooses to interpret, for example his work on knowledge and acknowledgement of other minds clearly prepares the ground for his reading of *King Lear* as a drama of the acknowledgement and the avoidance of love (and we shall examine this particular theme in more detail in later chapters). Even there, however, his focus is as much upon what his literary criticism reveals about literary criticism, and so about the connections between criticism and philosophy, as upon what it reveals about Lear. For his explicitly declared primary purpose in the essay is to identify the difficulties preventing critical appreciation of texts such as *King Lear*, in particular the temptation to succumb to the (ultimately incoherent) impulse to regard character analysis and verbal analysis as conflicting or even separable approaches to plays and poetry; and since such an impulse could be seen as one inflexion of a desire to consider language in isolation from the fact of its employment by particular people to accomplish particular purposes, to separate speech from speakers, then Cavell's attempt to put the two together again in his reading of *King Lear* generates a mode of criticism which precisely expresses the main impulse of ordinary language philosophy as he defines it in *Must We Mean What We Say?*

More generally, the examples of practical critical problems that Cavell chooses to discuss in his essays on poetry and music confront a question that I mentioned in the Foreword and that Cavell takes to be definitive of modern art—when the key question raised by certain objects that claim the status of art works is whether, and on what grounds, they might be said to be art at all. This issue arises in poetry, when certain critics take the resistance to paraphrase of the work of poets such as Hart Crane and Wallace Stevens as proof that they register the misdirection and so the complete failure of the poetic impulse; it dominates the visual arts, where—for example—Caro's constructions challenge prevailing conceptions of what features a work must possess in order to count as a sculpture at all; and it is particularly clear in modern music, where concern for the continued vitality and viability (i.e. the continued existence) of the human practices of making and appreciating music is given expression in battles over the question of whether such concepts as tonality or composition can be applied to the work of certain 'composers' in the twentieth century—in other words, over whether those central musical terms can be projected into these new contexts. These are areas of criticism in which the consequences of the critic's vulnerability to rebuff are most daunting, for here she is exposing herself to the charge that she is no longer capable of distinguishing genuine art from simulacra or fraudulent pretence; it is not so much the particular calibration or texture of her aesthetic responses that is at stake—it is their general (dis)orientation. However, these are also areas in which the critic's task is most closely convergent with that of the ordinary language philosopher: for what is placed in question by instances of modern art is the appropriate application and projection of the most basic of aesthetic terms.

Accordingly, Cavell's early essays in and on art criticism, which make up a substantial proportion of *Must We Mean What We Say?*, must be seen as something more or other than criticism as opposed to philosophy, or illustrations or applications of philosophical theses independently derived. He does not, of course, wish to deny that there are differences in the mode or form of the work done in such essays and that done in ones which directly address the writings and problems of other philosophers; but he does wish to deny that those differences can be captured by the suggestion that the former do not, whereas the latter do, make a contribution to determining what we would say when, to elucidating grammar. In particular, the fact that the critic draws upon the full extent and texture of her personal responses can no longer function as a means of distinguishing criticism from philosophy; on the contrary, given the intimacy of the relation between the two activities, that fact underwrites the suggestion we encountered in the previous chapter that a degree of self-reliance and self-awareness is required of philosophers by the practice of ordinary language philosophy. It implies that both practices are modes, however different, of (achieving and deploying) exemplary self-articulation or self-revelation.

The above is the central point about philosophical methodology that Cavell intends to highlight by means of his examination of, and engagement in, art criticism—but it is not the only one; for bringing philosophical and aesthetic judgements into a close relation also helps to underline the non-coercive and tentative nature of philosophical claims to community.

The philosopher appealing to everyday language turns to the reader not to convince him without proof but to get him to prove something, test something, against himself. He is saying: Look and find out whether you can see what I see, wish to say what I wish to say. Of course he often seems to answer or beg his own question by posing it in plural form ... But this plural is still first person: it does not, to use Kant's word, 'postulate' that 'we', you and I and he, say and want and imagine and feel and suffer together. If we do not, then the philosopher's remarks are irrelevant to us. Of course he doesn't think they are irrelevant, but the implication is that philosophy, like art, is, and should be, powerless to *prove* its relevance; and that says something about the kind of relevance it wishes to have. All the philosopher, this kind of philosopher, can do is to express, as fully as he can, his world, and attract our undivided attention to our own. (*MWM* 96)

In aesthetics, the good critic is powerless to prove her relevance to others, and may fail to do so; but the community which can be achieved by her claiming relevance makes her efforts worth while, and even if her audience decide that her world of responses is not one they (can) share, they will have made that decision by exploring, testing, and thereby improving their knowledge of their own world, their own selves. The practice of aesthetic debate thus contributes to the self-knowledge of all who participate and holds out the possibility of creating a freely willed community. And in so far as this characterization of aesthetics is applicable to the practice of ordinary language philosophy, we can say that the point of claiming to speak for others philosophically is to stimulate them to self-examination and to attempt to realize or recover a similarly uncoerced community.

When Cavell turns to the procedures of moral and political argument, his interest is similarly reflexive, in that he takes an examination of those practices to be useful in clarifying particular aspects of his own philosophical practice. In other words, his analyses of the social face of criteria—the face that aligns a speaker with other speakers—not only clarify certain specific ways in which human beings relate to their fellows, but also cast light upon that other specific mode of relating to others which these specific analyses themselves exemplify. When politics and morality are presented to us as drawing upon specific aspects of self-knowledge, as distinct modes of exploring the degree to which the individual can speak for others by speaking from the depths of her own self, and as particular attempts to forge and discover community whilst respecting individuality, we are also being asked to refine our understanding of philosophy by locating its own distinctive point or purpose by comparison and contrast with the procedures laid out before us. This is something worth bearing in mind as we attempt to trace out the details of those analyses in the following chapters.

2

Morality: Emotivism and Agreement

The central lineaments of Cavell's understanding of morality are laid out in the chapters which constitute part 3 of *The Claim of Reason*—chapters originally composed as part of his doctoral dissertation, and so roughly contemporaneous with the material collected in *Must We Mean What We Say?* (see *CR*, p. xii). Once again, the guiding assumption is that rationality in moral debate may be a matter of agreement on patterns of support for conclusions rather than guaranteed agreement in conclusions, and he begins by suggesting that it is only the contrary assumption—predicated upon an excessive emphasis on logic and natural science as models of reasoning—which leads so many philosophers to deny that moral argument can be seen as rational. In so doing, Cavell makes more explicit than in his essays on aesthetics the point that those who identify the ability of logicians and scientists to reach agreement on conclusions as the criterion of the rationality of their practices may be completely misidentifying rather than incompletely describing our concept of rationality.

The Logic of Moral Discourse

Cavell begins by arguing that someone who, when considering the concept of rationality, focusses upon the agreement on conclusions which characterizes natural science is failing to address the question of what permits or underpins that agreement. Scientists now agree, for example, that there are mountains on the moon; and anyone who disagrees with this judgement will be told to look through a telescope. What if such a person refused to accept the evidence of telescopes as telling us of the nature of the moon? She would be treated either as irrational or as incompetent in science: given the procedures and canons of science as that institution is now constituted, that person is no scientist.

Once these procedures and canons are established, then agreement is reached in familiar ways; but that simply means: agreement (or absence of disagreement) about what constitutes science, scientific procedure, and scientific evidence, is what permits particular disagreements to be resolved in certain ways. Being a scientist just is having a commitment to, and being competent at, these modes of resolution. (*CR* 261)

In short, the important locus of agreement is the canons and procedures of supporting and evaluating scientific conclusions rather than the conclusions themselves; the possibility of agreeing on the latter is a consequence of agreeing on the former.

Cavell is quick to spell out the implications of this re-evaluation of the rationality of science for our view of morality:

If what makes science rational is not the fact of agreement about particular propositions itself, or about the acknowledged modes of arriving at it, but the fact of a *commitment* to certain modes of argument whose very nature is to lead to such agreement, then morality may be rational on exactly the same ground, namely that we commit ourselves to *certain* modes of argument, but now ones which do not lead, in the same ways, and sometimes not at all, to agreement (about a conclusion). (*CR* 261–2)

This naturally raises the following question: If these modes of argument are not such as to guarantee agreement on a conclusion, then what is their point? Why should we commit ourselves to them if they do not necessarily lead to agreement? Any answer to this question clearly depends upon further exploration of the nature of these agreed-upon modes of argument. For if we are to appreciate the role that the practice of moral debate plays in human life, we must clarify its nature as a practice; and that means exploring in more detail what distinguishes appropriate ways of supporting a moral claim from those which are inappropriate or incompetent. What *makes* a reason relevant to a moral debate or disagreement? What are the dimensions in terms of which a *moral* position is to be assessed for adequacy or superiority?

Cavell moves towards such a specification by means of a contrast with the views of Charles Stevenson, whose emotivist system of ethics hinges around the claim that any kind of statement which any speaker considers likely to alter attitudes may be adduced for or against an ethical judgement. As Cavell points out, this claim is equivalent to the assertion that *any* statement about *any* matter of fact must be considered morally relevant, provided only that it is likely to be effective. Reformulated in this way, the deep implausibility of Stevenson's position is not only made evident, but also accounted for: it is implausible because it offers a mischaracterization of the modes of support which are appropriate to moral claims (i.e. of the sorts of consideration which count as *morally* relevant), and so mischaracterizes morality.

Someone who claimed that any matter of fact whatever might count in support of a moral claim, provided only that it be effective in altering attitudes, would be implying that the effectiveness of a given consideration was the sole criterion of its moral relevance. But this would be equivalent to implying that someone in a moral argument who, in considering how to support her claim, considers only whether a statement will be effective in getting what she approves of done (or at least approved of) by the other person, and who considers that other person solely to the extent of considering what will get her to alter her attitudes or deeds, is acting in accord with the spirit of morality. Such a claim is seriously awry—not because moral argument cannot sometimes be used solely to manipulate one's interlocutors (human beings are prone to such temptations), and not because the manipulation of attitude and action cannot sometimes be justified by extreme utility and practical urgency (this is what justifies propaganda); it is awry because it implies that the manipulation of attitude and action is morality's essence.

The disillusionment, the discouragement, comes ... from being told that one man may treat me morally and yet act only in terms of his attitudes, without necessarily considering me or mine. If this is so, then the concept of morality is unrelated to the concept of justice. For however justice is to be understood— whether in terms of rendering to each his due, or in terms of equality, or of impartiality or of fairness—*what* must be understood is a concept concerning the treatment of *persons*; and *that* is a concept, in turn, of a creature with commitments and cares. But for these commitments and cares, and the ways in which they conflict with one another and with those of other persons, there would be no problem and no concept of justice. One can face the disappearance of justice from the world more easily than an amnesia of the very concept of justice. (*CR* 283)

What this passage implies is that, for Cavell, morally relevant reasons for questioning a person's action are ones which speak to the cares and commitments of the person with whom one is engaging in moral argument; anyone who offers reasons which lack this feature shows herself to be incompetent at the practice of moral argument by showing herself to be ignorant of the canons and procedures (the modes of support) which govern moral criticisms of an action, and so ignorant of the nature of morality. On Stevenson's account, there would be no essential difference between giving someone reasons for taking a course of action she is committed to and one to which she has no obvious commitment, nor between reasons which point to something the person cares about and those which are essentially unrelated to what she cares about, or needs to care about; and this simply annihilates the features which distinguish morality from other ways of relating to our fellow human beings.

If Cavell's position is to be made at all plausible, however, the form and depth of the control which he takes such canons of relevance to impose upon practitioners of moral argument must be spelt out in more detail. First, commitments: for Cavell, a person's commitments are not more or less external to her wants, positions, or modes of conduct, but are rather implications of what she does and who she is. If, for example, someone makes a promise then she is committed to performing a course of action; should she fail to perform that action, then, in order to retain credibility as a moral agent, she must explain why the circumstances in which she found herself justified her failure to honour that commitment, why she could not have given advance warning to those relying upon her promise, and so on. Moreover, this feature of promise-making is by no means as distinctive as philosophers have tended to make it seem: as Cavell points out, and as we have already seen with respect to the act of saying that a given action is voluntary, precisely the same creation of a commitment and the attendant obligation to provide excuses or justifications of one's failure to honour that commitment hold in the case of innumerable everyday human actions.

... there are any number of ways, other than promising, for committing yourself to a course of action: the expression or declaration of an intention, the giving of an impression, not correcting someone's misapprehension, beginning a course of conduct on the basis of which someone else has taken action and so on. There is nothing sacred about the act of promising which is not sacred about expressing an intention, or any other way of committing oneself. The words 'I am going to ...' or 'I will ...' do not in themselves indicate that you are 'merely' expressing an intention and *not* promising. If it is *important to be explicit* then you may engage either in the 'rituals' of saying 'I really want to ...' or 'I certainly intend, will try to ...', or the ritual of saying 'I promise'. It is *this* importance which makes explicit promises important. But to take them more seriously than that, as the golden path to commitment, is to take our ordinary, non-explicit commitments too lightly. (*CR* 298)

Of course, the precise form and weight of a given commitment, and the routes of explanation, excuse, and justification that it leaves open, will vary from case to case; but each case will, in its own way, impose non-arbitrary and impersonal constraints upon the agent concerned—on pain of her exile from the realm of moral accountability altogether. And by the same token, unless a given agent's budget of commitments forms the reference point of my attempts to challenge her behaviour on moral grounds—unless, for example, I can justify my criticism of her in terms of what she really is committed to rather than in terms of what she has no obvious commitment to—then my challenge is morally incompetent.

Similarly, what human beings care about is not entirely arbitrary, unstable, flexible, or unpredictable; on the contrary, there are grammatical constraints upon what someone can (logically) care about. One might not think that Antigone should have placed as much weight as she did upon her relationship with her brother when deciding to disobey Creon, but anyone who failed to acknowledge the relevance of care for one's close relatives when advising her to act otherwise would be revealing incompetence in the practice of moral argument; and it would be similarly incompetent to attempt to convince someone to break her promise on the ground that it would be very time-consuming for her to keep it. Here, it is important to note that Cavell is not claiming that all moral argument with a given person is irrational unless it is supported by reasons which relate to that person's *existing* concerns; after all, a crucial part of moral disagreement involves convincing one's interlocutor that there are things (values, people, responsibilities) that she must or ought to care about, even though her present intentions or behaviour show that she does not. Cavell's point is that there are grammatical limits upon the reasons then cited, constraints upon what it makes sense to exhort someone to care about and upon how they might intelligibly justify a decision to reject or downplay them; and these limits vary not according to the occurrent psychology of the individual concerned or the types of preferences statistically prevalent amongst human beings, but according to the nature of the proposed object of care, the nature of the interlocutor's other declared concerns and values, and so on. These limits and their variations may be bewildering in their multiplicity and circumstance-relativity; but they are neither vague nor arbitrary nor purely empirical.

It should also be emphasized that, according to Cavell, the need to speak to someone's cares and commitments when confronting them morally controls more than the substance of one's reasons for disagreeing with them; it is equally determinant of their form or mode of presentation. He illustrates this by exploring the differences between saying 'You must do *X*' and 'You ought to do *X*'. In the domain of games, for example, it would be odd to say to a chess-player 'You ought to move the Queen in straight paths', but correct to say 'You must move the Queen in straight paths' and unexceptionable to say 'You ought to castle here'; this is because 'ought' implies that there is an alternative which the player would be justified in taking but which you are advising her (for specific reasons) to forgo, and there is no recognizable alternative to moving the Queen in straight lines that is also a licit move in chess. Transposing this insight to the practice of moral debate, we can say that 'You ought to do *X*' implies the existence of an alternative, morally justifiable action which the speaker is advising against, whereas 'You must do *X*' implies that there is no real alternative to doing *X*.

If, however, the speaker's reason for advising that *X* be done is that it is something to which her interlocutor is *committed* by virtue of other things she has said or done, then it would make no sense to present *X* as something she ought to do. That would imply that *not* doing *X* would be justified except in these specific circumstances, when in the case of the necessary implications of actions precisely the reverse is true. Honouring the implications of a previous action is not something which needs to be supported by specific reasons from case to case; such implications rather form the given background of commitment, determining courses of action which the agent *must* follow, except of course when specific reasons support the claim that in this particular situation she ought not to do what she has committed herself to doing (presumably because there is something else she should care about more). In short, when *X* is an implication of an agent's previous actions, it would make sense to advise someone that she ought *not* to do *X*, but not to advise her that she ought to do it. Conversely, it *would* make sense to say that she must do *X* (namely, when reasons exist which support the idea that the commitment should be overridden, but the speaker wishes to assert that they are not sufficient for so doing, i.e. that there really isn't an alternative); but it would *not* make sense to say that she must not do *X* (because when doing *X* is an implication of a previous action, it always exists as a legitimate alternative to not doing *X*).

These grammatical points lead to the following conclusions. First, when one's reason for advising that a certain action be done depends upon its being something to which the person addressed is committed, then 'must' rather than 'ought' is the appropriate mode of presentation of that reason; and second, when one advises a person that she 'ought' to perform a certain action, the reason upon which the advice is based must relate to that person's cares rather than to her commitments. When Cavell puts these points about the form of moral reasons together with his earlier points about the substance of such reasons, he reaches the following conclusion:

> In ... morality, there are two main sorts of reasons with which we may be confronted: the one I might call a 'basis of care'—it provides whatever sense there will be in your confronting someone with what he 'ought' to do; the second I call a 'ground of commitment'—it grounds what you say 'must' be done in that person's commitments, both his explicit undertakings and the implications of what he does and where he is, for which he is responsible. (*CR* 325)

And of course, the constraints here presented as determinant for the moralist when she confronts another person are also determinant for that other person when she responds to the moralist. The terms in which any competently entered moral query about a given action must be articulated must also be the terms of any competently entered moral defence of that action; and the mode of presenting that defence (e.g. describing one's action as something one *must* do rather than something one *ought* to do) will carry analogous implications about the substance of the defence. In short, whether one is criticizing or defending a moral claim, one must invoke the values, concerns, and commitments that human beings must and ought to honour in their actions.

The specific logic of moral argument therefore entails that anyone confronted with a challenge or query concerning their actions which is grounded in their cares or commitments is able to ignore that challenge only on pain of manifesting incompetence in the practice of moral debate; a competently entered query demands a competently entered response. What it does *not* demand, however, is *acceptance* of the criticism thus entered; for we can acknowledge the relevance of the basis of care or ground of commitment cited by our interlocutor without agreeing to the weight or significance she attaches to it in the present context. In short, agreement about the pertinence of the challenge can coexist with disagreement about its importance. Cavell puts it as follows:

> What is enough to counter my claim to be right or justifed in taking a 'certain' action is up to me, up to me to determine. I don't *care* that he is an enemy of the state; it's too bad that he took what I said as a promise; I know that others will be scornful, nevertheless ... suppose I *have* done more or less what he did,

my case was different. I can *refuse to accept* a 'ground for doubt' without impugning it as false, and without supplying a new basis, and yet not be dismissed as irrational or morally incompetent. What *I cannot* do, and yet maintain my position as morally competent, is to deny the *relevance* of your doubts ('What difference does it make that I promised, that he's an enemy of the state, that I will hurt my friends'), fail to see that they require a determination by me. (*CR* 267)

In other words, if both the person making a claim to moral rightness and the person challenging it are morally competent, then the person challenged cannot avoid responding to the challenger's grounds for doubt, but the challenger cannot avoid admitting the right of the person challenged to determine the significance of those grounds for doubt for herself. Her obligation to respond is dictated by the logic of the practice but the precise nature of her response is not. Accordingly, the response she makes—whether it is to accept the precise significance we have assigned to our ground for doubt, to contest it, or simply to deny that it has any significance—reveals not what the *practice* impersonally determines to be an adequate basis for the claim she has made, but what *she* personally regards as adequate. Making a claim to moral rightness, precisely because it carries an obligation to support that claim without determining any one way of so doing, thus says as much about the person making the claim as about the action which is that claim's object. In effect, participation in this practice involves declaring something about oneself and discovering something about others; moral discussion is an arena for the revelation of one self to another.

Questioning a claim to moral rightness (whether of any action or of any judgement) takes the form of asking 'Why are you doing that?', 'How can you do that?', 'What *are* you doing?', 'Have you really considered what you're saying?', 'Do you know what this means?'; and assessing the claim is, as we might now say, to determine *what* your position is, and to challenge the position itself, to question whether the position you *take* is adequate to the claim you have entered. The point of the assessment is not to determine *whether* it is adequate, where *what* will be adequate is itself *given* by the form of the assessment itself; the point is to determine *what* position you are taking, that is to say, *what position you are taking responsibility for*—and whether it is one I can respect. What is at stake in such discussions is not, or not exactly, whether you know our world, but whether, or to what extent, we are to live in the same moral universe. What is at stake in such examples as we've so far noticed is not the validity of morality as a whole, but the nature or quality of our relationship with one another. (*CR* 268)

If two people can explain and justify their differing moral judgements to one another in terms whose relevance to the matter in hand cannot itself be the subject of disagreement, then the structures which make such discussion possible also make it possible for those two people to continue to respect one another despite their differences. This outcome to the discussion is not guaranteed; but in the absence of those structures, even the possibility of such an outcome—the *possibility* of what one might call rational disagreement—would not exist.

Criticizing those structures because they do not guarantee agreement in conclusions about claims to moral rightness would only make sense if the critic thinks that such guaranteed agreement is both feasible and desirable; but such a thought presupposes that the world is fundamentally different from the place Cavell claims that we know it to be. It implies that human cares and commitments are not multiple and prone to conflict with one another, and that human beings are not prone to order, evaluate, and honour them in different ways; it implies that the notion of there always being one right thing to do in any conceivable circumstance makes sense. But why, Cavell asks, should we make such an assumption when the world we live in is informed with incompatible and yet equally legitimate claims, responsibilities, and wishes? If we perceive the world in such conflictual terms, the possibility of engaging in modes of explanation and defence which hold out the possibility of rational disagreement, of at least agreeing to disagree, will be seen as Cavell sees it—as one to be valued; for it gives us a way of removing unnecessary obstacles to agreement (i.e. misunderstandings or failures to understand) and a chance of maintaining mutual regard in the face of seemingly unavoidable disagreements.

> Morality ... provides *one* possibility of settling conflict, a way of encompassing conflict which allows the continuance of personal relationships against the hard and apparently inevitable fact of misunderstanding, mutually incompatible wishes, commitments, loyalties, interests and needs, a way of mending relationships and maintaining the self in opposition to itself or others. Other ways of settling or encompassing conflict are provided by politics, religion, love and forgiveness, rebellion, and withdrawal. Morality is a valuable way because the others are often inaccessible or brutal; but it is not everything; it provides a door through which someone, alienated or in danger of alienation from another through his action, can return by the offering and the acceptance of explanations, excuses and justifications, or by the respect one human being will show another who sees and can accept the responsibility for a position which he himself would not adopt. We do not have to agree with one another in order to live in the same moral world, but we do have to know and respect one another's differences. (*CR* 269)

In other words, the criteria of relevance shared by those competent in the practice of moral argument open a space in which the right to acknowledge and determine for oneself the relative importance of multiple and competing cares and commitments can coexist with the achievement of a community of mutual understanding and respect; once again, Cavell sees in a human mode of criterially governed interaction a way in which the search for community can be prosecuted without the sacrifice of individuality.

However, more is at stake than the laudable and valuable attempt to maintain one's regard for and relationship with *others* when one engages in moral debate with someone; Cavell's claim is that participation in such debates is essential for *self*-understanding—for discovering and maintaining one's relationship with oneself. The crucial point here is that, as well as being multiple and often incompatible (and partly because of it), the cares and commitments of a given individual can be *opaque* to her:

I have described moral arguments as ones whose direct point it is to determine the positions we are assuming or are able or willing to assume responsibility for; and discussion is *necessary* because our responsibilities, the extensions of our cares and commitments, and the implications of our conduct, are not obvious; because the self is not obvious to the self. To the extent that that responsibility is the subject of moral argument, what makes moral argument rational is not the assumption that there is in every situation one thing that ought to be done and this may be known, nor the assumption that we can always come to agreement about what ought to be done on the basis of rational methods. Its rationality lies in following the methods which lead to a knowledge of our own position, of where we stand; in short, to a knowledge and definition of ourselves. (*CR* 312)

Why might the extension of our cares and commitments, or the implications of our conduct, not be obvious to us? First, it may not be obvious to us how far our present and acknowledged cares and commitments do in fact extend: in contexts where their multiplicity has led to conflict, we may be able to see more clearly how best to order and honour the many things about which we feel we ought to care, how best to fulfil the many commitments we have, by discussing the possibilities with another person who cares enough about our well-being to engage us in a debate about it. Second, it may not be obvious how far our present range of cares and commitments ought to be further extended: we might not see that our action in a given context fails to make a commitment that we ought to make, or amounts to a failure to care about something we should care about; and attending to those who are prepared to point such matters out may be essential if we are to correct our perception of our situation. These possibilities exist precisely because the practice of moral argument does not determine right and wrong ways of fixing the significance of any given care or commitment. For example, the decision to regard any such value as fundamental and unconditional or as more significant than other considerations only under certain conditions, the belief that one course of action is something that must be done rather than one which generally ought to be done but not in these circumstances, is left to the agent concerned; and given that such decisions themselves fix the agent, determine her practice of morality, the advice and viewpoint of others may be of vital importance.

What you say you *must* (have to, are compelled to . . .) do, another will feel you *ought* to do, generally speaking, other things equal, etc., but that *here* you ought (would do better) *not to*. (That is a much more usual conflict than the academic case of 'You ought to do *X*', 'You ought not to do *X*'.) What you say you *must* do is not 'defined by the practice', for there is no such practice until you make it one, make it *yours*. We might say, such a declaration defines *you*, establishes your position. One problem of the freedom of the will lies in what you *regard* as a choice, what you see as alternatives you can take, and become responsible for, make a part of your position. This is a deeply practical problem, and it has an inexorable logic: whether what you say that you 'cannot' do you in fact will not do because of fear, or whether out of a consistent conviction that it is not for you, in either case that is then *your* will. If the alternative is blocked through fear, then your will is fearful; if from single-mindedness, then it is whole. It is about such choices that existentialists say, You choose your life. This is the way an action Categorically Imperative feels. (*CR* 309)

Precisely because such choices are deeply practical problems, because your inclinations may be based on fear rather than integrity, the opportunity to test your views and defences against the more detached (but none the less concerned) perspective of another person will always be useful and may be invaluable.

However, the third, and for Cavell perhaps the most important, sense in which the extent of our cares and commitments may be obscure to us depends upon seeing that our best intentions are not always enough to hold the consequences (and so the implications) of our actions within clear lines. What we do may have consequences which we didn't intend, or may fail to execute the intentions for which we acted, without our being aware of either fact; and there may be alternative courses of action available to us of which we are ignorant, so that choosing the course of action upon which we have fixed implies the existence of a set of preferences or concerns which are not really ours. In all these ways, that for which we *are* responsible can outrun or otherwise differ from that for which we wished or intended to be responsible, precisely because what we did can outrun or otherwise differ from what we intended to do or thought we were doing—and in a world where the consequences of action can be multiple, complex, interwoven, and widely ramifying in ways which an agent may be unable to predict or observe, what we did can therefore come as a complete surprise to us.

In short, what we might be said to have done can have the most various descriptions, and what we can be held responsible for doing will vary according to which description is settled upon. But the appropriateness of any one of those descriptions depends in part on what in fact happened as a result of our actions—on whether we *did* succeed in keeping our promise, whether we *did* cause the dismissal of a colleague, whether we *did* fail to choose the course of action which would have honoured our commitment to our children without failing to satisfy our friends' expectations; and those facts and results are not always obvious to the person who brought them about. In this sense, attending to others may be essential if we are to begin to comprehend what we are responsible for doing, the position for which we can be held accountable; for it may be our only way of discovering what we have in fact done.

In this respect, commitment to the practice of moral debate allows others to bring to our attention aspects of our situation and implications of our conduct of which we might not otherwise be aware but which materially alter that for which we might legitimately be held responsible. After all, if the confrontation is one which respects the logic of moral debate, our challenger's queries will necessarily raise issues that a person in our position—with our cares and commitments—cannot avoid facing; we are not forced to evaluate them in one specific way, but we cannot avoid the responsibility of *making* an evaluation, of determining what significance they are to have for us—we cannot avoid *taking* a position with respect to them. At the same time, however, the practice gives us a way of making the burden of these unlooked-for but unavoidable responsibilities bearable; for it gives us the opportunity and the right to explain ourselves, to correct our mistakes, and to apologize for that which we cannot correct—and to do so in ways which others cannot simply dismiss as irrelevant to the evaluation of our behaviour.

Whenever the practice licenses a query about our conduct, it also licenses certain responses to the query—chances to explain, defend, justify, or apologize for one's conduct: we can declare the purity of our intention in contexts where that intention failed of execution and our action seemed to be uncaring or faithless; we can apologize; and we can commit ourselves to behaviour designed to mitigate the damage we have unwittingly caused. In short, commitment to the practice of moral debate will not only allow us and force us to see more clearly what we have done, that for which we can be held responsible; it also permits us to respond to that knowledge in ways which will allow us to live with it—to live with ourselves as well as with others in a world where intentions can fail, alternatives be overlooked, and consequences outrun foresight. The very same practice which allows the self to be declared to other selves and thereby holds out the possibility of community is also a means of self-discovery and self-definition; making oneself known to others and making oneself known to oneself are two sides of the same coin.

Cavell summarizes these points about everyday human action by means of a contrast with actions in games, where such questions as what we are to do, what alternatives are open to us, and whether what we did was better than some other action are all settled by the practice:

> In morality, none of this is so. Our way is neither clear nor simple; we are often lost. What you are said to do can have the most various descriptions; under some you will know that you are doing it, under others you will not, under some your act will seem unjust to you, under others not. What alternatives we can or must take are not fixed but chosen; and thereby fix us. What is better than what else is not given, but must be created in what we care about. Whether we have done what we have undertaken is a matter of how far we can see our responsibilities, and see them through. ('Did you help him?'; 'Did you get him the message?'; 'Did you make your position clear?'; 'Did you do all you could?') What we are responsible for doing is, ineluctably, *what in fact happens*. But that will be described in as many ways as our actions themselves. And such total responsibility is bearable only because of the significance of elaboratives. (*CR* 324)

Cavell's point is that, although the root of responsibility is what you do or fail to do (those permanent facts of history), the trunk and branch of responsibility are what you are *answerable for*; his claim is that it is impossible to engage in action without opening oneself to queries about that action which relate to one's cares and commitments, i.e. without possessing the capacity to deploy what Cavell calls elaboratives—explanations of why one is doing something, and excuses or defences of it should these become necessary.

This impossibility is a function of the way in which the concept of human action is interwoven with the concepts of commitments and cares. As we saw when discussing the case of promising, part of what makes an action the action it is are the implications which follow from it: to promise is to commit oneself to act, and thus to ensure that one's future actions will be open to assessment in terms of that commitment. However, as Cavell also emphasized in that earlier discussion, in this respect promising is no different from a myriad other actions; all such deeds create commitments. But then any given action must always take place against a background of commitments created by previous actions; accordingly, as well as modifying that background by means of the obligations it creates, any action can also be evaluated as a response to it, a mode of acknowledging those existing commitments which can then be assessed for adequacy.

A similar point holds for cares: since human actions are essentially goal-directed, any given action is identifiable as the action it is only by reference to the goal to which it is directed—in the absence of that information, it would be impossible to say what the agent had done. However, it then follows that an action will reveal what the agent concerned wants—her desires, concerns, and cares; and since any given action is typically one amongst many possible actions, its performance can also reveal by implication the relative importance to the agent of the goal thus achieved as compared with the goals achievable by alternative courses of action. It must therefore be the case that an everyday human action is open to assessment with respect to the cares and concerns it furthers. In short, to act is to locate oneself in the space of cares and commitments and thereby to open oneself to moral assessment; and if such questioning is always a legitimate response to everyday human actions, then part of being a human agent must be the capacity to reply in kind—to explain, defend, or excuse one's action by reference to one's cares and commitments.

In this respect, however, the capacity that is at the foundation of one's competence as a *moral* agent is simply one aspect of a capacity that is essential to one's competence as an agent *per se*. For anyone who fails to understand that an action is something which the agent may be called upon at any time to account for has failed to grasp what the true nature of action is, namely, that actions are something for which agents are answerable. Cavell makes this point in his account of promising,

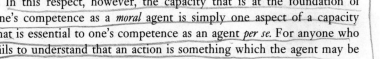
How is a biographer to describe an action? In terms of what the agent is answerable for. To lay this out is to reveal the moral position of the biographer; the biographer's ordering of significance.

when querying the idea that a child may be capable of making promises and yet may not grasp what counts as a legitimate reason for breaking promises:

That one must know what excuses and defenses and justifications (which I earlier called elaboratives) are, in order to know what promises are, does not make promising a special social practice; rather, it brings out the fact that the child is still not sufficiently a master of social intercourse to qualify him as a responsible and autonomous member of society. Learning what counts as an elaborative is a large part of what such mastery will require: in the absence of a mastery of elaboratives, we may question with respect to *any* conventional action (e.g., warning, thanking, giving, commending ...) whether the child knows what it *is*, what counts as doing it. And no one of these actions carries with it any particular set of defenses or excuses. (*CR* 310–11)

A person cannot be said to know how to make a promise if she does not know what breaking a promise is; and she cannot be said to know what breaking a promise is if she does not know when breaking a promise might be justified, or how such justifications might be entered, or when circumstances require an apology, and so on. But this knowledge of excuses, explanations, justifications—this knowledge of elaboratives—is not specific to the action of making a promise; for such defences are the ones we learn when learning to defend *any* of our actions. Acquiring the capacity to deploy elaboratives is part of becoming an adult, a person who is responsible for what she does; it is part of being an agent. And it is precisely these elaboratives which constitute the bulk of moral defence—of the procedures of accounting for one's actions whose logic we have been tracing out in some detail.

Self and Community: Art, Morality, Philosophy

In this last respect, the role of moral debate in our form of life contrasts sharply with that of aesthetic debate as it was outlined in the previous chapter. One might put it as follows: whereas it makes perfect sense to imagine a given person never participating in the procedures of aesthetic debate to any significant degree (she could always remain in or retreat to the domain of personal taste), it makes no sense to imagine that same person opting out of moral debate—for to do so is to opt out of the community of human agents altogether by abdicating from the responsibility of accounting for one's actions. It would be akin to self-imposed exile from the arena of everyday human life in society, from the stream of ordinary actions in which human beings, in their social settings, engage. In this respect, to ask the point of committing oneself to the criteria of relevance which inform the practice of moral argument is to ask the point of becoming a mature and responsible adult; a given person may fail to mature, may fail to become an autonomous and responsible agent, but this is not a matter over which she exercises a choice that might be guided by considerations of utility and point—it cannot itself be the result of an autonomous, responsible decision. By contrast, the practice of making and supporting aesthetic judgements is far less basic to our concept of human agency; it may draw upon the depths of our individuality and offer the chance of an intimate communion with others, so that someone who avoids engaging in such debates is missing something important, but such a person would not thereby be revealing her incompetence as an agent. She might well be asked to justify or account for this avoidance or refusal, but in responding to such questions, she would reveal herself to be a person capable of accounting for her actions; and she could not intelligibly so account for a refusal to deploy elaboratives.

This fundamental difference between morality and aesthetics is, however, only one element in a complex array of contrasts and analogies that can be drawn between the role of aesthetic debate and the role of moral debate in our form of life. To begin with the analogies: according to Cavell's interpretation of the matter, both practices manifest a very specific type of logic—one which permits rational disagreement without eradicating the hope of agreement on conclusions; and by submitting themselves to the constraints thereby imposed, human beings can explore and give expression to aspects of their individuality as well as exploring and creating their community with other individuals. In this sense, both practices show how the absence of guaranteed agreement permits the coexistence of individuality and community, for agreement in conclusions can be guaranteed only by submission to procedures in which any scope for the expression of one's individuality has been eradicated.

However, the ways in which individuality and community, speaking for oneself and speaking for others, are related to one another in each domain differ greatly; and this provides us with a series of contrasts. In the case of aesthetics, it is the courage and honesty of my attempts to give expression to my own responses which alone will make it possible for my claim to be speaking for others to be the foundation of a genuine community of response; only if I am true to myself in what I say will others find that I am true to them. In the case of morality, I need make no claim to speak for others when declaring my own position on the rightness or wrongness of an action, and when I do attempt to speak for another, I can only do so if I confront her declared position in terms of her own cares and commitments; if I am truly speaking for her in what I say, she may find her declared position to be false to herself, but in speaking for her I need not be speaking for myself. The achievement of a community of aesthetic response does not constitute the denial or repression of individuality because it can be attained only if individual responses can willingly be brought to coincide—only if differences in those individual responses freely disappear; whereas the achievement of moral community does not constitute a denial or repression of individuality because it consists in a respect for individual differences—it can be attained even if our differences remain. In the domain of aesthetics, individual self-knowledge is the basis upon which community is sought; by relying upon one's capacity to explore and express oneself, one opens up the possibility of community. In the domain of morality, individual self-knowledge is sought through discussion with those in the same moral universe; by relying upon community, one opens up the possibility of deepening self-knowledge.

One might summarize these contrasts in the following way: in aesthetics, a community of response consists in the attunement of individual responses, and is brought about by the controlled deployment of subjectivity and self-knowledge; whereas in morality, community consists in a mutual respect for individual differences which is brought about by the controlled avoidance of subjectivity, and which is relied upon for the achievement of self-knowledge. The shared criteria which constitute the two practices of making and supporting judgements permit the achievement of self-knowledge and the achievement of community in both cases; but in aesthetics, the former is a means to the latter, whereas in morality the latter is a means to the former. This implies that the nature of the community achievable in both cases will differ radically: in aesthetics, it will involve a certain depth and intimacy, a revealed or freely willed coincidence of selves; and in morality it will involve a certain absence of self, a refusal to fore-ground the idiosyncrasies of one's psyche, which has its own more austere attractions.

However, part of the reason for this sense of striking contrasts derives from the fact that the type or sense of community upon which Cavell concentrates in the domain of morality is very different to that which was his focus in the domain of aesthetics. In aesthetics, it was the community which exists when agreement on conclusions—although never guaranteed—is actually achieved; whereas in morality, it is the community which can be said to exist even when the possibility of agreeing on conclusions is unrealized. In other words, although both domains allow for the possibility of achieving rational disagreement *and* free agreement on conclusions (since neither excludes the latter), and so could both be said to permit the discovery and maintenance of community in both of those senses of the term, what seems to matter more to Cavell in aesthetics is the hope of agreement in conclusions, but what seems to matter more in morality is the hope of agreeing to disagree.

Clearly, Cavell's choice of emphasis here can be partially accounted for by the fact that in aesthetics, but not in morality, one's claim to rightness in judgement imputes universal agreement with that judgement. I may hope that others will come to share my judgement of an action's moral rectitude, believe that they ought to, and even regard agreement on that judgement as a touchstone for another person's continued inhabitation of my moral universe; but to claim that my judgement of the moral rightness of any given action is one with which all human beings ought to agree is at best to make clear the specific nature of my moral system (e.g. one presupposing a moral law which applies indifferently to all human beings)—for its denial would not be a sign of moral incompetence on the part of my opponent, but rather an indication that she cleaves to a different moral system. Under these circumstances, it is hardly surprising that one's attention should turn away from conceivable communities of agreement on moral conclusions, and towards the value of agreements to disagree; and the imputation of universal agreement which is evident in the practice of making aesthetic judgements makes it similarly unsurprising that one's attention should focus more on what the nature of such agreement might be when it *is* achieved.

Whatever the reasons for the shift, however, one consequence of it is that when we ask what light Cavell's philosophical investigation of morality casts upon the methods and structure of the investigation itself, we will find that it highlights matters which were much more in the background when we asked the same question about his investigation of aesthetics. When examining aesthetic judgements, Cavell found striking parallels between the imputation of universal agreement in such judgements and a tendency to employ the first-person plural form in making philosophical claims about what is meant by what is said; in both, reliance upon a mode of self-knowledge was seen to lead to the discovery or the establishment of community—in speaking for ourselves, we find that we are speaking for others. By contrast, what Cavell emphasizes in his examination of morality is not so much the achievement of a community of judgement through the tapping of self-knowledge but rather the achievement of self-knowledge through reliance upon those who live in the same moral world, those who need only agree to disagree about their judgements; in short, the emphasis falls upon self-knowledge as something to be achieved rather than relied upon, and upon the possible or likely failure of claims to speak for others when speaking for oneself.

And of course, both emphases are ones which highlight aspects of the nature of philosophical discourse—aspects which could also be seen by employing aesthetic discourse as a pole of comparison (and which were pointed out in the previous chapter), but which (for the reasons canvassed above) are much more evident when moral discourse is used instead. In the first place, it is essential in understanding the claim of a philosopher to speak for others when asserting what is said when to see that the claim may fail; it is simply an invitation to her interlocutor to see whether they *do* form a community in this respect, and when the invitation is accepted it is in the end up to the interlocutor to pronounce on that matter. In this respect, the philosopher has no more authority than her interlocutor is prepared to give her; an initial disagreement may be overcome, but if it persists there can be no appeal beyond the two parties to the disagreement. The resemblance with the form and nature of moral confrontation should be clear: the moralist too must accept the right of her interlocutor to determine the significance of the considerations raised by the competently entered query; and although she may come to think that the moralist's words are more faithful to her real position than her own initial pronouncements, it is all too possible that she may not. Furthermore, in the case of a persistent moral disagreement, what is at risk is never morality as such, but the nature and quality of one person's relationship with another: if the disagreement is sufficiently deep, that relationship may alter or end, but the availability of moral discourse as one viable mode of establishing community would persist. Similarly, the failure of a philosophical claim to speak for another spells the end of the idea that two specific people form a community on this issue, but not the end of the idea that it is possible for someone to speak for another when speaking philosophically; what is revealed is not the inadequacy of philosophical discourse as a way of establishing and exploring community, but the fact that a particular philosophical claim has been addressed to the wrong party. To make use of a formulation we first encountered in the context of morality: at stake in a philosophical claim to community is not the validity of philosophy as a whole but the nature or quality of two people's relationship with one another.

Of equal importance to understanding the nature of ordinary language philosophy is the fact that—whether or not it succeeds in its claim to community—it constitutes a method (or array of methods) for *acquiring* as well as giving expression to self-knowledge. The pressure of philo-sophical dialogue and self-questioning, by forcing someone to draw upon her knowledge of what she would say when, can lead a person to discover things about herself, her relation to others, and her relation to the world which she was not previously aware that she knew—and which hold for her (if they hold at all) regardless of whether they hold for others. In the present case, she would have begun specifically to appreciate things about the nature of morality, its role in her life, and the way in which it brings her closer to others; but she would also thereby have come to appreciate that her status as a language-using creature permits her to investigate many aspects of her life and world in this way—namely, by eliciting and elucidating criteria. Without the pressure of philosophical discourse, neither the specific deepening of her self-awareness brought about by eliciting the criteria which govern moral debate, nor the general deepening of her self-awareness brought about by knowing that she possesses knowledge of this sort that can be tapped in this way, would have occurred. In short, by applying Cavell's insights into the nature of morality to the methods by which he achieves them, we can come to see that they too are means of exploring and achieving self-knowledge, whether they result in the discovery or achievement of community or not.

It is, however, important to note in conclusion that a reflexive comparison of the results of Cavell's investigation into moral argument with the structure of his investigative method reveals at best a set of analogies or parallels between the two enterprises. Unlike the results of a similar comparison with the practices of aesthetic debate, which suggested that art criticism—particularly when focussed upon modern works of art—could be regarded as one mode of engaging in the practice of ordinary language philosophy, Cavell has no grounds for (and, at this stage at least, registers no desire to) interpret the processes of moral argument as a species of philosophical endeavour. To be sure, the different practices of moral and philosophical debate present a strikingly similar physiognomy at a certain level of abstraction, since both provide a domain within which human beings can explore and give expression to their individuality whilst simultaneously exploring and establishing a community with other individuals; in effect, both practices permit the coexistence of individuality and community. None the less, they do so in different ways; and this difference is crystallized in the fact that moral judgements—unlike aesthetic judgements and unlike philosophical claims about criteria—carry no necessary imputation of universal agreement. Any philosophical investigation of morality which registers and respects this fact thereby ensures that it will uncover nothing more—and, of course, nothing less—than a number of illuminating parallels between the object of the investigation and the investigation itself.

3

Politics: The Social Contract

Cavell's writings on the nature and role of politics in human life were, until very recently, much less extensive than his work on aesthetics and morality. Indeed, prior to the publication of his 1988 Carus Lectures (which we will examine in some detail in a later chapter), he engaged in an explicit treatment of political-theoretical matters only in sections of his book on Thoreau *The Senses of Walden*, passages in his essays on *Coriolanus* and *The Misanthrope* (in *TOS*), and in six pages of the opening chapter of *The Claim of Reason*. None the less, the importance of this material is far greater than its volume would suggest: for the focus and nature of his interests in this area serve to underline the specific themes that have already been broached in his writings on aesthetics and morality, to confirm the general need to interpret the results of his philosophical work in a given area as designed to cast light on the nature of philosophy itself, and to reinforce a sense of the startling degree to which Cavell's work embodies from the outset a unified vision of modern Western culture—one in which its various domains or spheres appear as differing inflexions of a single pattern or structure. We cannot therefore complete our survey of his early work and its focus on the social face of criteria, without attempting to elucidate his fundamental concerns in the domain of politics; but the task is made easier by the fact that those concerns are in fact relatively limited in scope. Indeed, since the central core of his reflections at this stage of his project remains essentially unchanged across the shifting contexts in which they are explicitly elucidated, and since they find their clearest expression in the relevant passage from *The Claim of Reason*, it is that text upon which we will be concentrating here.

Cavell begins with the observation that political theorists in the modern period have characteristically thought of the political community as founded upon a social contract, and he attempts to analyse the significance of this form of theorizing. On his reading, social contract theorists are obviously not to be regarded as offering a historical claim about how human society actually came into existence. Neither are they attempting to provide a general-purpose *answer* to the question

'Why should I obey the government?'—an answer of the form 'Because I am party to an agreement to that effect'; they are rather attempting to provide a set of terms in which we might *set about* answering a question about our obligation to obey a specific government, should such a question arise. In other words, for Cavell, writers such as Locke and Rousseau are in fact engaging in a philosophical form of political education: their aim is to provide a particular way of conceptualizing the relationship between the citizen and his society, a particular way of articulating the nature of citizenship. Cavell's aim is to elucidate the point and the consequences of this articulation.

In the first place, the consent which is involved in the social contract theorist's picture of society is not just a consent to obedience, the making of a promise to obey the government; it is also a consent to *membership* of society—and 'membership' understood in a very specific way.

What I consent to, in consenting to the contract, is not mere obedience, but membership in a polis, which implies two things: First, that I recognize the principle of consent itself; which means, that I recognize others to have consented with me, and hence that I consent to political *equality*. Second, that I recognize the society and its government, thus constituted, as *mine*; which means that I am answerable not merely to it, but for it. So far, then, as I recognize myself to be exercising my responsibility for it, my obedience to it is obedience to my own laws; citizenship in that case is the same as my autonomy; the polis is the field within which I work out my personal identity and it is the creation of (political) *freedom*. (*CR* 23)

For the social contract theorist, membership of the polis is internally related to the concept of consent: *only* someone who consents to membership can be a member, and *anyone* who consents to membership can be a member. Any member will know that her membership is solely a matter of her having consented to membership, and so will know that anyone else can (or has) become a member on the same basis. In this sense, membership is freely willed fraternity; because participation in the community is (and is understood to be) on an equal basis, it is *participation* in a community of equals. Moreover, the sense in which membership is a matter of participation is a very specific one: my membership of the political community is not just a matter of my having joined a community but of my being joined to it—it is *my* community, a part of me as much as I am a part of it. What I do and fail to do (*qua* citizen, politically) I do and fail to do in its name—I am answerable to it; and what it does and fails to do it does and fails to do in my name, on my behalf—I am answerable for it.

The idea that membership of the polis presupposes an acknowledgement of the polis as *mine* in effect gives expression to a vision of modern society as an artefact—as the creation of its members rather than a reflection of the divine or natural order of things:

Society ... is what we have done with the success of Locke and the others in removing the divine right of kings and placing political authority in our consent to be governed together ... The essential message of the idea of a social contract is that political institutions require justification, that they are absolutely without sanctity, that power over us is held on trust from us, that institutions have no authority other than the authority we lend them, that we are their architects, that they are therefore artifacts, that there are laws or ends, of nature or justice, in terms of which they are to be tested. They are experiments. (*SW* 82)

The members of a modern society are taken as no longer regarding the structure of their society as a reflection of sacred or supernatural facts, but as a reflection of their own joint purposes; they see themselves as its architects as well as its builders, not only its constructors but also the constructors of its blueprint. By characterizing society as a construction to which its members have consented, the social contract theorist therefore simultaneously puts that society at a distance from its members (conceptualizing its arrangements as provisional, contingent, capable of being modified—and so as unjustified unless humanly justifiable) and joins them deeply to it (conceptualizing its arrangements as implemented on their authority); such a theorist invites us to see ourselves as answerable *for* our government as well as answerable to it.

Conceiving of membership of the polis in this way involves conceiving of the polis as an arena within which each member might achieve and exercise autonomy: for if the polis can act in my name, if its structures, arrangements, and decisions are implemented on my authority, if what it does is something for which I can be held responsible, then in so far as I regard myself as *exercising* that authority I must regard the polis and its laws as embodying my will—and my obedience to it will then constitute obedience to laws which I have given to myself. In such circumstances, being answerable to the political community becomes an opportunity rather than a burden—an opportunity to forge, develop, and implement an aspect of my individual identity by constructing and maintaining a political community in which taking on and living up to the rights and duties of citizenship means realizing my best understanding of what my political identity should be (of who, politically speaking, I am). In short, in so far as I regard myself as exercising my responsibility for society and its government, citizenship is not a constraint on my autonomy but an aspect of it.

So, the idea of society as my society, as a construction to which I have consented with others and within which all have consented to stand on an equal footing, opens the possibility of membership in a political community on terms of freedom, equality, and fraternity—a trinity of ideas that encapsulates the view of society most famously identified with 'Locke and the others'. They are the blessings that a perfected modern polis brings for its members, the blessings in view of which they consent to membership and its burden of obedience.

Even in a perfected polis, of course, these blessings will cost the precedence of other blessings—those of God, of friendship, of family, of love; as in the case of morality, politics at its best is one way of achieving human goods, but it is only *one* way and the achievement of any given human good is not always compatible with that of every other. More pertinently, however, no actual political community has ever attained that perfection; any such community is riven with specific inequalities, lacks of freedom, and absences of fraternity. So when the question 'Why ought I to obey the government?' is raised in an actual case, it will be of no avail to point to these general advantages of citizenship. On the contrary, by invoking the notion of a social contract at this point, one sharpens the force of that question by recalling the advantages in view of which we are understood to have given our consent to obey the government, and highlighting their absence in our present social circumstances. The question is in effect reformulated to read: 'Given the specific inequalities, lack of freedom, and absence of fraternity in the society to which I have consented, do these outweigh the "disadvantages" of withdrawing my consent?'

What difference does this reformulation of the question actually make? First, it characterizes the present disadvantages of society, the specific inequalities and lacks of freedom and absence of fraternity in the community in which we find ourselves, as something to which we consent or have consented. Thinking of the polis as mine ensures that I am implicated in whatever the polis is and does: for even if its structures and pronouncements do not embody what I am prepared to recognize as my (political) will, my membership entails that they are made in my name and so are ones for which I am answerable.

Of course, when faced with the present state of society as a set of arrangements to which one has given one's consent, it is always possible to respond by withdrawing that consent. Indeed, that this *is* the choice we face in such circumstances is the second lesson to be drawn from our reformulation of the question of whether we ought to obey a given government. However, making such a choice involves computing the disadvantages of withdrawing consent; we know that citizenship in this polis involves consenting to specific inequities and injustices, but in order to determine whether or not these are outweighed by the countervailing benefits of citizenship we need to know what those specific benefits might actually be. In other words, if I am to answer the question I must determine the precise nature and extent of that to which I am at present committed by virtue of my participation in the polis, my status as one of its citizens—which means determining the precise nature and extent of my polis; and in the terms put forward by the social contract theorist, this means discovering what any member of that polis is obedient to (its constitutive laws and arrangements) and with whom (the constitution of the membership).

Since, however, this polis is mine—is something for which I am answerable, which acts on my authority and in my name—determining its nature and extent is the necessary first step on the way to determining the lineaments of my political identity, my political self; and in determining who I am *qua* citizen, I partially determine who I am *per se*. As Cavell puts it:

> ... the philosophical significance of the writing of the social contract theorists lies in its imparting of political education: it is philosophical because its method is an examination of myself by an attack upon my assumptions; it is political because the terms of this self-examination are the terms which reveal me as a member of a polis; it is education not because I learn new information but because I learn that the finding and forming of my knowledge of myself requires the finding and forming of my knowledge of that membership (the depths of my own and the extent of those joined with me). (*CR* 25)

According to Cavell, Rousseau is the social contract theorist who is most accurate in tracing out the answers which emerge when the task of finding and forming one's knowledge of one's political self is prosecuted within the terms set out by such theorizing. For Rousseau, in thinking of ourselves as members of a polis, we are constrained to think of ourselves as always already party to some social pacts or contracts; but the facts of everyday political life clearly reveal that we are not participants in the perfected polis. In his terms, we are not party to the genuine social contract, our polis is not the emanation of the general will; but it is none the less the emanation of the will of its citizens, something that results from the manner in which they exercise their political freedom. It follows that the non-existence of the perfected polis is the result of our not exercising our freedom to implement it. Since, then, we are not choosing freedom for all, we must be choosing freedom for some—we must be exercising our (political will) partially, in favour of some particular group or party in society.

The epistemological problem of society is not to discover new facts about it; the facts, as the Encyclopedists were globally showing, are there to be had. The problem is for me to discover my position with respect to those facts—how I know with whom I am in community, and to whom and to what I am in fact obedient. The existence of the prior contract is not an explanation of such facts. ... it is ... the fact that I now recognize myself to be party to some social contract, or pacts, which explains (what we take to be) the prior existence of the contract. But since the genuine social contract is not in effect (we could know this by knowing that we are born free and are everywhere in chains) it follows that we are not exercising our general will; and since we are not in a state of nature it follows that we are exercising our will not to the general but to the particular, to the partial, to the unequal, to private benefit, to privacy. We obey the logic of conspiracy, though we believe this to be true only of *others*. (You could call this Rousseau's self-diagnosis.) So we hallucinate the meaning of others to us (e.g. as equals) or have the illusion of meaning something to one another (e.g. as free fellow-citizens). (*CR* 25–6)

Since the bonds between us are (Rousseau claims) at once undeniable and undeniably inequitable, they must be secured by our obedience to agreements and compacts that are being made among ourselves as individuals acting privately and in secret, not among ourselves as citizens acting openly on behalf of the polis. We know that our citizenship does not in fact confer equality, freedom, and fraternity upon us, and—in so far as we conceive of our political lives in terms of the social contract—we are constrained to view this state of affairs as something willed by the members of our polis, something for which we and they are responsible; and since we are not aware of freely willing that our own freedom be fettered (since it would be crazy to do so), we conclude that the fetters we feel are the result of conspiracies by our fellow citizens against us. What we fail to see is that every other member of the polis is similarly fettered, and so must regard us as conspiring against them; we delude ourselves that we treat them as equal and free fellow citizens. So, if private conspiracy is the only possible explanation for the present state of society, then the logic of our position is that we are all conspirators. If this is false, then it is paranoid; if it is true, then we are crazy—crazy because, in failing to act on behalf of the polis, we are failing to act on behalf of a community which acts in our name and so are acting against ourselves, opposing one aspect of our identity with another, splitting our personality. What Rousseau's analysis highlights is the fact that membership of the sort of political community in which citizenship can be the same as autonomy is also one in which it can be the same as heteronomy; the promise of a political identity which is an integral aspect of personal identity is balanced by the threat of a personality divided against itself.

This analysis thus offers us peculiar and peculiarly intimate terms of self-criticism; and it leaves at least two key questions as yet unanswered. First, even if we find that the grammar of the myth of the social contract does articulate an aspect of our experience of politics and political relations, even if we sense a truth in Rousseau's conviction that the society in which we find ourselves is one to which we have consented, how and why did we go about doing so? Granted that it was not an explicit or specific act or agreement, what form of behaviour might constitute the investment of our consent in the polis—its authorization to act in our name? Second, if we find that injustices are being perpetrated in our name, if we are forced to the conclusion that we are conspiring against ourselves and others, how might we exercise our capacity and our right to withdraw our consent from such social arrangements—how might we declare that we are no longer answerable for such injustices and conspiracies? The answer Cavell gives to this second question flows from the answer he gives to the first.

On his account, Rousseau's conviction that our society is something to which we have consented manifests itself in a claim to know that he can speak for society and that society can speak for him—that they can reveal one another's most private thoughts. Political participation is thus pictured as a matter of simultaneously giving voice to the polis and giving one's voice *to* it; and its existence or reality is demonstrated in one's recognition that one's political voice is the voice of a political community. The question of how and why one consents to membership in the polis then can be reformulated as the question of how and why one consents to the giving over of one's political voice to the polis; and the answer of the social contract theorist is that it is a condition for the possibility of political speech *per se.*

At first sight, this seems paradoxical: it seems obvious that before one can consent to membership of a political community, one must be in a position to make up one's mind about it for oneself, and so must *have* a mind of one's own; to couch the point in terms of speech, one must have the capacity to speak for oneself before one can decide to give over that voice to the polis. For Cavell, however, the contrary is the case: the granting (or withholding) of consent does not presuppose, but is the condition of, speaking for oneself.

To speak for oneself politically is to speak for the others with whom you consent to association, and it is to consent to be spoken for by them—not as a parent speaks for you, i.e., instead of you, but as someone in mutuality speaks for you, i.e., speaks your mind. Who these others are, for whom you speak and by whom you are spoken for, is not known a priori, though it is in practice generally treated as given. To speak for yourself then means risking the rebuff—on some occasion, perhaps once for all—of those for whom you claimed to be speaking; and it means risking having to rebuff—on some occasion, perhaps once for all—those who claimed to be speaking for you. (*CR* 27)

Possessing a political voice is a matter of claiming to speak for others because it is equivalent to speaking as a citizen, and being a citizen is a matter of being one member of a community of fellow citizens; the extent of that community may be open to empirical exploration, but the implication that your speech is representative of *some* community or other is not. By the same token, one cannot possess a political voice without allowing that others may speak for you, since being a citizen involves consenting to be identified with the words and deeds of one's fellow citizens; once again, their identity and numbers may be open to dispute, but their existence is not.

This is why recognition of oneself as having a political identity at all is bound up with a sense of having always already consented to being answerable for the arrangements and pronouncements of the polis; for on this picture, if you have claimed a political voice in the polis in which you find yourself, then you have recognized it as yours, and it will speak for you until you say that it doesn't—or, more precisely, until you show that you do by rebuffing its claim to speak for you. However, when membership of the polis is understood in this specific way, what will count as withdrawing from the polis is equally precisely determined.

Since the granting of consent entails the acknowledgement of others, the withdrawal of consent entails the same acknowledgment: I have to say *both* 'It is not mine any longer' (I am no longer responsible for it, it no longer speaks for me) *and* 'It is no longer ours' (not what we bargained for, we no longer recognize the principle of consent in it, the original 'we' is no longer bound together by consent but only by force, so it no longer exists). (*CR* 27)

If 'speaking for others and being spoken for by others' is part of the content of political consent, then political dissent is not the undoing of consent but a dispute about its content—a dispute within the boundaries of the freely constituted polis about whether its present arrangements really are faithful to it. Dissent is also an attempt to speak for others, and if it involves rebuking some who claimed to speak for the dissenter, it is intended to bring them back to a position in which they can continue to do so; it is an attempt to restore or redefine the nature and extent of the polis, not an attempt to move beyond its bounds.

In other words, on this picture dissent is not a refusal of political speech, a refusal to give one's voice over to the polis, but a central deployment of it—a response to the inequities of citizenship which attempts to apply the resources of citizenship to heal the community from within. When citizens such as Thoreau resort to civil disobedience, they are not attempting to privatize their political voice, to transform it into something non-political, but are rather using it to rebuke their fellow citizens in the name of something to which they are jointly committed. Thoreau is refusing society his voice only in the sense that his words are intended to be such that his fellow citizens are unable either to attend to them *or* to leave them alone; his civil disobedience is embodied as much in the words of the essay he wrote about his night in Concord jail as in the night itself, and both are directed at his fellow citizens. Just as exercising our will to partial or private benefit is not a denial or transcendence of the political realm but a distortion of it and so an option within it, so speaking for oneself privately is not an alternative to speaking for oneself politically but a way of exercising one's political voice.

The alternative to speaking for yourself politically is not: speaking for yourself privately. (Because 'privately' here can only either be repeating the 'for myself', in which case it means roughly, 'I'm doing the talking'; or else it implies that you do not *know* that you speak for others, which does not deny the condition of speaking for others.) The alternative is having nothing (political) to say. (*CR* 27–8)

Of course, characterizing dissent and the withdrawal of consent as modes of speaking for others (as first-person plural forms of speech) does not provide an answer to the question 'Which specific political inequities and injustices demand that I withdraw my consent?' Nothing apart from our own conscience can tell us when we must claim that the present polis is unfaithful to our original agreement. What the social contract theorists do tell us is that the adoption of some relation or other to the facts which make up my society is a condition for the possession of a political voice at all (since the absence of any relation amounts to becoming politically mute); and that the exercise of my political voice is a way of finding and forming a knowledge of my identity by finding and forming a knowledge of whom I am in community with and to what I am prepared to be obedient. In this respect, exercising one's political voice is a way of learning about the self and that self's society; and failure to exercise it becomes a way of avoiding that knowledge—a way of blocking awareness of facts for which the self can be held accountable.

Rousseau's discovery is less a discovery of new knowledge than a discovery of a mode of knowledge, a way to use the self as access to the self's society. It is consequently the discovery of a new mode of ignorance. Marx and Freud will call this ignorance unconsciousness, the former of our social present, the latter of our private pasts; but these will prove not to be so different. (Both speak of this difference as the result of repression.) (*CR* 26)

As was the case with respect to aesthetics and morality, Cavell's elucidation of contractarian conceptions of the relationship between citizen and polis provides a striking set of parallels with the ordinary language conception of philosophy. According to Cavell, membership of the modern polis is most fundamentally understood to consist in the possession of a political voice, and the key condition for its possession is that one speak for others when speaking for oneself politically. This condition is unavoidable, but the identity of those others is a matter of empirical discovery; the exercise of one's voice is therefore a way of exploring rather than relying upon the bounds of one's political community, the limits of one aspect of one's mutuality with others. The obverse of this condition is that one allow others to speak for oneself— that the polis be authorized to speak and act in one's name unless and until one shows that it does not; and this answerability for the polis opens the possibility of one's obedience to it being a matter of obedience to laws one gives to oneself, so that citizenship becomes an aspect of autonomy and the polis functions as a field for the working out of an aspect of one's identity. In short, exercising one's capacity to speak politically is at once a means of exploring one's individuality and one's community; it constitutes a mode of establishing a sort of self-knowledge which is simultaneously knowledge of others.

This conjunction of self-knowledge and knowledge of others in politics is of course precisely analogous to the methodology of ordinary language philosophers: in both domains, claims drawing upon self-knowledge are made in the first-person plural mode, but the range of reference of the 'we' is a matter to be decided by the responses others make to our claims to speak for them, to speak their minds; in both, the self-knowledge concerned is worked out rather than simply assumed; and in both that working out is inseparable from the working out of the limits of one's agreement with others. Whereas Cavell's interpretation of aesthetic discourse tended to foreground the establishment of achieved communities of response, and his interpretation of moral discourse tended to focus on the achievement of self-knowledge, his interpretation of political discourse gives equal weight to the two themes: the political voice most resembles the aesthetic voice in its claim to be speaking for others, and it most resembles the moral voice in its acknowledgement of the need for others to speak on its behalf. In this respect, therefore, political discourse seems to epitomize the ways in which the grammars of these three criterially governed and constituted modes of human interaction closely parallel the grammar of philosophical practice.

We might capture the general position in the following terms: the structure of the problem of political consent seems to stand midway between that of eliciting agreement on the aesthetic status of a particular object and that of determining one's position with respect to a concrete moral problem. For one can think of all three issues as variations upon a general question concerning how one is to go on—how one is to apply or project one's (aesthetic, moral, or political) judgement in a new context; and one can distinguish the variants in terms of their similarity to that general question as it is posed in ordinary language philosophy, which asks us to exercise our linguistic judgement in particular imagined contexts. In the case of aesthetic judgements—particularly with respect to modern art—the degree of similarity is high, since making the judgement amounts to claiming that we should all extend the grammar of the relevant aesthetic terms in a particular way. In the case of morality the differences seem more striking than the similarities, for a moral judgement carries no necessary imputation of universality and serves more to fix a personal moral position than to project the shared grammar of moral terms. In this respect, political discourse resembles that of morality rather than of philosophy, for its emphasis is clearly upon substantive rather than grammatical issues—political consent and dissent focusses upon the content of the social contract, the substantive direction being taken by the political community; but the contractarian tie between one's own and others' voices characterizes political speech as speech on behalf of the political community, an attempt to recall one's fellow citizens to the terms of its founding charter, and such imputed universality aligns political discourse with that of aesthetics and so with philosophy.

Such a general summary of the matter does not, however, capture everything that is of reflexive interest about Cavell's interpretation of social contract theory. For he also employs that interpretation to draw attention to an aspect of ordinary language (and so of the philosophical method based upon it) which has not yet been noted, and which has to do with the presuppositions of entrance into the speech community. If my possession of a political voice has as its condition that that voice be given over to the polis, then the acquisition of that voice—my stepping over the threshold of the political community—has as its condition that I be prepared to recognize something of myself in the sayings and doings of those who are already members, and that they be prepared to recognize something of themselves in my first attempts to exercise my voice. In the absence of such mutual recognition or acknowledgement, I will be incapable of growing into citizenship, and the polis will be incapable of ensuring its continuance through my inheritance of it—I will lack a political voice, and the polis will find itself unable to speak for, to share a political voice with, its young. Thus the need of the political community to maintain its own existence generates inescapable responsibilities on the part of members and candidate members, elders and adolescents; no one can know how deeply agreement might run across the generations, but the penalty for its absence is such that our attempts to find it are worth the risks of rebuff, rebuke, and redefinition of the self.

This way of understanding the age of consent issues in a sketch of the logic of adolescence—an attempt to treat adolescence as a political concept rather than a piece of human psychopathology—which is most evident in the 'Cover Letter to Moliere's *Misanthrope*' in *Themes Out of School*. Within the context of *The Claim of Reason*, however, it sets up a way of highlighting the problem of the inheritance of one's natural language—a problem in which the role of one's political elders is taken by the elders who taught Augustine to speak:

I would like to say: If I am to have a native tongue, I have to accept what 'my elders' say and do as consequential; and they have to accept, even have to applaud, what I say and do as what they say and do. We do not know in advance what the content of our mutual acceptance is, how far we may be in agreement. I do not know in advance how deep my agreement with myself is, how far responsibility for the language may run. But if I am to have my own voice in it, I must be speaking for others and allow others to speak for me. The alternative to speaking for myself representatively (for *someone* else's consent) is not speaking for myself privately. The alternative is having nothing to say, being voiceless, not even mute. (*CR* 28)

For Cavell, taking this parallel seriously generates at least three important points. First, it suggests that the methods of ordinary language philosophy should be seen, not as an ornamental or otherwise optional aspect of one's capacities as a native speaker, but as a central aspect of their full flowering. The claims of the philosopher to speak for others when stating what is said when may be rebuffed in particular cases, but the claim to be speaking on *someone's* behalf is a condition for speech *per se*; in its absence, one would not be speaking privately (speaking a private language)—one would not be speaking at all. In this respect, Cavell's interpretation of contractarian politics comes to a conclusion which is parallel to his interpretation of morality; for in the latter case too, despite the fact that we may find our moral universe to be unshared by our interlocutor, our being open to moral debate and confrontation—our capacity to elaborate our actions—is not just a condition for moral agency but a condition for agency *tout court*.

Second, Cavell's talk of elders and children as needing to see themselves in one another re-emphasizes the way in which, and the degree to which, the foundations of our linguistic understanding are personal, to do with knowledge and awareness of self. In effect, he portrays our linguistic elders as, in the last analysis, offering themselves as paradigms of correct, intelligible speech. Rather than transmitting a body of impersonal, objective principles, their teaching amounts to displaying the body of their personal linguistic responses as an exemplary instance of how we should go on; and our capacity to absorb that teaching rests upon our ability to locate and draw upon those aspects of our own responses which are or can be attuned to theirs—upon that within us which is both personal and interpersonal, subjective and intersubjective.

On such an account, however (and this is the third lesson), we must think of the speech community as an inherently fragile thing. For if the ground of the inheritability of language, the basis of the continued existence of the speech community and its members, is the capacity of human beings to see and hear themselves in the words and deeds of other human beings, then the continuance of that community cannot be guaranteed either by nature or by grammar; it rests solely upon our capacity to take and maintain an interest in one another and in ourselves.

This portrayal of the foundations of ordinary language has clear and momentous implications for our understanding of the philosophical method that draws upon it. For it not only confirms Cavell's earlier commitment to the idea that the basis of that method is ineluctably personal; it does so in a way that simultaneously reveals its fragility and specifies what might be at stake in its preservation. For in so far as ordinary language philosophy draws upon a willingness and a capacity to speak representatively (to speak for others by speaking for one-self) that can be thought of as a core condition for speech *per se*, then a commitment to this philosophical method will appear as one, central form in which human beings express and renew the interest in one another and themselves that maintains human culture and community—not so much a species of second childhood as a form of education for adults, a means of reinheriting language and the life that it informs. But by the same token, the basis of the method, like the basis of its central resource, is a contingent and fragile thing—a matter of the interest one can take in oneself and others. So a continued commitment to this philosophical approach presents itself as at once deeply significant and sheerly contingent—something in which much is at stake and nothing is guaranteed. Against such a background, it is unsurprising that the question of the inheritability of ordinary language philosophy should constitute a pervasive background theme in Cavell's later work.

Conclusion to Part I
Philosophy's Affirmation of Modernity

Thus far, my juxtaposition of Cavell's remarks about aesthetics with his remarks on morality and politics has been subservient to a single purpose: that of making the best possible case for his claims that there are structural analogies between the procedures and concepts which go to make up each of those domains of discourse, and that these analogies also hold between those domains and that of ordinary language philosophy. However, as we have moved from aesthetics through morality to politics, what has become more evident is a particular feature or characteristic of Cavell's own remarks about the domains at issue; for by the time he turns to politics, he is plainly and explicitly engaged in elucidating a specific brand of political theorizing. Rather than attempting to outline the grammar of politics *per se* (whatever that might mean), he offers a way of understanding the nature of politics in a community arranged according to the specifications of contractarian liberalism; and it is with respect to this specification of the domain of politics that Cavell can find fruitful and illuminating analogies between it and ordinary language philosophy.

Some absolutely crucial insights flow from this simple observation, and I want to end this part of the book by drawing out some of their implications—in a necessarily preliminary way, but one that might none the less help the reader to orientate herself in the chapters that are to follow. First, it becomes obvious in retrospect that Cavell's remarks on morality and art also conform—although much less explicitly—to a liberal conception of the nature of ethical and aesthetic life. His portrait of the procedures of moral discourse is one which emphasizes the fundamental importance of the individual's right to work out her moral position for herself: ethical debate is primarily an essential part of a process of self-development, and although it is structured in such a way as to permit the possibility of moral community, that community is based upon an agreement to disagree and presupposes that one must confront others on their own terms rather than upon one's own. Most fundamentally, the procedures Cavell outlines are explicitly tailored for a world in which moral values, duties, and responsibilities are multiple, complex, conflicting, and ultimately incommensurable—a world of moral experience in which there is not one right thing to do in every conceivable circumstance but in which what it is right to do is open to argument, elaboration, and divergent but equally legitimate decisions. Individuals do not engage in moral debate in order to *discover* the one right thing to do; they do so in order to fix the relative importance of their cares and commitments for themselves, and to bear the responsibility for so doing. If one were to speculate about the best shape for a political community intended to accommodate individuals with this attitude to moral life, then anti-perfectionist versions of liberal democracy such as that outlined in John Rawls' *A Theory of Justice* (in which the state is forbidden to determine policy in accordance with any particular conception of the good) would seem to fit the bill.

And once this liberal inflexion is seen in Cavell's picture of morality, it is not hard to perceive that a similar mark has been left upon his picture of aesthetics; here, the importance of his decision to focus upon the circumstances and structure of modernist art becomes clear. For, as we saw in the Foreword, he interprets modernism as a response to the fact that the impersonal certainties and general principles that partly constituted the classical traditions in, for example, architecture and painting seem no longer able to elicit conviction from artists, critics, or audiences; as a consequence, individual art works cannot presuppose agreed conventions but rather embody intensely personal concerns whose claim to intersubjective intelligibility and power might none the less be granted by critics and audience and thereby become the ground of new conventions and so of a new aesthetic community. Against such a background, Cavell's portrait of the critic as an exemplar of self-mastery and of an aesthetic community as one in which subjectivity is not eradicated but brought to coincide with the individuality of others through the exercise of free will and self-exploration carries great plausibility; and the classically liberal emphases upon individual autonomy, personal conviction, and freely willed agreement that such a portrait so naturally embodies can all too easily be overlooked. In other words, seen against the wider sweep of Cavell's other interests, his emphasis on modernism in the arts comes into focus as an aspect of a wider concern with (liberal) modernity; artistic modernism just *is* a response to, and so a trace or manifestation of, the problem of modernity as it emerges in the domain of aesthetics.

Given, however, that Wittgensteinian grammatical investigations are typically understood to eschew the avocation of particular values (if any theses advanced in philosophy would receive universal agreement,[1] then surely no specific cultural formation should receive a philosophical imprimatur), then identifying a liberal inflexion in Cavell's characterization of the political, moral, and aesthetic procedures and concepts he has examined may lead us to conclude that he has failed to provide a suitably detached or impartial investigation of the relevant domains, and so that his characterizations are unreliable or inaccurate. There is, however, a way of deflecting or defusing this suspicion: not by denying that Cavell's picture of aesthetics, morality, and politics is essentially liberal, but by pointing out that this may be because that which he is attempting to depict—some of the central concepts and procedures which go to make up aesthetic, moral, and political thought and practice in the late twentieth century—are themselves inevitably and ineradicably liberal. After all, in the case of politics, the texts of the contractarian liberal theorists have had an influence which is not confined to scholarly life; they were the origin and precipitate of revolutionary political activity which resulted in the overthrow of absolute monarchies and their replacement by political systems which at the least pay lip-service to the ideas of liberty, equality, and fraternity, and which form the framework of contemporary political life in the Western world. By the same token, the aptness of the procedures of moral discourse outlined by Cavell to a world of conflicting and incommensurable values might well be thought to reinforce rather than detract from his claim merely to be exploring the structure of the concepts and practices which inform our present experience of the moral life. What would be truly surprising, and provide grounds for accusations of substantive bias, would be an account of the grammar of ordinary moral, political, and aesthetic practices which did not reveal concepts and procedures which were deeply imbued with the values that have dominated Western culture since the Enlightenment. Ordinary life in the late twentieth century, and the ordinary language which informs it, is—and could hardly be other than—run through with liberal preconceptions.

The real interest of Cavell's readings of these domains of ordinary life therefore lies not in the fact that they reflect the essentially liberal values and interests of modernity, but in the particular variant or inflexion of those values and interests that they emphasize. For example, Cavell's position reveals the possibility of accommodating a liberal

[1] As Wittgenstein claims in *PI*, sect. 128.

emphasis upon the individual whilst allowing scope for the development and sustenance of community. As becomes most obvious in his treatment of the contractarian political theorists, Cavell's liberalism is not atomist; individual identity is not something which can be achieved and maintained in the absence of participation in a community of individuals. And, as his treatment of aesthetics underlines, articulating the deepest and most intimate reaches of the self need not involve escaping from or transcending the community, but can rather be a means of rendering one's connections with other selves deeper and more intimate. In this respect, we can already see that Cavell's liberalism is not likely to be vulnerable to a communitarian critique.[2]

Furthermore, the undeniably liberal Cavellian emphasis upon the integrity and autonomy of the individual coexists with a strong sense that such wholeness or identity is something that is not simply given or to be taken for granted, but must rather be worked for and may be under threat. For example, the interactions of moral argument are presented not merely as a way in which an individual may declare her position to others, but also as something without which she may not succeed in establishing or fixing her position; and the myth of the social contract is interpreted as stressing the possibility that each citizen's individual voice may be suffocated by the private and partial conspiracies of her fellow citizens. More generally, Cavell's view that making use of one's voice in art, morality, politics, and philosophy offers a way of bringing one's individual identity and one's membership of a community into convergence implies that, if one does *not* make use of one's voice—if one does not make a claim on community and thereby avail oneself of the resources for self-understanding and self-expression that membership of the relevant community makes available—then one's own identity will be to that degree impoverished or diminished. In this sense, in Cavell's variant of liberalism, the autonomy and integrity of the self is presented as a provisional and threatened achievement.

These themes will be developed in greater detail as the book progresses; but a word of warning about this general defensive strategy with respect to Cavell's liberalism ought to be sounded. Whilst it is the very reverse of surprising to find that prevalent contemporary aesthetic, moral, and political concepts and practices are imbued with liberal values, it would be very surprising indeed if contemporary culture were

[2] An important source of dissension in the field of political theory throughout the 1980s. Those interested in exploring the issue further might wish to consult S. Mulhall and A. Swift, *Liberals and Communitarians* (Oxford, 1992).

monolithically liberal. Quite apart from influences deriving from non-Western cultures, and setting aside for the moment attempts to establish post-modern modes of thought and practice, Western culture also contains strands of thought and orientations towards life which are fundamentally hostile to liberal values—socialism and Christianity being two obvious examples. By focussing upon the predominantly liberal inflexion of modern culture, Cavell is not imposing his own prejudices upon modern cultural reality; but it may be that the elements of modern culture that he ignores will have things to say about the liberal values he is elucidating to which his elucidations are, as they stand, blind.

This leaves the question of the status of Cavell's understanding and application of ordinary language philosophy. For, it will be recalled, Cavell argues for the existence of structural parallels not only between the domains of aesthetics, morality, and politics, but also between all three of those domains and that of his own philosophical method; and if the former are fundamentally liberal, then the truth of the second claim will entail that the latter is equally implicated in the values of a liberal perspective. In short, the structural parallels between Cavell's philosophical method and the results of applying that method suggest that ordinary language philosophy is the paradigmatically *modern* philosophy. A philosophy which grounds itself upon modes of self-knowledge through which the individual can speak for others and discover surprising depths of community without sacrificing her right to speak for herself, a philosophy which does not impose or presuppose uniformity between individuals but which holds out the hope of establishing that individuals are deeply, internally related to one another—such a philosophy might have been expressly designed for the predominantly liberal culture of which it is a part. In a recent book, Charles Taylor has argued that a central aspect of the modern notion of the self, of human identity and the sources of human good, is the affirmation of ordinary life—a renewed sense of the centrality of domesticity and labour, a distinctive concern for the domains of work and family life, of production and reproduction.[3] We shall examine the relation of this thesis to Cavell's work in more detail later in this book; but even at this stage, it is possible to see that Cavell's reliance upon and preoccupation with ordinary language (and so with the ordinary world which it informs) allows us to interpret his understanding or inflexion of the

---

[3] Cf. C. Taylor, *Sources of the Self* (Cambridge, 1989).

Wittgensteinian philosophical method as an aspect of that affirmation of the ordinary—as philosophy's affirmation of the ordinary.

It is important to appreciate that such an interpretation of the Wittgensteinian approach does not contravene its declared refusal to advance particular theses, its self-imposed restriction to descriptions of that which we cannot fail to know, and its reiterated refusal of the desire to construct philosophical systems. For there is a distinction between the deliverances of a method and its guiding presuppositions: the fact that a method demands a certain species of detachment or neutrality from its practitioners does not entail that the method itself is detached from or neutral between the wider cultural forces and movements within which it operates. On the contrary: as Rawlsian liberalism exemplifies, a 'theory' which is designed to result in a species of neutrality within the domain of its application but which itself embodies a certain set of substantive values or interests is one possessed of a classically liberal physiognomy. We may, however, accept the feasibility of the general project of locating Wittgensteinian philosophy within a wider cultural framework, and none the less have qualms about the particular location assigned to it: it may, in particular, seem puzzling that what is supposed to be the philosophical reflection of a general cultural movement which began at the time of the Reformation was initiated only in the present century. If so, it may be worth remembering Hegel's suggestion that the owl of Minerva flies at dusk.

PART II
Criteria, Scepticism, and Romanticism

4

Criteria, Scepticism, and the External World

In Part I of this book, I tried to elucidate the social face of criteria—the various ways in which they might be thought to facilitate and partly constitute agreement between human beings, to create a human community. In this chapter, I want to commence an investigation of the vertical rather than the horizontal axis of the space opened up by criteria, to explore the sense in which they align a speaker with the world rather than with other speakers. To this end, I will be concentrating upon the material published as the first two parts of *The Claim of Reason*; although these chapters first appeared in 1979, the material they contain originally constituted a major part of Cavell's doctoral thesis and thus can be regarded as the foundation of his philosophical work in a chronological as well as a logical sense.

Cavell takes Wittgenstein to have developed his notion of a criterion in response to the threat of scepticism—the worry that we cannot be certain of the existence of the world or of other mind-endowed creatures (other people) in it. Although, as we shall see, Cavell does not take the notion to constitute (or to be intended to constitute) a *refutation* of scepticism, its significance and function can best be understood by relating it to this particular philosophical problematic; and, purely for ease of exposition, my attempt to elucidate his understanding of criteria will proceed by examining his analysis of external-world scepticism before going on (in the next chapter) to the issue of scepticism about other minds.

Identity and Existence

For Cavell, the notion of a criterion is an everyday one, and Wittgenstein's notion—although not exactly the same one—is importantly dependent on it. If one analyses the ordinary notion in the contexts in which it is employed—for example, in stating the criteria for entry to a college, the criteria for a government's stability, the criteria for assigning manuscript leaves to a certain chronological period, and so on—one finds a common structure which might be summarized as follows:

> ... criteria are specifications a given person or group sets up on the basis of which (by means of, in terms of which) to judge (assess, settle) whether something has a particular status or value. Different formulations bring it closer to other regions of Wittgenstein's surface rhetoric: Certain specifications are what a person or group mean by (what they call, count as) a thing's having a certain status; the specifications define the status; the status consists in satisfying those specifications. (*CR* 9)

To this degree, then, Wittgenstein's notion of a criterion is not a technical term, not a term of art. However, once this general similarity between the ordinary notion and that of Wittgenstein is granted, certain important differences can be seen more clearly and must be acknowledged.

First, the ordinary notion of a criterion typically presupposes a distinction between criteria and standards: the criteria set up by the given authority can be satisfied to a greater or lesser degree, and standards are needed to determine that degree. In this sense, both criteria and standards are means by which a group judges or evaluates an object's membership in some special status; but criteria determine whether an object is of the right general kind, whether it is a candidate for this status in the first place, whereas standards discriminate the degree to which candidates satisfy those criteria. In some situations, once the issue of criteria is fixed, the further issue of standards would not arise: for example, once the criteria for sorting manuscript leaves have been determined, then if we assume that the differences between the candidate leaves are sufficiently gross, no difficulties about assessing the degree to which the candidates satisfy the criteria are likely to emerge. In other contexts, the issue of standards is at least as vital as that of criteria: if, for example, American officials fix 'the capacity to raise and support effective armed forces' as a criterion of the stability of the Saigon government, then the question of how one determines the degree to which that criterion is satisfied is critical, and to leave the matter open would be either deluded or devious. Indeed, in some practices criteria are explicitly taken for granted and the emphasis falls wholly upon standards; for example, in the case of a diving competition or a dog show, when the judges have a certain amount of discretion in the area of applying standards but none whatever in the area of determining or altering criteria.

The first disanalogy with Wittgenstein's notion of a criterion arises here:

In no case in which he appeals to the application of criteria is there a separate stage at which one might, explicitly or implicitly, appeal to the application of standards. To have criteria, in his sense, for something's being so is to know whether, in an individual case, the criteria do or do not apply. If there is doubt about the application, the case is in some way 'non-standard'. This means that we have no decisive criteria for it, as we haven't 'for all eventualities'. And this is itself informative about the case, as it is sometimes to answer a question 'Yes and No'; for example, Is Schoenberg's *Book of the Hanging Garden* a tonal work?; Can you play chess without the queen?; some would say, Can machines think? is such a question. What would be the point of deciding upon a more definite answer—I mean, a shorter answer—to these questions? (*CR* 13–14)

The second disanalogy between Wittgenstein's notion of a criterion and the everyday one has to do with the nature of the candidate objects and the concepts which assign them a certain status. In the ordinary case, the object in question is clearly one which requires some sort of assessment or evaluation, and the point of establishing criteria is to make the determination of its ranking or status as rational (i.e. as consistent, coherent, impersonal, and non-arbitrary) as possible. Wittgenstein's candidates for judgements are unlike dives, dogs, governments, and students in the sense that they raise or permit no obvious question of status or evaluation; his 'objects', and the concepts under which we subsume them by means of criteria, are chairs, toothaches, instances of rule-following, believing, reading, attending to the shape of an object, and so on—they are just the ordinary objects and concepts of the world. In both the ordinary and the Wittgensteinian sense, criteria are object-specific; but in the ordinary case we *start out* with a known kind of object and then apply criteria in order to evaluate it, whereas in Wittgenstein's examples we use criteria in order to *learn* what kind of object anything is.

It is worth noting here that, for Wittgenstein, this learning process is a matter of mastering the use of a concept; but attaining this mastery is not separable from attaining a mastery of the relation between this concept and other concepts. Criteria tell us what kind of object anything is in part by determining which other concepts can intelligibly be applied in contexts in which the concept of that object has its application; for example, knowing what toothache is is in part a matter of knowing what counts as *having* a toothache, what counts as *alleviating* a toothache, and so on.

... the test of your possession of a concept (e.g., of a chair, or a bird; of the meaning of a word; of what it is to know something) would be your ability to use the concept in conjunction with other concepts, your knowledge of which concepts are relevant to the one in question and which are not; your knowledge of how various relevant concepts, used in conjunction with the concepts of different kinds of objects, require different kinds of contexts for their employment. (*CR* 73)

In this respect, learning by means of criteria what kind of object anything is is not a matter of learning the name of the object; it is a matter of learning how its concept fits into a web of other concepts, of knowing the grammatical post at which the concept of the object is stationed.

That point aside, this second disanalogy with the ordinary notion of a criterion implies that, for Wittgenstein, any concept we use in speaking about anything at all will require criteria; without the control of criteria (of standards governing the application of concepts) we would not know what counts as evidence for or against any given claim. Wittgenstein is therefore presupposing that all our knowledge of the world, every surmise and tested conviction we have about it, depends upon the same structure or background of necessities and agreements that judgements of value explicitly do. It is not that statements of fact *are* judgements of value, but rather that both fact-stating and value-judging presuppose the same capacities of human nature—that only a creature that can judge of value can state a fact. Wittgenstein's focus is upon our ability to identify or discriminate or classify different objects with and from one another; his criteria are criteria of judgement.

The focus upon judgement takes human knowledge to be the human capacity for applying the concepts of a language to the things of a world, for characterizing (categorizing) the world when and as it is humanly done, and hence construes the limits of human knowledge as coinciding with the limits of its concepts (in some historical period). The philosophical task in this case will be to provide an organon which will bring those limits to consciousness—not to show the confinement of our knowledge (as Locke more or less suggests and Kant more or less implies) but to show what in a given period we cannot fail to know or ways we cannot fail to know in. (*CR* 17)

The third disanalogy with the ordinary notion of criteria has to do with the authority or group which establishes or applies the given criteria. In the ordinary case, the identity of this group varies widely according to the kind of object involved and the point of evaluating or ranking it; but Wittgenstein's source of authority never varies in this way. His criteria are always 'ours', the group which forms his authority seems to be the human group as such, human beings generally; when I articulate my criteria, I do so as a representative language-speaker. As we have already seen in earlier chapters, this is a *claim* to community rather than an attempt to rely upon it; by speaking representatively, I invite others to recognize themselves in what I say, but they can refuse my invitation—show it to have been directed to the wrong parties.

None the less, the notion of a criterion as Wittgenstein relies upon it in his grammatical investigations, and his more general notion of grammar itself, both presuppose that ordinary language is shared and pervasively systematic; for when I say what 'we' can and cannot say I am voicing necessities which others recognize as ones which they themselves obey—I am drawing upon a background of pervasive and systematic *agreements*. What the feasibility and success of Wittgenstein's grammatical investigations show is that this agreement runs very deep and very wide; and yet it seems inconceivable that we can have agreed beforehand to all that would be necessary to establish it. There would have to be too many conventions in play, one for each shade of each word's meaning in each context of its use.

The mystery dissipates a little if we realize that the agreement about which Wittgenstein is talking (his term is *Ubereinstimmung*) is agreement *in* something rather than agreement *to* something; he is interested in the fact that human beings agree *in* definitions and judgements, that they agree *in* the language they use:

> The idea of agreement here is not that of coming to or arriving at an agreement on a given occasion, but of being in agreement throughout, being in harmony, like pitches or tones, or clocks, or weighing scales, or columns of figures. That a group of human beings *stimmen* in their language *uberein* says, so to speak, that they are mutually voiced with respect to it, mutually attuned top to bottom. (*CR* 32)

In short, appeals to criteria and to grammar are not attempts to explain or prove that human beings are attuned with one another in their words (and so in their form of life); they are, when successful, exemplifications of it. There is nothing deeper than that agreement upon which to found the human capacity to know the world. But such appeals are not always successful; and when they fail, what is revealed is the fact that human beings are not, in this respect, in agreement, that one person's words are not in attunement with those of others. And in philosophy, the appeal to criteria tends to occur precisely when this attunement is threatened or lost, when we seem not to know our way around with respect to our words and the world to which they apply. For Wittgenstein, criteria are interesting not just because of the depth of agreement which they reveal, but also because they can be forgone.

For Cavell, then, criteria are criteria of judgement; in using them, a human being counts something under a concept, e.g. judging someone to be in pain on the basis of her winces and groans. Such criteria are context-dependent in the following sense: groaning is a criterion of pain (a piece of pain-behaviour) only under certain circumstances. If, for example, the person groaning is (would correctly be described as) clearing her throat or calling her hamsters, then the groaning is not a criterion of pain—it does not justify us in judging the person groaning to be in pain—because it is not an *expression* of pain, not a piece of *pain*-behaviour. Criteria are *not* context-dependent if that is taken to mean that pain-behaviour is a criterion of pain only in certain circumstances. That could be true only if a piece of behaviour could rightly be called pain-behaviour, behaviour expressive of pain, and yet not be a criterion of pain; whereas, according to Cavell, if the circumstances are right and the behaviour counts as pain-behaviour, then it also counts as a criterion of pain—the criteria for pain have been satisfied. In other words, for something to be a criterion of pain just *is* for it to be pain-behaviour; in calling a piece of behaviour 'pain-behaviour' we must already have included the circumstances under which that behaviour is *pain*-behaviour (and not e.g. throat-clearing or calling behaviour). What is circumstance-dependent is the matter of whether groaning is pain-behaviour, not the matter of whether pain-behaviour is a criterion of pain.

This interpretation of the point at which context-dependence enters into an account of criteria has two important consequences. First, if the recognition of groaning as pain-behaviour is a matter of distinguishing those circumstances in which it is an expression of pain from those in which it is not, then it may be exceedingly difficult to specify what the relevant circumstances are. We may be able to identify specific situations as ones in which we would say that a given episode of groaning is not a piece of pain-behaviour, but it will be impossible to specify all such situations in advance, and impossible to specify our grounds for saying that a given episode of groaning *is* a piece of pain-behaviour. There seems to be no less general answer to the question 'How do we learn what the relevant circumstances are?' than 'In coming to talk'; and this answer seems not to differ from the response 'In coming to know what things are, what people do'. Here, once more, we come up against Cavell's conviction that our capacity for speech is grounded not in an impersonal body of rules but in our ineluctably personal capacity to go on from familiar contexts to new ones, to project our concepts and their criteria.

Second, if identifying a piece of behaviour as pain-behaviour is equivalent to identifying the presence of a criterion of pain, then criteria cannot guarantee the presence of real, existing, actual pain. It is perfectly possible for pain-behaviour to be manifest and pain to be absent; and on Cavell's interpretation, that is equivalent to saying that it is perfectly possible for the criteria of pain to be satisfied and pain to be absent. In other words, on this reading of criteria, there are no criteria for the existence or occurrence of pain which go essentially beyond the criteria for the behaviour's being pain-behaviour; criteria of pain are satisfied by the presence of pain-behaviour, and so cannot guarantee the presence of pain.

It is this second consequence which distinguishes Cavell's position from that adopted by orthodox Wittgensteinian philosophers such as Norman Malcolm. On the latter's view, Wittgensteinian criteria do confer certainty: if the criteria for someone's being in pain are satisfied, then that person is certainly in pain—and it is this feature of criteria which explains why Wittgenstein introduced the notion in the first place. Cavell, however, not only regards this as a misreading of Wittgenstein's purposes;[1] he also argues that this alternative reading cannot succeed in excluding the uncertainty it opposes, but only in relocating it. For of course Malcolm acknowledges, as anyone must, that someone can be behaving just as if she were in pain and yet not be in pain; but in order to preserve the tightness of the connection he proposes between criteria and that of which they are criteria, he is forced to describe such a situation as one in which the criteria for her being in pain only seemed to be satisfied and in fact were not. However, once a distinction between the apparent and the actual satisfaction of criteria is introduced, the very doubts about the reality of another's pain that he is attempting to combat will be restatable as doubts about whether what appears to be a case of the satisfaction of criteria really is such a case. In other words, even on the more usual, perhaps orthodox, reading of the notion of

[1] Cavell presses the argument against the orthodox view that Malcolm represents by examining in some detail a set of passages from Wittgenstein—particularly those relating to the context-dependence of criteria, upon a misinterpretation of which Cavell thinks the orthodox position depends—in *CR* 37–48.

criteria, they will not confer the certainty that some Wittgensteinian philosophers wish them to provide.

On Cavell's reading of the notion, however, criteria and their satisfaction do guarantee something, namely, the applicability of the *concept* of pain. The criteria of pain can be satisfied and pain may in fact be absent, but the satisfaction of the criteria entails that this fact can only be accommodated or made comprehensible—can only be *described*—in certain ways.

> If ... the groaning *was* not (turns out not to have been) in those circumstances a criterion of pain (pain-behaviour), then there is no reason to suppose the person to be in pain; pain is not, so far, at issue. But if the groan was in those circumstances a criterion of pain, an expression of pain, then pain is, and remains, at issue. And that means that only *certain* eventualities will normally count as his not being in pain after all ... Circumstances, namely ... in which we will say (he will be) feigning, rehearsing, hoaxing, etc. Why such circumstances? What differentiates such circumstances from those in which he is (said to be) clearing his throat, responding to a joke, etc.? Just that for 'He's rehearsing', or 'feigning', or 'It's a hoax', etc., to satisfy us as explanations of his *not* being in pain (for it to 'turn out' that he is not in pain) *what* he is feigning must be precisely *pain*, what he is rehearsing must be the part of a man *in pain*, the hoax depends upon him simulating *pain*, etc. These circumstances are ones in appealing to which, in describing which, we *retain the concept* (here, of pain) whose application these criteria determine. And this means to me: In all such circumstances he has satisfied the criteria we use for applying the concept of pain to others. It is because of *that* satisfaction that we know that he is feigning pain (ie. that it is pain he is feigning), and that he knows what to do to feign pain. Criteria are 'criteria for something's being so', not in the sense that they tell us of a thing's existence, but of something like its identity, not of its *being* so, but of its being *so*. Criteria do not determine the certainty of statements, but the application of the concepts employed in statements. (*CR* 44–5)

And of course, if criteria settle questions of identity rather than existence, they cannot be used to refute scepticism; appeals to such criteria cannot directly negate the sceptical conclusion that we do not know with certainty of the existence of the external world (or of other minds within it). On the contrary, this reading of Wittgenstein's notion of criteria makes that conclusion undeniable: if our relation to the world and to others in general presupposes a background of attunement in criteria, then it cannot be one of knowing, where knowing is construed as certainty; but by the same token, that relation cannot be subject to *failures* of knowledge. The problem with the sceptic is not that he fails to recognize that criteria can provide the knowledge he craves, but that he raises the question of knowledge at the level or depth at which human beings relate themselves to the world by means of criteria, and so at a level or depth at which knowledge is not and cannot be at issue. In so doing, in asking criteria to do what they cannot intelligibly be asked to do but taking that inability as a failure, the sceptic in effect repudiates our criteria; he refuses them as inadequate to their task. And, on this reading of the notion of criteria and grammar, they must always be open to such repudiation: 'If the fact that we share, or have established, criteria, is the condition under which we can think and communicate in language, then scepticism is a *natural* possibility of that condition; it reveals most perfectly the standing threat to thought and communication, that they are only human, nothing more than natural to us' (*CR* 47).

At this stage, then, Cavell's understanding of criteria implies that, although the conclusion of scepticism is in some way awry or confused, the progress of the sceptic to the point where he feels compelled to renounce the conceptual scheme he shares with others cannot be blocked simply by invoking criteria; for to think that criteria provide the certainty for which the sceptic is searching is to share in his confused assumption that issues of knowledge, certainty, and doubt have legitimate application at this level of language. What we must now go on to explore is the question why and how the sceptic comes to feel that criteria are failing him, that he must renounce his conceptual scheme; for only in this way can we determine whether and how his progress might legitimately be halted.

Specific and Generic Objects

What is distinctive about the external-world sceptic is that he takes the validity of human knowledge of the world in general to be at stake when he is examining the validity of a specific claim to know something about that world—and in particular, that he takes the failure of his specific knowledge-claim to signal the failure of human knowledge of the world *per se*. Some ordinary language philosophers have taken this to show that the sceptic is misunderstanding the nature and status of specific knowledge-claims from the outset; and Cavell takes Austin as paradigmatic of such philosophers. According to Austin,[2] someone

---

[2] In his influential paper 'Other Minds', in *PP*.

making a specific claim to knowledge (e.g. that there is a goldfinch in
the garden) must be capable of defending it by citing her ground for
identifying the bird as a goldfinch—her criterion (e.g. its eye-markings);
and she must furthermore possess certain background credentials (e.g.
her training or experience in this domain) and opportunities in the
current case (e.g. the bird must be clearly visible from her vantage-
point). However, if these bases for her claim to know are not validly
countered or disputed, in ways familiar to all competent speakers, then
her claim has been adequately supported; and if they *are* validly
countered, then her claim fails, but its failure has no obvious consequences for the whole of human knowledge. If, for example, I don't
know that bitterns have the same eye-markings as goldfinches, then I
was wrong to claim to know that the bird in the garden was a goldfinch;
but the discovery of an error along those lines will not make me chary
of ever claiming to know anything.

Cavell takes Austin to be right in his assessment of the strictly
localized consequences of such failures or errors; but he concludes from
this that such types of knowledge-claim are not what the sceptic is
focussing on. After all, if the ways of countering, defending, and
assessing such claims are known to all native speakers of a language,
then so must the fact that any failure to defend such claims can have
only limited consequences; and the traditional epistemologist is, in
general, no less competent a speaker than his Austinian opponent. So,
to suggest that he is simply ignoring, repressing, or overlooking these
points when he finds himself driven towards a sceptical conclusion is to
imply a degree of duplicity or ignorance on his part which it is difficult
to credit. Cavell's view is rather that Austin's examples of knowledge-
claims are not ones of the type that the sceptic has in mind:

Austin takes a case in which, as he says, you (can) have provided enough to
show that there is 'no room for an alternative, competing description of it'. This
is a case in which the *problem* of knowledge is one, and initially one solely, of
correct description (identification, recognition). The objects 'chosen as stalking
horses' by the classical epistemologist are never of this kind; they do not
confront the problem of knowing at this point; that is not the 'problem of
knowledge' which concerns them. The objects they work with have been e.g.
bits of wax, tables, chairs, houses, men, envelopes, bells, sheets of paper,
tomatoes, blackboards, pencils, etc. (*CR* 52)

According to Cavell, whereas Austinian examples are of specific objects,
the examples of the classical epistemologist are of generic objects. This

difference is not one between types or classes of object, but between the kinds of problem that may arise about such objects; it is a way of characterizing the different spirit in which an object can be under discussion. Austin's goldfinch is a specific object in the sense that, when a problem of knowledge is imagined to arise with respect to it, that problem is one of identity rather than existence: the criteria which settle the question do so by settling the question whether it is a goldfinch as opposed to, for example, a bittern, one specific type of bird as opposed to another. The classical epistemologist's tomato or bit of wax is a generic object in the sense that, when a problem of knowledge arises with respect to it, that problem is of existence rather than identity: the question is not whether we can identify it, say what it is by saying what distinguishes it from other classes of object, but whether we can say that we know that it exists, is real, is actually there.

A problem of knowledge arising from the identification of specific objects is one which can be solved by the provision of a particular piece of information: if you lack the criteria for an Austinian specific object, then you lack a bit of knowledge which can be conveyed to you by someone telling you what the object is called, what its name is— perhaps, in the case of a goldfinch, by giving you an ornithology handbook. However, you are only in a position to be given that piece of information if you already possess the criteria for an object of that general (generic) kind. Someone who lacks the concept of a bird, who lacks the criteria which distinguish a living creature of that sort from other things, lacks the possibility of acquiring any more specific information about such creatures of the sort which Austinian criteria provide: if she cannot tell a hawk from a handsaw, she cannot learn how to tell a sparrow-hawk from a sparrow. These criteria, the ones you must possess if you are to know anything else about objects of the sort they pick out, are Wittgensteinian criteria (more precisely, the type of criteria with which Wittgenstein is primarily concerned); and (because?) it is situations in which they are in play with which the traditional epistemologist is primarily concerned. The capacity to recognize a tomato or a table seems to require no more than the ordinary human capacities to see and to speak; anyone who has mastered a language can say what she sees when she sees such things, for anyone who cannot do this simply cannot be regarded as linguistically competent.

This difference in the logical priority of the criteria that have application to specific and to generic objects is vital to the generation of the traditional epistemologist's sceptical worries. For he raises his question about tomatoes and tables rather than goldfinches and bitterns precisely so as to ensure that no specialized knowledge, with which some speakers might be better acquainted than others, is at issue; after all, and as he knows as well as any other competent speaker, if such information *were* at issue then a failure of knowledge resulting from a lack of acquaintance with it clearly would not cast any doubt upon human knowledge *per se.* For exactly the same reason, he also chooses a knowledge-claim which is made in optimal circumstances: if visibility were poor or his interlocutor's position with respect to the generic object otherwise inferior, and this were the reason for doubting the claim to know that the object was really there, then once again the failure of knowledge thereby generated would not suggest a universal failure of human knowledge. With the epistemologist's generic objects, neither restriction on the ramifications of his sceptical worry can be invoked: anyone equipped with normal human perceptual and linguistic capacities, anyone capable of knowing anything at all, must know that this object is in front of her eyes—it will seem that if we know anything, we know that. And then, if the epistemologist can succeed in getting us to admit that we do *not* know that, to admit that our basis for claiming knowledge of that seemingly fundamental sort is inadequate, the conclusion that we do not know *anything* will be inescapable.

It is ... of the essence of the traditional epistemologist's investigations that the objects he uses as examples are not ones about which there is something more to learn in the way of recognizing them; *no-one's position,* with respect to identifying them, *is better than anyone else's.* And it turns out that no-one's position is better in any respect. An island of earth is faced by an island of consciousness, of sense experience. And this proves not to be enough for knowing. (*CR* 56)

It is this need to imagine a best case for knowledge which makes the sceptic's focus upon questions of reality or existence rather than upon questions of identity essential. For such a best case is one in which the criteria for something's being an object of a certain sort have been satisfied, and the only sort of doubts that can be raised about a knowledge-claim employing a concept whose criteria have been satisfied are ones that do not relate to questions that the satisfaction of criteria settle, i.e. ones that do not relate to questions of identity. The sceptic, then, cannot doubt its being *so*; but he can doubt its *being* so. He can do this by raising possibilities the description of which retains the relevant concept but alters the reason for its applicability, e.g. by raising the suspicion that it is not a real goldfinch (but a stuffed or mechanical one), not a genuine tomato (but one made of wax), not a real table (but a hallucinated or dreamt-up one). Just as the satisfaction of the criteria for pain do not guarantee the presence of genuine pain but do determine that our account of its absence must involve the presence of genuine *pain*-behaviour, so the satisfaction of the criteria in this case guarantees that the failure of the object to match up to the knowledge-claim be accounted for in ways which retain the concept of that object. The need for the sceptic's doubts to be focussed on the reality or existence of something rather than its identity is thus unavoidable.

The logic of the sceptic's position can also be elucidated in the following way. If doubt can be raised about a knowledge-claim directed at a particular generic object, then that doubt will immediately ramify vertically in the sense that it must simultaneously undercut any and all knowledge-claims directed at specific objects of this generic type: if you can't claim to know a hawk from a handsaw, you certainly can't claim to know a sparrow-hawk from a sparrow. If, however, the doubt is to ramify to all knowledge-claims directed at any generic objects (and thereby to all knowledge-claims), it must arise by reference to a feature which all generic objects possess—or, more precisely, which all objects possess generically, i.e. in so far as they are objects. In short, the doubt must be directed at the objecthood of the object, at the fact of its materiality, its externality to the perceiver:

When those objects present themselves to the epistemologist, he is not taking one as opposed to another, interested in its features as peculiar to it and nothing else. He would rather, so to speak, have an unrecognizable *something* there if he could, an anything, a thatness. What comes to him is an island, a body surrounded by air, a tiny earth. What is at stake for him in the object is materiality as such, externality altogether. (*CR* 53)

Once again, the sceptic's preference for raising doubts about existence or reality rather than about identity is not a dispensable feature of his approach to these matters.

To summarize: the need for sceptical doubt to have global ramifications entails that it must be raised by the epistemologist with respect to the reality or existence of an object rather than its identity; and this means that the knowledge-claim subjected to sceptical doubt must be a claim to know of the generic object that it exists, is real, is actually there. If such a claim can be made to arise and then legitimately be undermined, what will be cast in doubt is not a piece of knowledge or an aspect of one human being's cognitive, linguistic, or perceptual competence, but our assurance that there is a world of objects to which our concepts of objects can be trusted to relate us; for if we admit that situations in which, for all the world, our criteria are satisfied are none the less ones in which we cannot be sure that their objects are actually there, then our cognitive capacities will have been shown to be incapable of ever establishing reliable contact with the world. Of course, there may be problems in getting this particular kind of knowledge-claim to arise in these contexts, and there may be problems with the sceptic's grounds for doubting such claims to knowledge when made in such contexts; but the sceptic's inference from the failure of a specific knowledge-claim to the failure of human knowledge as such cannot be dismissed a priori on the Austinian grounds that it distorts or ignores the procedures that are appropriate to the assessment of the sort of knowledge-claim that is at stake.

> Proving a radical incoherence or some extraordinary use of language in the investigations of classical epistemology will now mean proving some radical incoherence in asking, about a generic object, how we know it exists. Asking it, of course, not when there is some real and obvious difficulty about knowing it (e.g., poor visibility, which might make my position better than yours), but when there is no special reason of *that* kind; when for all the world we are both in the same position, and an optimal position, facing it together. Doubtless there is something extraordinary about this question, and perhaps we should say that there must be some special reason for raising it. Then my question is: Is it obvious that the philosopher has no such reason? (*CR 56*)

What might make it seem reasonable to raise what are clearly odd or unusual grounds for doubting the existence or reality of a generic object—grounds that are odd or unusual not in the sense that they have no relevance to the knowledge-claim (for if the object in front of me is a piece of painted wax then it is not a tomato) but in the sense that it seems odd or unusual to raise such possibilities when the conditions for making that claim to know are optimal? There *are* cases in which, although you have no definite reason for thinking that the relevant ground for doubt does in fact apply, you have some reason to think that *something might be amiss* with your knowledge-claim; these are cases in which a worry has arisen and needs to be accounted for or dissolved. For example, you distinctly remember having put an envelope on the table, and now it isn't there; *there must be some explanation.* Maybe it was stolen; maybe you only put the letter itself there and not the envelope as well; maybe you only dreamt that you put it there. If someone were to say, in relation to such a case, that you have no reason to raise the question of existence or reality, she would seem to you to have missed the point because the context is one in which the question has already, and entirely reasonably, arisen—it has been forced upon you. Cavell's claim is that the original motivation of the sceptic derives from such a situation: not one in which an object has gone missing, but one in which a sense has arisen that something may be amiss with even the simplest case of knowledge under optimal conditions. The sceptic *begins* his investigation with this sense of something being amiss with human knowledge; and once he has this sense, then the odd or unusual possibilities he invokes will naturally and reasonably arise as possibilities which, if actual, would indeed confirm that his worries are not groundless, and which he discovers cannot, once invoked, be ruled out.

My major claim about the philosopher's originating question—e.g., '(How) do (can) we know anything about the world?' or 'What is knowledge; what does my knowledge of the world consist in?'—is that it (in one or another of its versions) is a response to, or expression of, a real experience which takes hold of human beings. It is not 'natural' in the sense I have already found in the claim to 'reasonableness': it is not a response to questions raised in ordinary practical contexts, framed in language which any master of language will accept as ordinary. But it is, as I might put it, a response which expresses a natural experience of a creature complicated or burdened enough to possess language at all. (*CR* 140)

The experience Cavell has in mind is, naturally enough, an experience or sense that one may know *nothing* about the world. Something analogous to this can arise, for example, when I turn out to be wrong in some obvious way about something I was totally convinced or assured of—when I discover that a friend's telephone number, written beneath her home address, is not in fact her home number; or it may be generated when I make a mistake about a matter of intimate knowledge—such as misidentifying the big band whose record was just played on the radio after a childhood and adolescence in which such music was part of my life. Such experiences are, however, at best analogous to the ones from which the sceptic begins: they produce a similar sense of something being amiss for which an account is needed, a strong desire to discover what could have precipitated the error, and a sense of one's cognitive capacities as being more fragile than one had supposed; but at most they produce a deepened sense that human beings are fallible rather than a sense that they are metaphysically deprived or inept. For the latter,

> an experience of a different order is needed, an experience that philosophers have characterized, more or less, as one of realizing that my sensations may not be *of* the world I take them to be of at all, or that I can know only how objects appear (to us) to be, never what objects are like in themselves. (*CR* 143)

Such characterizations are at work when one attempts to get sceptical worries off the ground in a seminar on epistemology—by asking students if they have ever considered that, although for all the world awake, they might in reality be dreaming; or that if our eyes had evolved differently we would see things other than as we see them now, so that how we see them now is in some sense accidental or dependent upon us rather than upon them; or that things would seem just as they do to us now if there existed a power large enough to keep us in a hypnotic spell or arrange the appearances of the world around us like an enormous stage-set. Setting aside for the moment the question of their ultimate intelligibility, what is common to such tales is their attempt to generate a sense of ourselves as sealed off from the world, each closed for ever within her own endless succession of experiences. The type of experience elicited and articulated by such thoughts may have a psychological explanation, but the mere existence of such an explanation would not demonstrate the epistemological insignificance of the experience; and although the thoughts themselves may seem absurd or nonsensical when raised with respect to specific knowledge-claims, if the experiences which they articulate have worked in the initial motivation of those claims—if we arrive at those claims already in their grip—then any attempts to prove their nonsensicality in this way will always be too late.

We might think of what is going on here as Cavell's attempt to recover the humanness of the sceptical impulse: instead of regarding it as no more than an intellectual game—a hypothesis whose only value is to dramatize or motivate a set of puzzles in a certain academic practice—he looks for its roots in ordinary human experience. Not, of course, a species of experience that is 'ordinary' in the sense that it is typical, common, or pervasive; rather, one that ordinary people (untouched by the demands and assumptions of professional philosophy) can recognize as an intelligible possibility for any and all human beings. In other words, just as the aim of ordinary language philosophy is to restore the words used by philosophers to their everyday contexts in human life, so Cavell attempts to return a familiar philosophical problematic to the realm of ordinary human experience from which it can and does grow, and thus to demonstrate that it has more than a purely academic significance.

Ultimately, of course, Cavell can do no more than claim to have undergone experiences of this order—experiences which cannot be dissipated by intellectual struggle but which must be left to go away in their own time. If, however, one can accept that the advent of such experiences and such a frame of mind is natural to human beings, then the need to reach for a particular type of knowledge-claim in relation to a particular type of object in order to reassure oneself will seem equally natural:

Ask, then, in the relevant frame of mind, or tone of voice (the stage directions for which are emblematized by, as well as anything else, the meaning of reflecting 'that I am here, seated by the fire, wearing a dressing-gown, holding a paper in my hands, and other things of this nature'), 'What do I actually know about what—if anything—really exists?'; follow this by asking 'How for example do I know that there is a——here?'; and I claim that you will find that you will always pick a generic object to fill the blank, never an object like a goldfinch; a table, yes; a Louis XIV escritoire, no. I claim, further, that the rest of the traditional investigation then follows Austin's model in perfect form. (*CR* 144)

What is this form? The relevant frame of mind leads me to investigate a best-case claim to knowledge. I ask for the basis of that claim: 'How, for example, do I know that there is a table there?' Answer: 'Because I see it' or 'By means of the senses'. Ground for doubt: 'But what do I really see? Mightn't I be dreaming, hallucinating?' or 'But that's not enough. Mightn't it be a dummy or decoy or stage-prop?' or 'But I don't see *all* of it. The most I see is . . .'. Conclusion: 'So I don't know'. Moral: 'I can never know. The senses are not enough to ground our knowledge of the world' or 'We don't really *see* what we think we see—we don't really see objects, because things could appear to our senses as they do and there be nothing there, or at least not what we take for granted is there'.

As this way of bringing out the moral of the sceptical recital makes clear, the sceptic's initial motivating experience ensures that he regards his investigation of the knowledge-claim as a re-examination of an actual situation rather than a consideration of a hypothetical one. He is not attempting to remind himself (by imagining what he would say when) of the circumstances in which the possibilities he raises when assessing his grounds for doubt would be real ones; he takes that knowledge for granted, and asks himself whether *this* situation is such a situation or not—for he has been forced to consider that this situation may not be the unproblematic one it seems, or is described, to be. The methods he employs to answer that question are also intended to be perfectly ordinary ones—the ways in which any competent speaker knows that he must (grammatically) proceed in order to establish a claim to know of something's existence; indeed, it is this reliance upon perfectly ordinary procedures which gives his investigation its force. However, what he is attempting to question by means of these methods and his knowledge of what we should say when is precisely whether what we ordinarily say about such familiar situations is true or fully appropriate or entirely accurate.

... the traditional philosopher is, as the ordinary language philosopher is, involved with investigating our conceptualization, or projective imagination, of problems or situations. But the traditional philosopher is led to this investigation by a problem which suggests to him that our description must be wrong, that we are misconceiving the real situation ... It is as though the traditional philosopher is saying: I know what it is to *see* something and so I realize we *don't* see objects. (*CR* 157)

It will therefore be futile for the ordinary language philosopher to say: 'But since we *do* sometimes see objects, you have misunderstood the concept of seeing something'. It may be true that, according to our ordinary ways of characterizing things, there is no problem about whether I see an object in a perfectly standard case of seeing an object; but if we have been brought to suspect the accuracy of such characterizations, this will simply beg our question. If we are to undermine the force of the sceptic's case, we must rather examine more closely the next steps in the queston-and-answer sequence by means of which he reaches the conclusion that our ordinary characterizations are indeed inaccurate: we must examine the basis for the knowledge-claim and the ground for doubting that basis to be adequate to the claim.

Grounds for Knowledge and Grounds for Doubt

As we saw above, the basis for such a knowledge-claim elicited by the sceptic tends most often to be 'the senses'; and Cavell accepts the naturalness of such a defence of our knowledge-claim to the following degree: If I accept the philosopher's request to go over a familiar situation in detail, then I will *have* to give a response such as 'Well, I see it, of course' in answer to his request for the basis of my claim to know, for example, that there is a table in front of me. 'Have to' here means 'Have to in order to remain reasonable, in order to honour the most natural demands of ordinary language as fully as possible'; given the context, the object and the question accepted as reasonably asked, I have no choice other than to produce this basis—the basis seems to be as determined by ordinary language as the kind of basis we can offer for claims about specific objects. If, however, my cited ground for the claim is natural in that sense, there is another sense in which it is unnatural: that basis as cited invokes the senses by contrast with other ways of informing ourselves about objects (e.g. the testimony of others), but the conclusion of the sceptical investigation—that we do not really see objects—talks of seeing as opposed to really or immediately or directly seeing. In short, the contrast with which we begin the investigation is significantly different from the contrast with which we end it; and this ought to seem unusual or striking. The ordinary language philosopher takes it to show that the sceptic is misusing language by changing the meanings of his words; but the sceptic takes the emergent contrast as a discovery that ordinary language is not fully trustworthy. Deciding which one is right is equivalent to deciding whether the emergence of the new contrast is as natural, as fully responsive to the demands of ordinary language with respect to the justification of knowledge-claims, as the emergence of the basis seems to be.

Cavell begins by questioning the intelligibility of the sceptic's ground for doubting the claim to knowledge that he is investigating; and he takes as his example the sceptical assertion that one cannot claim to know that an object in front of one exists on the grounds that one can see it, for one does not in fact see all of it. This assertion presupposes that there is some part of the object that is hidden, so the sceptic owes us an specification of which part that is; and a common way of doing this is to claim that it is the back half of the object that is hidden from view. The sceptic's mode of specifying the relevant part seems to supply everything he needs to generate universal doubt about the senses, for it seems to succeed in specifying a part of objects which will always be hidden from the viewer no matter what the viewer's particular position. If we regard the back half of a given object (e.g. a sphere) as that part of it which is established by imagining an outline (a great circle) drawn around it whose plane is perpendicular to the perceiver's line of vision, then the object's back half will always be hidden from the perceiver's view because every shift of the perceiver's position will involve a corresponding shift in what will count as its back half. It will then seem that one part of any given object is never visible to a perceiver, that we never really, directly see all of an object.

Cavell argues that this mode of specifying the part of the object which is hidden cannot do the work that the sceptic wishes it to do, because it does not establish that there is a part of an object which we can never see. In each case of perceiving an object, the sceptic has given us a way of establishing a part of it which we cannot see from our present position; but the region of the object thus specified is not something which we can *never* see, because we can shift our position in order to do so. In that new position, there will of course be another region of the object which we cannot there and then see, but that too can be seen if we move again. In other words, this way of establishing the back half of any given object entails that there is no particular part of it which is invariably the back half, no part which is *the* back half; and if there is no such part, then there is no particular part that is *never* seen and so no sense in which we can never see all of an object. The very feature of the sceptic's mode of specifying an object's back half which seemed to make it so apt for the generation of universal sceptical doubt thus turns out to render it incapable of performing that task.

We might say: The sceptic's *method* of establishing with respect to a particular object that a part of the object is not seen does not vary when the perceiver's position with respect to the object varies, but the particular region of the object thereby *established* as this part does; so the method does not establish that this part is *never* seen. But it would then follow that the method could be thought to establish the stronger conclusion only by someone who imagined objects and subjects as unchanging in their orientation to one another; for only if we were incapable of changing our position with respect to objects that always presented the same face to us would such a method establish a part of the objects that was *never* seen.

Thus this sceptical picture is one in which all our objects are moons. In which the earth is our moon. In which, at any rate, our position with respect to significant objects is *rooted*, the great circles which establish their back and front halves fixed in relation to it, fixed in our concentration as we gaze at them. The moment we move, the 'parts' disappear, or else we *see* what had before been hidden from view—from any other position than one perpendicular to *that* great circle, *that* 'back half' which it alone establishes *can be seen*: to establish a *different* 'back half', a *new* act of diagramming will be required, a new position taken, etc. This suggests that what philosophers call 'the senses' are themselves conceived in terms of this idea of a geometrically fixed position, disconnected from the fact of their possession and use by a creature who must *act*. (*CR* 202)

The reason for the sceptic's problem lies in his failure to provide any way of establishing the identity of the back half of a perceived object which is independent of the merely geometrical–physical fact that it is not visible from the perceiver's present position. For that position is not unalterable, and as a consequence the identity of the object's back half must shift each time the object turns a different face towards the perceiver and each time the perceiver changes her position with respect to that object. In other words, such a method fails to establish the 'back half' of an object as a definite part of it which retains an independent identity throughout our interactions with it; since every move we make will alter what counts as the object's back half, we can never establish what its back half is and then employ the frame of reference thus established in our life with the object. The concept of an object's back half can thus only be perpetually established and re-established, it cannot be used; it offers a purchase on the object which vanishes every time we move to grasp it, and so offers no purchase on it at all.

There are only two ways of avoiding this conclusion. One is to repress the fact that the position of the perceiver is alterable and to think of ourselves as never moving to grasp the objects which we diagram according to this method; we would then succeed in fixing only one particular part of any given object as its back half, but at the cost of treating all objects and all perceivers as geometrically fixed in relation to one another and thereby ensuring that the point of purchase thus specified is one for which we can have no use. The second way is to regard the method as a way of picking out a specific region of the object which we will continue to regard as its back half even after we alter our position with respect to it, so that the line drawn around the object in a plane perpendicular to the perceiver's line of vision at some given moment is to be imagined as a permanent feature of it for our future purposes. Then once again we have a definite part of the object which is its back half, and we can furthermore regard the concept as giving us a stable purchase on the object for which we might have some use in our interactions with it; but then the object's back half cannot be regarded as something we can never see (we cannot see it at the moment it is christened, but we can see it if we—or it—should move), and so no sceptical conclusion follows.

In other words, the sceptic faces a dilemma:

> Either the model in terms of which we, and he, must understand his statements fails to fit its original object, becomes a model of nothing—unless we *make* it fit by distorting our life among objects (and hence distorting our concept of an object *uberhaupt*?) or by constructing an idea of 'the senses' which extirpate them from the body; or else it fits its original faithfully, in which case it carries no implication about knowledge as a whole—no one would there suppose that because we couldn't see all of *that* object that therefore we never see 'all' of *any* object.
>
> In the latter case, what we say is true, it is a *fact*, flatly right about that specific object and our position with respect to it, and no general sceptical conclusion is suggested; in the former case, the sceptical conclusion is not a *fact*, and not about our world, in which eyes and bodies go together and in which objects do not inevitably keep exactly 'one side' turned towards us. (*CR* 203)

So much for the naturalness or intelligibility of the sceptic's grounds for *doubting* the knowledge-claim entered about a generic object; what of the naturalness or intelligibility of the sceptic's assumption that his imagined situations are ones in which someone can be said to know something? The sceptic is led by his sense of something being amiss with human knowledge to go back over a familiar situation, one in which—for example—someone is sitting at a desk on which there is a green pencil jar, and to ask himself how that person knows that the jar is really there; but is it right to say that this person knows any such thing? Of course, assuming that conditions are optimal, no one would say that she does *not* know that there is a jar in front of her eyes—after all, if asked, she could have said that the jar was there without looking; but would anyone say that she *does* know that the jar is on the desk? There are circumstances in which I might say this of her—if, for example, I knew that Mrs Greenjar was coming to tea and was very sensitive about references to her unusual name; but in the absence of a special reason of that kind, one which makes that description of her 'knowledge' relevant to something that she did or said or was doing or saying, no one would say anything of the sort. The sceptic may reply that, although no one would normally say so, it is true that this person knows that there is a jar on the desk; so why can we not say so as part of our investigation? Cavell responds as follows:

What I am suggesting is that 'Because it is true' is not a reason or basis for saying anything, it does not constitute the point of your saying something; and I am suggesting that there must, in grammar, be reasons for what you say, or be point in your saying of something, if what you say is to be comprehensible. We can understand what the *words* mean apart from understanding why you say them; but apart from understanding the point of your saying them we cannot understand what *you* mean. (*CR* 206)

Here we find ourselves returning to an issue that was central to the introductory chapter of this book. Cavell's point is that saying that the person behind the desk knows that there is a jar on it is a species of assertion, and so a speech-act; and like any other particular type of human action, not just anything people do will *be* (will count as) asserting something. For example, is the sceptic's utterance meant to be an instance of telling someone something? If so, then what is said must be something which the hearer is in a position to understand (can a scientist tell me what a pi-meson is?) and something which is, or might reasonably be thought to be, informative to the hearer (can one person tell another who is facing her 'I see you'?). But what information does the sceptic think that he is imparting when he tells me that the person behind the desk knows that there is a jar on the desk? How might he suppose that I might not have known that, when person and desk and jar are in full view? The sceptic might reply by claiming that he is simply remarking upon a fact about the situation before us both. Of course, it is perfectly possible simply to remark something; but this doesn't mean that just anything, any time, can comprehensibly be remarked or remarked upon. In the absence of a special context how might I intelligibly remark that the telephone receiver is hanging on the hook, or that the letter you are reading is in your hand? But the sceptic is not imagining any such context; indeed, he is precisely remarking upon something in an ordinary, familiar, resolutely non-special context—a context in which it is, one could say, precisely unremarkable.

What the sceptic is doing is violating the conditions under which something can intelligibly be said; he is not thereby depriving his words of meaning (they may mean what they always did, what dictionaries say they mean) but rather depriving his utterance (his saying of them) of any meaning. It is not that his words make no sense, because they have a use—they can be said meaningfully; but that just means that we can imagine circumstances under which it would make sense to say them. It does not mean that apart from such circumstances they have any (clear) sense. Saying something has its conditions, but the sceptic wants to speak beyond or outside those conditions (to speak outside language games); he wants to speak without the commitments speech exacts.

> I could express this by saying: In philosophizing we come to be dissatisfied with answers which depend upon *our* meaning something by an expression, as though what *we* meant by it were more or less arbitrary. (As we sometimes feel about our more obviously moral commitments that they are more or less arbitrary, and that if they are to have any *real* or full power they must be rooted in, or 'based upon', a reality deeper than the fact of morality itself.) It is as though we try to get the world to provide answers in a way which is independent of our responsibility for *claiming* something to be so . . .; and we fix the world so that it can do this. We construct 'parts' of objects which have no parts; 'senses' which have no guiding function; become obsessed with how we can know 'the pain itself' in a context in which the question 'Why do you think this expression of pain gives a false picture of it?' has no answer . . .; convince ourselves that what we *call* something does not tell us what it is in a context in which the questions 'What would *you* call it?' or 'What else might it be?' have no answers . . . And we take what we have fixed or constructed to be *discoveries* about the world, and take this fixation to reveal the human condition rather than our escape or denial of this condition through the rejection of the human conditions of knowledge and action and the substitution of fantasy. Why this happens, how it happens, how it is so much as possible for it to happen, why it leads to the conclusions it does, are further questions—questions not answered by claiming, for example, that we have 'changed the meanings of our words', 'been inattentive to their ordinary meanings', 'misused our language'. (*CR* 215–16)

Another way of making the point that Cavell is pressing here is to underline the fact that the situations which the sceptic wishes to re-examine are not ones in which a knowledge-claim is being entered; to imagine myself seated before Descartes's fire is not to imagine myself claiming to know that I am seated before the fire. Moreover, it would be extremely odd to imagine ourselves entering such a claim in such a context—a context in which, by hypothesis, there are no special reasons for believing that we might not know this.

The sceptic might reply by pointing out that he can give a serious basis for such a claim in such a context, namely, 'Because I see it'; and if such a basis exists, can it be wrong to imagine a claim based upon it being made? If, however, we bear in mind that such a basis is itself a species of claim, then we will appreciate that it too is subject to the same conditions as any other claim; and in the sceptic's imagined context, it suffers the same misfortune as the original claim it is held to support. There *are* occasions on which we would claim that we saw the fire or envelope or table, but they are ones in which there is some real question about whether we are in a position to see the relevant object, or are prepared to discover that a trick has been played on us, and so on; and in such contexts, no general suspicion *would* be raised about human knowledge. And the occasions in which such a suspicion would be raised are precisely ones in which the conditions for intelligibly making the claim are absent. Just as 'Because it is true' is not a reason or basis for asserting something, so 'Because it is true that I see it' is not a reason or basis for claiming to see something; to think otherwise would be to imagine a world in which, whenever any of us sees anything, we claim to see it—a world in which everything catches our attention every moment.

The sceptic may respond by pointing out that, in such contexts, we would certainly claim that we saw an object that was in front of our eyes *if we were asked* whether we did.

But what does this come to? Is [the sceptic] to be taken to mean that we are in a *position* to claim to see it? Is that enough for him? 'Being in a position' to lend you five dollars is not the same as lending you five dollars. And just as not anything I do will be lending you five dollars (I send you a cheque for five dollars in the mail out of the blue) ... so not just anything I say will be telling you, or confirming, or agreeing that I see the envelope in your hand. 'But it's so flamingly obvious that you do see it! You aren't going to say that you *don't* see it.' No; and I am not going to go up to a stranger and tell him that I won't lend him five dollars either. (Though that is true, too.) 'Alright, but don't you?' I could reply 'Are you really asking me?' for if you are, then I imagine a context in which that might be something you need to know, and that your asking implies that I may (am in a position to) know, and then considerations about how much I see may well be relevant. Or I might, by now, humour you, and say 'Yes, alright, I see it. Well?' But in *that* mood I'm not very receptive to the suggestion that all of knowlege is at stake in my affirmation. (*CR* 219–20)

In short, the sceptic can be said to face a reformulated version of the dilemma we identified earlier: his investigation of knowledge must be the investigation of a concrete claim if its procedure is to be coherent; but it cannot be the investigation of a concrete claim if its conclusion is to be general. Without the coherence it wouldn't have the obviousness that it seemed to have; without the generality its conclusion would not be sceptical.

To talk of the sceptic's imagined context as a non-claim context is simply to reiterate the earlier point that the sceptic is impelled to speak outside language games, outside the human conditions within which it is possible to say anything in particular. The sceptic's distortion of the ordinary conditions for human speech thus parallels his distortion of the ordinary human senses (disconnecting them from action, imagining himself as a disembodied pair of eyes); and the desire to confirm our capacity to make connection with the world in such unconditioned circumstances is precisely a desire to transcend our finitude—a desire to know the world as we imagine that God knows it. That desire will presumably be as easy to rid us of as it is to rid us of the prideful craving to be God without replacing that craving with a despair at our finitude.

A Refutation of Scepticism?

By this stage in Cavell's painstaking investigation, it may seem clear that the sceptical impulse has run into the sands. Not only the assumption that genuine grounds exist for raising a doubt about a claim to know of the existence of a generic object, but also the assumption that it is appropriate to articulate such a knowledge-claim about such an object in the first place, have both been shown to lack any substance; and as a result there appears to be no way in which the sceptical impulse might find intelligible expression. It might seem that if anything constitutes a refutation of scepticism, this does; and if it is interpreted this way, Cavell's work would stand four-square within the tradition of orthodox Wittgensteinian treatments of scepticism. But Cavell himself is insistent that this is the wrong way to understand his achievement. For example, having constructed the first dilemma for the sceptic (the one with which to confront him when he attempts to suggest that we never really see the back part of perceived objects), Cavell immediately remarks that this 'will hardly constitute a refutation of scepticism, much less of the traditional epistemological procedure as a whole' (*CR* 203)— for, amongst other things, it might be possible for the sceptic to uncover fresh reasons for thinking that the existence of objects is problematic, and so to avoid the dilemma by raising doubts about certain 'facts' concerning our life with objects upon which Cavell's construction of that dilemma relies. Nevertheless, such an acknowledgement of the need for further work at this point of his attack may seem to have been superseded by Cavell's later construction of an analogous dilemma for the sceptic with respect to his more basic assumption that knowledge-claims can intelligibly be made in relation to generic objects: for if we can undermine that assumption, then there can be no knowledge-claims about which the sceptic might raise intelligible doubts. However, this conclusion too is one that Cavell resists: in more than one context, he has explicitly denied that this more fundamental dilemma, and indeed anything else to be found in his book, constitutes a refutation of scepticism.

The ... work of Austin and Wittgenstein is commonly thought to represent an effort to refute philosophical scepticism, as expressed most famously in Descartes and in Hume, and an essential drive of my book *The Claim of Reason* is to show that, at least in the case of Wittgenstein, this is a fateful distortion, that Wittgenstein's teaching is on the contrary that scepticism is (not exactly true, but not exactly false either; it is) a standing threat to the human mind, that our ordinary language and its representation of the world *can* be philosophically repudiated and that it is essential to our inheritance and mutual possession of language, as well as to what inspires philosophy, that this should be so.[3]

It is worth examining the implications of this passage in some detail; for they constitute Cavell's most fundamental break with the orthodox Wittgensteinian tradition in philosophy.

Cavell's repudiation of the idea that he has refuted scepticism seems to have four main components. First, it is a repudiation of the idea that Wittgensteinian criteria in themselves constitute a refutation of scepticism. Cavell wishes to dissociate himself from any version of a claim often made by Wittgensteinian philosophers, namely, that criteria confer certainty, from which it would follow that the mere presence of criteria in any concrete case is enough to license a flat rejection of any attempt to articulate sceptical doubts, and that the continued desire to articulate such doubts must be symptomatic of a simple failure to apprehend the true nature of ordinary language. Since, according to Cavell, criteria do not confer certainty, no such licence is accorded us; there is no crucial piece of knowledge about language that sceptics lack or have forgotten, and that the rest of us possess. On the contrary, since our having criteria in common is ultimately a matter of our agreeing and continuing to agree in employing and deploying them, it is of the essence of criteria that they are open to repudiation; for anything ultimately founded in agreement or consent is unavoidably vulnerable to the

---

[3] S. Cavell, 'Psychoanalysis and Cinema: The Melodrama of the Unknown Woman', in *IIS* 21.

termination or withdrawal of that agreement or consent. This is Cavell's second reason for rejecting the idea of refuting scepticism: we cannot 'refute' the possibility that someone will decide (or find, or be driven to the conclusion) that he no longer agrees with others, that his attunement with them has limits; we cannot 'refute' the possibility of repudiating an agreement, however fundamental that agreement may be.

Of course, given that Cavell also regards agreement in criteria as the presupposition of mutual intelligibility, he is committed to thinking that the consequence of repudiating them will be a failure of intelligibility—an inability to mean what we think we mean, or to mean anything, by what we say; so a mismatch between what the sceptic says and what he wishes to mean remains the inevitable consequence of succumbing to the sceptical impulse, such that that impulse cannot be given intelligible expression. But this merely provides a third reason for rejecting the idea of refuting scepticism: for on this account of its necessary fate, the sceptical impulse is not best characterized as a commitment to a body of beliefs or hypotheses which might be based upon inadequate evidence or invalid arguments and so might be open to refutation; it is rather an impulse to repudiate or deny the framework within which alone human speech is possible, and so exemplifies one way in which human beings attempt to deny their conditionedness (their condition). In short, on Cavell's view, the sceptical repudiation of criteria embodies an inflexion of the human desire to transcend finitude, to deny the human; and although we may struggle against or succumb to particular outbreaks of such a desire, and although the desire itself may be subject to diagnosis and interpretation, it is not open to refutation.

On Cavell's view, therefore, neither a grasp of the true nature of criteria nor a successful demonstration of the emptiness of any particular attempt to articulate sceptical doubts amounts to a refutation of the sceptical impulse. But in the passage quoted above, he goes further than this: he also claims that while scepticism is not exactly true, it is not exactly false either—in other words, that there is something approximating to a truth or a moral embedded in scepticism, and so something which calls for acceptance rather than refutation. We can begin to see what he means by this if we ask ourselves whether Cavell's particular confrontation with the sceptic has allowed anything significant to emerge about the non-claim contexts within which the latter attempts to find a foothold. On the one hand, the propositions upon which the sceptic concentrates when he goes over familiar situations with his suspicion in mind are not ones which it makes sense to imagine being asserted; in those circumstances, the conditions for making a specific claim to knowledge do not hold. On the other hand, such propositions do seem to be true; and no one would say that a human being sitting at a desk does *not* know whether there is a green jar on it. The problem is that this piece of 'knowledge' does not function in our lives in the way that pieces of knowledge characteristically do.

For example, how might the sceptic—seated behind the desk—answer the question 'How do you know that there is a green jar on the table?' Perhaps by saying any one of the following: 'I just looked at it', 'I remember that it is there', 'I must look at it a hundred times a day', and so on. The oddity here is not that the sceptic has nothing to say, but that the hundreds of things that he can say seem to crowd in upon him: all seem equally pertinent (and so equally irrelevant), and yet none is more certain than the proposition that they are meant to support. In short, such 'reasons', *in the context in which the sceptic offers them*, are not operative as reasons for his 'belief':

... those hundred reasons are, roughly, the same reasons we would give to the questions 'How does he know his name?', 'How does he know he has five fingers', 'How does he know that the jar will fall if he releases it from his grasp?', 'How does he know the sun will rise tomorrow?'. Offering such 'reasons' is not offering grounds for eliciting belief in a particular claim I have made, but protestations of knowledge, entreaties that I be credible. No one of them, in their rootlessness, would remove a doubt; they are signs to ward off doubt. (*CR* 217)

A comparison with the status of a similarly placed proposition might clarify matters here. What would be wrong with saying that we know with absolute certainty, that we have conclusive evidence, that houses do not turn into flowers? If there is absolutely conclusive evidence that *S* is *P*, then that *S* is *P* is a well-established fact; on the basis of the evidence you can claim to know that *S* is *P*. But is it merely *in fact* the case that houses do not turn into flowers? What fact is conveyed when we are told that they do not? What would it be like if they did? What would 'house' and 'flower' mean in the language of such a world; what would be the difference between stones and seeds; where would we live and what would we grow in our gardens; what would 'grow' mean?

The point here is that although there may be nothing of which we are more convinced than that there is a jar on the desk, or that houses do not turn into flowers, these are not things which it makes sense for us to claim to know—for that would suggest that we relate to them as we do to such claims as 'There is a goldfinch at the bottom of the garden'. They are not specific beliefs at all: they are not arrived at or brought under suspicion by the gathering of specific evidence; they do not express 'facts' that some are in a better position than others to have learnt, or 'claims' that some are in a better position than others to make. This is what Cavell means by saying that the sceptic's contexts are non-claim contexts; and this realization is the truth or moral that can be derived from scepticism. For the sceptic is right in so far as he thinks that such propositions do not encapsulate something we can be said to know; and his persistence in the face of philosophers' attempts to treat his doubts as misplaced or false reveals an important flaw in the position of his opponents, both traditional and Wittgensteinian—namely, their belief that we do know, and with certainty, the things that the sceptic doubts. When, for example, Wittgensteinian philosophers attempt to refute the sceptic by arguing that criteria confer certainty, they interpret criteria in a way which presupposes that the concepts of knowledge, doubt, and certainty can be used to characterize our relation to the world at the level at which criteria operate; they merely assert that this relation is a matter of certainty rather than of doubt. Accordingly, in so far as confronting the sceptic helps to undermine the idea that certainty is an appropriate way of characterizing matters here, he is furthering our understanding of the true state of affairs.

None the less, in so far as the sceptic's final position amounts to substituting the concept of doubt for that of certainty, he participates in the misapprehension evinced by his opponents; in this sense, as Cavell puts it, the truth in scepticism is not exactly a truth. For in claiming that the multitude of propositions which spring to mind when we focus upon non-claim contexts cannot be said to articulate something that we know, Cavell does not intend to imply that they are something we do *not* know; his point is rather that they do not play the role of specific knowledge-claims at all. Of course, this does not make their role in our lives any less fundamental; attempting to imagine life in a world in which houses do turn into flowers involves imagining a radical disruption of our relation to the world. The truth of the matter is rather that this fundamental relation to the world (the human creature's basis in the world as a whole) is not one of knowing; but, as the tenacity both of the sceptical impulse and of the impulse to oppose scepticism in epistemological terms makes clear, nothing is more human than the compulsion to characterize this relation in that way:

Both Wittgenstein and Heidegger continue, by reinterpreting, Kant's insight that limitations of knowledge are not failures of it. *Being and Time* goes further than *Philosophical Investigations* in laying out how to think about what the human creature's relation to the world as such is (locating, among others, that particular relation called knowing); but Wittgenstein goes further than Heidegger in laying out how to investigate the cost of our continuous temptation to knowledge, as I would like to put it ... In the *Investigations*, the cost is arrived at in terms (e.g., of not knowing what we are saying, of emptiness in our assertions, of the illusion of meaning something, of claims to impossible privacies) suggestive of madness ... And in both the cost is the loss, or forgoing, of identity or of selfhood. To be interested in such accounts as accounts of the cost of knowing to the knowing creature, I suppose that one will have to take an interest in certain preoccupations of romanticism. (*CR* 241–2)

That final hint is something we will follow up in Chapter 6. For the moment, we might conclude by noting that here we can see another sense in which Cavell's Wittgensteinian account of the cost of our temptation to knowledge leads to issues of self-knowledge (and thus to issues of selfhood and identity). This interpretation of scepticism locates in it an impulse to transcend the human conditions of knowing and speaking, to transcend the merely human; and the result of that impulse—the attempt to speak outside language games—is that masters of a language think that they are informing themselves of something (think that they are saying something meaningful) when they are not. The sceptic does not realize that what he must say (in order to be fully coherent) is not what he means to say, or that what he means to say cannot fully be meant; he does not realize what he is saying. This, for Cavell, is one more way in which the problems of philosophy become problems of self-knowledge.

5
Criteria, Scepticism, and Other Minds

In the previous chapter, I focussed on Cavell's view of concepts in their application to the external world; in this chapter, I want—in effect—to narrow that focus even further and look at his view of concepts in their application to a certain sort of denizen of the external world, namely, creatures we regard as possessed of a mind. Since, however, the application of psychological concepts to such creatures amounts to acknowledging them as being in some way kin to ourselves (i.e. as fellow human beings), it is only to be expected that this narrowing of focus will highlight complexities and confusions whose treatment will require more than a mechanical application of lessons acquired through the study of external-world scepticism in the previous chapter. In short, scepticism about other minds should be seen neither as an instance of, nor as something entirely distinct from, scepticism about the external world.

Withholding Concepts of the Inner: Knowledge and Acknowledgement

The central respect in which Cavell's treatment of these two kinds of scepticism manifests a sense of their kinship is his initial acknowledge-ment that the criteria governing the application of psychological con-cepts do not confer certainty. If we understand the criteria for pain as determining when a given stretch of human behaviour is *pain*-behaviour (i.e. behaviour expressive of pain), then the possibility of such criteria being satisfied and pain none the less being absent cannot be excluded: indeed, situations in which someone is feigning pain can be character-ized precisely as ones in which behaviour expressive of pain is not expressive of *real* pain. On the other hand, and as we noted in the previous chapter, criteria do none the less impose very precise limits on the ways in which such situations can intelligibly be invoked or described; for satisfaction of the criteria for pain entails that the absence of pain can only be accounted for in certain ways (e.g. by claiming that the person concerned is feigning pain or rehearsing the part of a

character who is in pain)—in other words, by invoking ways of comprehending the situation which accommodate the indisputable fact that the
person's behaviour is expressive of *pain*. This obligation to retain the
concept of pain in articulating or describing such situations ensures that
the possibility of criteria for pain being satisfied and pain being absent
can be invoked only when certain very specific circumstances obtain;
and this in turn prevents us from drawing any *general* sceptical conclusions.

Thus, scepticism about other minds cannot—as many Wittgenstein-
ians are prone to think—be blocked by the invocation of criteria as the
guarantors of certainty, but it does *not* follow that such scepticism is
thereby vindicated; for the sceptic is wrong to view the fact that criteria
do not confer certainty as a failure of the criteria rather than as an
indication that the concept of certainty is not applicable at this level or
depth of the human relation to the world. On Cavell's view, what is
exposed—the truth or moral of scepticism about other minds—is the
limitation inherent in viewing our knowledge of others exclusively
under the aspect of certainty. However, the philosophical task is not
just to demonstrate the validity of this diagnosis, but to do so in a way
which does not entail dismissing the sceptic as duplicitous or linguistically incompetent. For, first, if that diagnosis is based solely upon
reminders of what we say when, then it is based upon something known
by any competent speaker, and it must remain a *question* how the
sceptic can have lost touch with this knowledge, i.e. how a competent
speaker can become a sceptic. And second, anyone who espouses
scepticism about other minds must, as a competent speaker, be supposed
to imagine that the circumstances in which he finds himself justify *both*
the application of the concept of doubt in this case *and* the immediate
conclusion that other minds can *never* be known. In other words,
Cavell's methodological self-understanding entails viewing the sceptic
as having got himself into a position in which, on the one hand, he sees
himself as being in an optimal position for judging that a given person
is in pain (i.e. a best case for knowledge), and, on the other hand, the
possibility that the person may none the less not be in pain has arisen
and cannot be dismissed. What we must understand is how such a
position comes to be occupied, and how one might extricate oneself
from it.

According to Cavell, however, this task can only be accomplished if
we recognize certain crucial features of the role of psychological
concepts in our lives—all of which might be thought of as highlighted

by sceptical doubts about other minds. The first such feature emerges in the following way. When a philosopher such as Cavell outlines in some detail the schematism of pain—i.e. the grammar of the concept of 'pain', its relation to other concepts—it is difficult to avoid a sense of disappointment, a feeling that all this talk of criteria leaves out something essential. The sceptic enunciates this disappointment by saying that all this talk of behaviour and the circumstances or context of behaviour seems to leave out the pain itself; we talk about words when there is a psychological reality with which those words are supposed to bring us into contact, and it is that contact which seems so fragile and open to doubt.

Cavell agrees that such a focus upon the grammar of 'pain' leaves something out; he would even accept that there is a sense in which such a focus concentrates upon words rather than upon that which gives life to them. But what is left out is not the pain itself, not if that means 'the pain as opposed to the pain-behaviour'; what is left out are my *responses* to the pain-behaviour—to the criteria of pain—as they emerge. The knowledge that such criteria confer imposes a call on me—for comfort, succour, healing; for a response which helps to assuage the pain or to acknowledge that it is unassuageable here and now.

> When I say 'He's in pain' (supposing I do, supposing that's what I have to say) my knowledge is expressed (roughly as his is; i.e., *analogously* with his?) by the fact that it is called from me, cried out (though we generally keep our voices down) ... Sometimes my problem will be *not* to cry it out, but to free my response *from* the other. Instead of responding to him from my freedom, I am engulfed by his suffering or his anxieties, or by his opinion of me, or his hope for me; as may be.—But all this makes it seem that the philosophical problem of knowledge is something I impose on these matters; that I am the philosophical problem. I am. It is in me that the circuit of communication is cut; I am the stone on which the wheel breaks. What is disappointing about criteria?
>
> There is something they do not do; it can seem the essential. I have to know what they are for; I have to accept them, use them. (*CR* 82–3)

The point is one which Cavell first broaches in 'Knowing and Acknowledging', a late essay in *Must We Mean What We Say?*; in the domain of psychological concepts, knowing takes the form of acknowledging—part of knowing that another is in pain is knowing that the other's pain demands a response from me. This does not entail that every sufferer whose pain is known to others either receives or ought to receive sympathy from those others; for, of course, the claim

that suffering imposes upon us may go unanswered—we may feel irritation, *Schadenfreude*, or nothing. The point is that such responses are
failures of acknowledgement; and the applicability of the concept of
acknowledgement is evinced as much by its failure as by its success.

It is not a description of a given response, but a category in terms of which a
given response is evaluated ... A 'failure to know' might just mean a piece of
ignorance, an absence of something, a blank. A 'failure to acknowledge' is the
presence of something, a confusion, an indifference, a callousness, an exhaustion,
a coldness. Spiritual emptiness is not a blank. (*MWM* 263–4)

In short, although it is possible simply to be ignorant of the fact that someone is in pain, it is not possible simply to know that fact; such knowledge must take a positive form, it must find its expression—whether in
an acknowledgement of the pain or in a failure to acknowledge
it.

Accordingly, knowledge of another's inner state is not reducible
simply to an intellectual awareness that certain criteria have been
satisfied; it involves a capacity and willingness to respond to the
presence of that which the criteria are criteria *for*—and this is not
something which the simple presence of the criteria can guarantee. But
the importance of acknowledgement goes deeper even than this. For
before one can respond or fail to respond to the *pain* which the other
person's behaviour makes manifest, one must be prepared to respond to
the other's behaviour as *pain-behaviour*, be prepared to apply the concept
of pain to it—one must be prepared to regard it as behaviour expressive
of an inner life; and on Cavell's view, this is not something that we
determine on the basis of criteria either.

There are not human criteria which apprise me, or which make any move
towards telling me why I take it, among all the things I encounter on the
surface of the earth or in its waters or its sky, that some of them have feeling;
that some of them 'resemble' or 'behave like' human beings or human bodies; or
that some exhibit (forms of) life—unless the *fact* that human beings apply
psychological concepts to certain things and not to others is such a criterion.
(*CR* 83)

This claim seems at first very counter-intuitive: if there exist criteria
for distinguishing one type of psychological phenomenon from another,
should there not also exist criteria for distinguishing those entities to
which psychological concepts apply from those which do not? Cavell's
question in response is: What *are* these criteria? What *are* the features

by reference to which we supposedly recognize certain behaviour as that of a living being, one capable of feeling and possessed of an inner life? We cannot be said to do it on the basis of knowledge of origins or bodily make-up (e.g. are they made of flesh and blood?), for in our everyday interactions with our fellow human beings we typically have no such knowledge. If these putative criteria are to be (as they must be) usable, they must specify features that *are* available to us—a distinctive way or set of ways in which a living creature behaves; but what are these ways? On Cavell's view, there is only one general answer to be given here, namely, 'The ways in which living creatures that I have known have done these things'—but, in so far as there is no further way of cashing this out, it will of course appear to be no answer at all.

As it stands, Cavell's mode of arguing for his view makes it difficult to arrive at a final verdict upon it: the risk in asking a rhetorical question is that the possibility of its receiving an answer in the future cannot be excluded. However, a more definitive conclusion might be reached if we stress the obvious problem that will emerge with any conceivable answer to that question: for any feature that might be specified as our means of distinguishing living beings from other entities could conceivably be simulated. It is this latter point that is registered in certain versions of scepticism about other minds: such scepticism might begin by focussing upon possibilities of pretence or dissimulation, possibilities which presuppose that the relevant creature possesses an inner life and raise doubts only about its true lineaments; but it usually moves on to raise the possibility of mutants, golems, and androids, i.e. entities possessed of human form and capable of human-like behaviour but without any inner life at all, to whom we mistakenly believe the whole schematism of psychological concepts is applicable. If we have been brought to suspect that the creature before us is a golem, then what we suspect is precisely that its humanoid behaviour—i.e. behaviour which appears to manifest psychological criteria, and which in every other conceivable respect resembles that of human beings—is deceptive; so the fact that its behaviour has that appearance cannot be used to remove our anxiety.

On Cavell's view, such possibilities may not be as intelligible as they seem, but the desire to invoke them illuminates just the point about the limitations of criteria at which he is driving. For it dramatizes the fact that, although once we decide to treat a given creature's behaviour as expressive of an inner life and so as capable of satisfying psychological criteria, we may then be able to distinguish between its various inner states on the basis of behavioural criteria, there are no criteria which determine whether or not we should so regard its behaviour. Anyone in the grip of the sceptical suspicion has, in effect, decided to withhold our concepts of the inner from that creature, to refuse to regard its behaviour as expressive of an inner life; and Cavell's point is that criteria do not and cannot offer us any leverage against such a person. To think that they do would be to think that criteria determine reality rather than identity, fixing not only what counts as something's being *so* but also what counts as something's *being* so. For Cavell, criteria can and do determine whether a given stretch of behaviour is expressive of pain as opposed to joy; but they cannot determine whether it is expressive of real pain as opposed to feigned pain—and they cannot determine whether it is genuinely expressive as opposed to a mere appearance of expressivity.

Of course, this does *not* mean that Cavell thinks that there is no distinction between animate and inanimate creatures, or that we do not know the difference between them: it simply means that this difference is not one for which there are criteria. Psychological criteria form a complex and subtle schematism of the forms and manifestations of the inner life, such that applying them to a given creature amounts to treating that creature's behaviour as expressive of an inner life; but there are no criteria to tell us when and how to do that, no agreed-upon and specifiable features on to whose detectable presence or absence the responsibility inherent in deciding to apply or withhold that schematism in a particular case might be displaced. It follows that that responsibility must remain, ineluctably, the burden of the person taking the decision: it is, in each case, the responsibility of the person using the concepts— yours and mine. Only through my acceptance of another creature's body as the home of my concepts of the human soul will those criteria have life; and in face of my withdrawal of that acceptance those criteria are dead. My condition is not exactly that I have to put the other's life there in her behaviour, and not exactly that I have to leave it there either: I have to respond to it, or refuse to respond—I have to acknowledge it.

So the sceptic is right to suspect that there is more to knowing that someone is in pain than the mere satisfaction of criteria; but by concluding from this that we cannot reach the inner life of others, by thinking that our knowledge of a human being's behaviour leaves us uncertain of the nature and even the existence or reality of her inner life, the sceptic himself refuses the responsibility of applying those criteria. His description of this situation as a failure of knowledge is itself a failure of acknowledgement.

To withhold, or hedge, our concepts of psychological states from a given creature, on the ground that our criteria cannot reach to the inner life of the creature, is specifically to withhold the source of my idea that living beings are things that feel; it is to withhold myself, to reject my response to anything as a living being; to blank so much as my idea of anything as *having a body*. To describe *this* condition as one in which I do not know (am not certain) of the existence of other minds is empty. There is now nothing there, of the right kind, to be known. (*CR* 83–4)

Withholding Concepts of the Inner: The Normal and the Natural

These two aspects of the role of the concept of acknowledgement in characterizing the place of psychological concepts in our lives (capturing our obligation to apply or withhold our psychological concepts in relation to a given creatures's behaviour, and our obligation to respond to the specific knowledge of another's inner state which flows from applying rather than withholding those concepts) might be summarized as the discovery of our own responsibility—our responsiveness—in the existence of others. A third feature that Cavell is concerned to pick out also has to do with this responsibility, but falls somewhere between the two features already mentioned, in that it links up with a sense in which our criteria of pain are related to some conception of normal human behaviour; and once again, the link emerges very naturally from sceptical qualms. For Cavell has claimed that the concept of pain must be retained in order to offer an intelligible description of circumstances in which pain criteria are satisfied but pain is absent; but the sceptic might dispute this by raising the possibility that the pain-behaviour exhibited in such circumstances isn't really *pain* behaviour at all. What if, in this particular case, the behaviour which we usually count as expressive of pain is indeed expressive of something, but of something entirely other than pain? The sceptical worry here is thus not that we may be faced with a dissimulating human being, and not that we may be faced with a creature simulating humanness; the worry is that this person's screaming may really be the way she clears her throat or calls her hamsters or sings Schubert.

   Cavell's initial response is to imagine circumstances in which such an alternative interpretation might make sense, i.e. in which the concepts used to characterize the alternative possibilities might have application. If, for example, we see this person writhing, perspiring, and screaming, and then looking around; and then her three hamsters trot up; and we observe this on several occasions; then we will probably have to admit that this is the way she calls her pets. But this doesn't show that there is no necessity to retain the concept of pain in circumstances where the criteria for pain have been satisfied; rather, it shows that we shall no longer call her screaming *pain*-behaviour. In other words, we will not give up our usual notion of what pain-behaviour is, but rather rule such a person out of our world of pain. 'In this respect, [s]he will not exist for us. In response to [her] there will doubtless be more that we will feel shaky about than our knowledge of when [s]he is and is not in pain. But ... these doubts are limited to [her], and have no tendency to make us wonder whether we ever can be sure' (*CR* 89).

Cavell's point is that the sceptic has invoked a real possibility (or at least has invoked a possibility which cannot be dismissed out of hand as incoherent) but misinterpreted its significance. Perhaps there are people who laugh at physical pain or rejection the way we laugh at a joke; but if there are, their difference from us will not be localized (Would they respond to an affectionate touch by screaming in pain? Would they cry at what slightly offends us, or collect and care for and eat objects which appal us?), and the question of how we are to talk to, act with, and treat them will be *deeply* problematic. The problem would not be epistemological or metaphysical but practical; it would be akin to the problems attendant upon our attempts to treat psychotics, our attempts to honour them as persons by entering their world.

To dismiss the possibility invoked by the sceptic by saying that 'normal people don't behave like that' may therefore be misleading, but it contains a grain of truth. It is misleading in that it implies that we have (or ought to have) a theory of normality, or a theory of pain which distinguishes between normal and abnormal cases of pain, in order to justify our assimilation of the hamster-lover or the pain-connoisseur to the category of psychotics. But this is to misread the thrust of Cavell's comparison. Our attempts to imagine someone who feels in a whip what we feel in a caress are in effect attempts to imagine a person for whom suffering and comfort are entirely independent of what we mean by 'pain' and 'pity'; and these attempts are guided only by the criteria governing the relevant terms, not by any theory about or underlying them.

There is, however, a sense in which the concept of normality does come in here; for if the pain-connoisseur's behaviour is sufficiently aberrant, then we will conclude not that she expresses pain abnormally, or that she finds certain unusual things painful, but that *she* is abnormal—we will withhold our concepts of pain from her. The crucial point is that the decision to withhold our concepts just is the decision to treat her as abnormal; and whether we do so or not is in the last analysis a *decision*. In facing the pain-connoisseur, we face a choice— either it's an abnormal sort of pain-behaviour, or she's abnormal; and our position is not cognitively deficient in any respect—no one could be in a better position to decide than we are now. No one can tell us just how far to go in our attempts to understand her, to make sense of her world (i.e. to regard her behaviour as abnormal pain-behaviour), before exiling her from our own (i.e. by regarding her as an abnormal person).

But then, what grounds our presumption that suffering is not inde-pendent of pain, that pity and comfort go together—the presumption that motivates our decision (if that is our decision) to exile the pain-connoisseur? Why is it, for example, that we balk at the idea that someone might experience a feeling of love or hope for one second, regardless of what happens before or after that second? Can't an ardent hope flare in the moment when my football team's striker suddenly finds space in the penalty-box and the possibility of a Cup-winning goal appears from nowhere? And can't that hope be snuffed out before a second has passed? Of course it can, but only because very specific stage-setting was in place: I had to care about the outcome, feel that what I hoped for was all but impossible, be convinced that this was my team's final chance; and afterwards, in the crushing of my hope, I will need time to go over that split-second in memory from every angle, to curse, to let the feelings of despair work themselves out. In short, the sheer *amount* of time is not critical: what is needed is enough time for a coherent 'before and after' to take place. A passion has a history, as an action has—a logical history.

But what is the status of the claim that passions and actions have histories? For Cavell, it records one of a multitude of

very general facts of *human* nature—such, for example, as the fact that the realization of intention requires action, that action requires movement, that movement involves consequences we had not intended, that our knowledge (and ignorance) of ourselves and of others depends upon the way our minds are expressed (and distorted) in word and deed and passion; that actions and passions have histories. That *that* should express understanding or boredom or anger (or: that it should be part of the grammar of 'understanding' that *that* should be what we call his 'suddenly understanding') is not necessary: someone may have to be said to 'understand suddenly' and then always fail to manifest the understanding five minutes later, just as someone *may* be bored by an earthquake or by the death of his child or the declaration of martial law, or *may* be angry at a pin or a cloud or a fish, just as someone may quietly (but comfortably?) sit on a chair of nails. That human beings on the whole do not respond in these ways is, therefore, seriously referred to as conventional; but now we are thinking of convention not as the arrangements a particular culture has found convenient, in terms of its history and geography, for effecting the necessities of human existence, but as those forms of life which are normal to any group of creatures we call human, any group about which we will say, for example, that they *have* a past to which they respond, or a geographical environment which they manipulate or exploit in certain ways for certain humanly comprehensible motives. (*CR* 110–11)

For Cavell, the phenomena which constitute the criteria of something's being so are fully in the nature of things—they are part of the backdrop of very general facts of nature (including human nature) in relation to which our concepts mean anything at all; and because they are facts, they are not necessary—one can imagine beings whose nature is not constituted in that way. What one cannot imagine is *human* beings whose nature is not constituted in that way—or, to put it more precisely, we can acknowledge other creatures as human only to the degree that we can find in the background of their lives the general regularities with which alone our psychological concepts can get any purchase. It is perfectly possible to imagine groups of humans who differ from us in hoping for a different future, fearing a different region of the past, questioning in forms different from ours; but hope will still be grammatically related to satisfaction and disappointment, and fear to some object or reason for fear which, though it may not be one we share or are affected by, we can understand as such a reason. If the pain-connoisseur's form of life is such that we can identify such connections in it, then we can treat her behaviour as (an abnormal) part of our world of suffering and pain; if it lacks the relevant patterns, then in this respect we cannot treat her as part of our world, and so in this respect she is *not* part of that world.

Being in the human world thus seems to be a matter of sharing or failing to share certain facets of human nature: normality seems to be a matter of finding certain things natural, as if the very distinction between normality and abnormality rests upon a distinction between the natural and the unnatural. This comes out most clearly when we recognize that a child's capacity to acquire the most basic linguistic and arithmetical skills (to learn how to go on) rests upon certain natural reactions.

> Our ability to communicate with him depends upon his 'natural understanding', his 'natural reaction', to our directions and our gestures. It depends on our mutual attunement in judgements. It is astonishing how far this takes us in understanding one another, but it has its limits ... And when these limits are reached, when our attunements are dissonant, I cannot get below them to firmer ground ... For not only does he not receive me, because his natural reactions are not mine; but my own understanding is found to go no further than my own natural reactions bear it. I am thrown back upon myself: I as it were turn my palms outward, as if to exhibit the kind of creature I am, and declare my ground occupied, only mine, ceding yours. (*CR* 115)

The deepest anxiety in such a situation is how to decide *when* one should turn one's palms outward, when one should simply allow the divergence to stand; it is an anxiety which derives, not from the fact that my understanding has limits, but from the fact that I must *draw* them—and seemingly on no other basis than my own nature, my self. Drawing the line between acknowledging a difference and withdrawing a set of concepts seems to indicate something about me as much as about them.

> It seems safe to suppose that if you can describe any behaviour which I can recognize as that of human beings, I can give you an explanation which will make that behaviour coherent, i.e., show it to be imaginable in terms of natural responses and practicalities. Though those natural responses may not be mine, and those practices not practical for me, in my environment, as I interpret it. And if I say 'They are crazy' or 'incomprehensible' then that is not a fact but my fate for them. I have gone as far as my imagination, magnanimity or anxiety will allow; or as my honour, or my standing cares and commitments, can accommodate. (*CR* 118)

What this implies most importantly for Cavell is that the process of attempting to educate or communicate with others is or should be a process of self-education and self-communication; for it is a means by which one's own reactions, what one takes to be natural or a matter of course, are brought to the surface, and their arbitrariness or peculiarity opened to question. In the case of teaching someone to add, I may be perfectly happy to take my stand upon my reaction as simply something that I do; but if the topic of teaching and interaction is more political, cultural, personal, then the discovery of a divergence may lead us to question ourselves rather than to exile the divergent other. Either way, in coming to see the dependence of ideas of normality upon ideas of naturalness, we might come to see what all teaching and learning isolates and dramatizes—the moment in which my power comes to an end in the face of the other's separateness from me.

Putting together these various aspects of the role of psychological concepts in our lives, we might say that knowledge of other minds must be understood as involving acknowledgement and imagination: recognizing the behaviour of another creature as expressive of mind—knowing that our criteria are satisfied—means accepting its behaviour as recognizably human and giving expression to that acceptance in one's own behaviour. It is within this distinctive framework that Cavell's later analyses of scepticism about other minds find their place. But before going on to examine those analyses, one final point must be made. Thus far, we have been examining third-person ascriptions of psychological predicates; but it is vital to note that Cavell takes the features that have thereby emerged to be equally significant in first-person cases.

It is relatively easy to see that knowledge takes the form of acknowledgement, that it calls for expression, in the first-person as well as the third-person case. For in the latter case, talk of acknowledgement does not pick out a particular sort of response to another's pain, but rather picks out a category in terms of which any given response is to be evaluated: it highlights the fact that another's pain-behaviour demands a response from us, that our knowledge must find expression in our behaviour. And, of course, precisely the same sort of point can be made about a given person's relation to her own pain:

to say that behaviour is expressive is not to say that the man impaled upon his sensation must express it in his own behaviour; it is to say that in order not to express it he must *suppress* the behaviour, or twist it. And if he twists it far or often enough, he may lose possession of that region of the mind which that behaviour is expressing. (*MWM* 264)

For Cavell, just as our knowledge of another's pain finds expression in our behaviour, so our awareness of our own pain finds behavioural expression; and just as the absence of any response to another's pain is a failure of acknowledgement, so the absence of an expression of one's own pain is a suppression of it. The psychoanalytic concept of repression confirms this in so far as it offers a new way of understanding certain forms of human behaviour as suppressions (or displaced expressions) of mind, as failures of (self-)acknowledgement. In both first- and third-person cases, then, talk of behaviour as expressive indicates a category in terms of which to evaluate that behaviour.

In asserting such parallels between first-person and third-person perspectives, Cavell is brought to oppose any blanket denial of the legitimacy of employing the concept of knowledge in first-person cases, and thus to oppose the standard Wittgensteinian position on this matter. In so far as typical Wittgensteinian claims that '"I know I'm in pain" is senseless' are meant to capture the fact that the sufferer's relation to her pain is more intimate than talk of knowledge and certainty allow—in so far as it captures the sense in which such a person is not so much possessed of an instance of pain as possessed by it, impaled upon it—Cavell is happy to agree; this, after all, is part of his reason for emphasizing that such a sufferer's behaviour is *expressive* of pain, that the pain is (manifest) in her winces and screams. However, it seems to him wrong to claim—as even Wittgenstein himself sometimes seems to do—that 'I *know* I'm in pain' has no legitimate, and philosophically significant, uses. For example, 'I know I'm in pain', said in response to someone who has seen through my attempts to suppress my pain and is pressing me to admit it, is perfectly legitimate; it is, one might say, a mode of acknowledging that I am in pain, and thus provides a sense in which one can say that knowledge takes the form of acknowledgement in both first- and third-person cases.

Moreover, once we move into wider ranges of psychological concepts, Cavell wishes to go even further than this. He finds it misleading to claim, for example, that 'I know what I am thinking' is wrong, when it would be correct to say 'I can't quite put my finger on what I'm trying to say—Ah yes, now I know what I'm thinking'.

And when it comes to regions of the soul like envy or charity or ambition or self-destructiveness, or coldness covered with affectionateness, or loneliness covered with activity, or hatred covered by judiciousness, or obsessiveness covered by intellectuality ... one's lack of knowledge about oneself may fully contrast with one's beliefs about oneself. My condition then is not that I need no criteria for such states, but that I fail accurately to allow of myself the ones I have. And here my relation to myself is expressed by saying that I do not know myself. (*CR* 101)

Of course, for Cavell, the criteria in play here are not analogous to the criteria we employ when making knowledge-claims about the world— we do not have to turn inwards and make an inventory of the contents of our mind as if plotting the movements of planets in an internal solar system; but there *are* criteria in this region which are *analogous* to those which we employ when making knowledge-claims about other minds. An example which brings out the precise import of this claim is that of expectation. What can we imagine a person to know when she says that she is expecting someone or something? As Wittgenstein admits, there may well be characteristic feelings which go with the concentration, anticipation, release, etc. involved in such cases. The person concerned will not need or use criteria to identify such feelings *as* feelings characteristic of expectation; but the presence of those feelings may lead her to say that she is expecting something, and whether they do or not will depend upon the *circumstances* in which they occur. If she has an experience characteristic of waiting for a guest to arrive whilst washing the dishes after a dinner party, she may say 'I have a queer feeling that someone is about to arrive', whereas if she has the experience whilst laying the table for a dinner party she may say 'I can't wait for my guests to arrive'; and what makes the former experience 'queer' is not its intrinsic nature but its inappropriateness to the context—there is nothing in the circumstances to be expected. In other words, what leads her to say, or to refrain from saying, that she is expecting something is the presence or absence of circumstances in which anyone could, in terms of our usual criteria for 'expecting', see how *whatever* experience she is having adds up in those circumstances to her expecting something.

If it is true that the having of my feelings *alone* cannot make possible my knowledge of myself (of what I am doing, what I am expecting . . .), this says something about the nature of self-knowledge; that it depends upon my knowing or appreciating the place or reach—I want to say, the normality or abnormality—of those feelings to the situation in which those feelings occur. (*CR* 107)

This does *not* mean that I know about myself the way that others do, that what justifies me in saying what I feel is what justifies you in saying what I feel. My use of criteria is not to establish that I (rather than anyone else) am feeling such-and-such, and not to establish that it is concentration, release, and anticipation (rather than something else) that I am feeling, but rather to establish that in these circumstances these feelings add up to expectation (rather than something else); and even then, the criteria relating feeling to circumstance are not employed by me in the way that they are employed by you (i.e. not on the basis of observation of their presence). But none the less, what leads me, for example, to call the pain in my tooth a toothache is just what will lead you to call it toothache, namely, a particular history associated with the pain. In short, according to Cavell, I rely upon those general facts of nature and human nature, and the ways in which criteria relate behaviour to circumstance against the background of those general regularities, that we saw earlier were at the basis of our attempts to make sense of the behaviour of other creatures as human or expressive of mind. The same criteria, and the same appreciation of normality and its limits, are in play.

> Knowing oneself is the capacity, as I wish to put it, for placing-oneself-in-the-world. It is not merely that to know I have in fact *done* what I intended ... I have to look to see *whether* it is done; it is also, and crucially, that I have to know that *that* circumstance is (counts as) what I did. How can *that* (the spilt milk) be 'what I did'?; how can *that* (the sobbing child) be 'what I expected'?; how can *that* (the empty room) be 'what I said' (that he had already left)? How do I *relate* or compare what goes on in my mind to the phenomena of the world? And at the level at which this is asked, it does not mean 'How do I know that the milk is spilt; that the child is crying; that he has left?' but rather how do we know of the 'possibilities of these phenomena' ... that there are, and which phenomena are, phenomena of this kind? (*CR* 108)

So, for Cavell, just as knowledge of other minds involves acknowledgement and imagination, so knowledge of one's own mind is a matter of expression and imagination. In this area as a whole, knowledge finds expression in behaviour and in an appreciation of the (ab)normality of fit between what goes on in the mind and what goes on in the world; and it is within this framework that Cavell goes on to place scepticism about the possibility of such knowledge.

Private Languages and Seeing Aspects

As we saw earlier, on Cavell's view the sceptic is right to think that criteria do not confer certainty but wrong to think that criteria therefore fail to provide the conditions under which we can know of the existence and nature of another's inner life. The sceptic is thus to be applauded in so far as he maintains, in the face of philosophical resistance, a stance which illuminates certain obvious and not-so-obvious truths that might be subsumed under the first heading (namely, that another may be in pain and fail to express it, or feign to be in pain and thus mislead me; and more generally, that knowledge of other minds requires acknowledgement and imagination); but he errs in attempting to give expression to these truths in terms of access to knowledge (namely, by claiming that the sufferer knows something that others don't). The interesting question is: Why? Why should the sceptic interpret my desire to know the other and his state of mind as a desire to know what that other knows?

Cavell's answer—one already hinted at in earlier sections of this chapter—is that the sceptic takes our criteria for pain, expectation, and so on to relate behaviour to *something else*, something that is not visible to those 'on the outside' but with which the person concerned is immediately or directly acquainted. Only such a picture of the relation between mind and body—a picture of two different worlds or processes standing in some relationship to one another—can provide an object or set of objects of which the person concerned might be thought to know and of which others might be thought to be ignorant. Accordingly, it is this picture that Cavell takes to be the central assumption of other-minds scepticism; and he interprets Wittgenstein's famous private language argument as an attempt to unearth the desires and needs which lead us to think of the matter in this way.

Cavell looks in some detail at section 258 of the *Philosophical Investigations*, in which Wittgenstein confronts someone defending the intelligibility of a private language (i.e. one which can be understood only by the person using it) who imagines himself making a note 'S' in his diary whenever he has a particular sensation. This would-be private linguist believes that in order for the annotation to function at all, i.e. in order for it to succeed in recording the presence of that sensation, he must establish a firm connection between 'S' and the relevant sensation; and he goes on to imagine that this can be done by means of a private ostensive definition, which will permit him to 'impress upon himself' the sign–sensation correlation. Wittgenstein's response to this carries an air of definitive rebuttal:

But 'I impress it upon myself' can only mean: this process brings it about that I remember the connection right in the future. But in the present case I have no criterion of correctness. One would like to say: whatever is going to seem right to me is right. And that only means that here we can't talk about 'right'. (*PI* 258)

Cavell's interpretation of this passage is striking. Rather than treating it as the core of an argument against (perhaps even a refutation of) the private linguist, he takes it to be designed to draw out a hidden assumption or presupposition of the private linguist's position for the purposes of diagnosis; the crux is not whether or not such a criterion of correctness is available, but why it might be thought to be needed. And what the passage demonstrates is that this need emerges only because the private linguist wants to get the sign and the sensation definitively linked—to get them stamped upon one another so firmly that their faces, so to speak, can be seen to match independently of any decision of his. In other words, the private linguist hits trouble only because he feels the need for this special 'impressing'; and according to Cavell, what creates that feeling is a crucial assumption or presupposition that is dominating his view about language and its expressiveness:

In each of Wittgenstein's attempts to realise the fantasy of a private language, a moment arises in which, to get on with the fantasy, the idea, or fact, of the *expressiveness* of voicing or writing down my experiences has to be overcome. In 243 [of *PI*] this is quite explicit; in 258 the idea of formulating a definition of the sign overcomes the fact that the sign already has all the definition it needs—if, that is, I am actually employing it as I said I was. (*CR* 348)

If I do indeed regularly experience a certain sensation, and I have some reason for wishing to record its occurrence, then I have a use for the sign 'S' and I can embark upon the practice of employing it as an annotation in my diary. Sometimes I may forget to note down the occurrences of the sensation, and one day when I am struck by this forgetfulness I may decide to make a note of those occasions on which it happens, so that my diary becomes dotted with various instances of the sign 'S', sometimes accompanied by my new sign 'F' and sometimes not; but unless some *further* complication arises about this new practice, I would feel no need to impress upon myself the connection between 'F' and my forgetfulness—so why should I feel the need to do so in the case of the old practice with 'S'? In both cases, the connection is surely as clear as the original sensation itself.

This thing of our 'writing "S"', and other things that we do and experience no deeper metaphysically than this, is all there is for our confidence in our experiences to go on. And it is enough; it is in principle perfect. But we keep passing over this supposition of our example, as if the incident of writing kept getting mentioned only to fill in the image of a diary. But the writing of the 'S' just is the *expression* of S, the sensation. It may, in fact, be the only S-behaviour in our repertory. (*CR* 350)

If asked for our reason for calling 'S' the name of a sensation, we need only point out the kind of way it is used in the diarist's practice; and if asked why we think that it is the same sensation every time, we can point to that fact that the diarist writes 'S' every time (cf. *PI* 270). That is all; but what more could we want?

In other words, what establishes that 'S' refers to the sensation is the fact that writing down 'S' is a mode of giving expression to that sensation—just as my references to my pain are my expressions of pain itself, and my words refer to my pain just to the extent that they are (modified) expressions of it. The private linguist's problem in impressing the sign–sensation correlation on himself arises precisely because it amounts to an attempt to rely upon reference alone (here an inner pointing), and reference cannot establish any such connection in the absence of expressive behaviour. His problem is that he passes over or represses the dependence of reference upon expression in naming our states of consciousness.

If, however, the private linguist's desire to forge connections between sign and sensation functions primarily to cover over the fact that those connections are already in place, then those existent expressive connections must be ones that he is unwilling or unable to acknowledge. As the very notion of a private language suggests, this unwillingness or inability will have two fundamental roots: first, a worry that merely natural expressive language is not enough to allow him to give expression to himself in language, to make himself known (here, the desire to impress a connection between sign and sensation manifests a desire to ensure that his signs really do have the faces of *his* sensations stamped on them); and second, a worry that merely natural expressive language makes him known regardless of any contribution on his part, that giving expression to himself is beyond his control (and here, the emphasis on establishing a sign–sensation correlation himself is a way of denying the knowledge that his expressive behaviour already *has* the faces of his sensations stamped upon it). In short, the fantasy of a private language—which encapsulates a desire to deny the publicness of language—is a fantasy or fear either of inexpressiveness or of finding that what I express is beyond my control. And the mood of such fantasies can thus be encapsulated in the following question: Why do we attach expressive significance to *any* words or deeds, of ourselves or of others? How can some of our behaviour fail to express anything, and the rest be condemned to meaning?

Cavell's claim is not that such questions are ultimately coherent; but he takes it that they could only be asked by someone in a frame of mind in which the relation between the human mind and the human body has become opaque. The only way forward is thus to provide a way of understanding that relationship which will stop us from wanting to ask those questions; and in his view that means invoking Wittgenstein's treatment of aspect perception:

Imagination is called for, faced with the other, when I have to take the facts in, realize the significance of what is going on, make the behaviour real for myself, make a connection. 'Take the facts in' means something like 'see his behaviour in a certain way', for example, see his blink as a wince, and connect the wince with something in the world that there is to be winced at (perhaps a remark which you yourself would not wince at), or, if it is not that, connect the wince with something in him, a thought, or a nerve. (*CR* 354)

The crucial point here is that the criteria for pain do not relate bodily movement to pain itself, but rather behaviour expressive of pain to something that might have occasioned it, e.g. a painful thought, experience, or event. In other words, criteria do not relate behaviour to 'something else', establishing links between the stream of human speech and action and an inner realm; they relate what someone says and does—understood as expressive of mind—to other things going on in and around him, connecting elements within the stream of life. Properly understood, criteria are the terms in which I relate what is going on (e.g. make sense of it by giving its history or circumstances) and in which I relate *to* what is going on. We might say that applying criteria is a matter of seeing behaviour as expressive, i.e. is an instance of seeing something as something; and this is the topic of much of part 2 of the *Philosophical Investigations*.

In those sections, Wittgenstein engages in an extensive and intensive discussion of experiences of aspect-dawning (e.g. suddenly being struck by the fact that a figure of a duck is also a figure of a rabbit) and what he calls 'continuous aspect perception' (e.g. taking the duck aspect of a duck-rabbit figure entirely for granted), primarily as a preparation for studying analogues to these experiences and attitudes (and the position of those lacking such experiences and attitudes) with respect to words. Cavell takes this idea of an analogical investigation a step further: on his view, the topic of our relation to our words should itself be regarded as 'allegorical' of our relation to ourselves and to other persons.

The idea of the allegory of words is that human expressions, the human figure, to be grasped, must be read. To know another mind is to interpret a physiognomy, and the message of this region of the *Investigations* is that this is not a matter of 'mere knowing'. I have to *read* the physiognomy, and see the creature according to my reading, and treat it according to my seeing. The human body is the best picture of the human soul—not, I feel like adding, primarily because it represents the soul but because it expresses it. The body is the field of expression of the soul. The body is *of* the soul; it is the soul's; a human soul *has* a human body. (*CR* 356)

How do these connections with aspect perception and attachment to our words help to illuminate the motivations and confusions of the sceptic about other minds? In the first place, perceiving an aspect is more than mere knowing; or to be more precise, continuously perceiving an aspect is manifest in one's actions and orientations towards the given object—one's life with the object makes manifest one's awareness of it as the particular object it is.[1] In this sense, my knowledge of the object is necessarily given expression in my behaviour, in an attitude; and Cavell's claim is that, in just the same way, my knowledge of other minds—and of particular states of others' minds—will itself find expression in my attitude. It is not a matter of merely knowing something about a given creature's behaviour, not a matter of affirming a proposition or drawing an inference from that behaviour to something else; it is a matter of treating that behaviour as expressive of mind, i.e. as expressive. It is an inflexion of myself towards others, an orientation which affects everything.

Second, the analogy with words allows Cavell to introduce the concept of reading, and the idea of 'reading' the human body or human behaviour captures three important features of psychological concepts:

Part of the reason that I want the word 'read' is, I feel sure, recorded in its history: it has something to do with being advised, and hence with seeing. But part of the reason has also to do with an intimation that I am to read something particular, in a particular way; the text, so to speak, has a particular tone and form. The form is a story, a history. You can tell who someone is by describing him and saying what he does for a living, etc. If you know the person, understand him, your knowledge will consist in being able to tell his story. (*CR* 363)

The concept of reading captures the immediacy of our relation to the other's mind in so far as it brings with it the idea of seeing: I do not infer from my perceptions of the other's behaviour that she possesses a

---

[1] For a detailed justification of this claim, and a general examination of Wittgenstein's remarks on this complex topic, see the opening chapters of my *On Being in the World* (London, 1990).

mind, I *see* her behaviour as expressive of mind. And the same concept can be used to capture the sense in which the criteria for psychological concepts involve relating behaviour to circumstance, to what comes before and after the behaviour in question; this is another way of putting the earlier point that human actions and passions have histories. Finally, the concept of reading carries with it a sense of the specificity of the other: just as reading properly or closely is a matter of responsiveness to the specific form and tone of each instance and type of text, so reading the physiognomy of a given other involves a responsiveness to the specificity of that other—the particular inflexion that human expressiveness takes in her bodily frame, the individuality of the ways in which what she does relates to what is going on in and around her.

Third, and perhaps most important for Cavell, however, is the light cast by these analogies upon the sorts of thing that might interfere with or block the immediacy of one's relation to the other's expressive behaviour. For when we fail to see the rabbit aspect of the duck-rabbit, it is not—it cannot be—because that aspect of the figure is hidden; on the contrary, the aspect is completely visible, the figure is wearing it on its face. In such cases of what Wittgenstein calls aspect-blindness, the failure is a failure of perception on our part:

The block to my vision of the other is not the other's body but my incapacity or unwillingness to interpret or judge it accurately, to draw the right connections. The suggestion is: I suffer a kind of blindness, but I avoid the issue by projecting this darkness upon the other ... We may say that the rabbit-aspect of the figure is hidden from us when we fail to see it. But what hides it is then obviously not the picture (that reveals it), but our (prior) way of taking it, namely in its duck-aspect. What hides one aspect is another aspect, something on the same level. So we might say: What hides the mind is not the body but the mind itself—his his, or mine his, and contrariwise. (*CR* 369)

The sceptical picture of mind and body as two distinct but parallel domains leads to the view that the other's body veils her mind; it *can* reveal it, but it need not, and its signals may be systematically misleading. In effect, the other's body stands between me and her, it separates us. The truth in this picture is that we are indeed *separate*—we are each embodied, each this body and not that, each here and not there, each now and not then. But we are not separated *by* our bodies:

If something separates us, comes between us, that can only be a particular aspect or stance of the mind itself, a particular *way* in which we relate or are related (by birth, by law, by force, in love) to one another—our positions, our attitudes, with reference to one another. Call this our history; it is our present. (*CR* 369)

We are endlessly separate, for *no* reason; but then we are answerable for everything that comes between us—if not for causing it, then for continuing it; if not for denying it then for affirming it; if not for it then to it. This is the primary lesson of the analogy with figures and words.

It might seem that placing such weight upon the example of aspect perception requires Cavell to misrepresent a vital part of Wittgenstein's treatment of that topic: for is it not essential to Wittgenstein's view that aspect perception is a strictly limited phenomenon? We do not, for example, see the cutlery on the table *as* cutlery—it just is cutlery; and it seems equally implausible to imply that we see a human being as angry when she just is obviously angry, with no two ways about it. In short, claiming to see *X* as *a* seems to make sense only if there is some other, competing way to see *X*; and this condition does not seem to hold in the case of expressive human behaviour. Cavell has two responses to this worry. First, the case of the human being differs from that of the cutlery in that there is no difficulty in the idea of knowing what cutlery is—knowledge which one can easily manifest in one's use of cutlery during a meal, for example; but in the case of a human being, it is not yet obvious whether we know what it is to know what a human being is—what sort of behaviour, for example, would manifest that knowledge? In short, the aspect under which we are regarding a human being, and our relation to it, is by no means as clear or unproblematic as the analogy with cutlery suggests. Second, Cavell claims that there *are* competing ways of viewing human beings: there are ways of regarding human creatures and their behaviour which do not amount to regarding that behaviour as giving expression to a soul.

He cites two examples and discusses them at length—the issue of abortion and the issue of slavery. On Cavell's view, conservatives on the abortion issue are in the business of trying to get their liberal opponents to see a human embryo as a human being, and the liberal—whilst able to admit that the embryo is *human*, even that it is a human in embryo—is unable or unwilling to see it in that way. Slave-owners, on the other hand, see and to some extent treat certain human beings as slaves, i.e. see them as not purely human, as a different *kind* of human being from themselves.

I have not wished to argue from the fact that it is correct to say that one can see and to a certain extent treat human embryos as human beings that it follows that human embryos are not human beings; nor to argue from the fact that another can see and fully treat certain human beings as slaves that it follows that human beings are not slaves. I have wished to say that it is not a fact that human embryos are human beings and that it is nothing more than a fact that certain human beings are slaves. (*CR* 378)

In other words, for Cavell, whilst it makes perfect sense to say that it is a fact that a given knife is a piece of cutlery, the notion that a given creature is a human being cannot be so flatly treated as analogously matter-of-fact. Since there are contexts in which it makes perfect sense for someone to say that another person is *failing* to see a human being as a human being, the notion of *seeing* human beings as human beings is to that extent not out of place—talk of seeing-as is at least not obviously meaningless or incoherent.

Given this amount of leeway, the central point that Cavell is concerned to make is that the knowledge that something is human can fail, fluctuate, be taken for granted, and be striven for in just the sorts of ways suggested by the duck-rabbit figure:

What is implied is that it is essential to knowing that something is human that we sometimes experience it as such, and sometimes do not, or fail to; that certain alterations of consciousness take place, and sometimes not, in the face of it. Or in the presence of a memory of it. The memory, perhaps in a dream, may run across the mind, like a rabbit across a landscape, forcing an exclamation from me, perhaps in the form of a name. (*CR* 379)

Empathic Projection

Cavell goes on to develop his sense of the analogy between knowing other minds and perceiving aspects in great detail, some of which will emerge in later chapters. At this point, however, I want to examine the comparisons and contrasts which emerge between scepticism about the external world and scepticism about other minds when the latter is understood within the framework that has already been put in place. In particular, I want to ask whether, for Cavell, there can be a best case for knowing another mind—whether there are circumstances in which a universal doubt about the existence of other minds can be generated by the failure of a specific claim to know another mind.

In the case of external-world scepticism, the only available basis of a claim to knowledge was the deliverances of the senses, in particular that of vision; any competent language-user, if asked by the sceptic how she knows that there is a tomato on the table in front of her, would answer 'Because I can see it'. In the case of other-minds scepticism, things are less clear; if the sceptic were to ask someone to cite the basis of her claim to know that another humanish creature was possessed of a mind or soul, what might she say? Since minds are not visible objects, such a claim cannot be grounded in the exercise of one's senses. It seems that I must do more than simply identify what is before my eyes, I must also identify *with* the creature I see, see a kinship between it and myself, see it as a creature just like me. It seems likely that some such basis will emerge under sceptical pressure; it may in the end be no less reliable than the forced appearance of 'Because I see it' in the earlier sceptical recital, but its appearance here is at least no *more* forced than its analogue in the external-world case. Cavell labels it 'empathic projection', on the understanding that the phrase is no more than a label for *something* that must be the basis of my claims to read the other, something that I go on in myself in adopting or calling upon my attitude towards other human beings in any particular case; and he accepts the aptness of its invocation at least to the degree that it reflects the importance of the response of the knower in this domain of knowledge.

The sceptic's problem is that, if he then attempts to generate a universal doubt by suggesting, in a given case, that I may go wrong in my empathic projection—that I may be projecting upon an android or mutant or alien of a new kidney rather than upon a human being—the doubt will not generalize. In the case of external-world scepticism, the senses are my access to the external world as a whole; so, if doubt is cast upon them by invoking the possibility of dreaming or hallucinations, the world as a whole vanishes, i.e. the doubt generalizes. The role of empathic projection, however, is to affix a seam or division *within* the world: on the basis of that capacity for projection, I segregate human from non-human things in the course of my daily life. Looked at this way, mutants and androids appear to be a new variant of a perfectly familiar kind of thing, namely, the non-human kind. So, pointing out in a given case that I might be empathically projecting upon a mutant amounts to a dramatic way of claiming that a specific humanish being might really be non-human. But this merely invokes the possibility of just the sort of error which might be expected in such a continuous process of categorization, i.e. the possibility of a specific *mis*categorization; it would not of itself show the general implementation of that

basic categorial distinction—the affixing of such a seam to my experience at all—to be mistaken. In other words, although the invocation of
mutants would certainly show that I can never be certain that I never
make a projective error, it would not convince me that I am never right
in projecting; this doubt will not generalize.

We might summarize this by saying that the others do not vanish
when a given case fails me—which amounts to the admission that this
sceptical approach has failed to generate or focus upon a best case of
knowledge of other minds. This does not, however, entail that such a
best case does not exist; for thus far in the sceptical recital we have
failed to take seriously the sense in which knowledge of other minds
takes the form of acknowledgement. Casting the recital in terms of
mutants and androids makes the issue seem one of correct
identification—of taking an accurate, purely cognitive inventory of the
furniture of the universe; if, however, we focus upon the point that the
concept of acknowledgement is designed to highlight, namely, the need
to give expression to the knowledge at its core, then the true nature of
a best case in this domain (as well as of the difficulties involved in
securing one) may become clearer.

In his earlier essay on *King Lear* (in *Must We Mean What We Say?*),
Cavell argued that my acknowledgement of another calls for recognition
of the other's specific relation to myself (since the fact of the acknowledgement's being called for from me is otherwise left unacknowledged),
and that this may entail the revelation of myself as having denied or
distorted that relation: this is his interpretation of the structure and
development of Lear's relationship with Cordelia. This necessary reflexivity at the heart of acknowledgement already helps to account for the
difficulties involved in finding a best case of acknowledging other
minds, for it highlights the fact that acknowledgement *singles out* knower
and known. If acknowledgement is always a function of one person's
specific relation to another, its successes and failures seem destined to be
similarly localized: my acknowledgement of a specific person need have
no obvious implications for my acknowledgement of other people, and
none for that other person's relation to people other than me. In this
sense, it seems that both knower and known can step out of their
confinement from each other; the notion of a generic other (analogous
to that of a generic object, an object about which a doubt—once
raised—could be generalized because it can stand for objects in general)
seems a contradiction in terms.

A second difficulty flows from the fact that the sceptic is in search of an unusual—and perhaps mythical—mode of acknowledgement of the other; since his worry is about the sheer reality or existence of other minds, it would seem that his best case must be one of acknowledging the sheer *humanity* of the other:

For in the case of, for example, 'acknowledging another's pain', I know in a general way what I am called upon to do that goes beyond my feat of cognition, viz., to express sympathy, or impatience, something that incorporates his suffering. And in the case of Lear, I know in a general way what he has to reveal about himself in order to acknowledge Cordelia as his unjustly banished daughter, viz., that he is her unjust banishing father. Whereas in following the case of the sceptical recital I have been led to ask whether, and on what basis, I can acknowledge the other (simply) as a human being. It is not settled what, if anything, would go beyond empathically projecting his humanity; nor what, if any, relation I bear to him; nor how, if at all, I can reveal myself to him as having denied this relation. (*CR* 429)

For Cavell, however, these two worries create difficulties for rather than definitive rebuttals of the sceptic; they might make us unwilling simply to accept the intelligibility or attainability of a best case for knowledge here, but they do not amount to a licence to dismiss the idea of a best case out of hand. Moreover, the nature of these difficulties makes it clearer just what a best case for knowledge in this domain would look like; it would be one which could accommodate the idea of being singled out by a generic other and challenged to acknowledge the bare humanity of that other. It would therefore seem that the search for a best case in the domain of other minds amounts to a search for the following:

Is there a case in which a given other compresses within himself or herself my view of psychic reality as a whole; a given other who exemplifies all others for me, humanity as such; a given other upon whom I stake my capacity for acknowledgement altogether, that is to say, my capacity at once for acknowledging the existence of others and for revealing my existence in relation to others? (*CR* 430)

If such a case could be found, it would give the sceptic what he wants, precisely because it will allow the consequences of a failure of acknowledgement to generalize; and it will do so not despite but rather *because* of the fact that any relationship with another person that one regarded with such seriousness would be extremely unusual—the very reverse of generic. For what would happen if such an other fails me—if I cannot believe, or feel that I cannot know, what *this* other shows and says to me?

... the consequence will not extend to different others. I am thrown upon just *this* other's body. Nor here, in being thrown back upon myself, does the consequence extend to different others in my position. No one else *is* in this position with respect to this other. I and this other have been singled out for one another. This is what a best case comes to. If it fails, the remainder of the world and of my capacities in it have become irrelevant. That there are others, and others perhaps in my position in relation to them, are matters not beyond my knowledge but past my caring. I am not removed from the world; it is dead for me. All for me is but toys; there is for me no new tomorrow; my chaos is come (again?). I shut my eyes to others. (*CR* 430)

As Cavell's final sentences imply, relationships of the sort which seem to call out for characterization in the terms we have been outlining are central to certain literary genres—including, but also ranging far beyond, that of Shakespearean drama (e.g. Othello and Desdemona, Lear and Cordelia); in this way he manages simultaneously to suggest that the idea of a best case of knowing other minds is not merely an incoherent product of sceptical confusion but a possibility of central significance in our culture, and to begin forging a fundamental connection between (these types of) literature and (these areas of) philosophy—a connection that we will attempt to explore in later chapters. For present purposes, however, it is important to see that, despite the fact that such relationships are often portrayed in literature as ending in murder or death, it is no part of Cavell's view that the failure of a best case of knowing another mind would always and necessarily condemn the other person to literal non-existence; in the vast majority of such cases—whether in literature or life—failures of acknowledgement will leave the other person still living, and still knowing of her own existence. But she will remain as unacknowledged, as denied; the fact that I have shut my eyes to her will be part of her knowledge. So, to acknowledge her now would be to know this, to acknowledge her not only as someone I have denied but also as someone who knows this about me (and so about us); and to deny her now would be to deny this, to deny my denial of her and her knowledge of my denial—in effect, to remove myself from her world, to shut her eyes to me. Thus, even if I succeed in acknowledging her as someone I have denied, that denial is now part of her knowledge of herself and of her continuing life with me; and if I go on denying this denial, I will put myself past her caring and find that I remain only as unacknowledged by her. Either way, it would seem that the failure of a best case for acknowledgement will implicate me in the other's existence; either way, I will have to live with the knowledge that, in the very case upon which I was prepared to stake my capacity for acknowledgement as such, that capacity failed me.

But if the consequences of failure are so serious, then it is only to be expected that we will avoid best cases for acknowledgement—we will avoid the best in order to avoid the worst, we will have to *be* singled out. The possibility of such avoidance already distinguishes other-minds scepticism from external-world scepticism: it makes no sense to avoid a best case in relation to the external world because the best case just *is* my everyday life with objects. In the case of other minds, however, I can not only avoid the *occurrence* of a best case, I can also avoid *knowing* that a given occurrence is a best case. I can attempt to restrict my relations with others, control my caring for or about them; and I can avoid acknowledging that my attempts at such restrictions have failed, when and if they ever do. But of course, neither strategy is guaranteed to succeed; despite my best efforts, I may simply *be* singled out.

Such forms of avoidance are responses to a sense of being exposed to the other—exposed to the possibility of a best case. But knowing other minds involves exposure of another sort: what Cavell calls exposure to my *concept* of the other. This exposure results from the fact that any knowledge of 'other minds' rests upon my assurance in applying the relevant concepts; the other can present me with no mark or feature on the basis of which I can *settle* my attitude. In one sense, of course, this reliance upon assurance is a universal human condition, something that is true of us all; but in another sense it singles each of us out, for it raises the possibility that the limits or uncertainties of my assurance are merely *my* limits and uncertainties—that they constitute a failure to measure up to ordinary human capacities rather than a measure of them. The sense of exposure here is redoubled when we recognize our general unclarity about the nature of the assurance that forms the basis for acknowledging others—is this 'empathic projection' something we can rely upon, or is it mythical, an attempt to dramatize or repress the true nature of our situation when knowing others?

This double sense of exposure—to the other and to my concept of the other—becomes particularly acute when what is supposed to stand in need of acknowledgement is the sheer humanity of the other. Is this a real aspect of our responsibilities here, a separable or inseparable part of the business of acknowledging that another is in pain, unhappy, joyous; or is it just a Romantic myth, an ideal which covers our avoidance of that everyday business?

It is as a general alternative to sceptical doubt that Austin was moved to say that, in substantiating my claims to know, 'enough is enough'; I must have said enough to rule out other reasonable, competing possibilities. But how much is enough when it comes to knowing and acknowledging the humanity of another? How many times, and about just which matters, must I pity another, help another, accept another's excuses, before concluding that enough is enough? 'Give me another day; another moment; another dollar; another chance ...' If I do not answer such appeals, is this because I have found the other, this other, not to be worth it or entitled to it, or myself not to be up to it? (*CR* 438)

If we step back a little from the detail of the possibilities that we have raised, then Cavell's sense of the general structure of our situation with respect to knowing others may emerge more clearly. First, the sceptic cannot hope to raise his universal doubt in this domain if he formulates that doubt in terms of a purely cognitive failure; a best case does not emerge merely from invoking the possibility that our empathic projection might be misdirected in any given case. If we reconceptualize matters in terms of acknowledgement rather than simple knowledge, however, things look different. On the one hand, it can seem that the very notion of acknowledging someone's bare humanity, together with the embedded notion that such an acknowledgement might take an ideally full or unrestricted form, is a chimera. Even if we accept Cavell's hints that characters in Shakespearean drama provide models of a best case for knowing others, such models—and the ideals they instantiate—seem to place ordinary interpersonal relationships against a scale or standard which has more to do with adolescent yearnings or Romantic myths than the grammar of psychological concepts. On the other hand, the grammar of acknowledgement implies that, if a best case in this area *were* a real possibility, we would have very good reason to refuse to admit it: avoiding the very idea of the best makes sense if it allows us to avoid the very idea of the worst. Furthermore, the way in which acknowledgement has its basis in the willingness or capacity of the knower to apply the relevant concepts, together with the way in which it singles out knower and known, introduces a structural uncertainty: how can we distinguish, in any given case of acknowledgement, between doing as much as we can to give expression to our knowledge of the other and merely thinking that this is the case in order to avoid the knowledge that we are unwilling to do so; or between reaching the limits of *our* capacity to acknowledge and reaching the limits of the humanly acknowledgeable?

Cavell is not attempting to deny that we typically find ourselves living lives in which our relations with others do not manifest continued and unrestricted acknowledgement of those others; he is arguing that there is a real question about how we are to interpret that undoubted fact. How can we know whether the restricted relations in which we find ourselves with a given other show that this is not (and there is no such thing as) a best case for knowledge, or that we are imposing those restrictions in order to avoid such a best case, or that we are imposing an interpretation of this relationship as restricted in order to avoid knowing that it is a best case?

Our position is not, so far as we know, the best. But mightn't it be? Mightn't it be that just this haphazard, unsponsored state of the world, just this radiation of relationships, of my cares and commitments, provides the milieu in which my knowledge of others can best be expressed? Just *this*—say expecting someone to tea; or returning a favour; waving goodbye; reluctantly or happily laying in groceries for a friend with a cold; feeling rebuked, and feeling that it would be humiliating to admit the feeling; pretending not to understand that the other has taken my expression, with a certain justice, as meaning more than I sincerely wished it to mean; hiding inside a marriage; hiding outside a marriage—just such things are perhaps the most that knowing others comes to, or has come to for me.—Is there more for it to come to; more that it *must* come to? (*CR* 439–40)

In other words, to the question whether there is such a thing as a best case for acknowledging others, Cavell's answer is 'I don't know; and neither does anyone else'. The question cannot simply be dismissed as nonsensical, and neither can it be given a general answer; it is rather a question which every individual faces (or refuses to face) in her relationships with others *in each case*, and nothing about the features of each relationship can settle the answer. In short, the possibility which the question invokes haunts our everyday lives with others: if it is impossible simply to dismiss it, it is also impossible simply to embrace it. In this sense, the doubt and ignorance which the sceptic is prone to express in purely cognitive terms is seen by Cavell as integral to the texture of ordinary life when it is understood in terms of acknowledgement; in contrast to scepticism about the external world, in the case of other minds we live our scepticism.

In saying that we live our scepticism, I mean to register this ignorance about our everyday position towards others—not that we positively know that we are never, or not ordinarily, in best cases for knowing of the existence of others, but that we are rather disappointed in our occasions for knowing, as though we have, or have lost, some picture of what knowing another, or being known by another, would really come to—a harmony, a concord, a union, a transparence, a governance, a power—against which our actual successes at knowing, and being known, are poor things. (*CR* 440)

Knowing and Being Known

One crucial aspect of the reflexivity that is inherent in acknowledge-ment, and so also in any scepticism about acknowledgement, has yet to be dealt with. Thus far, we have been focussing upon the nature and limits of my capacity to know of the existence of others; but since I am an other to those others (and they, in this respect, are I's to me), this investigation should also be seen as exploring my capacity to *be* known and acknowledged. Indeed, it is plausible to claim that the scepticism which emerges in third-person cases gains much of its grip and impor-tance precisely because it articulates a threat which we experience in first-person terms: the anxiety it embodies is an anxiety over our own transparency or comprehensibility to others. And coming to see this reflexive aspect of other-minds scepticism immediately highlights a lacuna in our account of knowing and acknowledging. By focussing upon what is involved in my coming to know others, the whole weight of our investigation has been upon the role of the knower; little or no attention has been devoted to the role of the known—to the ways in which a given person might facilitate or block the attempts of another to know or acknowledge her existence. I want to end this chapter by mentioning some of the elements of Cavell's account of this facet of knowing and acknowledging, since they play a vital role in the later development of his thought.

His account takes off from the central Wittgensteinian perception that the human body is the field of expression of the human soul. My inner state or life is to be understood as something to which I give expression—or to be more precise, it is something which I must either express or suppress: in this respect, 'expression' (like 'acknowledgement') is a way of categorizing a dimension or mode of behaviour rather than a specific type of response within that dimension. Of course, certain qualifications must be made to this generalization—in particular, we must acknowledge that what I express is not necessarily determined by what I intend to express. My way of concealing a pain may precisely reveal it to anyone who is acquainted with me; and if there is something about me that I do not know (my meanness with money, my hatred of my father, my need for love), my words and deeds may make it manifest to others even though I am not in a position either to reveal it or to conceal it. Even in these cases, however, what is given expression is what matters; and it remains true of a great deal of what goes on in me that normally if it is to be known I must tell it or otherwise give expression to it.

The vital importance of being known has, perhaps, been sufficiently emphasized in the preceding pages; but it is worth reiterating here, if only to dilute the comfort in the thought that, even if no one knows or acknowledges my inner state, at least I do. Cavell does not claim that if I am not known or acknowledged by others, then I am condemned to non-existence: his point is rather that I would then exist as unacknowledged, as denied by others, and that this would then be part of my own knowledge of myself. If my pain is treated as unworthy of response by others, if its reality is denied in this way, then what reality will it have for me? And if I am treated as unworthy of acknowledgement by others, if my existence as a human being is denied in this way, then what does my existence as a human being amount to? In other words, if, through knowing others, I am implicated in their existence, then my existence is implicated in others' acknowledgements of me. This makes the decision to make myself known—to express myself—one which is fraught with risk, since it opens me to rebuff; but deciding not to make myself known, to suppress myself, would close me off from the very possibility of acceptance (it would *ensure* that my existence was and remained unacknowledged)—and systematically suppressing my expressions of (even a part of) my soul or mind could lead to my losing possession of (that part of) it altogether.

For Cavell, then, being known is of central importance because one's inner life can find its full reality only through its being given expression to, and acknowledgement by, others. My existence as a human individual is not just a fact about me or about the world, and it is not something that I can simply be thought to grasp entirely independently of the reactions and responses of others; on the contrary, if I am to possess it I must declare it, as if taking it upon myself. Doing so therefore involves running two risks, overcoming two anxieties—the anxiety that my expressions of myself will be unacknowledged, and the anxiety that my expressions do not capture me, that they are not truly expressions of me:

you must let yourself matter to the other. (There is a very good reason not to do so. You may discover that you do not matter.) . . . To let yourself matter is to acknowledge not merely how it is with you, and hence to acknowledge that you want the other to care, at least to care to know. It is equally to acknowledge that your expressions in fact express you, that they are yours, that you are in them. This means allowing yourself to be comprehended, something you can always deny. Not to deny it is, I would like to say, to acknowledge your body, and the body of your expressions, to be yours, you on earth, all there will ever *be* of you. (*CR* 382–3)

In other words, part of the import of my scepticism about the possibility of knowing other minds is the expression it gives to my scepticism about my capacity to give myself expression in the only way in which it is possible for me to do so, namely, through my body and its body of expressions. This anxiety of necessary inexpressiveness is one of the roots of the fantasy of a private language: rather than treating my body as the field of expression of my soul (i.e. believing in my expressions of myself, having confidence in or working to achieve an alignment between my soul and my body, and so taking real possession of a sense of myself as flesh and blood), I see any expression of myself as a distortion, a theatricalization of myself. Such theatricalization is of course possible, and it would result in responses from the other which would be directed to the wrong thing—to the part I played, the character I enacted, rather than to me myself. But there is another, more passive approach to self-expression: rather than *making* yourself known, trying to direct the other's responses (thus converting her and her responses into another character in your production), allow yourself to *be* known—wait to be known.

Of course, your waiting may be in vain—the role of the knower cannot be eradicated—but at least you do not exclude the possibility of the arrival of what you desire. And this waiting need not be thought of as purely passive, for *becoming* passive can itself be thought of as an activity, and an activity of a very important sort:

activity just here may well prove to constitute knowing oneself. It is the ability to make oneself an other to oneself, to learn of oneself something one did not *already* know. Hence this is the focus at which knowledge of oneself and of others meet. I should think a sensible axiom of the knowledge of persons would be this: that one can see others only to the extent that one can take oneself as an other. (*CR* 459)

Here, Cavell is picking up his earlier claim that it makes perfect sense to talk of knowledge and of *failures* of knowledge in the first-person case. It is not the case that one cannot fail to know oneself, although it is the case that one cannot *just* fail to know oneself; in the sense in which one can simply fail to know (not stand in any relationship to) another person, one cannot fail to know oneself because one cannot just fail to stand in some relation to oneself. Ignorance is therefore something I must work at, knowledge something I must work to avoid; but if I were to imagine that it is impossible to discover something new about myself, that it is impossible for me to surprise myself or come upon myself anew, I would be imagining a world in which I bored myself to a colossal degree. I could sometimes amuse myself, but I could hardly take an interest in myself.

If, therefore, my ignorance about myself is something I wish to avoid, if self-knowledge is something I wish to work for, then I must work at comprehending my expressions of myself. In short, and just as the reflexivities of acknowledgement would lead us to expect, self-knowledge should be understood in a way parallel to that of knowledge of others: self-knowledge is a matter of making oneself an other to oneself, and presupposes the self's avoidance of self-suppression. Knowledge of self and knowledge of others intersect: the appropriate method is that of acknowledging the field of expression of a soul.

6

Criteria, Counting, and Recounting

As I acknowledged at the beginning of Chapter 4, my separation of Cavell's treatment of scepticism about the external world from his treatment of scepticism about other minds was a highly artificial strategy, motivated solely by the desire to enhance the surveyability of this complex material. It is, however, impossible to track the development of Cavell's thought beyond *The Claim of Reason* without taking very seriously the degree to which he sees these two modes or aspects of scepticism as inextricably interwoven. Accordingly, in this chapter my aim will be to isolate and examine Cavell's reasons for holding this view, and to trace out some of the consequences which flow from it. In particular, I want to examine what would follow if we could legitimately transfer a version of the idea of empathic projection (which is central to Cavell's investigation of other-minds scepticism) into our understanding of external-world scepticism. For it is with this speculation that Cavell begins to draw his work in *The Claim of Reason* to a close.

Doesn't the concept of empathic projection make the idea of knowing others too special a project from the beginning, as if the knowing of objects could take care of itself, whereas what goes into the knowing of others is everything that goes into the knowing of objects *plus* something else, something that, as it were, animates the object? ... This idea may have the whole process of perception ... backwards. It makes equal sense—at least equal—to suppose that the natural (or, the biologically more primitive) condition of human perception is of (outward) things, whether objects or persons, as animated; so that it is the seeing of objects as objects (i.e. seeing them objectively, as non-animated) that is the sophisticated development ... (*CR* 441)

Of course, the crucial objection to such an idea is that it seems to introduce the notion of animism into the sceptical problematic. Cavell's investigation thus becomes focussed on the question of whether the (perhaps biologically primitive) idea of perceiving objects as animated can itself be given a sophisticated development in anything other than a merely 'literary' or 'metaphorical' sense. Is there anything in that idea from which philosophy can draw genuine guidance?

Doubt and Jealousy

Towards the end of *The Claim of Reason*, Cavell begins to unearth a sequence of symmetries and asymmetries between the nature and structure of the two facets of scepticism with which he has been grappling:

Over and over, an apparent symmetry or asymmetry between scepticism with respect to the external world and scepticism with respect to other minds has collapsed, on further reflection into its opposite. (For example: There is no best case for knowing another because there is no example that carries the right representativeness.—Ah, but there is! There is the Exemplar himself, or herself! ...) It would not hurt my intuitions, to anticipate further than this book actually goes, were someone to be able to show that my discoveries in the region of the sceptical problem of the other are, rightly understood, further characterizations of (material object) scepticism, of scepticism as such. So that, for example, what I will find in Othello's relation to Desdemona is not just initiated by the human being's relation to the world, in particular by that phase of its career in which the human being makes to secure or close its knowledge of the world's existence once and for all, only to discover it to be closed off for ever; but also that their relation remains to the end a certain allegory of that career. The consequent implication that there is between human existence and the existence of the world a standing possibility of death-dealing passion, of a yearning at once unappeasable and unsatisfiable, as of an impossible exclusiveness and completeness, is an implication that harks back, to my mind, to the late suggestion of the possibility of falling in love with the world, blind to its progress beyond our knowledge. (*CR* 451–2)

The implications Cavell draws from his claim to find scepticism about other minds to be an allegory or further characterization of scepticism about the external world are startling, to say the least; but before they can be assessed, a prior question must be dealt with. For it also seems clear from the passage that the claim from which those implications are drawn itself presupposes the acceptance of two separable steps or leaps. First, we must accept that what philosophy studies as sceptical doubt about the existence of other minds is studied in literature under the form of (certain forms of) tragedy; and second, we must accept that the terms in which that study is carried forward in literature can be carried back to the philosophical study of sceptical doubt about the existence of the external world. In short, it seems that what underwrites Cavell's attempt to redefine or refocus philosophical understandings of scepticism in this way is the conviction which his readings of certain Shakespearean texts can elicit.

In this matter, appearances are not so much deceptive as ambiguous. On one level—a level that is absolutely vital to Cavell—things are exactly as they seem: indeed, his resolve to rely upon a literary reading to further a philosophical analysis is precisely designed to court philosophical (and literary) outrage, and thus to bring into question our conviction that the boundaries or relations between these two domains are obvious and obviously fixed. On this level, in fact, my attempt to break down the progress of Cavell's thinking into two phases which I characterize as steps from one of these domains to the other ought itself to be broken down, since it relies upon the very conviction that is under suspicion. It follows that any further analysis of Cavell's thought on this level would have to proceed through an examination of his literary readings, and in particular through an examination of his grounds for characterizing the nature and progress of Othello's relations with Desdemona in terms which create or uncover their resemblance to the nature and progress of Cartesian or Humean sceptical doubts.

My study will not be taking this path. This is not because I feel that Cavell's convictions in this area are groundless; on the contrary, his sense that Shakespearean tragedy can be usefully and plausibly interpreted as examining what philosophy describes as scepticism seems to me to be an insight of the first order. However, what conveys this weight of conviction to Cavell's readers is pre-eminently his writing on the relevant plays; and that prose is even more resistant to exegetical summary than it is in the writings we have looked at hitherto. Even in his more obviously 'philosophical' works, any attempt to prise the core of his conceptual or grammatical analyses from the texture of his prose can at best be partially successful, and is to be regarded primarily as an encouragement to the reader to return to the original texts; but such partial and instrumental success in relation to Cavell's more obviously 'literary-critical' works (and so, of course, in relation to his more recent writings, whose every sentence places the philosophy/literature distinction in question) is barely to be hoped for.

There is, however, more to my avoidance of this path than the recognition that adopting the perspective of the exegete on this material would be both entirely ineffectual and indicative of the most profound misunderstanding. In particular, there is the recognition that there are other paths for me to take—that an assessment of the plausibility of Cavell's Shakespearean readings is not the only way of uncovering and evaluating his reasons for asserting and exploring a mutually revealing connection between the two facets of scepticism. In fact, Cavell points out such an alternative path in comments he makes on the above passage from *The Claim of Reason* in the introduction to a collection of his readings of Shakespeare, *Disowning Knowledge*. For the comparison or equation of Othello with the external-world sceptic in that cited passage is of course designed to highlight features of the position and progress of the latter which otherwise tend to be passed over; and this implies that those features are none the less present and detectable in the terms in which the sceptic generates and prosecutes his project in philosophy. So it ought to be possible to specify those features in ways which do not *presuppose* but rather *prepare us for* Cavell's equation of scepticism with tragedy; and this is the path that I will take in the remainder of this chapter.

The most striking feature of Cavell's comparison or equation of Othello with the sceptic is its implied comparison or equation of the sceptic's world with Desdemona. This suggests that the sceptic's world is somehow alive or at least animate, that he is responding to the world as if it were capable of responding to him. On Cavell's view, this may be startling, but it is in effect no more than an accurate characterization of the attitude that the sceptic adopts to the world and its objects when engaged in his quest for certainty.

Here one would one day have to look at the philosopher's extraordinary treatment of objects, as in Descartes's wax that is melting, in Price's tomato with nothing but its visual front aspect remaining, in Moore's raised moving hands, in Heidegger's blooming tree, to explore the sense of hyperbolic, unprecedented attention in play. It is not just careful description, or practical investigation, under way here. The philosopher is as it were looking for a *response* from the object, perhaps a shining. (*DK* 8)

Of course, as it stands this is a claim about what one might call the phenomenology of scepticism; it cannot easily be argued for—it can only be checked against one's own experience of the attempt to generate and resolve sceptical worries, whether in a text, a classroom, or one's study. And even if such checking turns out to validate the claim, its importance can be denied on the grounds that such phenomenological matters are irrelevant to the essence of the sceptical problematic. But the impulse to issue such a denial would be weakened if it were possible to point out other aspects of the sceptical scene in philosophy which confirmed the applicability of the concept of animism in what might be called a grammatical rather than a phenomenological way, and which did so in tolerably precise terms; and this is something Cavell undertakes to do. For as he emphasizes, the comparison of the sceptic and his world with Othello and Desdemona carries implications that are more specific than the general notion that the sceptic's world is animate; for example, it implies that the sceptic's doubt is a cover for or function of jealousy, and that his desire is to establish an exclusive and complete relationship with the world, as if the world were not just an animate other but an Exemplar (just as Desdemona is Othello's Exemplary other). But Cavell's view is that these implications too are derivable from the ways in which the external-world sceptic generates and manifests his doubt in philosophy.

This grammatical derivation depends for its initial plausibility upon seeing the animism that is implicit in the philosophically foregrounded concepts of doubt and belief.

Doubt, like belief, is most fully, say originally, directed to claims of others, of speakers; an appropriate reaction to, for instance, rumour, Iago's medium. If you tell me that there is a table in the next room I may or may not believe you; hence I may say I believe or do not believe there is a table there. But philosophers are led to say that they believe that there is a table *here* (the presence that is for all the world *this* table), before the very eyes. (*DK* 7)

The philosopher's situation is a best case for knowledge, a scene in which our relation to the table exemplifies our most immediate and intimate relation to the world as such because the table is functioning as a generic object. And the course of the sceptical argument transforms what we hold to be true of the world into (at best) opinion, guesswork, hypothesis, belief, or (at worst) into something in which we can no longer believe. However, on Cavell's view, belief and doubt are attitudes most at home when directed to claims made upon us by others, other speakers; our talk of believing a given proposition is parasitic upon our talk of believing someone who enunciates it, and not vice versa. This specific claim to logical priority clearly harmonizes with Cavell's more general emphasis upon the idea that interaction between speakers is the context in which language is most fully itself, and it fits happily—if a little loosely—into an Austinian framework (within which the concepts of belief and knowledge are seen not as marking lower and higher points that a given knowledge-claim might occupy on a single scale of epistemic validity, but as indicating different stances a speaker takes up towards that claim—as ways in which a speaker claims differing degrees of reliability or trustworthiness; cf. *IQO* 161); but when encountered in isolation, it may seem to lack any independent plausibility. If so, it is worth pointing out that many philosophers talk in ways which seem to presuppose its truth. For example, sceptics often talk of believing or doubting the 'testimony' or the 'deliverances' of the senses: but such terms have their primary application to human utterances or speech-acts, and it is difficult to think of any reason for using them to characterize the information we obtain through our perceptual organs unless it signals a subliminal sense on the sceptics' part that their deployment of the concepts of belief and doubt in this context would otherwise appear unnatural or forced.

But the cost of constructing an unforced application of those concepts is exactly what the sceptical tendency to talk of the testimony of the senses already encapsulates. For characterizing our perceptions of the world as if they were part of an exchange between speakers amounts to placing the world in the position of a speaker, of someone lodging a claim on us; and if the attitude of belief is most at home when directed to another speaker, then the sceptical philosopher's general need to employ the concepts of belief and doubt in this context will have exactly the same import. This is because the philosopher's context as Cavell has specified it is a non-claim context. He is not speaking with anyone whose position is inferior to his with respect to the table, so he cannot be telling anyone anything; and neither is his position with respect to the table inferior to anybody else's, so nobody is able to tell him anything. In other words, there is no other human being with whom the philosopher might be thought to be (or might think of himself as) interacting, no human other who is in a position to receive or originate a claim; but he is driven by his scepticism to invoke a concept which suggests that something in this non-claim context is none the less making a claim upon him—and that something can only be the world.

In turning the concept of belief to name our immediate or absolute relation to the world, say our absolute intimacy, a relation no human other *could* either confirm or compromise, the philosopher turns the world into, or puts it in the position of, a speaker, lodging its claims upon us, claims to which, as it turns out, the philosopher cannot listen. (*DK* 7–8)

Such a use of the term 'belief' turns it from its usual course. As Cavell has emphasized, it is essential to language that words *can* be so turned, that they can be used apart from their ordinary language games; but such linguistic errancies have a logic. For the sceptic's desire to turn the word 'belief' in this way is a desire to relate one particular word (with its specific meaning as determined by its ordinary criteria and its grammatical relations with other concepts) to one particular context; and since the word's ordinary grammar would not license this turn, its motivating impulse must lie in the sceptic's interpretation of the alien context—the turn reveals that there is something in or about that context which seems to him to call for a word with just those conceptual connections. Since the concept of belief primarily hangs together with the concept of a claim that is believed and so of a person making a claim, its use in a 'best case for knowledge' context (where other human beings are irrelevant) suggests that the sceptic must be interpreting *the world* as making claims on him; and since in such a context the world appears in the guise of a generic object, he must be interpreting those claims as issuing from the world understood as an *Exemplary* other—an other in whom the whole of reality is compressed, apart from whom no one and nothing else could be relevant, and so with whom there exists a relationship of exclusive intimacy. In short, the philosophical sceptic's specific yoking of concept to context stands revealed as having been produced by a vision of the world as animate in a very specific way, as making claims upon him within a relationship of exclusive intimacy.

This exclusivity is already enough to prepare the ground for the applicability of the concept of jealousy as an interpretation of sceptical doubt and its origins. Let us first remind ourselves, however, of the extremity of the jealousy that the comparison of scepticism with tragedy would impute to the sceptic, by citing Cavell's reading of Othello's version of this emotion: '[Othello] seeks a possession that is not in opposition to another's claim or desire but one that establishes an absolute and inalienable bonding to himself, to which no claim or desire *could* be opposed, could conceivably count; as if the jealousy is directed to the sheer existence of the other, its separateness from him' (*DK* 9). Regardless of the plausibility of this passage as an interpretation of Othello, the points that we have already established about the sceptical scene in philosophy make this interpretation immediately transferable to it. For that scene is one of a best case for knowledge, and such a context excludes the very possibility of any other human being's claims being relevant to determining the true nature and reality of the sceptic's link with the world. It follows that any relation the sceptic could establish with the world in such a context would instantiate an extreme of intimacy; it would be of a sort to which no other claim or desire could conceivably be opposed, an absolute intimacy or bonding of the world with himself. But that context is one which the sceptic himself is forced to choose or construct (on pain of failing to generate scepticism), so this absolute intimacy must be what he desires, what fuels his project. And since this absoluteness is a fantasy (since it would involve overcoming the very separateness of the world from him, its sheer externality, without which it would not *be* the world with which he wishes to be bonded at all), his doubt must be seen as inevitable, a necessary disappointment dictated by and so originating in and so expressive of the necessary insatiability of his jealous desire for possessive intimacy with the world.

It might be worth pausing here for a moment, in order to acknowledge the degree to which Cavell's grammatical justification of the claim that other-minds scepticism is allegorical of external-world scepticism builds upon his separate analyses of these two facets of scepticism examined in the previous chapters. For turning the concepts of belief and doubt in the sceptic's way only results in the animation of the world if that turning is understood as taking place within the context of a best case for knowledge—only if it is a turn to a generic object; and such notions as generic objects, best cases, and Exemplary others are of course Cavellian constructions or interpretations. But once these elements *are* put together in the way summarized above, then the striking characterizations of scepticism which Cavell puts forward as resulting from his readings of Shakespearean tragedy can be seen as immediately and independently derivable from his work on scepticism as it reveals itself in philosophy. For if the philosophical sceptic *is* interpretable as treating the world as if it were responsive or animate in the sense specified above, then we are already forced to conclude that the impulse to philosophical scepticism can and should be made to bear a less cognitive, more affective interpretation; and if the best-case context of the sceptical claim *does* mean that the intimacy of the sceptic's relation to this animate(d) world is hyperbolically exclusive and exemplary, then the suggestion that the desires and emotions which shadow or dominate this intimacy are similarly extreme gains in plausibility. In short, if the philosophical sceptic's quest for certainty about the world's existence does conceal a desire to overcome the world's separateness from him, to possess it utterly, then it becomes illuminating rather than confusing to understand his desire as a jealous one. So, Cavell's grammatical analysis suggests that his general assumption that the sceptic's motives require diagnosis and interpretation cannot be dismissed on the grounds that the move to Shakespeare (which helps to justify the assumption and further specify the interpretations) is entirely unmotivated by recognizably philosophical considerations. On the contrary: the analysis reveals philosophical considerations which show that philosophical scepticism must *not* be interpreted as motivated only by intellectual scruple. The taint of madness in scepticism, a taint which every sceptic acknowledges and attempts to accommodate, is here diagnosed as a derangement of the intellect by extremities of feeling.

Doubt and Death

Staying on the general path of this investigation, what I want to turn to now is a further set of implications that flow from the equation of the sceptic's world with Desdemona, and the corresponding question of whether these too can be independently supported by or derived from grammatical or otherwise more 'purely' philosophical considerations. For, regardless of the question of determining the precise nature of the motives that lead Othello to his final tragic deed, the nature of that deed is indisputable—he murders Desdemona; so Cavell's equation of scepticism with tragedy implies that the sceptic's passionate desire for possessive intimacy with the world is death-dealing. Is there a grammatical basis for claiming that the result of sceptical doubt in philosophy is the death of the world at philosophy's hands, and so presumably for the further claim that the task of recovery from scepticism is to be understood as one of restoring life to the world?

Let us begin with death before contemplating the possibility of resurrection. The grammatical consequences of turning the concept of belief into the context of a best case for knowing of the world's existence ensure that the generic object the sceptic confronts there is transformed into an Exemplary other; and this implies that the results of the failure of his capacities for knowledge and certainty should be understood in the terms appropriate to a failure of a best case for acknowledgement. In those terms (as specified in the previous chapter), the world as a whole should be thought of as becoming not so much unknown or unknowable but no longer relevant; he is past caring for it, it is dead to him. Of course, *the sceptic* will interpret this loss of concern as a consequence of his being betrayed by the world, of the world's failure to live up to his passionate expectations; he will find that his investment of trust in it was misplaced. But the world's deadness, its inability to attract and maintain his interest, is in fact caused by him—a point which we saw to be a further grammatical consequence of his turning the concept of belief into the context of a best case for knowledge. The world disappoints him precisely because he interprets his goal of achieving and maintaining certainty about the world's existence as a matter of achieving and maintaining an undispossessable possession of that world—a literally fantastic, necessarily unattainable ideal. So his quest was always already doomed to disappointment; his jealousy ensured that the world could not possibly satisfy him. Here is one interpretation of what the world's death, and scepticism's responsibility for that death, amounts to.

I will return to this idea of the world's death as resulting from and so being centrally constituted by a withdrawal of the sceptic's interest in it. But before doing so, I must examine another aspect of Cavell's characterization of philosophical scepticism which licenses the idea of scepticism as death-dealing. This has to do with the sense in which the sceptic is led to speak outside language games—to employ ordinary terms in ways which strip them of their criteria, so that his utterances are in some peculiar way empty or otherwise incapable of meaning what he wants to say with them. We have gone into some detail about this Wittgensteinian term of criticism in previous chapters; and the vicissitudes of the concept of belief which we have been tracing in this chapter illustrate what it is intended to capture. By translating the term into a context in which the usual criteria governing its use are unavailable and then attempting to articulate his doubt in utterances which employ it, the sceptic ensures that those utterances are either empty (if no effort is made to adapt the term to its new context) or meaningful in ways which do not fulfil his declared purposes but rather betray his undeclared ones (if the effort of adaptation is made).

When, in Chapter 4, we examined the case of one specific version of scepticism about the external world, we saw the results of such attempts to speak outside language games. This was the version of scepticism which says that one cannot ground a claim to know that an object (a sphere, for example) before one's very eyes exists on the fact that one can see it, for one does not in fact see all of it. Such a sceptical argument depends upon specifying that part of the object which is not seen, a task performed by constructing around the object a great circle whose plane is perpendicular to the perceiver's line of vision. But, as we argued earlier, such a construction method can produce a part of the object which is *never* seen only if we imagine the sphere and the perceiver as unchanging in their orientation to one another; for the part so specified would come into sight whenever either object or subject moved. As Cavell puts it (in a passage I quoted in Chapter 4):

Thus this sceptical picture is one in which all our objects are moons. In which the earth is our moon. In which, at any rate, our position with respect to significant objects is *rooted*, the great circles which establish their back and front halves fixed in relation to it, fixed in our concentration as we gaze at them ... This suggests that what [sceptical] philosophers call 'the senses' are themselves conceived in terms of this idea of a geometrically fixed position, disconnected from the fact of their possession and use by a creature who must *act*. (*CR* 202)

The fixity that is so central to this sceptical picture is simply a dramatic exemplification of what Cavell takes to be the consequence of any species of scepticism, because he takes it to be the consequence of any attempt to speak outside language games. When a term (any term) is stripped of its criteria, it is thereby deprived not only of a set of rules governing its use but also of the natural forms of life within which alone both the words and the rules which govern them have their point or significance. The specific form of scepticism adduced here results in the freezing or fixation of subjects and objects because it represses or ignores the fact that words are the possession of creatures who must act in a changing world which acts upon them. But *any* attempt to speak outside language games will result in a similar freezing or fixation of the world, because to speak outside language games is to use words apart from and in opposition to the complexities of practical interaction with an active world which are precisely what the notion of a 'language *game*' is designed to capture. Words have meaning only in the context of language games because criteria have point only in the context of active human life; apart from that life both words and world are frozen, fixed, fixated—themselves deprived of life. Here is a second interpretation of what the world's death, and scepticism's responsibility for that death, amount to.

The intimacy of the relation Cavell sees between the question of how and why scepticism results in the death of the world and and that of how and why scepticism refuses a reliance upon criteria is not, however, fully captured by what has been said so far. Here, we need to recall the point that has been made over and over again in this book—namely, that criteria determine what it is for anything to fall under a given concept and so to constitute an instance of a particular sort, that essence is expressed by grammar. This alignment of language and world is prior to any particular empirical investigation, for in its absence we would have no idea what to look for when attempting to discover what the facts are in any particular case; in order to be able to discover whether there is a table in the next room, we must know what would have to be the case for anything to *count* as a table. This prior alignment of words and world is, as we saw earlier, precisely what scepticism puts in question. It is this level or aspect of our relation to the world which is highlighted in the context of a best case for knowledge, a context in which nothing but our capacity to tell what is in front of our eyes—our capacity to apply the concept of a table to the world—is at stake; and it is the refusal of the agreement which facilitates this basic linguistic capacity that is part of what Cavell means by claiming that the sceptic is driven to speak outside language games.

We might summarize the role of criteria by saying that criteria tell us what *counts* as an instance of something. But this link between the concept of criteria and the concept of counting involves two facets of the meaning of the latter term; and both facets relate to the question of the life and death of the world. On the one hand, criteria are criteria of individuation: in determining what counts *as* a table, they determine whether any given object falls under that particular concept or rather under some other—they determine what makes one thing a table, another a chair, this thing a human animal, that a non-human animal. On the other hand, criteria manifest what counts *for* human beings: by determining how human beings count one thing from another, how they conceptualize the world, criteria trace the distinctions and connections which matter to them—the distinctions which count. The structure of the concepts themselves is an expression of human interests, of which aspects of the world we deem significant enough to wish to get a grip on; and the agreement or attunement in criteria upon which our shared conceptual structures rests is ultimately an expression of the ways in which our interests in and reactions to the things of the world are in agreement. Agreement or attunement in criteria is thus a matter of our sharing routes of interest and feeling, modes of response, a sense of similarity, significance, outrageousness, and so on—much of what Wittgenstein means to capture with the idea of forms of life.

These two different aspects of the concept of counting are *both* part of what Cavell means by saying that our criteria tell us what counts. As he puts it:

To speak is to say what counts ... Something counts because it fits or *matters* ... I think of the concept [of counting] in this criterial occurrence as its nonnumerical use—it is not here tallying how much or how many, but membership or belonging. This is a matter both of establishing what Wittgenstein speaks of as a grammatical kind of object, and also of attributing a certain value or interest to the object. (*IQO* 86–7)

It follows that, by refusing criteria, the sceptic refuses both aspects of the concept of counting, both facets of the sense in which concepts manifest what counts. In the first place, he refuses that which alone permits him to individuate one object from another, to distinguish one thing or event or mood or thought from another; by speaking outside language games, he annihilates the difference between one thing and another, and so can be said to annihilate the world which those things make up. And by the same token, he refuses his participation in the modes of interest and response to which criteria give expression; by speaking outside any and all language games, he denies that the phenomena of the world matter to him in any way—he completely withdraws his investment of interest in the world. Putting the two aspects of his refusal together, we can say that the sceptic's drive to strip words of their criteria strips the objects of the world of their variegated specificity and value. He annihilates the world by annihilating its capacity to elicit his interest; he is driven past caring for it, it goes dead for him and recedes from his grasp. Here is a third interpretation of what the death of the world, and the sceptic's responsibility for that death, amounts to—one which harks back to and underwrites Cavell's earlier, differently grounded intuition that the failure of a best case for knowledge has results which resemble the failure of a best case of acknowledgement.

And of course, all three of these interpretations—all three senses of the world's death at the hands of scepticism that we have distinguished—are interrelated; the claims that scepticism constitutes a failure to acknowledge the world, that it freezes or fixes the world, and that it annihilates the specificity and value of the world are—rightly understood—simply different ways of characterizing or picturing the same thing. I will attempt to buttress this assertion by showing how all three formulations can be shown to apply to the work of one central figure in the history of philosophy—Kant; for this way of drawing together the main strands of our investigation thus far will have the further advantage of preparing the terms in which we might make sense of the idea that, and the ways in which, philosophy is equipped to bring the world back to life.

The choice of Kant as an example is intended to register Cavell's sense of Kant's founding importance for modern philosophy, that phase of philosophy whose characteristic shadow is the sceptic; as Cavell expresses it, philosophical settlements subsequent to Kant's own have not displaced it, or rather have only displaced it. However, to choose Kant as an example of philosophical scepticism may seem strange; after all, did not Kant regard it as a philosophical scandal that scepticism had not yet been thoroughly discredited, and so dedicate his work to the task of accomplishing scepticism's downfall? From Cavell's point of view, however, Kant's achievement did not (at least, not fully) match his intention, and the mismatch followed necessarily in so far as he attempted to bring about scepticism's downfall by refuting it. Such an approach merely contests scepticism's conclusion that the existence of the world as such cannot be known; it does not contest the assumption that our primordial relation to the world is to be thought of as one of knowing (or not knowing). Since, on Cavell's view of scepticism, it is this assumption which is both its distinguishing feature and its originating misconception, Kant's refutation of scepticism can be no more than a further expression or manifestation of the sceptical impulse.

Cavell's interpretation of Kant is summarized in the following passage, one which he presents as a version of two paragraphs from Kant's *Prolegomena to Any Future Metaphysics*:

You can take these paragraphs as constituting the whole argument of the *Critique of Pure Reason*, in four or five lines: (1) Experience is constituted by appearances. (2) Appearances are of something else, which accordingly cannot itself appear. (3) All and only functions of experience can be known; these are our categories of the understanding. (4) It follows that the something else—that of which appearances are appearances, whose existence we must grant—cannot be known. In discovering this limitation of reason, reason proves its power to itself, over itself. (5) Moreover, since it is unavoidable for our reason to be drawn to think about this unknowable ground of appearance, reason reveals itself to itself in this necessity also. (*IQO* 30)

This Kantian picture is designed to secure empirical knowledge against the threat of scepticism, and seems successful in so doing. For if such knowledge is limited to experience, and experience is constituted by appearances, and appearances are constituted by the application of the categories of the understanding to the deliverances of the senses, then we can be sure that our categories do deliver knowledge of the world; in fact, we can claim that in the absence of those categories there would be no world to know. But there is a price to pay for this security—that of ceding any claim to know things-in-themselves, any capacity to acquire knowledge of the internal constitution of that of which appearances are appearances. We may be able to rely upon empirical knowledge, knowledge of appearances; but that knowledge is not of things as they are in themselves.

Now, of course, the role of the thing-in-itself constitutes a central tension in Kantian thought. On the one hand, Kant declares it to be beyond the limits of experience, and so to be beyond the sway of the categories which themselves form the conditions for the possibility of experience of an objective world, of a world of objects. So it would seem that the very idea of an object is illicitly employed when used to characterize that which is beyond experience; it would seem that things-in-themselves are not things at all but something we know not what—something that Kant at times simply labels 'X'. On the other hand, the world of experience is defined by Kant as a world of appearances, and appearances must be appearances of something; and Kant is often happy to talk of this something as composed of things (e.g. things with internal constitutions, as he puts it in the paragraphs from the *Prolegomena*). So Kant himself is strongly tempted to project a noumenal realm of objects-in-themselves which exists beyond the boundaries of human knowledge; the limits of application of the categories are then not the limits of the intelligible application of the concept of knowledge but rather limitations on knowledge, barriers which exclude human beings from the ultimate reality of the world.

And the picture of knowledge which transforms those limits into limitations simultaneously secretes a very specific vision of the reality beyond those limits. For in the Kantian system, it is not only the categories which are limited in their application to the phenomenal world, the world of appearance; it is also the concepts of space and time. Space and time are characterized as the forms of sensible intuition, the two interrelated modes in terms of which all experience is shaped or ordered, and of which all twelve categories are to be understood as modifications or inflexions; so the very idea of a spatio-temporal framework, as well as that of the system of nature it frames, is limited to the realm of possible experience. It follows that the realm of the thing-in-itself is not only one in which any possible means of distinguishing objects one from another is unavailable, but is also one from which any possibility of objects changing over time or interacting in space has been removed. The noumenal realm is thus fixed and frozen, a domain from which activity is expunged and difference annihilated; and such a fixated, undifferentiated plenum is not one which might attract or sustain human interest—it is not a world we might care about or value. In other words, the Kantian settlement with scepticism is itself tainted with scepticism: it not only bars us from the world, but also envisions that world in the threefold set of death-dealing terms that we isolated earlier in this chapter.

Cavell traces the nature and results of the Kantian settlement back to his foundational conception of the relationship between human under-standing and human sensibility in the comprehending perception of the world; for the construction of the realm of the thing-in-itself is entailed by Kant's particular conception of the ways in which human knowledge is, and is not, dependent upon the specific sensuous and intellectual endowments of the human creature. On the one hand, intuitions without concepts are blind: without the synthesis of intuitions brought about by means of the imposition of categories originating in the understanding, there could be no experience of objects in a phenomenal world. But on the other hand, concepts without intuitions are empty: the categories of the understanding are entirely incapable of delivering any knowledge of the phenomenal world without an initial and ultimately inexplicable reception of bare intuition. It is the brute, originating role played by such intuition that captures and grounds Kant's sense that what we encounter in experience are appearances—not self-contained or self-originating phenomena, but rather representations of whatever unknow-able something is their source.

But if this conception of the relation between intuitions and categories is the origin of the Kantian noumenal realm, then it must also be the origin of the death-dealing violence to which that picture of the world gives expression.

This violence in human knowing is, I gather, what comes out of Heidegger's perception that philosophy has, from the beginning, but, if I understand, with increasing velocity in the age of technology, conceived knowledge under the aegis of dominion, of the concept of a concept as a matter, say, of grasping a thing. In Kant, this concept of the concept is pictured as that of synthesizing things, putting together appearances, yoking them, to yield objects of knowledge: Knowledge itself is explicitly, as opposed to the reception of sensuous intuitions, an active thing—Kant says spontaneous; intuitions alone occur to us passively. (In a motto, there is no intellectual intuition; or, there is no world without the suffering, the sensuous reception, of intuitions together with the active emplace-ment of concepts upon them.) (*DK* 9)

Cavell's suggestion is that the world dies at our hands because we picture our relation to it as an appropriation of it—as if the only way in which we might have access to it is by forcing our intuitions of it to yield objects (of knowledge). But then the death of the world is not inevitable: it may be that an alternative picture of our relation to it will orient us in such a way that we come to see that there are other modes of access to it—ones which restore or return it to life. In the terms set out by Kant, this alternative picture would be one of intellectual intuition, intuition that is not blind or blank but inherently and independently intelligible; and this picture would suggest that we gain access to the world not by imposing conditions that something must satisfy in order to be an object of knowledge for us, but by our satisfying the conditions necessary for there to be a world of things for us. Rather than imposing conditions on our intuition, we should accept and respect the conditions which we elicit from our intuition; there is nothing but intellectual, intelligible intuition.

Acknowledgement and Life

Of course, within the strict terms of the Kantian settlement, the very idea of an intelligible intuition is unintelligible; so as it stands, this alternative to death-dealing scepticism remains obscure. Cavell attempts to dissipate the obscurity in many ways, some of which depend much more upon the plausibility of his readings of Romantic writers than others; and true to my intentions in this chapter, I shall concentrate upon the latter. If, for this purpose, we return to Cavell's original comparison of the sceptic with Othello, and ask what this comparison has to tell us about how philosophy might reanimate the sceptic's world, the answer would seem to be that the philosopher should acknowledge the world—acknowledge it as his necessary other whose existence is thus both separate from and essential to his own. Acknowledging that it is essential to him would presumably mean acknowledging his interest in and need for it, which means accepting the fact that it attracts him—that he is drawn to and by it; and acknowledging its separateness would mean accepting the independence of what attracts him, not imposing his interests and needs upon it but rather allowing it to elicit the responses it requires and requests from him in its own way and according to its own nature. Such ideas constitute the transference of one way of conceptualizing a loving relation between human beings to the domain of relations between a human being and the world—a vision of falling in love with the world, as Cavell put it in the passage from *The Claim of Reason* with which we began this chapter. But how might the application of such ideas to our relation to the world and its objects be made out philosophically?

One of the best clues to a more 'grammatical' understanding of this vision of acknowledging the world occurs towards the end of *The Claim of Reason*, when Cavell articulates one of the worries which might arise from his invocation of the idea of empathic projection in his investigation of the problem of scepticism about other minds.

... the view of others as based upon empathic projection ... seems to take the idea of an attitude towards a soul as some appropriateness of my response. But why shouldn't one say that there is a required *appropriateness* with respect to each breed of thing (object or being); something appropriate for bread, something else for stones, something for large stones that block one's path and something for small smooth stones that can be slung or shied; something for grass, for flowers, for orchards, for forests, for each fish of the sea and each fowl of the air; something for each human contrivance and for each human condition; and, if you like, on up? For each link in the Great Chain of Being there is an appropriate hook of response. I said that one's experience of others puts a seam in experience. Why not consider that experience is endlessly, continuously seamed? Every thing, and every experience of every different thing, is what it is. (*CR* 441–2)

This is the possibility which I take Cavell's more recent work, primarily but not exclusively on Romantic poets and authors, to be elucidating. In *In Quest of the Ordinary*, for example, Cavell utilizes a text of John Wisdom's[1] in order to spell out what we might think of as the hook of response that is appropriate to flowers. Wisdom describes a context in which someone's treatment of flowers (his way of caring for them) elicits from an observer the assertion 'You believe that flowers feel'. This description already brings into the open what must be the basic suspicion about any attempt to rescue or revivify things-in-themselves by taking on some concept or other of animism—namely, that the rescue is founded upon the pathetic fallacy. From within this suspicion, there are only two ways of making the observer's assertion comprehensible: either it imputes a crazy belief to the flower-lover (roughly, the belief that flowers have minds) or it registers an inappropriate projection of emotion on the flower-lover's part. Cavell wants us to see something

[1] J. Wisdom, *Other Minds* (Oxford, 1952), ch. 1.

suspicious in this desire to explain (or explain away) the observer's response:

> let us hold off the explanatory hypothesis about believing that flowers feel (explanatory of what would make a certain way of treating them rational, anyway comprehensible) and instead imagine, if we can, someone's finding himself or herself struck by a treatment of flowers (a particularly nervous handling of them, or a special decorum in their presence, or a refusal to cut them, or perhaps a horror of cutting them, or a panic upon dropping them) in such a way that he is led to *consider* what flowers are, *what* it is he takes himself to know about what is and is not appropriate in our treatment of them. To consider, for example, that it is on the whole normal upon our meeting flowers to seek their odour; but on the whole not, with special exceptions, in the case of our meeting animals or persons; and on the whole not, it is worth adding, in the case of meeting stones and metals. (*IQO* 69)

What this striking treatment of flowers leads us to consider is what our ordinary, typical treatment of flowers amounts to; and that ordinary attitude not only includes certain responses which, when held up to scrutiny, might seem interpretable as undeveloped roots or primitive versions of the flower-lover's 'excesses', but also and more generally stands revealed as extremely specific. It might have seemed obvious in advance of any consideration that we do not treat flowers in the way we treat sentient beings—if flowers could feel for us what we feel for them we would not, for example, arrange them, not even lovingly; but it is likely to have been far from obvious that we do not treat flowers in the way that we treat other non-sentient beings—our feelings for them are expressed in arranging them and taking their odour, not in collecting them or polishing them. In our eagerness to confirm the seam in our experience between creatures possessed of minds and the mindless world they inhabit, we fail to see that our experience of that world is itself multiply seamed—that our responses to non-sentient living beings are very different from our responses to non-sentient, non-living ones, and that our responses to different beings within each of *those* categories are also categorially different.

Here, then, we have an instance of what acknowledging the world might be thought to amount to; rather than imposing our general preconceptions about objecthood on to a given object, we bring ourselves to consider what our everyday experiences of and with that object (our intelligible intuitions of it) can teach us about its specific, distinct nature. By reconsidering our responses to it, the treatment and attitude it can and does elicit from us, we simultaneously acknowledge that and how it attracts us; acknowledging that we are drawn to it leads us to consider how it draws us, to reconsider what it is about it that draws us, and so to consider anew precisely what it is.

And, for Cavell, such a reconsideration of our treatment of any given type of object can be thought of as a contribution to an investigation of the grammar of our word for that type of object. This may at first sight seem to violate the grammar of the word 'grammar', for knowing that it is appropriate to take the odour of a flower but not that of a person seems to amount to knowing something about the ways human beings typically interest themselves in flowers rather than to knowing one aspect of how we use the word 'flower'; but this is to ignore the scope and complexity of grammar and so of criteria. As we have repeatedly argued, knowing what something is is a matter of knowing what counts as something, what the criteria in our language for that something really are; and this means knowing how the criteria for the relevant word interweave with the criteria for a range of interrelated words. Someone who knows what an opinion is must know more than what counts as an opinion; or rather, to know what counts as an opinion, she must know, among other things, what in our everyday life counts as arriving at an opinion, holding firmly to an opinion, suddenly changing an opinion, having a low opinion of someone, being opinionated or indifferent to opinion, and so on. And if it is part of the grammar of 'opinion' that *this* (this stance of the mind or heart) is what is called 'holding an opinion'—as it is part of the grammar of 'chair' that *this* (this act or action) is what is called 'sitting on a chair'—then it is part of the grammar of 'flower' that *this* (this response) is what is called 'smelling a flower'. So reminding ourselves that we arrange flowers (but not animals) and take their odour (but do not paint or polish them), reminding ourselves of their distinctive place in our form of life, is a way of reminding ourselves of (certain aspects of) our shared criteria for the word 'flower'.

In effect, this is just another way of bringing out the point that criteria do not merely establish a grammatical kind of object but also attribute a certain kind of interest or value to the object—that criteria tell us what counts in both senses of the latter term. More generally, it is a reminder of the fact that our agreement or attunement in criteria is ultimately a matter of sharing certain routes of feeling, reaction, and response—that what must be accepted is our form of life. The aspect of the meaning of 'form of life' that Cavell is highlighting here is the biological rather than the social one—'forms of *life*' rather than '*forms* of life': not promising as opposed to intending, or coronations as opposed to inaugurations, but rather human as opposed to 'lower' or 'higher' life forms.

> The biological or vertical sense of form of life recalls differences ... between, say, poking at your food, perhaps with a fork, and pawing at it, or pecking at it. Here the romance of the hand and its apposable thumb comes into play, and of the upright posture and of the eyes set for heaven; but also the specific strength or scale of the human body and of the human sense and of the human voice ... everything humans do and suffer is as specific to them as are hoping or promising or calculating or smiling or waving hello or strolling or running in place or being naked or torturing. This listing is to recall patterns in the weave of our life, modifications of the life of us talkers, that are specific and confined to us, to the human life form, like running in place or hoping, as well as patterns we share with other life forms but whose human variations are still specific, like eating or sniffing or screaming with fear. (*NYUA* 41–2, 48)

In being reminded that and how we arrange flowers and take their odours, we are reminded not only of what counts as a flower but also of the specific manipulability of our hands, of our capacity to transform an upright posture into a bending or crouching one, and of our capacities for deriving specific sorts of pleasure from our specific senses. Recalling that we can sling or shy small stones but only drag large ones from our path recalls us to the range of terms like 'large' or 'small' in relation to stones, and so to the specific range of our physical strength. In short, reconsidering our attitudes to objects in the world brings back to consciousness not only (aspects of) the true nature of those objects but also (aspects of) the nature of human beings. Acknowledging the world and acknowledging our life in it are two sides of the same coin; considering what it is that draws us to flowers cannot be divorced from considering who we are to be so drawn.

And such consideration is a way of restoring life to both—to the world in which we live our lives and to the lives we live in it. The sceptic deprives the world of life by attempting to speak outside language games, and so divorces himself from his own life of practical interaction with the world—deprives himself of life. The practice of recovery or reanimation that Wittgenstein offers is that of reminding us of the criteria which govern our words, the means by which and the terms in which the things of the world count for us, matter to us; and in reminding us of this, in getting us to acknowledge this, he gives us the opportunity of reviving our interest in the world, of reinvesting it with our care and concern and so reviving our interest in our own lives. If we were to put this alternative to scepticism in Kantian terms, we might say that, rather than stopping after having elucidated the conditions of the possibility of objecthood in general (i.e. after the transcendental deduction of the categories), we should go on to elucidate the conditions of the possibility of each specific kind of object—provide a deduction of every one of our concepts in their application to the world. In Wittgensteinian terms, this means recalling our criteria, recounting what counts as any (and every) specific kind of object, reminding ourselves of the grammar of each and every word in the language; for each has its own investment of interest or value, each makes manifest the hook of response that is appropriate to one particular piece of the world and of our life within it.

Cavell's Wittgensteinian practice of recounting criteria can therefore be viewed as instantiating precisely the mode of thinking which we earlier sought in order to replace or overcome the violent picture of that activity instantiated in Kant's concept of the concept. Rather than yoking intuitions together to yield an object, rather than imposing our unquestioned and undifferentiated picture of objecthood upon each and every differentiated phenomenon we encounter, recounting the criteria governing each word in our language amounts to a practice of allowing ourselves to recall what differentiates each phenomenon we encounter from every other. Recounting criteria means recalling the specific place of each specific thing in our form of life, and so recalling simultaneously the precise lineaments of its nature and the precise contours of our own life form. It means recalling what counts, reminding ourselves that the world attracts us and how it does so in each particular case; it shows that the world is worthy of our care and concern, that it can and should bear the reinvestment of our interest in it and so in our own lives.

Recovery and Transfiguration

Even if this connection of Wittgensteinian philosophizing with Romanticism seems plausible, it may be questioned whether the practice of recovery it offers is sufficiently attractive to draw us to it. In particular, it might be thought that recalling our criteria rather than refusing them would merely amount to the substitution of one form of fixation for another; where the sceptic fixes and freezes the world in an undifferentiated plenum, Wittgenstein counsels the unquestioning reiteration of existing or given structures of language and life. If criteria must be accepted, then so must the form of life in which they are embedded; and the return from scepticism will take on the aspect of reaction, of an essentially conservative reinvestment in the status quo. Who is to say that the way we now treat the objects and events of the world, the fish in the seas, and the fowl in the air is a way which acknowledges, which responds to and elicits, their true nature? Who is to say that the violence Wittgenstein detects in (human pictures of) human thinking hitherto is not also embedded in the human form of life as it now presents itself?

These worries fail to appreciate the fact that the Wittgenstein who made conservative pronouncements about the need to accept given forms of life is also the thinker who claimed to have revolutionized philosophy—to have turned our philosophical (self-)examination around the fixed point of its real need. In particular, they fail to acknowledge that his concept of 'forms of life' carries a biological meaning which contests its social one and so contests any conservatism embedded in that social one.

In being asked to accept [the human form of life], or suffer it, as given for ourselves, we are not asked to accept, let us say, private property, but separateness; not a particular fact of power but the fact that I am a man, therefore of *this* (range or scale of) capacity for work, for pleasure, for endurance, for appeal, for command, for understanding, for wish, for will, for teaching, for suffering. The precise range or scale is not knowable a priori, any more than the precise range or scale of a word is to be known a priori. Of course, you can *fix* the range; so can you confine a man or a woman, and not all the ways and senses of confinement are knowable a priori. The rhetoric of humanity as a form of life, or a level of life, standing in need of transfiguration—some radical change, but as it were from inside, not *by* anything; some say in another birth, symbolizing a different order of natural reactions—is typical of a line of contradictory sensibilities, ones that may appear as radically innovative (in action or in feeling) or radically conservative: Luther was such a sensibility; so were Rousseau and Thoreau. (*NYUA* 44)

On this interpretation, by returning us to the everyday, to the ordinary life of our language and ourselves, Wittgenstein is returning us to a sense of what our real possibilities are. At this particular historical or cultural conjuncture, our lives may be dead or confined or in need of radical change; but recalling the human form of life reminds us that its species-specific endowment can support a wide variety of cultural or social formations. One such endowment is the capacity to acquire and deploy language—talking, we might say, is the distinctively human form of life; but such a capacity is precisely open to an indefinite series of variations, each human speaking some particular language and inhabiting some particular modification of society and culture that the talking form of life makes possible. In this sense, the only thing natural to the human being is its capacity to change its nature, to take on certain forms of social, linguistic life (patterns of reaction and response) as natural and to cast them off in favour of others, e.g. when they come to seem unnatural, chafing, confining. The limits of the human life form must be accepted, but the present form of human life, that particular inflexion of our capacities, reactions, interests, and needs, need not.

Reconsidering our responses to flowers, for example, may transfigure our present form of life in one of two ways: it may bring us to realize that our (personal or cultural) language and life embodies a memory of achieved richnesses of response which are at present unattained (Do we merely sniff at flowers, or do we take their odour?); or it may show that our present, attained modes of response contain the possibility of their own further enrichment (If we take their odour rather than sniffing at them, why do we not take more care with their cultivation or their cutting—why are we not more like the 'crazy' flower-lover?). In short, the terms of our present life with these objects contains the terms for transfiguring that life (developing or recovering it) in ways which retain their truth to its nature; and a grammatical investigation of those terms can accordingly have a revolutionary, life-restoring and/or life-enhancing potential.

So, the scene of our ordinary life of language need not be regarded as beyond criticism; if Wittgenstein's notion of a form of life has a biological as well as a social aspect, then the *actual* everyday is not only not necessarily what must be accepted but may even be what must be refused in favour of the real possibilities of our given life form. However, the terms of criticism by which we would so refuse the actual everyday in favour of what it might become are themselves to be found within the everyday. The possibilities our criteria hold out are ones to which we are recalled or of which we need only to be reminded, ones which we always already knew: in this sense, the actual everyday contains the terms of the eventual everyday—and may even instantiate it if those possibilities have only been forgotten by philosophy and not by our culture as a whole.

Accordingly, we must admit that Wittgenstein's practice of reminding us of what we say when, of recalling or recounting our criteria, *is*—as the reiteration of the 're-' prefix indicates—a reiterative task in at least two senses: it involves recalling that which we already know, and it may be required at any point of our language and at any time in our lives; it is a return to the everyday which may itself be required every day. That said, however, it is a mode of repetition which does not itself reiterate but rather competes with or contests the mode of repetition (the frozenness and fixation) of which it was earlier accused and which we (even earlier) identified with scepticism. For it is a recovery—a rediscovery—of that by means of which the reiterated impulse of scepticism might be overcome in each place of its coming (whether that place is philosophy's fixation on a word stripped of its criteria or our present culture's fixation on a deadened response to a piece of nature).

Sharing the intuition that human existence stands in need not of reform but of reformation, of a change that has the structure of a transfiguration, Wittgenstein's insight is that the ordinary has, and alone has, the power to move the ordinary, to leave the human habitat habitable, the same transfigured. The practice of the ordinary may be thought of as the overcoming of iteration or replication or imitation by repetition, of counting by recounting, of calling by recalling. It is the familiar invaded by another familiar. (*NYUA* 46–7)

In short, when Cavell's Wittgenstein says that philosophy leaves everything as it is, he is characterizing philosophical thinking as a matter of forbearance—a matter of letting-things-lie-before-us (as Heidegger might put it). He thereby pictures philosophical thought as—and advocates a practice of thought which is—a mode of accepting or acknowledging the world and our life within it.

Thought and Existence

Cavell is thus claiming that the mode of philosophical thinking to which he is committed combines acknowledging the world with acknowledging one's own existence within it; by recounting criteria, we simultaneously reanimate the world and ourselves. Of course, this conjunction has an extremely Romantic ring to it. The picture of the author or artist as a world-creating *and* a self-creating genius is central to Romanticism's understanding of its own nature; and Cavell has simply universalized or democratized it by attributing the capacity for such reanimation to anyone possessed of language (and thereby of the capacity to recount the criteria they employ). But by establishing the conjunction through the practice of recounting criteria, he has also stripped the notion of self-creation (as well as that of world-creation) of inappropriately metaphysical implications. Just as the notion of reanimating the world has been shown to be capable of bearing a sense other than that of creating the heavens and the earth from the void, so the notion of self-creation in play here does not depend upon a literalized anthropomorphism of God's creation of mankind—as if creating myself could only mean transfiguring the dust of myself with magic breath.

However, Cavell also attempts to buttress the connection between recounting criteria and acknowledging one's own existence in the world by examining the work of the founder of modern philosophy—Descartes; and here the importance of characterizing the practice of recounting criteria as a mode of thinking reveals itself, for the concept of thought plays a famously fundamental role in Descartes's writings. More precisely, in Descartes's view as popularly summarized, 'I think, therefore I am': anyone who ventures to think that her own existence may be in doubt thereby undermines that doubt, since thinking presupposes the existence of thought and so (according to Descartes) of a thinker—an argument against scepticism which leads to the view that human beings are most fundamentally thinking things. However, Cavell's reading of Descartes's thought on this issue highlights—in a manner analogous to much recent work on the subject—the way in which Descartes formulates his claim in the Second Meditation: '*I am, I exist*, is necessarily true every time that I pronounce it or conceive it in my mind.' For what this formulation brings out is the fact that the 'I think' from which Descartes's argument proceeds marks the scene of some kind of performance.

The point here is not to deny that the cogito is an inference of some kind; it is rather to emphasize that, in so far as it *is* an inference, it is one which each individual must perform for herself. The conclusion of the cogito cannot be taken as established as a general truth for all humankind merely by Descartes's meditations upon it; it cannot be detached from its premiss and relied upon by those who are not taking the step which the cogito's premiss marks. Only by *saying* 'I am, I exist'—only by pronouncing those words or conceiving them in one's mind, only by engaging in such an act of thought—can one's existence be guaranteed or certified. Placing the emphasis this way raises the following question: If the cogito is essentially performative, what can be said of my existence if and when I am not engaged in the relevant performance—what happens if and when I do *not* say 'I am, I exist' or conceive it in my mind? The obvious answer would seem to be that I will then not know or be certain of my existence; but the answer Cavell wants to consider is that perhaps I will then not exist. In short, he wants to suggest that the thinking in which Descartes urges us to engage does not so much confirm our existence as create it.

This may seem an extravagant interpretative hypothesis, to say the least; but it is by no means alien to the progress of the Meditations themselves. For soon after introducing the cogito, Descartes offers the following speculation: 'I am, I exist—that is certain; but for how long do I exist? For as long as I think; for it might perhaps happen, If I totally ceased thinking, that I would at the same time completely cease to be.' Cavell's comment on this passage is instructive:

> This does not quite say that my ceasing to think would cause, or would be, my ceasing to exist. It may amount to saying so if I must think of myself as having a creator (hence, according to Descartes, a preserver) and if all candidates for this role other than myself dropped out. These assumptions seem faithful to Descartes's text, so that I am prepared to take it that the cogito is only half the battle concerning the relation of my thinking to my existing, or perhaps 'I think, therefore I am' expresses only half the battle of the cogito: Descartes establishes to his satisfaction that I exist only while, or *if and only if,* I think. It is this, it seems, that leads him to claim that the mind always thinks . . . (*IQO* 108)

Of course, the idea that human beings are their own creators is one which Descartes explicitly rejects: for him God plays that role. But his attempts to introduce the assumption of God's existence into the epistemological vacuum surrounding the cogito are famously held to defy belief; and the philosophical and cultural world which inherited the cogito as its fulcrum of certainty understood itself more generally as being in no position to share Descartes's confidence in the divine. By contrast, however, his more general idea that human existence stands in need of creation and preservation by someone or something does not seem to have lost its power to elicit conviction.

We can be brought to see this in several ways. At the very least, it seems clear that we retain an intuition that our existence is somehow uncertain, that its reality is not something on which we can unproblematically depend—that it stands in need of a proof; why otherwise would we regard the Cartesian project as worthy of continuing study (and sometimes of continuation)? Moreover, Descartes's intuition might seem less alien if we reformulated it as the idea that genuinely human existence (a form of existence which successfully and fully manifests humanity) is something which cannot be taken for granted, as if it were a biological endowment automatically conferred on all members of our species, but must rather be achieved and maintained (and is more often unattained, incomplete).

This reformulation may still seem more like an idealistic Romantic aspiration than a grammatical remark. However, the underlying general idea that the reality of one's own existence requires activity of some sort on one's own part is in fact a consequence of the conceptual considerations adduced towards the end of the previous chapter. In that chapter we noted that, for Cavell, the human body is the field of expression of the human soul and knowing that soul takes the form of acknowledging its embodiment; for inner states are criterially related to their behavioural expression, and those expressions are such as to require specific responses from other human beings—knowing that someone is in pain, for example, involves acknowledging that pain in one's own behaviour towards that person. It follows that *failing* to acknowledge others condemns them (not to non-existence but) to an existence that is unacknowledged; and if another's pain is treated as unworthy of response by her fellow human beings, if its reality is denied in this way, then what reality can it have for the person concerned?

If, however, this reconceptualization of knowing as acknowledging places heavy responsibilities on the shoulders of the person doing the knowing (as it were), it places equally heavy burdens on the person being known. For if my inner life is to be understood as having no reality apart from the field of expression bequeathed by my body, and if its full reality requires that its behavioural expressions be acknowledged by others, then there is a dual sense in which my own ability and willingness to give public expression to my inner life is an essential prerequisite for the achievement and maintenance of its real existence in the world. In short, if my inner life can find its full reality only through my giving expression to it to, and receiving acknowledgement of it from, others, then my full or genuine existence as a human individual is doubly dependent upon my own capacity to declare that existence—to lay claim to it by actively making it manifest and passively waiting to be acknowledged. And this combination of activity and passivity involves more than acknowledging that one wants to be acknowledged, that one wants the other(s) to care; it also means acknowledging that my expressions of my inner life (of myself) do in fact express me—that they are mine, that I am in them. It means acknowledging my body and its body of expressions as my own, as me on earth; it means acknowledging my own (embodied) existence.

So, lacking Descartes's confidence in God but sharing his intuition that fully human existence stands in need of creation and preservation, Cavell takes the Cartesian emphasis on human beings as thinking things to have opened up for modern philosophy an understanding of human beings as ones who must create themselves by thinking—as beings who to exist must say so, who must enact their own existence in and through thought. And, of course, the mode of thought he has in mind to perform this (re-)creative or (re)animating function is the practice of recounting criteria, so that we enact our existence by attending to our words and their grammar.

The practice of recounting criteria should not seem at all unsuited to this proposed role. To begin with, it clearly displays the economy or interpenetration of activity and passivity, of knowing and being known. On the one hand, the determination of what we say when involves the active declaration of our criteria: we must make a claim, stake our capacity as a speaker upon our ability to articulate the agreements which underpin our shared language. But, on the other hand, in so doing we draw upon ourselves as a source of knowledge, allow ourselves to learn something from ourselves which we had not previously known (in the sense that we needed to be reminded of it)—and this is tantamount to becoming an other to one's own self, to passively allowing oneself to be known (in this case by oneself). In the terms established in the previous chapter, by engaging in this practice I take an interest in myself, permit myself to learn something about myself by becoming actively passive, and thereby prevent myself from being bored by myself.

Moreover, the resulting switch of focus from behavioural expression in general to linguistic expression in particular is neither as restrictive nor as much of a switch as it may sound. For, as we have already seen, talking is the distinctively human form of life: the human species is (it seems uniquely) endowed with a capacity for language which permits the development and articulation of a multiplicity of specific languages and of the specific forms of social and cultural life which hang together with them; so the practice of recounting the criteria which underpin each such formation will recall us simultaneously to the real possibilities of our human nature and to the more specific fulfilments and deforma- tions to which they have given rise in our historical period. By reminding us of what counts, this method of philosophical thinking will remind us of what our investments of interest in the world have been, are, and might be; and by drawing us to reinvest our interest in that world, it will allow us to reinvest our interest in the lives we are leading within it. In effect, by declaring what we say when we allow the things of the world to attract us once more, and so might succeed in turning away from our fixated lives of boredom and disappointment—lives in which we haunt the world, in which we exist as not fully present to a world that is not fully present to us—and turning towards a practical re-engagement with the everyday.

Writing, Reading, and Being Read

In spelling out the conceptual basis of Cavell's belief that the Romantic notion of animism could be rendered intelligible, I relied quite heavily upon the idea that our experience of the world was endlessly and continuously seamed—that there is some appropriate hook of response for each and every specific kind of object and phenomenon that we encounter in the world, and that those hooks can be forgotten, ignored, or otherwise go dead. I then pointed out that recalling ourselves to those specific hooks of response could be understood as a mode or extension of Wittgensteinian grammatical investigations, since part of knowing the criteria for the use of a given object-word is knowing which ways of treating the relevant object are appropriate to it and which are not. In this sense, the project of reanimating the world should be seen as an essentially linguistic or grammatical matter, no matter which particular piece of that world happens to be at issue.

But, of course, this essentially linguistic project must include as part of its general attempt to reanimate the world a more specific attempt to reanimate the linguistic elements of that world. For words, sentences, and texts are the object of our experience and concern just like flowers, chairs, and any other species of worldly phenomenon; indeed, in certain respects they play a role in our form of life which is of unique importance—as we have already seen, talking is the distinctively human life form, and the grammatical framework of language is the fulcrum upon which the whole of our experience of the world turns. Of course, *fully* re-animating our life with words would mean not only recalling how we relate to words as opposed to flowers and furniture, but also recovering the hooks of response that are appropriate to one word as opposed to another; and on both levels, the recounting of criteria is indispensable. For distinguishing words from flowers and furniture is a matter of knowing what counts as 'a word', knowing the criteria for 'a sentence', knowing the grammar of 'grammar'; and the absolute specificity of each and every word in our language is determined precisely by its criteria and the ways in which its criteria differ from those of every other member of that particular species of object. So, placing the full complexity of our seamed experience of language in front of our eyes so as to subject ourselves to its lessons could only be accomplished by asking ourselves what we would say when—recounting our criteria; in this domain, Cavell's essentially linguistic practice takes a linguistic object.

In his more recent writings, however, Cavell has supplemented this particular criterial method of acknowledging the specificity of words with a series of others. To put it more precisely, he has begun to develop alternative ways of attending to the specificity of words which do not involve simply recounting *their* Wittgensteinian criteria, but which none the less cast light upon the nature of words and language and so should be understood as further elucidations of what counts as a word or a language, i.e. as attempts to recount the criteria of such words as 'word', 'sentence', 'language'. Some of these new methods are more closely related to the practice of ordinary language philosophy than others; and I will begin to explore them by examining an example of the former sort of approach.

The practice of asking what we say when has always had a crucially diagnostic aspect for Cavell; emphasizing Wittgenstein's concern for therapy, he has devoted as much time to unearthing the pressures which drive the philosopher to speak outside language games as to pinpointing the emptiness of the resultant misuse of words. As a consequence, he has always paid very careful attention to what one might call the latent significance (as opposed to the patent incomprehensibility) of philosophical utterances: if what this person says (being empty or otherwise distorted) is not and cannot be what he means, what could he have it in mind to say that leads him to employ just these words in just this way? *The Claim of Reason* is in effect an extended attempt to perform this interpretative, diagnostic task on the philosophical sceptic.

The importance of this tendency in Cavell is that it forms part of what one might call a more liberal attitude towards certain unusual modes of employing words than tends to be exhibited by other ordinary language philosophers. Rather than instantly condemning such uses of words as nonsensical or merely metaphorical, he is prepared to pay careful attention to the ways in which they function in the discourse of the person concerned—their interrelation with other words in specific contexts, their appearance in some rather than other circumstances, the projections or displacements of meaning which have resulted in their emergence, and so on. In *The Claim of Reason*, Cavell baptizes one genre of such employments of language as 'mythological'—using a term which Wittgenstein offers as one way of characterizing his interlocutor's claim that 'With a rule, all the steps are really already taken' (*PI* 221). Here, to say that the claim is mythological is, in effect, to say that it should not be taken as a literal account of the actuality (the grammar and essence) of rule-following but rather as a symbol or picture of how that actuality strikes us. The relevant question about it is accordingly not whether it fits the facts about rules but rather what particular attitude, intuition, complex of thought and feeling about rule-following on the part of the competent rule-follower it expresses.

In this particular case, what seems to be given expression is that the conclusion reached by a rule is always foregone, that the rule determines that conclusion in such a way that following it amounts to forgoing our freedom. This mythology of rule-following is not false, because it is not in competition with a literal or grammatical account of rules and their employment; on the contrary, since it expresses a sense of the role that rules play in our lives (records how the facts about rule-following strike us) it must presuppose at least an implicit grasp of what rules are (since it could only be offered by someone who knows those facts). None the less, it may mislead us—the myth may be dangerous or pernicious if it is taken or developed in certain ways, e.g. as blurring the distinction between the self-imposed constraints of convention and those imposed by nature; but it may also be a precisely apt, economical, and potent manifestation of the way we relate to the constraints and emancipations of convention—an important indicator of what rules do and might mean to us, and therefore of what rules are.

In short, such mythological expressions are not philosophy, but they are its raw material; they are not themselves grammatical reminders, but they can make manifest the ways in which grammar is embedded in our lives and how our minds have either accommodated or distorted that actuality. But these traces can only be brought out by attending closely to the words of the mythological expression; for if it is functioning mythologically, then the words employed will have been utilized because of their aptness for this expressive task, and that aptitude will be a function of their precise meaning. In this sense, Cavell sees his task to be that of allowing any such myth to teach him by allowing the precise weight of its words to unfold their significance and thereby reveal possible paths of illumination and distortion which criss-cross the grammatical area with which he is concerned. In effect, this is how he conducts much of his investigation of other-minds scepticism in the final part of *The Claim of Reason*; when, for example, he is brought to say that the human body—in order to be interpreted or understood—must be 'read', he takes himself to be using the word 'read' mythologically and so is prepared to allow this inclination to remind him of certain important features of his life with others:

the idea of reading seems to tell me what *kind* of understanding or interpretation I might aspire to. Then what I need is not a paraphrase or translation of the word 'read', but an account of why it is that *that* word is the one I want—after which I may move away from it or move on from it. (The willingness and the refusal to exchange one word or expression for another, as well as the usefulness or futility in doing so, are themes running throughout the *Investigations*.) (*CR* 363)

We could, in fact, regard the business of this present chapter as an attempt to attend closely to and to allow ourselves to be taught by the inclination to use the word 'animism' in the context of scepticism. The Romantic impulse is being interpreted philosophically as a myth which can lead us on to (rather than away from) the truth and reality of our lives.

However, interpreting words and sentences as mythological expressions does not exhaust Cavell's armoury of methods. Indeed, in more recent work other modes of interpretation have assumed a significant role in his work; and two in particular are worth mentioning. The first is an inclination towards etymological explorations: Cavell often allows the historical vicissitudes of the words under his examination to guide its further progress. For example, the transition we noted earlier from a Kantian transcendental deduction of twelve concepts to a Wittgensteinian account of the criteria of any and every concept-term is sometimes presented as emerging from the consideration that Kant's term for the role of his categories in human knowledge ('conditions') itself means 'speaking together' (con-ditio) and so directs us towards our common language. In this case, as we have seen, the transition can be effected in alternative ways, but in other contexts, etymology is the sole engine of Cavell's further interpretative progress. This strategy has clear Heideggerian overtones; but it is worth pointing out that it is also resonant of a key element in Austin's methodological armoury. In 'A Plea for Excuses' (in *PI*), for example, he mentions as one lesson that might be

drawn from a study of his topic the insight that words come 'trailing
clouds of etymology'—a metaphor that he unpacks in the following
way: '... a word never—well, hardly ever—shakes off its etymology and
its formation. In spite of all changes in and extensions of and additions
to its meanings, and indeed rather pervading and governing these, there
will still persist the old idea. In an *accident* something befalls; by *mistake*
you take the wrong one; in *error* you stray ...' (*PP* 201–2). In that
context, Austin goes on to stress the philosophical problems that can be
caused by the simple models or pictures that are so often found to be
embedded in the history of words, and which lead us to distort the
more complex facts to which they also apply. We might think of Cavell
here as stressing the way in which the still-operative history of words
can also embody philosophical illumination.

The second of these more recent strategies is probably the most
surprising: it involves refining the etymological technique by permitting
oneself to decompose words into elements which have a meaning of
their own but cannot easily be read as participating in the given word
for that reason. This process of atomization appears in Cavell's comments on a story by Poe, whose title ('The Imp of the Perverse') is
taken to mark the importance of a series of words in the story all of
which begin with the three-letter sequence 'imp'—a linguistic atom or
word-imp which has other lives (e.g. as the multiply meaningful abbrevia-
tion 'imp.') and which in turn contains a two-letter sequence 'im' that is
possessed of opposite meanings (sometimes signifying negation, as in
'immediate', and sometimes intensification, as in 'imprison'). The contribution of such elements of meaning to a word in the Poe story such as
'unimpressive' can hardly be thought of as directly etymological, let
alone as grammatical; but Cavell none the less takes it to be a general
mode in which language addresses its users:

'Word imps' could name any of the recurrent combinations of letters of which
the words of a language are composed. They are part of the way words have
their familiar looks and sounds, and their familiarity depends upon our mostly
not noticing the particles (or cells) and their laws, which constitute words and
their imps—on our not noticing their necessary recurrences, which is perhaps
only to say that recurrence constitutes familiarity. This necessity, the most
familiar property of language there could be—that if there is to be language,
words and their cells must recur, as if fettered in their orbits, that language is
grammatical (to say the least)—insures the self-referentiality of language. When
we do note these cells or molecules, these little moles of language (perhaps in
thinking, perhaps in derangement), what we discover are word imps—the

initial, or it may be medial or final, movements, the implanted origins or constituents of words, leading lives of their own, staring back at us, calling upon one another, giving us away, alarming—because to note them is to see that they live in front of our eyes, within earshot, at every moment. (*IQO* 125)

Together with the original ordinary language impulse to diagnosis, these three modes of interpreting words—the mythological, the etymological, and what one might call the atomic—form a part of the array of approaches Cavell adopts in his attempts to reanimate our life with words. Taken as a whole, they might be thought of as constituting a practice of reading—a practice of reading words which reveals the ways in which their specific meanings are constituted and maintained, and which accordingly leads to a deepened understanding of the nature of words and language; so that this practice of reading any and all words can be seen as a way of appreciating the specific meanings of the words 'word' and 'language'—a way of recounting their criteria. And what these methods of reading reveal most strikingly about the nature of words and language is the degree to which what our words mean, and what we may thereby be held responsible for meaning by them, can run beyond our initial knowledge (although not beyond our eventual comprehension); their grammar, their possession of a history and of a ramifying internal complexity, and their mythological potency all function to constitute their specific meaning—but they do so in ways which we only discover or recover through these modes of reading.

For Cavell, this has two crucial consequences. First, it shows the independent life of language—a life in which words necessarily relate to those who inherit, employ, and bequeath them but in which they possess a relative autonomy. Attending to language in the ways outlined above brings this independence to our notice, but the act of attending itself allows us to confirm and affirm that this autonomy is only relative—that the life of words is inextricably bound up with human beings. In this respect, these modes of responding to language precisely resemble the reanimating practices outlined earlier in the case of non-linguistic pieces of the world; they amount to allowing language to reveal its true nature by permitting it to attract us, recalling its worthiness to elicit our interest and so regaining our interest in it—in short, they facilitate the reanimation of words and of our life with them in a way which acknowledges them as the necessary other of beings whose life form is linguistic. Indeed, this resemblance provides a sense in which the practice of reading words can function as an allegory of the more general practice of acknowledging the world, and leads Cavell to characterize the latter in terms of the former, i.e. to label that more general practice of philosophical thinking as a mode of reading the world.

Second, it shows that the more specific practice of reading words can best be understood as a practice of allowing oneself to be read by words. For such reading is a matter of waiting on words, allowing them to manifest their own independent life to us—in short, being passive so that they may be active; but the life they thereby exhibit is their life in our common language—their life in the language of their readers. So that in so far as our labours reveal a feature of those words (whether criterial, mythological, etymological, or atomic) which we are able to acknowledge as an aspect of their sense, we are acknowledging that this word has activated for us a hitherto unknown aspect of our own (actual and potential) responsibilities and commitments as a speaker of the language to which the word belongs—revealed and revivified an aspect of our lives as speakers, and so of ourselves. By allowing words to draw us through their complexities of sense in this way, we allow them to make or recover connections and associations of meaning in ourselves—we are brought to recognize our (linguistic) soul in the body of expressive significance that is their meaning. Reading words in this way is thus a matter of allowing them to interpret aspects of our own life back to us in a way which reanimates it; our reanimating attention to them amounts to holding ourselves open to their reanimating attention to us—a mode of reflexivity or mutual implication which is inevitable for a creature whose life form is essentially linguistic. It does not seem unduly fanciful to think of such reading as a matter of allowing ourselves to be read.

But of course, our life with words involves employing them as well as responding to them; so acknowledging and reanimating that life must also involve a specific mode of using words—it must involve a practice of writing or speech as well as one of reading or listening. This connection is already evident from the fact that our account of Cavell's mode of reading is itself made possible because he has enacted its results in his own writing; and this merely instantiates the more general point that these two moments or aspects of life with language are inseparable. If, for example, one's writing is to reanimate language, it must demonstrate a respect for the absolute specificity of each and every word it employs—it must amount to an acknowledgement of the criteria which govern each word and distinguish it from every other member of that species of object, to a continuous assumption of responsibility for and responsiveness to the full meaning of every linguistic mark one makes. But that can only result from attending to each such word, allowing it to communicate the full freight of its particular significance as that is manifest in the manifold contexts of its interrelations with other words and its applications to the world—in short, by reading it. Furthermore, writing is something which finds its fulfilment in being read, when it attracts or discovers a reader who can acknowledge (and thereby preserve and re-create) the animation of words which the writing enacts; but such re-creation will itself find its fulfilment in the furtherance or continuation of that enactment—specifically in the reader's account of her reading, and more generally in her continued animation of her life with words i.e. in writing.

Cavell summarizes these points in the following passage: 'Reading is a variation of writing, where they meet in meditation and achieve accounts of their opportunities; and writing is a variation of reading, since to write is to cast words together that you did not make, so as to give or take readings' (*IQO* 18). Such reading and writing will together constitute a reanimation of language—and they will also constitute a reanimation of the language-user, for the recovery of criterial precision which reading and writing prepare and enact replaces a fixated, frozen use of language (in which we simply reiterate the words we encounter in the careless, reduced, and rigidified way in which they circulate amongst us) with one which endlessly takes on and attempts to live up to the specific and complex burden of meaning that each word carries with it. Cavell encapsulates these themes of repetition, animating language and the enactment of one's existence in the following commentary on the ideas contained in Emerson's remark (or gag) that 'Man dares not say . . . but quotes':

First, language is an inheritance. Words are before I am; they are common. Second, the question of whether I am saying them or quoting them—saying them firsthand or secondhand, as it were—which means whether I am thinking or imitating, is the same as the question whether I do or do not exist as a human being and is a matter demanding proof. Third, the writing, of which the gag is part, is an expression of the proof of saying 'I', hence of the claim that writing is a matter, say the decision, of life and death, and that what this comes to is the inheriting of language, an owning of words, which does not remove them from circulation but rather returns them, as to life. (*IQO* 113–14)

And it is vital to note that, in so far as this practice of reading and writing (this facet of the practice of recounting criteria) *can* be thought of as a central mode of enacting one's own existence, it must also be thought of as placing my own existence and the existence of others in a relationship of mutual implication. As we have already seen in more general terms earlier in this chapter, if I enact or acknowledge my own existence by declaring my criteria, I give expression to a particular aspect of myself, acknowledge this particular body of my expressions to be mine (to embody me), and so declare myself available to be known by others; and the full reality of my existence will depend upon other people's ability and willingness to acknowledge me. However, in such declarations I claim to be speaking for a community of speakers (to be declaring what *we* say when); and asking others to acknowledge such declarations amounts to asking them to acknowledge that I do speak for them, to acknowledge that they too are embodied in my body of expressions. So, in declaring my own existence in *this* way I not only rely upon others to acknowledge *my* existence but also claim to be making the existence of others known in and through me; this mode of enacting my own existence is simultaneously a mode of calling on others to acknowledge me and of drawing them to enact their own existence by acknowledging that they are known by me. This complex reflexivity of acknowledgement flows from the fact that words and their criteria have two faces—they not only link the individual speaker to the world, they also link him with other speakers; it is because of this that the tasks of reanimating the world and acknowledging the existence of myself and of others within it simultaneously resolve themselves (or fail to do so) in Cavell's practice of recounting criteria.

It follows that the task of proving one's existence through the more specific practice of reading and writing will exhibit a similarly reflexive structure. Such a writer will necessarily require the acknowledgement that only a reader can provide, the acknowledgement that and how she has embodied herself in a given body of expressions; and such a reader will only be able fully to acknowledge herself in the words and sentences of the text to which she is attending when it has been written in a way which allows those words and sentences to manifest the full freight of their significance. And from both points of view, the existence and activity of the necessary other can not only underwrite or certify the existing state of one's self-knowledge but also extend it in ways hitherto undreamed of. For if the life of language is relatively independent of the life of any one of its users, then the writer's reader will be able to recover from the text reaches of meaning of which the text's author was unconscious, and the reader's writer will draw out reaches of meaning from her reader's consciousness of which the latter was initially unaware or in which she was uninterested. Cavell sees the latter point as captured in Emerson's claim that 'In every work of genius we recognize our own rejected thoughts; they come back to us with a certain alienated majesty'; and he sees the former as embodied in Emerson's related claims that 'He who has more obedience than I masters me' and 'Men imagine that they communicate their virtue and vice only by overt actions, and do not see that virtue and vice emit a breath every moment.'

For Cavell, these claims comprise a picture or theory of reading and writing as being read in which he is prepared to acknowledge himself:

> On the reading side ... mastery happens by obedience, which is to say, by a mode of listening ... a matter of discerning the whim from which at each word [the text] follows. On the writing side, the idea of communicating as emitting a breath every moment means that with every word you utter you say more than you know you say ... [These ideas] bring into investigation ... how it is that one writes better than one knows (as well as worse) and that one may be understood better by someone other than oneself (as well as worse) ... I find this a frightening notation of an anxiety in writing [and reading]; an acknowledgement that one must give over control of one's appropriations, as if to learn what they are. (*IQO* 116, 25)

Accordingly, if such a writer's reader fails to live up to her expectations, or if such a reader's writer fails to live up to her responsibilities, neither encounter will deliver the experience of reanimation. But if such a reader does encounter such a writer, then both will achieve their goal—and in so doing, each will be implicated in the enactment or manifestation of the other's existence (as well as in the reanimation of language). The writer who recounts criteria encounters a reader who is prepared to acknowledge those criteria as hers, and so to acknowledge her own existence in the writer's body of expressions; and the reader who recounts her criteria in this way thereby acknowledges the writer in her body of expressions. In short, because any attempts to recount criteria relate to a language that is claimed to be common between speaker and hearer, writer and reader (because they amount to claims about what we say when), the successful enactment of one's existence in language brings a community into existence—even if it is only a community of two. If such claims fail, then we are alone in the world and not fully existent within it; but our claims at least maintain the possibility of a future existence in a future community. And here, Cavell's most recent practices of reading and writing can be seen to manifest the same structure as that which we saw in his earlier analyses and applications of the philosophical method of asking what we say when in the realms of aesthetic, moral, and political discourse. What we have described as the practice of recounting criteria is itself a deeper recounting or recovery of Cavell's earliest vision of ordinary language philosophy as creating the space within which the simultaneous achievement of a genuine or deeper individuality and a genuine or deeper community is possible.

PART III
Common Themes, Competing Perspectives

Introduction to Part III

Redemptive Reading: Refractions and Reflexivities

In the first part of this book, I outlined the ways in which Cavell employs the procedures and concepts of ordinary language philosophy to illuminate certain aspects or dimensions of the procedures and concepts of contemporary aesthetic, moral, and political practices, and emphasized the surprising degree to which the former can be seen as mirroring the latter. Since the latter bear the hallmarks of the modern, liberal individualist culture in which they are embedded—defining a space in which the free achievement of individual identity coexists with the acknowledgement of membership in a community of equals—it seemed that ordinary language philosophy must be understood as similarly implicated in post-Enlightenment values. The second part of the book was designed to show that Cavell also sees the practices of ordinary language philosophy as everywhere set in opposition to the sceptical impulse—to show that for him, in the face of each specific outbreak of what seems to be a fundamental human desire to repudiate that which aligns speakers with one another and with the world they inhabit, ordinary language philosophy reaffirms the tenability of those alignments through the reiterative recounting of criteria. Of course, thinking of the conflict in this way presupposes a very distinctive understanding of the nature of scepticism as it has appeared and developed since its modern renaissance in Descartes; but it is one that seems to illuminate the phenomenon and to emerge very naturally from a Wittgensteinian perspective upon it. What can also be said at this point, however, is that it is an understanding of scepticism that dovetails very smoothly with the conclusions established in Part I, since it amounts to characterizing the sceptical impulse as a drive to deny or negate the terms in which the modern liberal individualist vision finds expression in the field of philosophy. And by characterizing ordinary language philosophy's opposition to scepticism (thus understood) as its defining mission or endeavour, Cavell can be seen as attempting at once to underwrite and to deepen the most far-reaching implication of his earlier work, namely, that his own Wittgensteinian philosophical method is unavoidably committed to the defence of that quintessentially modern vision.

Bringing the conclusions of these two parts together in this way generates a series of interrelated questions, of which two seem the most pressing. First, if the structure of ordinary language philosophy both reflects that of other contemporary cultural practices and is formed in response to scepticism, then we should expect to find versions of the sceptical impulse and of the corresponding impulse towards its overcoming in the formation of non-philosophical dimensions of our culture; and a comparative analysis of them might therefore cast light on the nature of that culture in both its philosophical and its non-philosophical forms. Second, if the philosophical practice of recounting criteria does indeed stand in some intimate relation to the ethics of liberal individualism, then a fuller understanding of the spiritual impulse underlying it is most likely to emerge by locating it in relation to other contemporary manifestations of liberalism in morality and politics.

I will attempt to address these questions in the next two parts of this book. In Part III, I will offer a brief characterization of the nature of Cavell's interests in the related fields of Shakespearean literary criticism, psychoanalysis, and cinema (in Chapters 7, 8, and 9 respectively). Here, the goal will be twofold. First, to stress the degree to which these seemingly 'non-philosophical' domains of modern culture none the less bear the traces of the guiding philosophical conflict that I have explored in this book: that between the sceptical impulse and the model or image of redemptive reading to which Cavell opposes it—the recovery of self, community, and world through acknowledgement of and by another self and its body of expressions. And second, to reveal the ways in which Cavell's work in these various fields has generated productive reconceptualizations of that philosophical theme—significantly advancing his argument rather than merely illustrating it. In Part IV, I will go on to prepare the ground for, and to engage in, an examination of the set of lectures that embodies the furthest reach of those reconceptualizations, and that also constitutes Cavell's attempt to locate his (refined) model of redemptive reading in relation to Rawls' *A Theory of Justice*— his 1988 Carus Lectures on Emersonian Perfectionism entitled *Conditions Handsome and Unhandsome*.

It is, however, important to bear three general points in mind as these matters unfold. First, by suggesting that traces of an essentially philosophical problematic are to be found in the domains of literature and literary criticism, psychoanalysis, and cinema, I do not mean to imply that Cavell takes this to justify subsuming these supposedly independent disciplines under the banner of philosophy. After all, in so far as those issues can be seen to be internal to non-philosophical modes of human thought and expression, they provide an equally compelling ground for subsuming philosophy under their banner. Cavell's position is rather that annexation in either direction would be a mistake: more precisely, that it would amount to a failure of acknowledgement. In effect, he conceptualizes the issue of relations between disciplines in the terms that emerged earlier in his account of interpersonal relations, and regards the traces of analogous or shared problems and tasks as providing a reason for each discipline to acknowledge those other disciplines *as other*—that is, as related to it rather than entirely detached from it or entirely subsumable within it, as separate but similar. Just as he previously set about charting the relations between philosophy and the realms of aesthetics, morality, and politics (as we saw in Part I), so here Cavell's detailed investigations are designed to establish the fact, to delineate the nature, and to explore the consequences of acknowledging such otherness (or othernesses) in a different but related region of the intellectual economy of the humanities. However, the word 'explore' should here be emphasized. For, of course, one of the key consequences of any such acknowledgement will be that each discipline is led towards a revised understanding of its own nature; and the precise contours of that new self-understanding (like any fundamental shift in a person's self-understanding) will be difficult to determine and to accept—indeed, if the revisions are sufficiently radical, they may be experienced by those within the discipline as amounting to its denial or destruction. But precisely because of this, Cavell regards himself as raising questions to be held open and considered rather than as providing definitive answers. In other words, the form taken by his acknowledgement as a philosopher of the otherness of the disciplines that abut his own is that of posing or asking questions about them; on his view, giving answers to those questions (whatever they may be) would amount to severing rather than maintaining those relationships, and so failing to acknowledge them. Accordingly, when Cavell ends *The Claim of Reason* by asking 'But can philosophy become literature and still know itself?' (*CR* 496), his words should be acknowledged as posing a genuine rather than a rhetorical question—one that his work is designed also to pose with respect to philosophy and psychoanalysis and to philosophy and cinema, and to which he does *not* claim to know the answer.

The second general point to be borne in mind in the following chapters is related to the first, and has to do with the nature of Cavell's approach to the texts he is studying. As a first approximation, we might say that, in his readings, Cavell appears to address himself to (that is, to take himself to be addressed by) unitary texts produced by single individuals. This formulation is not, of course, intended to suggest that he concentrates upon individual texts as opposed either to related series of texts (*œuvres*) or to words and sentences (and moving images)—for those oppositions are not obviously intelligible ones; it means rather that he tends to treat words and sentences primarily as parts of an essentially integral single text, and to treat extended bodies of work as a series of such integral single texts. It also means that he tends to treat each such text primarily as the intentional product of a single organizing intelligence, as the creation or composition of an individual human being. The degree to which this is a controversial choice rather than the inevitable starting-point of any critical enterprise becomes particularly apparent in Cavell's writings on film, in which his frequent references to the director as the author of her movie seem strikingly untroubled by the many criticisms that have been levelled at the *auteur* theory and its relatives (e.g. pointing out the essentially collaborative nature of the film-making process, or emphasizing the determining influence of bureaucratic, economic, and social structures on its end-product); but similar points could be developed with respect to the Shakespearean corpus, Freud's psychoanalytic writings, and the work of the American Transcendentalists. In other words, Cavell's general interpretative emphasis upon the integrity of the text and upon the individual author as its primary source, which has helped to earn him the label of a 'liberal humanist' literary critic, has also made it seem that his approach is vulnerable to two main criticisms: first, that it lacks any genuine awareness of the complexities of the social, historical, and political contexts within which the production and reception of these texts took place and by which they were consequently marked; and second, that it fails to acknowledge the essentially discontinuous, self-undermining, and uncontrollable nature of linguistic meaning and subjectivity—as argued by the proponents of Post-Structuralism in the humanities.

It is therefore important to note that the first of these criticisms is largely misplaced, and that the second fails to appreciate the depth and sophistication of Cavell's articulation and defence of his own assumptions. To begin with the first: the absence of any significant references to or engagements with historical or sociological analyses of these texts in Cavell's work does not, of course, mean that he is unaware of such analyses, or that he regards them as incoherent, irrelevant, or uninteresting; it shows only that he has chosen a different approach—one with (it is to hoped) virtues of its own, and one that no more occludes sociohistorical perspectives than they occlude it. And in fact, it is simply false to say that he completely ignores the chronological location and order of his texts: his interest in the cultural phenomena of modernity and modernism has already been demonstrated, and he often argues that two of his authors might be thought of as engaged in a precise and complex historical interaction, with one picking up and elaborating upon or contradicting certain facets of another's earlier words. Moreover, even if those interactions do seem to be modelled on a conversation between two individuals whose identity and relationship seems relatively unmarked by social and economic forces, the example of the Carus Lectures will show that Cavell regards the substance and the consequences of those conversations as ineradicably political. Further, it should be noted that, although Cavell's emphasis upon the authors of his texts does indeed proclaim his commitment to the idea that those texts are, before anything else, the creations of human individuals, this does not signal an attempt to introduce biographical analysis as an alternative to or substitute for social and political analysis; he does not leave his readings free of references to class structure in order to fill them with references to his authors' sexual proclivities or family background. When Cavell talks of 'Shakespeare', 'Freud', or 'Cukor', those words are used primarily as names of the authors of a certain body of plays, books, or films rather than as the proper names of individuals—so that Cavell's Shakespeare, whilst not exactly not a creature of the Elizabethan era, is always capable of putting the defining assumptions of that era into question (e.g. his use of cultural stereotypes such as the Bastard and the Moor) and is anyway primarily identified by (and so with) his texts, as 'the burden of the name of the greatest writer in the language, the creature of the greatest ordering of English' (*DK* 2). In short, the Cavellian emphasis upon a single controlling human intelligence behind the texts he studies is, at least in part, a reflection or displacement of his tendency to regard those individual texts and *œuvres* as essentially integral and self-comprehending human compositions.

This brings us to the second criticism mentioned earlier; and here, my explanatory remarks must be equally brief, for this is not the point at which a careful evaluation of the rival merits of Cavell's Wittgenstein-

ian philosophy and the varieties of Post-Structuralist thought which
have generated the terms of this criticism can be made. I will accordingly
restrict myself to pointing out that Cavell himself does not leave the
question of the nature and legitimacy of his approach unaddressed or
undefended; it is in fact a manifestation in his interpretative practice of
certain conclusions for which he argues at length in his early considerations of modernism in the arts. There,[1] his discussion focusses upon the
role of the concept of 'intention' (in particular, the author's intention) in
art criticism; Cavell finds himself (along with many others) strongly
inclined to employ that concept in aesthetic discussions, and so equally
strongly inclined to believe that only an erroneous theory of the nature
of intentions could lead others to reject its legitimacy. On his view, the
impulse to reject the invocation of an artist's intentions when attempting
to explain or understand a work of art depends upon thinking of
intentions as something that exist inside the artist's head whilst the art
work exists outside, in the public realm; for if this picture were correct,
then the relation between the two could at best be causal, and the
project of focussing upon intentions could only lead someone into the
realms of speculative psychobiography and away from a closer examination of the very thing that intentions were invoked in order to
explain—the work of art itself. In effect, those who cleave to this
picture construct a dilemma: either the artist's intention was effective,
in which case it was realized in the work and can be seen there, or it
was not, in which case the attempt to identify it takes the critic outside
the work in search of something that had no effect upon it. But for
Cavell, this dilemma presupposes a picture of a conceptual gap between
intention and outcome that simply does not normally exist (even if the
relation between the two can be complex and difficult to plot): in the
case of ordinary conduct, nothing is more visible than what was meant
and what was not meant by a certain action, *visible* in the correctly
executed action or in the slip, the mistake, the accident that marred its
execution. In other words, asking a question about the intention of a
particular act typically does not drive us outside the action itself but
further into it; in asking the question, we are asking about the meaning
of that particular action, about its significance, and not about the
existence or non-existence of a particular psychological episode. Correctly understood, talk of the author's intentions in the specific context
of art is simply a way of focussing more closely upon the work of art itself.

---

[1] Particularly in the essays 'Music Discomposed' and 'A Matter of Meaning It', in *MWM*.

It does more than this, however; it also registers what Cavell calls 'the first fact of works of art ... that they are meant, meant to be understood' (*MWM* 227–8). This claim includes an idea of meaningfulness and an idea of creation or composition; the point is that works of art are one sort of thing that people make and in which other people can take a certain sort of interest. There is thus a strong connection between work conducted in the field of the arts and the other sorts of actions that human beings perform; but there are also important differences between the activities of artists and the more everyday actions of human beings. Cavell specifies one such difference by providing a particular gloss on the famous Kantian notion of 'purposiveness without purpose': he takes this notion to register the fact that a work of art does not express a particular intention or achieve a specific goal, but rather celebrates the fact that people can intend their lives at all, that their actions can attain coherence and effectiveness in the face of the indifference of nature and social constraints. This claim is further unfolded by means of a comparison between the role of the concept of intention in moral assessments of human action and its role in aesthetic judgements:

The creation of art, being human conduct which affects others, has the commitments any conduct has. It escapes morality; not, however, in escaping commitment, but in being free to choose only those commitments it wishes to incur. In this way, art plays with one of man's fates, the fate of being accountable for everything you do and are, intended or not. It frees us to sing and dance, gives us actions to perform whose consequences, commitments, and liabilities are discharged in the act itself. The price for freedom in this choice of commitment and accountability is that of an exactitude in meeting those commitments and discharging those accounts which no mere morality can impose. You cede the possibilities of excuse, explanation, or justification for your failures; and the cost of failure is not remorse or recompense, but the loss of coherence altogether. (*MWM* 199–200)

Since neither the artist's goal or purpose, nor the means or resources needed to achieve it, are dictated to her, and since in a modernist context no set of conventions can be relied upon to carry an agreed significance, so that her task is in effect to find a way of creating something capable of earning the title of a work of art from scratch, she finds herself in a situation where her freedom is dilated, where the chances she takes are entirely her own; but since she is inviting others to take those chances with her, and cannot base that invitation on power or authority but only on attraction and promise, she must bear the responsibility of ensuring that every risk she takes be worth while, every infliction of tension lead to a resolution, and so on. In other words, the task of composing a work of art in the era of modernism is the task of composing something that can take responsibility for its every feature or element, something that can bear up under a reading which seeks to find its promise of meaningfulness to be fully made out.

It should be clear that these early ideas—regarding references to the intention of the artist as a means of penetrating further into the art work, and regarding such art works as wholes whose every feature invites the search for meaning—form one root of Cavell's general interpretative emphasis upon the integral text and the individual author. Of course, his conception of the implications and significance of these ideas, as well as of the details of their working out, is importantly modified by the points he establishes in his considerations of Romanticism (of which more in a moment), and by what he discovers in the particular texts he examines in his more recent work (as we shall see in the coming chapters); but those later readings should none the less be seen as inheriting or inflecting a method whose justifications were laid out far in advance. It should also be clear from this excursus that, in adopting this method or approach, Cavell is not presupposing that any and all texts will or must meet these exacting standards, but rather testing certain texts against those standards and finding that they at least are capable of living up to them; his employment of this method is thus a wager on the feasibility and power of a certain ideal of human creativity, rather than a sign that he thinks the bet is won in advance. If, however, we do regard these readings as attempts to locate concrete examples of a general template or paradigm that was defined in advance, this in turn suggests that, for Cavell, the real weight of proof, the level or dimension at which we can most properly assess the conflict between his interpretative approach and those of others, is that of the penetration and insight derived from applying those methods to particular texts. In other words, although it seems clear that he would suspect that many of the radical conclusions reached by Post-Structuralists are dependent upon erroneous philosophical pictures of meaning and subjectivity (and so upon a failure to trust the grammar of these terms as that is manifested in our ordinary lives with language) in just the manner exemplified by those suspicious of the concept of intention,[2] Cavell also takes it that the best way of justifying the working hypothesis

[2] See e.g. postscript A to 'Being Odd, Getting Even', in *IQO* and 'Macbeth Appalled' (unpublished manuscript).

that human beings are capable of composing texts that form a coherent, comprehensible, and self-comprehending whole is to provide a reading of certain texts in just those terms which can elicit or even compel conviction. And if we should indeed judge such methodological controversies by their practical fruits, then there is no substitute for the sort of detailed assessment of specific readings that I hope to provide in the chapters to come.

This brings us to the third general point to be borne in mind in the following pages—and again, it has to do with the nature and status of Cavell's interpretative approach. As we saw in Part II, his investigation of modern scepticism leads him to think of his Wittgensteinian practice of recounting criteria as a mode of thinking whose prosecution constitutes a reanimation of words, self, and world—a way of declaring and so enacting one's own existence and that of others through the full acknowledgement of the life in (that is, our life with) words. As we also saw, Cavell understands this acknowledgement to require a certain practice of reading (or listening) and writing (or speaking), one in which we are continuously responsible for and responsive to the absolute specificity of each and every word we employ; and he takes it that one vital aspect of such writing and reading would be the attempt to bring the full range and specificity of our experience to words. As we work through the following examinations of Cavell's writings on (his enacted readings of) Shakespeare, psychoanalysis, and cinema, what we must always bear in mind is that—beyond their specific thematic content—they constitute his own attempt to engage in the reanimating practice of writing and reading that he has already described in his examinations of Romanticism.

Looking at those readings in this way brings two important features of them into clearer focus. The first derives from a point that we noted at the end of the previous chapter, namely, the peculiarly reflexive conception of the task of reading that is secreted by this reanimating practice and its acknowledgement structure. For, according to Cavell, just as someone attempting to write in a way which is responsive to the full freight of her words' meanings can only completely succeed in her aim in so far as her efforts are acknowledged, i.e. in so far as she secures a reader who responds to her texts in the spirit in which they are written, so those attempting to read texts in this reanimating way can fully achieve their goal only in so far as they encounter texts that were written in the same spirit. More particularly, when such a reader encounters such a writer, she encounters someone who claims to be speaking for others as well as herself, someone who therefore asks her readers to acknowledge that her words embody and enact something of their own thoughts and existence: the phrase from Emerson that crystallizes this point is his claim that in every such work we 'recognize our own rejected thoughts . . . come back to us with a certain alienated majesty'.

Accordingly, when we come to see that Cavell's readings of Shakespeare, Freud, and Emerson reveal in their words structures of thought and feeling remarkably similar to his own, we should at least hesitate to dismiss this discovery of his own thoughts in others as a sign of narcissistic misreading. In the first place, of course, this phenomenon could as easily be interpreted as proof of the intersubjective reality of Cavell's problematic; and the only way of settling such a conflict of interpretations is by relying not on a priori argumentation but on the degree of conviction elicited by the readings themselves. Second, anyone who understands the acknowledgement structure underlying Cavell's model of reading would expect him to search for and to use texts which participate in his own attitude and approach to reading; for according to the terms of that approach, only texts written in the spirit in which he reads would be capable of calling forth heightened or exemplary experiences of reading—only texts motivated by the thoughts and feelings that are crystallized in Cavell's own conception and practice of reading could provide words capable of testing and drawing out the full potential of that practice. And third, the model of redemptive reading that Cavell advocates is one to which he takes himself to have been drawn by the particular texts he cites; this conception of reading is itself part of what these texts have taught him, the most important of the alienated, majestic thoughts which they have elicited from and returned to him. In this sense, he presents these readings of these particular texts not just as examples to test the success of his model of reading in practice, and not just as apt arenas for pursuing certain self-determined goals as a reader and writer; he also offers them as recountings of specific pivotal steps on the personal path which brought him to his present understanding of thinking, writing, and reading.

Noting this last, autobiographical element in the complex reflexive tapestry of Cavell's recent writings makes for a suitable transition to the second point that is highlighted when we look at Cavell's readings through the lens of his own model of redemptive reading—a point which might be expressed in the following way. In his writing on these particular texts, Cavell is attempting to acknowledge the absolute specificity of his particular experience of reading them; and—since such reading is the most fundamental activity of his life, since it is that to which he has most deeply committed himself—he is thereby attempting to declare and so to enact the specific texture of that life, the particular constellation of thoughts, feelings, and experiences that go to make him up as a person. He is, in short, not only furthering a philosophical argument and engaging in a mode of cultural analysis: he is also attempting to enact his own existence as an individual by bringing his personal world of experience to our common words, and acknowledging us, his readers, by asking us to acknowledge his words, and so himself, through reading them in the spirit to which their writing aspires.

Accordingly, as we work through the material of the following chapters, we must remember that the model of redemptive reading outlined in the previous chapter is one that Cavell offers us as a mode of understanding our own relation to his texts as well as his relation to the texts he studies. And it follows from this that not only the familiar questions of reanimation, recovery, and mutual acknowledgement (and so of lifelessness and failures of acknowledgement), but also the particular reconceptualizations of the reading model that emerge from Cavell's studies of these texts, are applicable to both relations.

7

Shakespeare: Scepticism and Tragedy

The Nature of Shakespearean Tragic Drama

We saw in previous chapters that Cavell understands the problematic known to philosophy as scepticism to be under examination in Shakespearean texts in the form of tragedy. His early essay characterizing *King Lear* as a drama pivoting around failures of acknowledgement, and his later interpretation of Othello as a diagnosis of the sceptic as in the grip of death-dealing jealousy, have already been shown to be pertinent to our philosophical concerns; and these have been followed by readings of *Coriolanus, The Winter's Tale, Hamlet,* and *Antony and Cleopatra,* in each of which Cavell's understanding of the emotional or spiritual drive of scepticism is deepened as he forges connections between it and certain interpretations of narcissism, cannibalism, and revenge. Although I lack the space in which to offer any critical exegesis of most of these connections, it will not be possible to make progress in providing even a brief surview of Cavell's interests in this and other 'non-philosophical' domains without examining his reading of *The Winter's Tale* in some detail. But before I do so, I want to note a fundamental element of Cavell's general approach to Shakespeare upon which I have as yet laid little emphasis: for Cavell is convinced not only that scepticism is a topic within these plays, but also that the Shakespearean corpus of which they are members—this particular mode of poetic drama, this particular body of expressions—itself constitutes an effort to overcome the sceptical impulse in our culture.

This doubling of issues within the plays and issues generated in and by an audience's relation to the plays themselves was already at work in 'The Avoidance of Love'.[1] Cavell there takes the events of *King Lear* to be driven by Lear's inability to acknowledge the love of his youngest daughter, because he is unable or unwilling to respond to that love and unable or unwilling to reveal this fact about himself; he wishes to avoid this recognition and revelation of himself, and so must avoid recognizing

[1] In *MWM*; repr. in *DK*.

or acknowledging others, those who are other to him, who relate to him and so place him—but by denying the reality of their relation to him, he denies (that aspect of) their reality, and so in some sense deprives them of it. If, however, this reading of the play carries conviction, if it makes sense of the motivation and interaction of the characters, it raises a question—namely, why it has not been advanced or accepted before. The matters Cavell raises are not recherché, and the pieces of evidence he collates are easily accessible—as salient as the words on the page. If they have not hitherto been seen, that cannot be because they are obscure; it must rather be because they are obvious. Our difficulty is the difficulty of seeing what is right in front of our eyes.

And for Cavell, this effect is something for which the play itself works; Shakespeare employs the medium of poetic drama in such a way as to locate the members of his audience in a position which is structurally analogous to that of the play's characters: 'The medium is one which keeps all significance continuously before our senses, so that when it comes over us that we have missed it, this discovery will reveal our ignorance to have been wilful, complicitous, a refusal to see' (*DK* 89). Of course, this doubling of the theme of failures of acknowledgement presupposes that human beings can stand in (at least some of or some version of) the same relations to fictional characters as they can to fellow human beings—that we can acknowledge or fail to acknowledge Lear just as we can acknowledge or fail to acknowledge our own fathers. And this seems to fly in the face of the obvious truth that fictional characters do not really exist, that they are not real. But in Cavell's view, such a reaction is simply another way of failing to acknowledge those characters; for it takes it to be obvious what fictional existence means, and what our relation to fictional characters is, rather than allowing our experience of plays such as *King Lear* to teach us the beginnings of answers to these questions.

For example, does the claim that such characters are not real mean that they are not in nature, not to be met with in space or time? But neither is God in nature, neither are square roots, the spirit of the age, or the correct tempo of the 'Great Fugue'; and if any of these are not real, it is not because they are not in nature. The truth in the claim is that, unlike our fellow members of the audience, these characters are fictional, that that is the particular mode of their existence; but then the interesting question is not *whether* fictional characters are real or exist, but rather *what* the nature of their (fictional) existence might be. Cavell's answer runs as follows.

Unlike other human beings, characters are not and cannot become aware of us, the audience: this is symbolized by the lowered house-lights, and dramatized in the story of the yokel who rushes on stage to save the nice lady from the murderous Moor. Cavell summarizes it by saying that we are not in the presence of the characters. They, however, are in our presence: and this means not only that we can see and hear them, glimpse the wince of pain under her smile, and sense the undertone of cruelty in his caring words, but also that we do not simply see and hear them—that merely registering her pain is in fact a mode of responding to or acknowledging it, more specifically a failure to acknowledge both its and her reality at this moment in the play's progress. It may be felt that these two claims work against one another: for how can we acknowledge characters if we cannot go up to them, cannot put ourselves in their presence—must not any such acknowledge-ment be essentially incomplete? On Cavell's view, however, this does not show that the concept of acknowledgement is misplaced in this context; it shows rather what acknowledgement in a theatre (as opposed to acknowledgement in 'real' life) amounts to. 'When we had the idea that acknowledgement must be incomplete in a theatre, it was as if we felt prevented from approaching the figures to whom we respond. But we are not prevented; we merely in fact, or in convention, do not approach them. Acknowledgement is complete without that; that is the beauty of theatre' (*DK* 105).

What *is* true is that in a theatre something is omitted which must be made good outside. Both inside and outside the theatre, we confront someone's pain or joy, and that involves responding in some way to the claim they make upon us; but outside the theatre, actually acknowledg-ing someone's pain (as opposed to responding to it by avoiding it and them) is inseparable from revealing ourselves to that person, allowing ourselves to be seen, making ourselves present to them (this is what, on Cavell's reading, *King Lear* is telling us)—and this is not possible inside the theatre. So what counts as the expression or completion of acknowl-edgement there?

Here, we need to examine more closely the force of the claim that we are not in the presence of the characters in a play. This claim amounts to pointing out that we cannot go up to them, that nothing would count as approaching them: there is no path from our position to theirs, we and they do not occupy the same space. But there is a sense in which we and they can and do occupy the same time. Of course, the events of the play may be set in the past or the future; but the characters in the play live through a sequence of moments each of which constitutes the present for them, and if the audience is genuinely to confront those characters, it must confront each presented moment of the play's events as the present moment of its characters. If, for example, I import my knowledge of the play's ending into my judgement of a character's motives at its outset; or if I regard events already presented as determining present and future events so that I completely expunge the character's freedom to have chosen differently at each moment of decision and action; or if in assessing her deeds I apply an a priori grid of expectations which frees me from attending to the specificity of her responses—then I fail to acknowledge her and her fellows as particular individuals located but not locked in time and space; I fail to acknowledge them as people.

I will say: we are not in, and cannot put ourselves in, the presence of the characters; but we are in, or can put ourselves in, their *present*. It is in making their present ours, their moments as they occur, that we complete our acknowledgement of them. But this requires making their present *theirs* . . . In failing to find the character's present we fail to make *him* present. Then he is indeed a fictitious creature, a figment of my imagination, like all the other people in my life whom I find I have failed to know, have known wrong. (*DK* 108)

However, the events of *King Lear* have taught us that the completion of acknowledgement of others involves self-revelation, so there must be an analogue of this inside the theatre; making the characters present must involve allowing (something about) ourselves to be seen. Clearly, no personal revelations are required—no whispered or shouted declarations of the identity of the Cordelia in my life; but it may be that in making the characters present I reveal something about myself which is impersonal—something I share with others (including them). This is Cavell's suggestion:

What I reveal is something I share with everyone else present with me at what is happening: that I am hidden and silent and fixed. In a word, that there is a point at which I am helpless before the acting and suffering of others. But I know the true point of my helplessness only if I have acknowledged totally the fact and the true cause of their suffering. Otherwise I am not emptied of help but withholding it . . . In another word, what is revealed is my separateness from what is happening to them; that I am I, and here. It is only in this perception of them as separate from me that I make them present. That I make them *other*, and face them.

And the point of my presence at these events is to join in confirming this separateness. Confirming it as neither a blessing nor a curse, but a fact, the fact of having one life—not one rather than two, but this one rather than any other. I cannot confirm it alone. Rather, it is the nature of this tragedy that its actors have to confirm their separateness alone, through isolation, the denial of others. What is purged is my difference from others, in everything but separateness. (*DK* 109)

This suggests a complex relation between acknowledgement inside and outside the theatre. In a theatre, it is not possible for us to go up to the people who require acknowledgement from us; we can neither declare our presence to them nor hide it, as we must outside the theatre. We might express this difference by saying that, in the theatre, our hiddenness, silence, and isolation are enforced—they are its conditions. But then these conditions can be thought of as literalizing the conditions we enact and exact outside the theatre, the conditions that we so often enforce on ourselves and upon others; so that a failure of acknowledgement outside the theatre can be thought of as a theatricalization of others—leaving ourselves in darkness, converting them into characters on a stage, fictionalizing their existence. But by enforcing these conditions, theatre absolves us of responsibility for them; it relieves us, not of the necessity for acknowledgement, but of the necessity for revealing ourselves to those we acknowledge—and this relief might be thought of as providing a respite within which we can prepare ourselves to face that necessity when it confronts us outside the theatre. 'Theatre does not expect us simply to stop theatricalizing; it knows that we can theatricalize its conditions as we can theatricalize any others. But in giving us a place within which our hiddenness and silence and separation are accounted for, it gives us a chance to stop' (*DK* 104).

In other words, Cavell detects a twofold relation between our responses to Shakespearean drama and the sceptical impulse. In the first place, he detects as much scope for the expression of scepticism within the theatre as without: because it makes sense to characterize our relation to the characters in these plays in terms of (a recognizable inflexion of) the concept of acknowledgement and its cognates, it makes sense to talk of our living out a sceptical relation to those characters—whether by failing to make specific characters present to ourselves, or by denying that questions of confrontation are even at stake in our relations with fictional beings. At the same time, however, the conditions of theatre literalize the conditions we create by succumbing to scepticism outside the theatre, and so make the nature of the rest of our existence plain—make it available for us to acknowledge; and since those same conditions also define a space within which acknowledgement does not involve putting ourselves in the presence of the beings we confront, they simultaneously make the overcoming of scepticism in that space (the refusal to theatricalize theatre) more feasible, and offer the hope that such a localized recovery can be extended into the world outside theatre (can be the harbinger of a more extensive refusal to theatricalize).

In other words, this mode of poetic drama is something that Shakespeare offers his society as a medium of recovery from scepticism. This body of his expressions is designed to draw together a community from the wider community and to hold out the opportunity for its members to stop theatricalizing their existence, both inside the theatre and outside it; it creates a place within which citizens can affirm the inevitable fact of their separateness as the unity of their condition, and acknowledge their joint responsibility for the further avoidable facts of differentiation, of denial and separation, that pervade their society. In short, Cavell understands our relation to Shakespearean dramatic art in terms of his model of redemptive reading.

The Winter's Tale

This aspect of Cavell's interest in Shakespeare is woven into every one of the readings of particular plays that he has published since 'The Avoidance of Love'; and just as his understanding of the nature of scepticism is altered by its specific appearance and development in each of those plays, so his understanding of the process of redemption or recovery that the plays themselves work to achieve in their audience is differently inflected in each case. But perhaps the most important of these readings, in terms of its influence on Cavell's conception of both levels of his interpretative project, is his essay on *The Winter's Tale* entitled 'Recounting Gains, Showing Losses'.[2] The two levels come together in Cavell's interpretation of the climactic resurrection scene; but if that conjunction is to be properly appreciated, we must trace in a little more detail the nature of the play's preceding interpretation of the scepticism it seeks to overcome.

Cavell understands Leontes' jealous banishment of Hermione in just the way he understands Othello's jealous denial of Desdemona: as a

---

[2] In *IQO*; repr. in *DK*.

portrayal of scepticism. But in Leontes' case, this jealous doubt focusses on his wife through her (and his) son—his doubt about her faithfulness takes the form of a doubt about whether his child is really his; and for Cavell this means not only that the figure of Leontes provides one of the most explicit Shakespearean confirmations of his earlier claims about the nature of the sceptical impulse, but also that it places those claims within an entirely new framework. Let us begin with the confirmations. In the following passage, Cavell summarizes the play's presentation of the development of that doubt:

> Leontes' first question to his son is 'Art thou my boy?' And then he goes on to try to recognize the boy as his by their resemblance in certain marks and features, at first by comparing their noses. That speech, distracted, ends with a repetition of the earlier doubt: 'Art thou my calf?' Already here we glimpse a Shakespearean pathos, a sense that one may feel sadness enough to fill an empty world. Upon the repetition, Leontes compares their heads. These efforts are of course of no avail. Then he rules out the value of the testimony of anyone else, as if testifying that he must know for himself; and as he proceeds, he insists that his doubts are reasonable, and he is led to consider his dreams. It is all virtually an exercise out of Descartes's *Meditations*. (*DK* 203)

And as the emphasis on telling and on distinguishing marks suggests, Cavell sees the notion of criteria in the background as well as that of Cartesian exercises. Leontes' inability to recognize his son as his amounts to an inability to establish his claim to know in a best case of knowledge, an inability or an unwillingness to effect or maintain a connection between the world and the most fundamental or basic categories in terms of which he conceptualizes it. But when a best case for knowledge fails, it is not a particular claim to know that suffers a defeat: it is our general capacity to determine what counts as an instance of our concepts, our general capacity to apply language to the world. This outcome of the sceptical impulse, an inability to say whether language applies to anything—an inability to say what exists—is precisely the vision to which Leontes himself gives expression:

> Why then the world and all that's in't is nothing,
> The covering sky is nothing, Bohemia nothing,
> My wife is nothing, nor nothing have these nothings
> If this be nothing.   (i. ii. 293–6)

As Cavell has already argued, however, the recession of the world from the sceptic is something willed (even if it is something he is driven to will); it is a refusal of criteria, a refusal to accept or acknowledge the human conditions of speech, an attempt to speak outside language games. What this suggests is that Leontes *wants* not to count, wants to lose the power of relating words to the world. But why does he desire this outcome? What is it from which this nothingness gives him relief? Here, we need to recall that his jealousy is expressed as a doubt and denial of his and Hermione's son; and that this focus upon procreation is embedded in a set of terms concerning breeding, generation, and issue which ramify widely in the language of the play. These references to parturition remind us that the ability to count implies multiplicity or differentiation, and that nature's capacity to bring forth issue, to be fruitful and to multiply, is what most centrally provides that differentiation. Putting these reminders together, Cavell leads us to the conclusion that Leontes' denial of his child and his creation of a state in which counting is impossible together amount to an attempt to deny nature's fruitfulness, to a wish for a world without pregnancy or issue; scepticism is thus explicitly figured as a form of revenge upon life.

This death-dealing revenge is of course taken most immediately upon Hermione herself; so that when, in the play's closing scene, we are presented with Leontes' (at least partial) recovery from scepticism, it takes the form of his presiding over Hermione's resurrection. Cavell takes these events as a form of marriage ceremony—or more precisely, given the relation between the participants, as a ceremony of remarriage. In other words, he suggests that this play proposes simultaneously to equate (re)marriage with (re-)creation and to present marriage, thus understood, as constituting a recovery from scepticism. Accepting this interpretation depends in part upon perceiving the sense in which marriage is a form of social grafting, and so can embody a vision of legitimized natural fecundity to set in opposition to scepticism's vengeful denial of it. But it also depends upon seeing that the equation of marriage and creation which this interpretation embodies is not lacking in authoritative precedent:

Can Hermione be understood as Leontes' issue? But this is the sense—is it not?—of the passage from Genesis in which theology has taken marriage to be legitimized, in which the origin of marriage has been presented as the creation of the woman from the man. It is how they are one flesh. Then let us emphasize that this ceremony of union takes the form of a ceremony of separation, thus declaring that the question of two becoming one is just half the problem; the other half is how one becomes two. It is separation that Leontes' participation in parturition grants—that Hermione has, that there is, a life beyond his, and that she can create a life beyond his and hers, and beyond plenitude and nothingness. The final scene of *The Winter's Tale* interprets this creation as their creation by one another. (*DK* 220)

But, of course, this final scene is a creation in another sense—the creation of a dramatist; and on Cavell's view, this fact about it is also one of its preoccupations.

The resurrection of the woman is, theatrically, a claim that the composer of this play is in command of an art that brings words to life, or vice versa, and since the condition of this life is that her spectators awake their faith, we, as well as Leontes, awake, as it were, with her. A transformation is being asked of our conception of the audience of a play, perhaps a claim that we are no longer spectators, but something else, more, say participants. (*DK* 218)

Just as Leontes' faith is needed to bring about Hermione's resurrection, so our willing participation in this piece of theatre is needed to bring it, and so both her and him, to life; and just as this resurrection is impossible without Leontes' acceptance of his own re-creation, so it demands a reconceptualization of our own parts in this drama. It demands that we see ourselves in Leontes, see ourselves both as participating in his desire for revenge upon life and as capable of overcoming that desire; it demands that we acknowledge our own power of life and death, both in this theatre and outside it. Shakespeare calls us to recognize his theatre as holding out to his society the possibility of overcoming the scepticism which engulfs Leontes; but its power to do so is not one which can operate without us and our faith in its power—and even then, its power is not one whose successful exercise can be guaranteed.

Some good readers of this play who would like to believe in it further than they can, declare themselves unconvinced that this final scene 'works' (as it is typically put). But I take some mode of uncertainty just here to be in the logic of the scene, as essential to its metaphysics as to the working of its theatre. Its working is no more the cause of our conviction, or participation, than it is their result; and our capacity for participation is precisely a way of characterizing the method no less than the subject of this piece of theatre. (*DK* 220)

Thus far, I think we can say, *The Winter's Tale* offers an unusually clear grounding for the claim that the nature, development, and overcoming of scepticism (as this is specified in Cavell's writings) is both a central topic within and a central part of our relation to Shakespearean theatre. But the form in which Leontes' sceptical jealousy is given expression also provides resources for deepening and altering our sense of its significance. For doubting whether one's child is one's own is simply not a doubt to which a woman has access: it is the doubt of a father, a man's anxiety. And this suggests that scepticism is not a female business at all.

Prior to *The Winter's Tale*, the centrality of a relationship between a man and a woman in Shakespeare's portrayal of scepticism (most obviously in *King Lear* and *Othello*) was read by Cavell primarily in terms of the fact that such a relationship emblematized a best case of knowing (i.e. acknowledging) other minds, which in turn emblematized human knowledge (i.e. acceptance) of the external world. What mattered about these pairs of people was the fact that they were a pair—and so that one of them could be seen, in accordance with the model of redemptive reading, as finding and losing a relation to himself and to the world according to his capacity to acknowledge his other in her body of expressions; but the further fact, that the person who succumbed to scepticism was a man and that the person who was simultaneously immune to and victimized by it was a woman, was (although not by any means ignored) not similarly foregrounded. What Leontes' spiritual trajectory suggests is that such foregrounding is no longer avoidable— that there is an as yet untraced intimacy between the economy of scepticism and knowledge and the economy of relations between men and women.

It suggests, to begin with, that the male sceptic's tendency to engage in a jealous interrogation and victimization of a woman is not just a contingent result of his madness but is internal to his motives for succumbing to it. More specifically, it suggests that the woman's immunity to scepticism may be precisely what brings about her victimization by the male sceptic—the man jealously desiring to possess what he conceives of as immunizing knowledge that he lacks. Or perhaps (following Freud's equation of the production of a child with female sexual fulfilment—an equation present, according to Cavell, in Shakespeare's play), Leontes' obsessive desire to be convinced that he fathered Hermione's child should be read as a desire to be certain that Hermione finds her satisfaction in him—as if the man can find a proof of his own existence only through such an acknowledgement by and from the woman. However, such suggestions would require reformulation if two matters which they take for granted were placed under question. In the first place, Hermione's immunity to Leontes' specific brand of sceptical doubt need not be read as entailing that scepticism is a male affair; it may rather be read as entailing only that *that form of scepticism* is a male affair. So it is open to us to argue that scepticism might none the less have a female inflexion, one given expression in relation either to a different object (e.g. not one's child but the identity of the *father* of one's child) or a different passion (e.g. not doubt or jealousy but love—a love that is as unconditioned, as hyberbolic, as Leontes' jealous doubt). And second, instead of talking of men and women, we could equally well talk of the male and female sides of the human character, and thus conceptualize the differing inflexions and logics of the forms of scepticism we have distinguished in terms of their relation to the masculine and feminine aspects of each human individual rather than as being inaccessible to one or other half of the human race.

Clearly, these are only some of the issues and questions which arise when the notion that scepticism is inflected by gender comes into play; and (setting aside his reading of *Antony and Cleopatra*) Cavell has on the whole not utilized Shakespearean texts in his attempts to order and answer them. He has instead turned to certain regions of psychoanalysis and cinema; and we shall do the same.

8

Psychoanalysis: Practices of Recovery

The concepts and practices of psychoanalysis have fed into Cavell's work from its earliest stages, although it is only in recent years that their intersection with philosophy as he conceives it (as well as with his conception of other domains and disciplines in which he has a stake) has become an explicit focus of his writings. In terms of my interest in the matter, it will be useful to distinguish three different levels or dimensions on which this influence has operated.

Psychoanalytic Readings and Reading as Psychoanalysis

On one level, specific Freudian diagnostic and therapeutic insights have helped to guide Cavell's readings of specific texts and the interpersonal relationships that are presented in them. I mentioned earlier that Cavell's epistemological interpretations of Shakespearean drama have invoked psychoanalytic concepts such as narcissism to identify components or facets of sceptical doubt; and a crucial part of the flexibility and subtlety evinced in his readings of specific speeches and behaviour patterns in these plays derives from his acceptance of such notions as repression, denial, the formative influence of maternal figures, and the intersubjective validity of Freud's analyses of dream-narratives and other symbolic systems (Cavell's interpretation of Leontes' doubt about his fatherhood of Hermione's child as an expression of anxiety about the reality and trajectory of the woman's desire is a key example of this last strategy). And much the same can be said—as we shall see in the next chapter—about Cavell's readings of specific films; in general, his work as a reader of texts is imbued with a sense (often acknowledged by Freud himself) that the poets and artists preceded Freud in many of his most important discoveries.

We might summarize this first level of intersection by saying that Cavell regards psychoanalysis as providing a set of indispensable tools for establishing the meanings of texts—for identifying their basic structure and content. But he also regards it as an essential resource for understanding the general relationship between a reader and a text; in short, for Cavell, psychoanalysis is not just a means of generating readings, it is also a paradigm for the general business of reading. To put things more precisely, he understands (a certain dimension or ideal version of) the relationship between a reader and a text as being strongly analogous to the relationship between analysand and analyst in psychoanalytic therapy.

But, as Cavell begins to spell out in an essay entitled 'The Politics of Interpretation', the analogy he has in mind locates the text rather than its reader in the place occupied by the analyst; on his picture, it is the reader who is analysed.

I imagine that [a] credible psychological model of [reading] will have to be psychoanalytic in character; yet psychoanalytic interpretations of texts have seemed typically to tell us something we more or less already knew, to leave us pretty much where we were before we read. It ought to help to see that from the point of view of psychoanalytic therapy the situation of reading has typically been turned around, that it is not first of all the text that is subject to interpretation, but we in the gaze or hearing of the text. I think good readers, or a certain kind of reader, have always known and acted on this, as in Thoreau's picture of reading by exposure to being read. But it is my impression that those who emphasize the psychoanalytic possibilities here tend to forget what a text is, the matter of its autonomy; while those who shun psychoanalysis tend not to offer a practice of reading that I can understand as having the consequence of therapy.

The practice suggested to me by turning the picture of interpreting a text into one of being interpreted by it would I think be guided by three principal ideas: first, access to the text is provided not by the mechanism of projection but by that of transference (which is why the accusation that in one's extended interpretations one is turning a work of art into a Rorschach test is desperately wrong but precisely significant and deserving of careful response); second, the pleasures of appreciation are succeeded by the risks of seduction; and third, the risks are worth running because the goal of the encounter is not consummation but freedom. Freedom from what, to do what? In the picture of psychoanalytic therapy, casting ourselves as its patient, its sufferer, its victim (according to the likes of Emerson and Heidegger, this is the true form of philosophical thinking), the goal is freedom from the person of the author ... Presumably we would not require a therapy whose structure partakes of seduction, to undo seduction, unless we were already seduced. (*TOS* 51–3)

There is much to comment on in these lines. First, how are we to understand the crucial difference between projection and transference? According to Laplanche and Pontalis, projection is 'an operation whereby qualities, feelings, wishes or even "objects", which the subject refuses to recognise or rejects in himself, are expelled from the self and located in another person or thing. Projection so understood is a defence of very primitive origin which may be seen at work especially in paranoia, but also in "normal" modes of thought such as superstition' (*LP* 349). Transference, on the other hand, is 'a process of actualisation of unconscious wishes. Transference uses specific objects and operates in the framework of a specific relationship established with these objects. Its context *par excellence* is the analytic situation . . . Classically, the transference is acknowledged to be the terrain on which all the basic problems of a given analysis play themselves out: the establishment, modalities, interpretation and resolution of the transference are in fact what define the cure' (*LP* 455).

On these definitions of Cavell's terms, it should be clear what is significant about conflating projection and transference and what is desperately wrong with that conflation. Both projection and transference involve the actualization of unconscious wishes in the context of a relationship with another entity, and if a subject employs projective mechanisms generally (e.g. projecting certain fears and wishes, or certain unacknowledged aspects of her own character, on the objects, institutions, and people around her and then relating to them in terms of those projections) they will inevitably be activated in the context of a relationship with an analyst. But projection is a defence, a means of denying or rejecting unconscious material by locating it outside the subject; and in so far as the subject understands others only in terms of her projections upon them, it also involves a denial of their separateness and autonomy. In itself, therefore, it is merely an extreme manifestation of the problems which that material poses for the subject, a failure of self-acknowledgement which leads to a failure to acknowledge others; it is simply reiterated whenever the psychic pressure becomes unbearable and so offers no possibility of development or amelioration. When, however, such mechanisms are placed within the context of a psychoanalytic relationship, the entity upon whom the projections are made is no longer unaware of the mechanisms at work and incapable of understanding how they are functioning in the subject's world; it is someone who is equipped to bear up under them, capable of maintaining a relative autonomy under the onslaught and responding to it in ways which might disrupt the mere reiteration of the mechanism. In such a context it becomes possible to *analyse* the subject's projections, to work with and upon them in ways which are directed towards the goal of eliminating the problems which led to their employment in the first place.

None of this means that transferential relationships cannot deteriorate into merely projective ones; it is perfectly possible for an analyst to fail in her efforts to maintain her autonomy under projection—perhaps she fails to see the mechanism at work, perhaps she fails to hold back from responding to that projection in its own terms, i.e. the terms that the analysand is forcing upon her. If, then, we transpose this psychoanalytic model to the domain of reading, we must acknowledge that projective interpretations are precisely the threat to which reading in accord with this model is most vulnerable; if one believes that access to the text involves being prepared to allow that one's own repressed or denied unconscious wishes may be found to be part of that text's concern or topic, it is easy to see that one might slip into forcing the text to conform to one's own wishes. But by the same token, if one is alive to this risk, if one recognizes that the purpose of this process is to allow one's unconscious wishes to be identified and put in question rather than to be unquestioningly reflected back to one by the text, then the possibility of therapeutic progress lies open.

It is this process of allowing oneself to be questioned or interpreted by the text which is part of what Cavell means by respecting its autonomy; the relation between reader and text is dialogical and dialectical, and if either party is to be thought of as possessed of initial authority, it must be the text (the analyst) rather than the reader. But another aspect of the text's autonomy emerges if we return briefly to the psychoanalytic paradigm; for, as Cavell points out elsewhere,[1] wherever transference is to be found, counter-transference must also be expected.

The idea of countertransference here is meant as a gloss on a moment in an earlier essay of mine ... in which I interpret reading as a process of interpreting one's transference to (as opposed to one's projection onto) a text. That idea implies that the fantasy of a text's analyzing its reader is as much the guide of a certain ambition of reading ... as that of the reader's analyzing the text. In now specifying the transference in question as of the nature of countertransference (that is, as a response to an other's transference to me) I do not deny the reversal of direction implied in the idea of the text as my reader, but I rather specify that that direction already depends upon a further understanding of a text's relation to me, and that that further relation cannot be said either (or can be said both) to be prior or/and posterior to any approach (or say attraction) to a text. (*TP* 257–8)

---

[1] In a footnote to an excerpt from his essay 'Psychoanalysis and Cinema: The Melodrama of the Unknown Woman', in *TP*.

Laplanche and Pontalis define counter-transference as 'the whole of the analyst's unconscious reactions to the individual analysand—especially to the analysand's own transference' (*LP* 92); and of course, the autonomy of the analyst and the dialogical nature of the relationship between analysand and analyst makes it inevitable that such counter-transference should occur. Indeed, one might say that the cure itself depends primarily upon the management of the dialectic of transference and counter-transference. As Cavell points out, this notion does not reverse the directedness initially suggested by the transferential nature of analysis—it is still the case that the analyst analyses—but it does further specify the nature of that analytical process as one in which the analyst is as subject to the mechanisms of the unconscious as is the analysand. More specifically, just as the analysand approaches analysis with certain preconceptions and expectations as well as certain established projective mechanisms (i.e. engages in some sort of initial transference to the analyst, for example understood as an authority figure), so the analyst will approach each analysis with some conception of her own position in relation to the analysand and of the structure or form of the material which the analysand is likely to transfer to her (i.e. engages in some sort of initial transference to the analysand, for example as someone in need of certain sorts of help). But this aspect of the analyst's transference to the analysand will inevitably shape or inflect the latter's own transference to the analyst, so that the question of which transference has priority will have no obvious answer; for if counter-transference is both a response to the other's transference and a factor partly determining its nature, then it cannot be said to be either prior or posterior to it.

What might these complexities lead us to expect if we adopt a psychoanalytic model of reading? Most importantly, it suggests that any reader approaching a text in accordance with this model will expect the text itself to contain an image (or fantasy) of its readers—will expect part of a text's conception of itself to be its conception of its readers—and will understand that this conception is always already shaping her transference to that text. We have already seen how this idea guides much of Cavell's work on Shakespeare, and we shall see its centrality in his work on Emerson and Thoreau a little later.

So much for Cavell's conception of—and emphasis upon—the autonomy of the text throughout one's interpretations of it. However, the notion of transference upon which that conception is founded was only one of three ideas which he held to be central to his psychoanalytic model of reading; and the other two help him to specify the sense in which such reading is therapeutic or redemptive. More precisely, Cavell regards one's transferences to texts as a matter of submitting to their seduction in order to attain one's freedom. The notion of seduction is clearly central to psychoanalytic therapy—in part because it operates upon the desires of the analysand (attempting to detach them from certain objects and obstacles), in part because it utilizes her desires in order to do so (her desires to submit to, to react against, and otherwise to transfer to her analyst); the analysis is essentially a matter of seducing the analysand away from that which has already seduced her, with the analyst (by virtue of the transferential relationship) functioning as a provisional object for the refocussing of those fixated desires. But if a therapeutic practice conceives of itself as reorienting our desire, it clearly presupposes both that desire is its business or medium and that our problem is that our desire is already oriented wrongly; in other words, that for which we require its therapy must be some species of seduction to which we have already succumbed and which is conceived of as debilitating, obstructive, or otherwise harmful. These implications can be thought of as further specifications of the analyst's counter-transference; accordingly, in terms of Cavell's model of reading, they constitute further specifications of the text's image of its readers.

This leaves the question of our freedom—the freedom purportedly given to us by psychoanalytic therapy. Cavell specifies this not just as a freedom from our misaligned or fixated desires, but also as a freedom from the person of the analyst. The practice itself depends upon an initial and continued (even if continually developing) relationship with the person of the analyst, one in which profoundly powerful emotions and fantasies are at work in the transferential relationship; but the cure crucially depends upon going beyond that relationship—upon taking everything that the analyst as representative of the practice can be and do for you, but taking it in order to maintain yourself in the orientations and relationships which your newly freed and acknowledged desires desire. In other words, the message which the analyst delivers must not be entangled with her person in a way which derogates from the analysand's autonomy. Translated into the domain of our relations with texts, such a conception suggests that the redemptive or therapeutic message of the text must itself be detached from the messenger. It suggests that the (author of the) text must not attempt to assert the wrong sort of authority over us, that a part of its message must be that each reader must find her own way to achieve and to make use of the freedom it attempts to bestow; the text must, in other words, respect the autonomy of its readers. And this in turn suggests that its initial attractiveness or seductiveness must be matched by its eventual repulsiveness or aversiveness.   .

Apart from the ideas of transference, seduction, and freedom, just two further elements are needed to complete our sketch of Cavell's understanding of the nature of psychoanalysis and so of the nature of a therapeutic reading practice moulded in its image—the concepts of the uncanny and of mourning. Freud defines the phenomenon of the uncanny as that of the return of the repressed familiar; and this experience is central to his understanding of psychoanalytic practice precisely because the aim of that practice is to facilitate the recovery (the return) of unconscious (because repressed) material from the analysand, and the mark of its success is the analysand's free acknowledgement of that material as hers (as familiar). In effect, then, this experience is what the transferential relationship is designed to elicit; and correspondingly, experiences of the uncanny will constitute a sign of insight and progress in any reading which takes the psychoanalytic relationship as its model. Cavell, once again utilizing words of Emerson's, characterizes it as an experience of our own rejected thoughts coming back to us with a certain alienated majesty. The concept of mourning is similarly central to psychoanalytic practice; for the goal of identifying, reiterating, and thereby unfreezing each and every one of the analysand's fixated desires in order to bestow on her the freedom to attach her desires elsewhere is a brief summary of what Freud means by mourning.

... the repetition of each fact in one's attachment to an object gone, an effort to undo or release the ties of association strand by strand, is part of the work of realization of loss that Freud and principally after him Melanie Klein recognize as the work of mourning. They call it reality-testing, a subjection to the verdict of reality that one's attachment to an object is to undergo severing ... mourning is the only alternative to our nostalgias, in which we will otherwise despair and die. (*TOS* 54)

Thus, the psychoanalytic process is pictured as an attempt to undo the self's despairing attachment to a pattern of desires which ties it to outmoded, non-existent, or otherwise illusory objects and thereby reduces its present and its future to a mechanical, deathly reiteration of its past; it is an attempt to transform this lethal nostalgia by means of a mourning process which opens the self to possibilities of change and rebirth. What is to be mourned is a fixated (state of the) self, and what is to be hoped for is the subject's freedom to attain a new (state of the) self.

These ideas—transference, seduction, and freedom, mourning and the uncanny—thus form the psychoanalytic foundation of Cavell's image or paradigm (or fantasy?) of reading; as we shall see later, he finds confirmation of their validity in the texts of American Romanticism—in Emerson and Thoreau—and it is clear that the specific readings of plays and films which form a substantial part of his own *œuvre* are intended to be results of the model at work. But it is also worth underlining the degree to which this psychoanalytically derived model converges upon the model of philosophical reading (or rather, of philosophical thinking as reading) which I earlier labelled 'recounting criteria', and which I attempted to show can be developed solely from the resources provided by Cavell's understanding of Wittgensteinian criteria and the nature of scepticism in its philosophical guise. The main points of convergence can quickly be spelt out.

The practice of ordinary language philosophy is structured as a dialogue (whether between two selves or between two sides or voices of the same self) in which the person in the grip of philosophical confusion is reminded of what she would say when; in other words, she is recalled to a knowledge (of criteria, and so of herself as a competent speaker) which she was not aware that she possessed, by an interlocutor whose therapeutic power is founded upon a claim to know such things about her—a claim to know that she knows something that she doesn't know that she knows. Under the spell of scepticism, she denies or represses that (self-)knowledge, and as a result she loses her ability to differentiate objects and people from one another and from herself; she creates a frozen, fixated world—one from which she has withdrawn the investment of her interest (her desire). Her recovery, the return of the repressed familiar, requires that she rotate the axis of her investigation around the fixed point of her real need (her true desire): she must acknowledge the relative autonomy of language, other people, and the world, and reinterpret them by allowing herself to be reinterpreted by them—read them by allowing herself to be read by them. Philosophically speaking, this means allowing herself to be reminded of her criteria and so of the true nature of that for which they are criteria; she will thereby acknowledge the world's capacity to elicit or attract the investment of her interest in it (her desire for it), to seduce her from her self-imposed fixated state and free her for the relative autonomy which is rightfully hers. But this reorientation is not a once-for-all event; it is rather a practice to be employed on each occasion of her being overcome by scepticism. Recounting criteria is thus a form of life-giving repetition which stands in opposition to the mechanical, deathly fixation of the sceptic.

The parallels with Cavell's psychoanalytic model of reading thus extend to every one of the five concepts we identified as central to it—transference, seduction, freedom, mourning, and the uncanny all find their analogues in the practice of recounting criteria. At the very least, Cavell's awareness of the structure of either one of these practices must have sharpened his eye for its twin in the other; but, as I stressed at the beginning of this part of the book, his view is very definitely not that these parallels reveal that philosophy is really psychoanalysis or vice versa—that no distinction can or should any longer be drawn between philosophical and psychoanalytical perspectives. Drawing such a conclusion would be no more sensible than concluding, on the basis of the parallels Cavell unearthed between ordinary language philosophy and discourse in the domains of art, morality, and politics, that the distinctions between these domains no longer existed. None the less, such parallels do suggest that the relevant domains of discourse are more intimately related than they are likely to acknowledge. And in the specific case of philosophy and psychoanalysis, the fact that the two perspectives have developed a set of concepts and a self-understanding which manifest a real family resemblance strongly suggests that they are each responding in their own distinctive way to the same environmental pressures or questions. More precisely, Cavell is concerned to argue that these paradigmatically modern practices are responding to what he takes to be the most fundamental cultural problematic of modernity—scepticism.

A Reading of Psychoanalysis

The above claim introduces us to the third level of intersection between Cavell's work and his conception of psychoanalysis. In his view, just as the Cartesian Meditations and the Shakespearean corpus signalled the simultaneous advent of scepticism and of attempts to overthrow it at the inception of the modern era, so the development of the Freudian science of the mind can be seen as a further stage in the story of scepticism's impact on post-Enlightenment culture.

It is from a perspective in which our culture appears as having entered on a path of radical scepticism (hence on a path to deny this path) from the time of, say, Descartes and Shakespeare—or, say, from the time of the fall of Kings and the rise of the new science and the death of God—that I see, late in this history, the advent of psychoanalysis as the place, perhaps the last place, in which the human psyche as such (the idea that there is a life of the mind, hence a death) receives its proof. And it receives proof of its existence in the only form in which that psyche can (any longer) believe it—namely, as essentially unknown to itself, say unconscious. As Freud puts it in the closing pages of *The Interpretation of Dreams:* 'The unconscious is the true psychical reality'... This can seem like a mere piece of rhetoric on Freud's part, arbitrarily under-rating the reality of consciousness and promoting the unconscious out of something like a prejudice that promotes the reality of atomic particles over the reality of flesh and blood and its opposable things—and certainly on less, or no, compelling intellectual grounds. Whereas, seen in relation to, or as a displacement of, philosophy, Freud's assertion declares that for the mind to lose the psychoanalytic intuition of itself as unconscious would be for it to lose the intuition that it exists. (*IIS* 25–6)

Even if there were any way of lessening the audacity of this claim, it would be entirely contrary to Cavell's intentions to make use of it; his central purpose is precisely to subvert our sense that we fully understand the nature and cultural significance of psychoanalysis, to recover a sense of the extraordinariness of this (by now) familiar enterprise. We can, however, make his claim seem less implausible if we relate it to two key elements of our discussion thus far.

The first such element is provided by the structural parallels unearthed earlier in this chapter between psychoanalysis and philosophical reading; the degree of family resemblance—at the level of basic concepts, method, and general orientation—between Freudian analytical practice and redemptive reading, together with the explicit connection established between such reading and recovery from scepticism, is itself enough to generate some conviction in Cavell's claim. But this is much strengthened by the second element, which emerged in his discussion of scepticism about other minds when the constraints imposed upon the range of application of our psychological concepts by our conception of 'normal' human behaviour were under examination. Here, the point was made that those constraints are ones determined by us, for which we are responsible; faced, for example, with the aberrant behaviour of the pain-connoisseur, we face a choice—either her behaviour is an abnormal sort of pain-behaviour, or she is abnormal; and our position is not cognitively deficient in any way—no one could be in a better position to decide than we are now. No one can tell us just how far to go in our attempts to understand her, to make sense of her world, before exiling her from our own. In effect, what Cavell's audacious reading of psychoanalysis does is to honour that practice as an institutionalized commitment to extend and deepen the range of the human capacity to make sense of seemingly aberrant behaviour as a part (however distorted or twisted a part) of our shared world. For the Freudian project as a whole can be characterized in the terms appropriate to the clinical situations in which it originated: the successful attempt to render humanly comprehensible (as a pre-condition for curing) modes of pathological behaviour with no detectable physiological causes and no evident psychological meaning. And for this reason, Freud can be thought of as having constructed a concrete method for acknowledging the humanity of seemingly aberrant others; and psychoanalysis can then stand as an example of how the seemingly unintelligible Romantic myth of acknowledging the other (simply) as a human being can be given practical content, an example of what acknowledging the sheer humanity of the other might look like. In so far as that myth emerged as a crucial element in the characterization of a best case of knowing other minds, and so as something whose enactment seemed vital to the overcoming of the sceptical impulse in that domain, psychoanalysis can thus be seen to earn the title of a practice devoted to the fight against scepticism.

We might also think of the matter in relation to the history of philosophy. Descartes's attempt to overcome scepticism was based upon a picture of the mind as essentially conscious; but his attempt failed, and no further attempts in the same vein have avoided that failure. But psychoanalytic practice embodies an intuition that there are regions of the mind which go beyond or before consciousness—indeed it is so fundamentally dependent upon that intuition that it can be thought to stake the whole of its existence on their existence; and as a result, any success that it may have in generating effective therapy is by the same token a practical proof of the existence of the unconscious mind, and so a practical proof of the existence of the mind (as essentially unconscious).

It is important to appreciate the precise form, and so the precise limits, of this founding psychoanalytic claim. On the one hand, the therapeutic practice it motivates depends upon its being possible to bring some of the contents of the unconscious to consciousness, i.e. depends upon its being possible to lift the barriers of repression and denial which generate obsessions, neuroses, etc.; but on the other, the theoretical work which underpins it suggests that the construction of society and culture presupposes the repression of certain human desires and so the creation and maintenance of an unconscious mind in every individual. In other words, psychoanalysis proves that the mind exists as unknown; it does not prove that it exists as unknowable, although it does presuppose that it will never exist as fully or completely known, known once and for all. The process of bringing to light that which conditions the conscious lives of individuals may always need to be reiterated; and that standing need highlights an essential ambiguity in any proof of the mind which reveals it as essentially unknown. For, as such a formulation implies, in the absence of successful psychoanalytic therapy, many people (or rather, all of us much of the time) are cut off from whilst being unknowingly determined by the unconscious regions of our minds; and according to the terms Cavell has set up, this means that most of us most of the time do not enact our existence—we do not know that we exist, and so we do not exist. As a result, Cavell is moved to describe the achievement of successful psychoanalytic therapy in the following terms: 'In Freud's practice, one human being represents to another all that that other has conceived of humanity in his or her life and moves with that other toward an expression of the conditions that condition that utterly specific life' (*IIS* 28). But what the terms of this heroic vision imply is a vision of what human life in a culture which has not accepted psychoanalytic insights and practice must be like: a world in which people's true individuality is not acknowledged (and so not enacted) by them, one in which, accordingly, there are no true individuals—a world in which individuals exist only as ghosts and haunt their own lives. It is a world in which scepticism holds sway.

Again, it is worth reminding ourselves that many of these elements in the psychoanalytic vision of modern culture and of its own practice are ones which Cavell has built into his portrait of philosophical reading. The practical nature of the Freudian proof accords with Cavell's view (examined in Chapter 6) that even Descartes's 'cogito' embodies a picture of thought as proving one's existence only if one enacts it; and the reliance that Freud's practical proof places upon a region of the mind which, although initially unknown, can and must be recalled to consciousness through dialogue with another is strongly reminiscent of the reliance placed upon just such a region of the minds of competent speakers in the philosophical practice of recounting criteria. Moreover, if the Freudian practice can be thought of as one of acknowledging the conditions which condition each individual's utterly specific life, the Wittgensteinian philosopher's reminders of what we say when can be thought of as representing to any given interlocutor the specific linguistic conditions of her life as a speaker (and so as an embodied mind). Finally, since the practice of philosophical reading understands itself as a practice of being read—since the practitioners of such philosophical thinking conceive of its enactment as a matter of suffering or being victimized by thought—that activity can be said already to have incorporated the element of passivity that is so fundamental to the Freudian emphasis upon transference.

Despite the force of these parallels, Cavell is perfectly aware that his claim that philosophy and psychoanalysis can be seen as convergent and so as competing perspectives will meet with opposition from both philosophers and psychoanalysts. Freud himself was at pains to distinguish his enterprise from that of the philosophical tradition, and to do so at precisely the points at which Cavell sees most convergence, e.g. with respect to his conception of the unconscious; and philosophy will not find it easy to see the threat of competition in the therapeutic efforts of an empirical science. But Cavell's concern is not simply to draw the two perspectives together: it is to permit them to learn from one another. His model of philosophical reading is in effect an epitome of what Cavell thinks psychoanalysis can teach philosophy; and he regards certain concepts and distinctions that are central to psychoanalysis (e.g. the division between appearance and reality, or between fantasy and reality) as ripe for further philosophical work. In short, the encounter which he has attempted to engineer is meant to be of benefit to both parties; for a discipline, as for an individual, acknowledgement of one's others as other is crucial to enhancing one's self-knowledge.

However, in his most recent work, the main issue in this weave of cross-questioning to which Cavell has devoted himself is the role of psychoanalytic practice in the development and overcoming of scepticism; and the feature of that practice which has seemed most significant to him in this respect is its emphasis upon women. Given his insistence that psychoanalysis is now the central cultural place in which human existence receives its proof, it would be difficult for him to avoid noticing that the series of case histories and psychopathological studies upon which Freud founded his science are primarily studies of women. When this fact is seen in the light of Cavell's reading of *The Winter's Tale*, and its revelation that philosophical scepticism is inflected by gender, then the parallel between Leontes' persecution of Hermione and Freud's interrogation of women such as Dora is equally difficult to ignore: 'It is at this juncture that psychoanalysis ... can be taken as asking of the woman: How is it that you escape doubt? What certainty encloses you, whatever your other insecurities, from just this torture?' (*IIS* 32).

In so far as psychoanalysis provides a proof of human existence, the centrality of women at the site of that proof suggests that this mode of enacting or affirming human existence is to be thought of as female; so that part of what psychoanalysis uncovers is that, at this late stage in Western culture, human existence can only be proved through the adoption or acceptance of the position of the woman. Then, however, questions arise about the relevance of Freud's own gender; for if the proof that psychoanalysis provides is from the female side of human existence, then Freud's need to interrogate women in order to elicit it suggests that he does not have it in his own possession—that his interrogations represent the male side of human existence, jealously desiring something that men think of themselves as lacking. The structural analogy here between Freud and Leontes suggests that Freud is, to this degree, succumbing to rather than overcoming scepticism— that the presence of women at the origins of psychoanalysis shows the sceptical provenance of that practice. And this suggestion seems to receive confirmation in the fact that Freud's avowed practice in case histories such as that of Dora involves the imputation that his patients possess knowledge of some sort—for (as we saw in earlier chapters) it is precisely a mark of scepticism to think of the other's certainty of her own existence as her possession of a piece of knowledge which one lacks oneself.

However, Cavell thinks that such a conclusion, although not false, is importantly incomplete; for it fails to take seriously the idea we mentioned when discussing *The Winter's Tale*—namely, that the gender-inflexion of scepticism could be read as relating not to men and women but rather to the male and female sides of human character. Viewed from that perspective, the fact that Freud's women patients seem to manifest an immunity to sceptical doubt will prompt only the more cautious conclusion that they are immune to masculine versions of scepticism rather than to scepticism *per se*; if the passion of doubt cannot express a feminine sense of separation from others and from the world, perhaps another passion (e.g. love) can. And the question of who wants to know what the woman knows, the identity of her sceptical interrogator, may require a similarly cautious answer; for Freud may then be representative not of men as opposed to women but of the masculine as opposed to the feminine side of human nature.

In fact, Cavell goes on to suggest that Freud might sometimes even be attempting to represent or take up that feminine side of human nature, even when he seems most vulnerable to the charge of enacting male persecution of women. In the Dora case, for example, Freud gives a fictitious name to his patient and explicitly invokes as his paradigm his sister's choice (and imposition) of a new name for one of her servants. This can easily be read as Freud treating his patient as if she were his servant; but Cavell thinks that another motive can as easily be imputed to Freud even here.

> A less impatient interpretation would have turned Freud's act of naming around again, taking it not as, or not alone as, a wish to dominate a woman, but as a confession that he is thinking of himself in the case through an identification with his sister. As if the knowledge of the existence of a woman is to be made on the basis of already enlisting oneself on that side. (*IIS* 34)

If the psychoanalytic proof of human existence invokes not the female but the feminine side of humanity, then that proof is not unavailable to the male side of humanity. What is required is that men renounce their present identification with the masculine version of scepticism and avail themselves of the feminine side of their own character. They will thereby gain access to a viable mode (according to psychoanalysis, the only viable mode in the present state of human culture) of simultaneously enacting their own existence and acknowledging the existence of other men and women. On this reading, if human existence in general (and the existence of women in particular) is at present unknown, it is at least not unknowable.

This recuperative strategy is of course fraught with difficulties: most particularly, it courts the criticism of feminist critics of Freud, who may not find the idea of Freud appropriating the identity of his sister, or of men appropriating a universally available female inflexion of humanity, as redemptive as Cavell suggests. We shall turn to this issue in more detail in the concluding chapter of this book; but for now, we must address a more pressing internal difficulty that Cavell's suggestion also confronts. For if this reading of Freud as avoiding rather than succumbing to masculine sceptical doubt is to be maintained, it must be possible to identify within his work something that opposes the (sceptical) interpretation of a woman's immunity to scepticism as her possession of a piece of knowledge. In Cavell's own work, this opposing conception is the Wittgensteinian idea that the best picture of the human soul is the human body, i.e. an emphasis upon the human body as expressive of mind; and his claim is that Freud identifies in women a particular capacity to demonstrate or enact precisely this aspect of peculiarly human existence. Freud labels this capacity 'hysterical conversion'— what he defines as 'a psycho-physical aptitude for transposing very large sums of excitation into the somatic innervation' ('The Neuro-psychoses of Defence', in *SE* iii. 50). Cavell glosses this as a capacity to modify the body as such rather than allowing the excitation to transpose into consciousness or to discharge into practice, and adds: 'While this capacity is something possessed by every psycho-physical being—that is, primarily human beings—a particular aptitude for it is required for a given sufferer to avail herself or himself of hysteria over other modes of symptom formation, as in obsessions or phobias' (*IIS* 35). It is important to note, first, that such a capacity is perfectly consistent with psychical health, and second, that it is one possessed by any human being; Freud stresses both points. None the less, he also regards this capacity as a human power possessed to a distinctive degree by women; and its exercise provides the crucial case material from which his science of the mind, of psychic reality, is built. In the Wittgensteinian terms emphasized by Cavell, such a capacity can be thought of as a talent for, and a will to, communicate; it is a capacity for expressiveness which constitutes a standing counter to the sceptical anxiety of inexpressive-ness that he found to be at the heart of the fantasy of a private language. In other words, the proof of human existence from its feminine side that psychoanalysis provides as a counter to the scepticism that can even infect its own practice is founded upon the capacity of human beings to enact their existence as specific individuals by acknowl-edging their bodies, and the specific body of their expressions, as theirs.

9
Cinema: Photography, Comedy, Melodrama

Cavell's work on cinema divides up relatively neatly into two parts or levels—analyses of specific films and examinations of the medium of cinema itself (with particular reference to the relationship between the screened image and the viewer of that image). However, his work none the less possesses a real unity: in part, this is because he finds that the films he studies themselves study their relation to their medium and its audience; but it is also because his work focusses upon precisely the same issue at both levels—that of scepticism. In other words, Cavell claims to detect a thematic doubling or mirroring which is itself a version of the doubling we examined with respect to Shakespeare: scepticism is not simply a topic examined by certain films but an issue that is central to any real understanding of our relationship to the medium of cinema. I shall begin by examining Cavell's reflections on the medium, before going on to examine the two genres of film to which he has paid most attention in his work.

Photography and Film

Cavell's first book on cinema, *The World Viewed*, is subtitled *Reflections on the Ontology of Film*, and it opens with the assumption that, since our experience of any film is an experience of a projected sequence of photographic images, the best way to understand our relationship with works produced in that medium is to examine the nature of photographs. In particular, Cavell raises the question of the relationship between a photograph and that of which it is a photograph. A photograph of an object is a visual record of that object: it is therefore similar to a painting (in that a painting too can be a visual record of an object—e.g. a portrait or a still life—and of the very same object as that captured in a photograph), and yet dissimilar (since the causal role played by that object in the making of the painting is entirely unlike its role in the taking of the photograph). We can express this dissimilarity by saying that a photograph is not so much a visual *representation* of an object (a photograph of an object does not stand for that object, and neither does it form a likeness of it) but rather a visual *transcription* of it.

The notion of 'transcription' is in part meant to highlight the fact that the photographic recording process is inherently mechanical. In this respect a photograph resembles a record of a concert or an opera, it is analogous to aural transcriptions; but it is also importantly different from them. For a record can be said to reproduce a sound, it can copy that sound perfectly; but we cannot say that a photograph reproduces a sight, or a look or an appearance. A sight, if it is anything, *is* an object (e.g. the Grand Canyon) or an extraordinary happening (e.g. the aurora borealis); and what we see, when we sight something, is not the sight of an object but the object itself.[1] To put it another way, whereas objects can be said to make sounds or have sounds, they cannot be said to make or to have sights; so there seems to be nothing of the right sort for a photograph to be a photograph *of*, short of the object itself. And yet it would seem flatly wrong to claim that a photograph presents us with the thing itself: a photograph of Garbo is not Garbo in the flesh.

Cavell gives expression to this impasse in a way which suggests how it might be overcome:

I feel like saying: Objects are too *close* to their sights to give them up for reproducing; in order to reproduce the sights they (as it were) make, you have to reproduce *them*—make a mold, or take an impression. We might, as Bazin does on occasion, try thinking of a photograph as a visual mold, or a visual impression. My dissatisfaction with that idea is, I think, that physical molds and impressions and imprints have clear procedures for getting *rid* of their originals, whereas in a photograph, the original is still as present as it ever was. Not present as it once was to the camera; but that is only a mold-machine, not the mold itself. (*WV* 20)

To say that a photographed object is not present to someone looking at the photograph as it once was to the camera, or to the person using that camera, is just to say that a photograph of Garbo is not Garbo in the flesh; to say that, none the less, the photographed object is present in the photograph is to say that when we look at a photograph of an object, we see that object (that particular real thing, the original item present to the camera) and not some surrogate for it, some aspect or apparition or likeness of it. The first claim simply notes that a photo- graph of an object and the object itself are different things (different

[1] Introducing talk of 'sense-data' at this point would not help matters, for if a photograph worked by reproducing the sense-data of its object, we could not tell a photograph of an object from the object itself.

objects); the second offers a partial elucidation of what seeing a photo-graph of an object amounts to. Such an elucidation does not commit us to asserting that we see the object *rather* than the photograph (which is what the first claim denies); it means that the object is what we see when we see a photograph of it.

As it stands, however, this elucidation does not seem to distinguish photographs from (at least some) paintings, for when we see a painting of a real object we see that which it represents; we can, for example, point to Greta Garbo in a portrait just as easily as in a photograph. But according to Cavell, visual representations and visual transcriptions of a given real object or person emphasize very different aspects of (the reality of) their subject: 'A representation emphasizes the identity of its subject, hence it may be called a likeness; a photograph emphasizes the existence of its subject, recording it, hence it is that it may be called a transcription' (WPT 4). As it stands, this formulation seems intuitively—phenomenologically—plausible but far from clear; more work is needed, and Cavell does it by focussing on a related aspect of photographs and paintings. For, of course, photographed and painted objects do not typically appear in a void; they form part of a world that is recorded along with them—and Cavell detects an analogous difference of emphasis in the way photographs and paintings record their worlds. According to him, when we look at a photograph of an object, the world in which we see it is (a portion of) the real, physical world; and this is not something that can be said about the world which we see in a painting of an object. In a still life, we see an object, and we see it in its world, the world that the painting depicts; but we do not see (the painting does not present us with) reality, with the real world. If we examine this specific claim a little more closely, what Cavell means by his general talk of differences in emphasis may become clearer.

You can always ask, pointing to an object in a photograph—a building, say—what lies behind it, totally obscured by it. This only accidentally makes sense when asked of an object in a painting. You can always ask, of an area photographed, what lies adjacent to that area, beyond the frame. This generally makes no sense asked of a painting. You can ask these questions of objects in photographs because they have answers in reality. The world of a painting is not continuous with the world of its frame; at its frame, a world finds its limits. We might say: a painting *is* a world; a photograph is *of* the world. What happens in a photograph is that *it* comes to an end. A photograph is cropped, not necessarily by paper cutting or masking but by the camera itself ... The camera, being finite, crops a portion from an indefinitely larger field; continuous portions of that field could be included in the photograph in fact taken; in principle it could all be taken. Hence objects in photographs that run past the edge do not feel cut; they are aimed at, shot, stopped live. When a photograph is cropped, the rest of the world is cut *out.* The implied presence of the rest of the world, and its explicit rejection, are as essential to the experience of a photograph as what it explicitly presents. (*WV* 23–4)

The most obvious worry with this way of distinguishing a painting from a photograph, a visual representation from a visual transcription, is that it seems to further obscure the distinction between seeing an object in a photograph and seeing the object. If the object we see in a photograph is (i.e. cannot be anything short of) the object itself, and if (the portion of) the world that we see in a photograph is (a portion of) the real world, then have we not deprived ourselves of any and all means of specifying the difference between seeing a particular portion or arrangement of the world and looking at a photograph of it?

According to Cavell, this worry results from asking the wrong question—or more precisely, from looking for the wrong sort of answer to it. He summarizes his ground for this judgement when he attempts to characterize our relationship to the world of a photograph projected on a surface or screen. 'A screen is a barrier ... It screens me from the world it holds—that is, makes me invisible. And it screens that world from me—that is, screens its existence from me. That the projected world does not exist (now) is its only difference from reality. (There is no feature, or set of features, in which it differs. Existence is not a predicate)' (*WV* 24).

These formulations clearly echo two other facets of Cavell's work that we have examined elsewhere. First, by denying that the projected world differs in any feature from reality, Cavell is in effect denying that the invocation of criteria might resolve or dissolve our confusion here. Criteria determine questions of identity (by determining specific differences between one entity or phenomenon and another): but any criteria we employ to distinguish real objects from one another (including those which distinguish photographs from other objects, e.g. from drawings or other visual records) can be and are employed to perform exactly the same task with respect to the objects *in* a photograph; and there are no *criteria* which distinguish a photographed object from the object itself (Is there some specific *respect* in which Garbo in a photograph differs from Garbo in the flesh?). But that does not mean that seeing an object and seeing that object in a photograph are not distinguishable; it means that the distinction must be specified not in terms of visible differences between them but rather in terms of the different relationships in which we stand to them.

And the terms in which Cavell spells out our relationship to the world of a photograph recall his earlier discussion of our relation to the fictional world of characters on a stage—the world of theatre. There too, he takes his discussion to amount to an elucidation of a specific mode of existence (that which we label 'fictional'), and there too he defines that relationship in terms of presence and presentness: in a theatre, the audience are those to whom the characters are present whilst they are not present to the characters. Now he claims that the viewers of a photograph of an object see that object but are themselves invisible, that they are absent from its world; in other words, they are those to whom that object is present whilst they are not present to it.

This makes it look as if our relations with the world of a play and with the world of a photograph are themselves indistinguishable; but this appearance is dispelled if we recall Cavell's further gloss on his claim about the world of theatrical characters in terms of space and time. The audience of a play cannot approach its characters, they do not share a space with them; but they can share their time, they can make their present moments present, and if they fail to do so that is a failure of acknowledgement on their part, it is something for which they as subjects are responsible. Whereas the viewers of a photograph share neither a space nor a time with the object in the photograph; they are not in its physical presence, and the moment at which the object was captured by the camera is not made present to them and cannot be made present by them. In Cavell's words, the world of a photograph does not (and cannot) exist *now*. 'The reality in a photograph is present to me while I am not present to it; and a world I know, and see, but to which I am nevertheless not present (through no fault of my subjectivity), is a world past' (*WV* 23).

Another way of putting this point would be to say that in a theatre, our absence from the world of the play is conventional, but in a cinema our absence is mechanically assured.

The fact that I am invisible and inaudible to the actors in a film, and fixed in position, no longer needs accounting for; it is not part of a convention I have to comply with: the proceedings do not have to make good the fact that I do nothing in the face of tragedy, or that I laugh at the follies of others. In viewing a movie, my helplessness is mechanically assured: I am present not at something happening, which I must confirm, but at something that has happened, which I must absorb (like a memory). In this, movies resemble novels, a fact mirrored in the sound of narration itself, whose tense is the past. (*WV* 25–6)

Against this background, the often-noted connection between film and nostalgia can be seen to be an internal one.

We are now in a position to clarify the connection between Cavell's complex characterization of our relationship with the world that is to be seen in the sequence of projected photographs that constitutes a film and his conception of scepticism. For according to the terms thus far invoked, we can say that the motion picture camera makes a world present to us from which we are absent; it causes live human beings and real objects in actual spaces to appear to us when they are in fact not there, it makes present a no-longer-existent world. But for Cavell, our relation to such an image of the world—to something which presents our senses with nothing less than reality but which is nevertheless nothing more than an image—exemplifies scepticism's understanding of our relation to the world itself; for the sceptic, what we take to be the world is but an image of it. In short, film is a moving image of scepticism.

In fact, the connection is even more precise than this.

... photography satisfied ... the human wish, intensifying in the West since the Reformation, to escape subjectivity and metaphysical isolation—a wish for the power to reach this world, having for so long tried, at last hopelessly, to manifest fidelity to another ... At some point the unhinging of our consciousness from the world interposed our subjectivity between us and our presentness to the world. Then our subjectivity became what is present to us, individuality became isolation ... Photography overcame subjectivity ... by automatism, by removing the human agent from the task of reproduction ... Photography maintains the presentness of the world by accepting our absence from it. (*WV* 21–3)

The wholly mechanical basis of photography removes human subjectivity from the process of reproducing reality, and thereby in a sense perfects it—it captures a world which is in every feature indistinguishable from reality; but the price to be paid for the world's presentness is the screening of human subjectivity from that world—it is a world from which viewers are helplessly, mechanically absent. In other words, photography's automatism accomplishes the overcoming of human subjectivity that the sceptic (mistrustful of human finitude, of what strikes him as the ineluctably perspectival nature of human consciousness) deems necessary for the re-establishment of our conviction in the presentness of reality; but the world thereby captured is a world to which human subjectivity can acknowledge no relation—one which recedes beyond its grasp. For the sceptic, that recession of reality is the revelation of a hideous truth; for Cavell, the nature of film confirms that it is rather the result of the sceptic's own assumption that a true connection with the world requires the transcendence of our finitude. When the role of that ordinary human subjectivity in maintaining our relation to the world is not acknowledged but denied, the human subject is transformed into an absent viewer of the world rather than simply one of its inhabitants.

It is, however, important to see that when Cavell calls film a moving image of scepticism, he does not mean that anyone viewing any cinematic product is necessarily succumbing to the spell of scepticism. There is nothing inherently sceptical about the relation between camera and subject, or between viewer and world viewed; what matters is rather how we understand and acknowledge these relations. If, for example—concerned to deny that the camera merely represents reality or that it captures something less than reality—we assert that it presents us with reality itself (see *WV* 166), then we are taking our relation to the world of film to be an accurate representation of our relation to the real world, and that is to succumb to scepticism. If, however, we come to perceive that film makes the world present to us in a way which mechanically defeats our presence to it, and so see it as a moving image of scepticism, then we are accurately representing the true nature of our relation to the world of a film without regarding it as a model of our true relation to reality; in other words, we are allowing ourselves to be recalled to the criteria which make manifest *this aspect* of our experience of the world, and we thereby precisely avoid scepticism.

Of course, given that this is the true nature of film, it may be perfectly plausible to claim that its popularity as a medium of entertainment in a culture which is permeated with scepticism is at least partly derived from the way in which a viewer's relation to the world of a film satisfies certain sceptical fantasies and wishes about our relation to reality. But this simply shows that film can feed the sceptical impulse; it does not show that it must do so. On the contrary: if the motion picture camera presents us with no more than an *image* of reality, it is nevertheless an image of nothing less than *reality*; so precisely the same aspect of photography's power which makes film an image of scepticism (its exclusion of subjectivity) also allows it to represent an acceptance of the world's independent existence.

The fact that in a moving picture successive film frames are fit flush into the fixed screen frame results in a phenomenological frame that is indefinitely extendible and contractible, limited in the smallness of the object it can grasp only by the state of its technology, and in largeness only by the span of the world. Drawing the camera back, and panning it, are two ways of extending the frame; a close-up is of a part of the body, or of one object or a small set of objects, supported by and reverberating the whole frame of nature. The altering frame is the image of perfect attention. Early in its history the cinema discovered the possibility of *calling* attention to persons and parts of persons and objects; but it is equally a possibility of the medium not to call attention to them but, rather, to let the world happen, to let its parts call attention to themselves according to their natural weight. This possibility is less explored than its opposite. Dreyer, Flaherty, Vigo, Renoir and Antonioni are masters of it. (*WV* 25)

  Just as the philosophical practice of recounting criteria can be thought of as a method of allowing any specific phenomenon (such as that of film) to call attention to itself according to its natural weight, so the nature of film (understood according to the terms that emerged from Cavell's application of that philosophical method to our experience of it) suggests that it is usable in the same enterprise. It is thus perfectly possible to combine the claim that film is a moving image of scepticism with the claim that certain of the possibilities which the medium of film opens up to human beings contest the sceptical impulse—and thus to stake a claim about film which is strongly analogous to Cavell's earlier claim about Shakespearean theatre.

  Of course, it is important to emphasize that this is no more than a possibility of the medium of film; if photography's overcoming of human subjectivity is automatic, its contributing to a practice of overcoming scepticism is not. More generally, Cavell's position is that it is not possible to know whether any given product of the medium constitutes a contribution to this or any other enterprise in advance of detailed study of the specific nature of that product. As should be obvious by now, this is no more than a reapplication at the level of specific films of the method that Cavell employed in his study of the medium of film as such: it is a thumb-nail sketch of a practice of interpreting films which allows them to draw attention to themselves according to their natural weight, a way of viewing products of the medium that constitutes a moving image of scepticism without being overcome by the sceptical impulse. It is, in short, a manifesto for a practice of redemptive reading; and it is what guides Cavell's own sequences of essays on two specific genres of film, to which we now turn.

The Comedy of Remarriage

When Cavell talks of a 'genre' of film, he does not mean a particular
cinematic form definable in terms of certain features, by analogy with
the definition of a type of object in terms of some set of properties that
any candidate object must possess if it is to qualify as an instance of the
type. In his use of the term, there is no such thing as *all* the features of a
genre; its members are related to one another in a very different way.

> ... a narrative or dramatic genre might be thought of as a medium in the visual
> arts might be thought of, or a 'form' in music. The idea is that the members of a
> genre share the inheritance of certain conditions, procedures and subjects and
> goals of composition, and that in primary art each member of such a genre
> represents a study of these conditions, something I think of as bearing the
> responsibility of its inheritance ... (*PH* 28)

What distinguishes one member of such a genre from its fellow members
is that it bears that responsibility differently, by bringing with it some
new feature or set of features; and what makes it none the less a
member of a given genre is that this new feature can be understood
('read') as compensating for any hitherto-standard feature that it lacks
and/or as contributing to a deeper characterization of the genre as a
whole. Of course, such readings of discrepancies between candidate
members of the genre will not be assessable independently of the
overall reading of those specific films of which they form a part; so this
aspect of Cavell's general approach to the study of film cannot be given
an a priori justification. We need to take note of this point here,
however, in order to explain why any attempt to characterize a given
genre must eschew talk of necessary features and focus instead on a
common inheritance of conditions, procedures, subjects, and goals.

 In the case of the comedy of remarriage, Cavell offers the following
initial characterization of that inheritance.[2]

> ... the genre of remarriage is an inheritor of the preoccupations and discoveries
> of Shakespearean romantic comedy, especially as that work has been studied
> by, first among others, Northrop Frye ... Frye follows a long tradition of critics
> in distinguishing between Old and New Comedy: while both, being forms of
> romantic comedy, show a young pair overcoming individual and social obstacles
> to their happiness, figured as a concluding marriage that achieves individual

---

[2] The six films that he takes to be the primary members of this genre are: *The Lady
Eve, It Happened One Night, Bringing Up Baby, The Philadelphia Story, His Girl Friday*, and *The
Awful Truth*.

and social reconciliations, New Comedy stresses the young man's efforts to overcome obstacles posed by an older man (a senex figure) to his winning the young woman of his choice, whereas Old Comedy puts particular stress on the heroine, who may hold the key to the successful conclusion of the plot, and who may undergo something like death and restoration. What I am calling the comedy of remarriage is, because of its emphasis on the heroine, more intimately related to Old Comedy than to New, but it is significantly different from either, indeed, it seems to transgress an important feature of both, in casting as its heroine a married woman; and the drive of its plot is not to get the central pair together, but to get them *back* together, together *again*. Hence the fact of marriage in it is subject to the fact or threat of divorce. (*PH* 1–2)

The importance of the Shakespearean background should be obvious from Chapters 6 and 7, but the fact that it is Shakespearean *comedy* which forms Cavell's most immediate object of comparison gives that reference a new inflexion. For whilst it leads us to expect the relationship between the central pair in these films to be treated as a best case of knowledge of other minds, and so as related to the problematic of scepticism in just the way that, for example, Othello and Desdemona's relationship was claimed to be, it also suggests that the tragic outcome of sceptical doubt in such cases will be avoided. In these films the couple in whom the human capacity to be assaulted by scepticism is exemplified also exemplify the human capacity to withstand that assault.

The precision with which Cavell takes the narrative of these films to track the logic of sceptical doubt is made clear in his summary of what he calls the founding myth of the genre—the primal story upon which the plots of each individual film can be thought of as variations or revisions.

A running quarrel is forcing apart a pair who recognize themselves as having known one another for ever, that is from the beginning, not just in the past but in a period before there was a past, before history. This naturally presents itself as their having shared childhood together, suggesting that they are brother and sister. They have discovered their sexuality together and find themselves required to enter this realm at roughly the same time that they are required to enter the social realm, as if the sexual and the social are to legitimize one another. This is the beginning of history, of an unending quarrel. The joining of the sexual and the social is called marriage. Something evidently internal to the task of marriage causes trouble in paradise—as if marriage, which was to be a ratification, is itself in need of ratification. So marriage has this disappointment—call this its impotence to domesticate sexuality without discouraging it, or its stupidity in the face of the riddle of intimacy, which repels where it attracts, or in the face of the puzzle of ecstasy, which is violent while it is tender, as if the leopard should lie down with the lamb. And the disappointment seeks revenge, a revenge, as it were, for having made one discover one's incompleteness, one's transience, one's homelessness. Upon separation the woman tries a regressive tack, usually that of accepting as a husband a simpler, or mere, father-substitute ... This is psychologically an effort to put her desire, awakened by the original man, back to sleep ... (*PH* 31–2)

If we take such a best case of knowing another mind as allegorical of a best case of knowing the existence of the world, then we see here the pattern Cavell has been at pains to lay out in other contexts. An original intimacy with the world is found disappointing, experienced as lacking or confining; and within that intimacy, one's separateness or individuality is experienced as a form of incompleteness. This disappointment produces a need for revenge, one which destroys the world (of intimacy): it demands the euthanasia of one's real desire for and interest in that world, denies one's separateness, and thus transforms it into isolation, and (since it amounts to a failure to legitimize incestuous desire, a failure to accommodate oneself to the existence of related and independent others) signals the loss of society. We might think of this last point as a democratic version of the way in which, in Shakespearean tragedy, the lives of kings and their queens stood for the health of their kingdoms.

And just as the founding myth of these films tracks the onslaught and the consequences of sceptical doubt, so it provides a vision of its overcoming.

It is the man's turn to make the move—the woman had presumably started things with something called an apple, anyway by presenting a temptation. The man must counter by showing that he has survived his yielding and by finding a way to enter a claim. To make a correct claim, to pass the test of his legitimacy, he must show that he is not attempting to command but that he is able to wish, and consequently to make a fool of himself. This enables the woman to awaken to her desire again, giving herself rather than the apple, and enables the man to recognize and accept this gift. This changing is the forgoing or forgetting of that past state and its impasse of vengefulness, a forgoing symbolised by the initial loss of virginity. (*PH* 32)

What is being modelled here is, most immediately, the acknowledgement of another person; but it also models the acceptance of the world. World-consuming revenge is overcome by acknowledging one's responsibility for it and by forgoing it; one's original intimacy with the world is recovered by acknowledging one's real interest in it, its capacity to elicit and satisfy one's desires, and by finding a way to make one's claims upon it which is not the imposition of a demand but the expression of a wish to be claimed by it.

The echoes of Cavell's understanding of the redemptive practice of recounting criteria should be clear; and they are reinforced by the aspect of the pairs' relationship which constitutes its foundation and anchor—their conversation. The films which make up this genre are talkies—not just in the sense that they presuppose the techniques of synchronized visual and aural recording, but in the sense that they constitute one mode of perfecting the possibilities opened up by that technical development; the most basic source of the pleasure they give is the endless and endlessly responsive verbal intercourse of their central couples. Cavell's claim is that the term 'conversation' here carries the dual (sexual and social) sense that is more obvious in some of its synonyms; in these films talking together (which means both speaking and hearing) is fully and plainly being together, a mode of association, a form of life. But if their achieved acknowledgement of one another is essentially a matter of learning to speak the same language, and this mutual acknowledgement is an emblem of the overcoming of scepticism more generally, then these films are locating language at the centre of any practice of recovery from scepticism in just the way envisaged in Cavell's practice of recounting criteria. In short, these couples' meet and happy conversation is a mode of redemptive reading.

Since, on this understanding of the films in this genre, divorce symbolizes the threat of scepticism, marriage must symbolize that to which scepticism is a threat—the domain of ordinary life and ordinary language. In other words, these films interpret the ordinary as the domestic (the life of a household, the domestication of desire in married life). But of course, they also offer a specific interpretation of marriage, of what the realm of the domestic might be or amount to. Most importantly of all, they understand marriage as remarriage—an interpretation which we first encountered in relation to *The Winter's Tale*, but the implications of which are spelt out in much more detail in these comedies. For first, such a reading shifts the weight of our interest in determining whether two people are married away from its initiating ceremony and towards what comes after or out of that ceremony—as if to say that no such festival, whether religious or legal, any longer has the power to ratify the union of a man and a woman, that this ratification is rather provided from within the continuous festivity of the union itself, by the willingness of both partners to keep on rededicating themselves to it. Second, this rededication is not merely to one another, to union in a isolated world outside or other to the common world, but also to an ordinary life with one's other—to a domestic life, a life in which one's desire is domesticated; it is a devotion to everyday life. Together, these two points imply a third; for if marriage is to be understood not as a ceremony but as a mode of repetition, and if it is also be be understood as a devotion to the domestic or to everyday life, then it must be to (some version of) the repetitiveness that is hidden in the concept of the everyday that such devotion should focus—to its dailiness or diurnality, to the unending succession of days that makes up the everyday.

These connections are ones which Cavell sees as most clearly developed in *The Awful Truth*. It is a film which presents neither a marriage ceremony at the beginning nor a remarriage ceremony at the end; its climactic scene involves the transformation of the moment at which the writ of the original (public) ceremony runs out into the moment of its (private) renewal; and this scene is presided over by a cuckoo clock in the form of a house from which a pair of skipping people recurrently depart and return, until eventually the male figurine re-enters through the female figurine's door and inhabits (household) life and time anew. Furthermore, Cavell sees the film as a whole, beyond its specific words and scenes, as designed to emblematize this devotion to dailiness. For that is what, in his view, explains the film's lack of a climactic or knock-out comic scene of the sort possessed by other members of the genre; that lack can be read positively as a way of contesting the irregular outbreak of extraordinary comic events with a continuous line of unbroken comedic development, in order to suggest that the rhythmic recurrences of ordinary diurnal life provide fun and interest enough to inspire life and a commitment to its continuation. What matters is establishing the correct relationship or attitude to the everyday, the daily—the correct perspective on time.

It is centrally as a title for these three features of diurnal comedy, the comedy of dailiness—its conclusion not in a future, a beyond, an ever after, but in a present continuity of before and after; its transformation of a festival into a festivity; its correction not of error but of experience or of a perspective on experience—that I retain the concept of remarriage as the title for the genre of films in question. The title registers, to my mind, the two most impressive affirmations of the task of human experience, the acceptance of human relatedness, as the acceptance of repetition. Kierkegaard's study called *Repetition*, which is a study of the possibility of marriage; and Nietszche's Eternal Return, the call for which he puts by saying it is high time, a heightening or ascension of time; this is literally *Hochzeit*, German for marriage, with time itself as the ring. As redemption by suffering does not depend on something that has already happened, so redemption by happiness does not depend on something that is yet to happen; both depend on a faith in something that is always happening, day by day. (*PH* 240–1)

The parallel between this cinematic vision of a reiterated return to the everyday and the unending recovery of ordinary language that is pivotal to the philosophical practice of recounting criteria is perhaps the central point at which the comedies of remarriage feed back into Cavell's conception of what overcoming scepticism might amount to.

The Melodrama of the Unknown Woman

The second genre of film upon which Cavell has concentrated is one which he thinks of as having been derived by negation from the genre we have just been examining. Here, the mechanism of derivation is meant to contrast with the mechanism of compensation: a particular member of a given genre may lack a feature that is central to its founding myth, but it must compensate for that lack by introducing another feature which permits the myth to be further explored or examined; whereas if a specific film does not merely lack but positively negates the central features of a given genre and its founding myth, then it does not constitute a member of that genre but rather a member of an adjacent genre—a genre which can be understood as opposing its neighbour's founding myth with another one altogether. Cavell regards the genre which he names 'the Melodrama of the Unknown Woman' as standing in just this relationship of systematic negation with the comedies of remarriage; but in order to appreciate the full force of this claim, we must pay closer attention to certain features of the comedies which have hitherto remained in the background.

In particular, it is important to note that the fundamental purpose of the relationship between the central pair in the comedies of remarriage is the creation or re-creation of the woman. This is part of the framework of Old Comedy, which understands its heroines as having to undergo something like death and resurrection; and it also shows these films to be inheritors of a more recent dramatic myth, that of *A Doll's*

House, in which Nora leaves her husband in search of what she calls an education, but which might as easily be called a transformation or metamorphosis—an entry into a new mode of existence. However, Nora justifies her departure from her husband by saying that he is not the man to provide her with the education she needs; and this implies that, even if Thorvald is not able to do it, the task of her education is none the less in the hands of men. This, too, is a feature that the comedies take over from Ibsen; in every case, and despite the strong sense that the woman's capacity to match the man in the endless witty responsiveness of their conversations emblematizes the real equality in their relationship, the woman is presented as standing in need of a certain sort of education by the man.

This demand for education has to do with the woman's sense that her life asks for some transformation, that she stands in need of creation, or re-creation. I say of this need that it marks a new step in the construction of the human. My use of the word 'creation' in speaking of these films is variously determined. Narratively, as said, it interprets the depth of the woman's demand for education; cinematically, it records the action of the motion picture camera upon a flesh-and-blood actress; historically, it invokes the issue of the formation of the social, particularly, of its constructions with the rise of Protestantism and capitalism; theologically, so to speak, it harks back to the passage in Genesis of the woman's creation from the man, that passage traditionally taken by theologians as justifying, or providing the image of, marriage. The theologian I invoke in particular is John Milton, whose great tract justifying divorce emphasizes most unforgettably for me the idea that marriage is—is constituted in—'a meet and happy conversation'. Now comes the moral cloud. Does creation from, even by, the man somehow entail creation *for* the man, say for his use and pleasure and pride? If not, how does the woman attain independence; how does she complete, as it were, her creation? This is what remarriage comedy, and the derived unknown woman melodrama, ponder. (UDFB 216)

Even though the fitness of the man for his educative task is a central *question* for the comedies—that is, even though what authorizes the woman's choice of him to provide or authorize the conditions of her new existence is open to investigation and criticism rather than merely taken for granted—his role suggests a privileging of the male even within the films' general atmosphere of gender equality. And this taint of male villainy seems to be confirmed by the fact that the women in the comedies are virtually never shown with their mothers and never shown to be mothers; it may remain unclear whether this is the permanent price of the women's happiness in their marriages or simply a temporary and mysterious aberration of the disordered world which surrounds the pair, but it ensures that the happiness achieved in remarriage comedies is not uncontaminated or uncompromised.

If we think of the issue of the woman's creation (the new creation of the woman and so the new creation of the human on its female or feminine side) as that which the two adjacent genres share (i.e. as that topic or theme around which they construct their opposing myths), then we now have a provisional list of the features of the remarriage comedies which the melodramas will negate; and we can think of those negations as themselves forming the framework of a founding myth, the myth of Nora's descendants who could neither manage nor relish the relationships within which the women of the comedies find happiness.[3]

> ... a woman achieves existence (or fails to), or establishes her right to existence in the form of a metamorphosis (or fails to), apart from or beyond satisfaction by marriage (of a certain kind) and with the presence of her mother and her children, where something in her language must be as traumatic in her case as the conversation of marriage is for her comedic sisters—perhaps it will be an aria of divorce, from husband, lover, mother or child. (*IIS* 18)

Just as the meet and happy conversation of the comedies emblematizes the central pairs' acknowledgement of one another in a union of real responsiveness, so the emblematic linguistic mode of the melodramas is irony—a mode in which communication and interaction are systematically negated, one which figures the woman's lack of a shared language with the men in her world and indeed with any other people in that world. In short, the irony serves to isolate the woman of the melodramas from (almost) everyone around her; and it raises the question of whether she is also isolated from us, her viewers. That is why Cavell thinks of this genre as a study of the unknownness of the woman.

The connections between this new genre and the development of the story of scepticism in modern culture are manifold. In the first place, it is significant that the genre of these films is melodrama: 'If some image of marriage, as an interpretation of domestication ... is the fictional equivalent of what ... philosophers understand to be the ordinary, or the everyday, then the threat to the ordinary named scepticism should show up in fiction's favourite threat to forms of marriage, namely, in forms of melodrama' (*IQO* 129–30). The chief negation of the comedies

---

[3] The nine films that he takes to be the primary members of this genre are: *Blonde Venus, Stella Dallas, Showboat, Mildred Pierce, Random Harvest, The Marquise of O, Now Voyager, Gaslight,* and *Letter from an Unknown Woman.* Of these, Cavell has so far published readings of the final four.

by the melodramas is the negation of marriage itself: marriage is not reconceived and provisionally affirmed but rather transcended. But that transcendence is effected in service of precisely the same goal to which marriage is in service in the comedies—namely, the re-creation of the woman. So what the melodramas show (even when their protagonists fail to achieve the transcendence for which they strive) is a mode of metamorphosis which is a route towards a new or original integrity that can be (at least provisionally) achieved in isolation—a personal change without social interchange. If this self-reliant route towards a new identity is understood as a mode of affirming the existence of the self, and so as an attempt to overcome scepticism, then we can begin to see a close connection between these events on film and the philosopher who originated the modern sceptical problematic—a connection which under-writes a very specific set of terms for thinking about his central achievement. As Cavell goes on to say immediately after the previously quoted passage: 'Accordingly, melodrama may be seen as an interpreta-tion of Descartes' cogito, and contrariwise, the cogito can be seen as an interpretation of the advent of melodrama—of the moment (private and public) at which the theatricalization of the self becomes the sole proof of its freedom and its existence' (*IQO* 130).

This is the point at which the possibilities of the medium of film open up further points of convergence with the concepts and narratives that we earlier saw developed within the domains of psychoanalysis and philosophy. To begin with, the fact that this cinematic proof of human existence is offered or enacted by women, in the face of male persecu-tion and incomprehension, and in a way which might be thought of as amounting to the theatricalization of the human self (its manifestation or display) calls to mind both Freud's fascination with the female capacity for hysterical conversion and the Wittgensteinian emphasis upon the expressiveness of the human body. But these reference points in turn suggest a particular way of understanding what these films reveal about the possibilities of the medium of film—namely, its own fascination with the study of individual women who represent the highest reaches of glamorous independence registered in the idea of a star, and its capacity to record and transfigure the human body.

That capacity is one which we saw that Cavell notes under the more general heading of the camera's ability to attend to the world—to let the world and its inhabitants draw attention to themselves in accordance with their natural weight; and of those inhabitants, human beings are amongst the most cinematically attractive. It is part of the power of moving pictures to find interest in the most insignificant repetitions, turnings, pauses, and yieldings of human beings.

Think of this interest or power as the camera's knowledge of the metaphysical restlessness of the live body at rest, something internal to what Walter Benjamin calls cinema's optics of the unconscious. Under examination by the camera, a human body becomes for its inhabitant a field of betrayal more than a ground of communication, and the camera's further power is manifested as it documents the individual's self-conscious efforts to control the body each time it is conscious of the camera's attention to it. I might call these recordings *somatograms* (cf. cardiograms, electroencephalograms), to register the essential linking of the pattern of a body's motions with the movements of the machine that records them ... Psychologically, submission to a somatogram—to the synchronization between body and camera—demands passiveness, you may say demands the visibility of the feminine side of one's character. (WPT 14, 19)

In other words, a somatogram is a transcription of the expressiveness of the human body. The capacity to allow one's embodiment to manifest one's self (even the unconscious or unknown reaches of that self)— what psychoanalysis studies as the capacity for hysterical conversion— is one which can be exercised only by permitting oneself to suffer or be victimized by it; and the camera's transcription of its exercise requires a capacity to allow oneself to be read by the camera. In both respects, therefore, we are dealing with essentially passive forms of activity, which can accordingly be thought of as related to the feminine side of human character (not to the female half of the human race); and they can also be said to constitute a proof of psychic reality—a proof from the feminine side of the reality of human existence.

In the genre of melodramas that Cavell has identified, this general capacity of film is applied to the study of this general human aptitude as it is manifest in those stars who may be understood to have raised it to its highest art—Bette Davis, Marlene Dietrich, and particularly Greta Garbo; and what results is the record of an enactment of human existence, a theatricalization of the self which constitutes an attempted proof of its reality and freedom.

It is as if Garbo has generalized this aptitude beyond human doubting—call this aptitude a talent for, and will to, communicate—generalized it to the point of absolute expressiveness, so that the sense of failure to know her, of her being beyond us (say, visibly absent) is itself the proof of her existence ... Such in my philosophy is the proof of human existence that, on its feminine side, as conceived in the appearance of psychoanalysis, it is the perfection of the motion picture camera to provide. (*IIS* 36)

This compact passage amounts to a multi-layered interpretation of the unknownness of the women in these melodramas in the light of psychoanalysis and its reading of feminine unknownness.[4] Understood as characters within the world of their films, they are unknown to those around them in the sense that they are unacknowledged; their existence as independent autonomous beings is systematically denied or missed, particularly by the men with whom they are paired. But although these failures of acknowledgement are culpable, the expression of masculine jealousy and revenge, it would be wrong to think that these women's unknownness is purely a function of the failures of their particular men—as if their fate is wholly in the hands of others. For the absoluteness of the capacity for expressiveness which these women deploy in enacting their existence seems to demand an equally (perhaps unattainably) absolute degree of acknowledgement from others; it generates a sense that, no matter how they might respond to her, she will outstrip their capacity for acknowledgement—and thus raises the question whether this reveals their personal inadequacy or the limits of the humanly acknowledgeable. For Cavell, it seems that Garbo's capacity for absolute expressiveness (and so Garbo herself) can only be acknowledged as being beyond our powers of acknowledgement; so her unknownness is the inevitable mode of her existence rather than a sign that she has not attained existence. By enacting it, she appears as a standing rebuke to our sense that we are always capable of fully acknowledging others—a reminder of the uncertainty that we saw in Chapter 6 to be inherent in the logic of acknowledgement.

So, Garbo's unknownness does not imply that she cannot be acknowledged by others at all; it is rather a way of specifying how she must be acknowledged if she is to be acknowledged at all. To acknowledge her as unknown amounts to acknowledging her existence as beyond doubt (i.e. acknowledging that her expressivity not only proves beyond question the reality of *her* existence but also epitomizes the irrelevance of the concepts of knowledge and doubt in determining the existence of *any* other mind) and as beyond acknowledgement (i.e. acknowledging that her expressivity outstrips the fullest acknowledgement we can give). It is this mode of acknowledgement that she fails to find in the world of her films; but what of us, the audience of her films? Her absolute expressivity as a film star is captured by the camera and so the reality of her psyche is fully revealed to us, revealed to us beyond

---

[4] My discussion in this paragraph, and the two following on from it, is indebted to Karen Hansen's illuminating article 'Being Doubted, Being Assured', in *IIS*.

doubting (she is before our very eyes, and we do not feel that there is any piece of knowledge about her existence that we lack) and beyond acknowledgement (we know that we do not measure up to the absolute acknowledgement her photogenesis seems to call for); but since our absence from her world is mechanically effected, our sense of her as beyond our acknowledgement is not permeated by any anxiety that it is caused by a feature of our subjectivity, a failure of our powers of acknowledgement. It thus provides (although in a very different, more automatic, way) the insight which Shakespearean tragedy is designed to elicit from its audience—a consciousness of human separateness: of our separation from her, and hers from us. The image of Garbo is thus an image of the autonomous human other; her screened unknownness is a demonstration of the separateness of embodied individuals understood as a metaphysical finitude rather than an intellectual lack.

We might think of this as the way in which the woman of the melodramas attempts to prove her existence for and to others—the others in the world of her film and the others in her audience; so that the relationship with those others that her theatrical display of self is designed to bring about is to this degree analogous to the two-person, interactive model of acknowledgement at the heart of Cavell's under-standing both of what it is to know another's existence (where the relevant others are her fellow characters in the film) and of what it is to interpret a text (where her others are her audience). But if enacted unknownness is truly to parallel the cogito, it must also and primarily function as a proof for and to the women themselves; their expressivity must demonstrate their existence to their own satisfaction. Even here, however, Cavell's conception of this essentially self-reliant proof con-forms to his interactive model of redemption from scepticism.

This conformity depends upon the fact that these women's enactment of their existence takes the form of metamorphosis. It is a matter of self-creation that has to be understood as self-re-creation, as an enactment of a new integrity, a new state of her self. It can thus be thought of as involving a relation between two selves, or rather two states of her self: condemned by the world of her film to a mode of existence in which she at best haunts the world, she stakes her life on her capacity to envision a further state of her self which it is within her power to realize or enact. She permits this vision of an unknown but knowable future self to attract her away from her present self, to initiate her self-transformation, her refusal of her world and its conditions—to initiate and maintain her refusal to conform. Thus the melodrama of self-

reliance involves a doubleness within the self, a capacity for self-transcendence which amounts to a movement from one state of the self to
another, an avoidance of fixation or repetition and an openness to the
unknown future. The essentially self-reliant metamorphoses of the
unknown woman thus remain recognizably congruent with the structures of Cavell's essentially interactive model of acknowledgement and
redemptive reading.

None the less, the theme of self-reliance in these melodramas specifies
one of the central differences between the women of the melodramas
and their comedic sisters.

> The comedies envision a relation of equality between human beings that we
> may characterize, using favourite terms of Emerson, as a relation of rightful
> attraction, of expressiveness, and of joy ... The relation ... is not, in the
> comedies, perceived as pervading society, but it is shown to hold between a pair
> who are somehow exemplary of the possibilities of this society at large. The
> melodramas envision the phase of the problematic self-reliance that demands
> this expressiveness and joy first in relation to oneself. (*LU* 344–5)

Here, Cavell simultaneously specifies the subject of the melodramas as
self-reliance—a certain negation of the social—but implies that the
existence of such individuals is at least as important a sign of the health
of the social or political realm as is the emblematic achievement of
marriage in the comedies. How are we to understand the politics of
such self-reliance? What is it that these women prove or enact to themselves?

Presumably we must once again begin by interpreting what they
enact as their unknownness; but here, Cavell reads this concept as
relating neither to the expressivity of the unconscious nor to failures of
knowledge and acknowledgement nor to an individual's unknown but
envisioned future. Instead, he interprets it as privacy. To see the full
implications of this interpretation, we must return to Garbo—surely
one of the most self-reliant, self-possessed, and private of screen
stars—and to what Cavell finds that her visible absence emblematizes.

> I find ... that I see her *jouissance* as remembering something, but, let me say,
> remembering it from the future, within a private theatre, not dissociating
> herself from the present moment, but knowing it forever, in its transience, as
> finite, from her finitude, or separateness, as from the perspective of her death.
> As if she herself were transformed into a mnemonic symbol, a monument of
> memory ... What the monument means to me is that a joyful passion for one's

life contains the ability to mourn, the acceptance of transience, of the world as beyond one—say, one's other. (*IIS* 36)

In other words, Cavell characterizes her enactment of her existence as a piece of private theatre, and its privacy amounts to a declaration of her sense of herself as separate and finite; what she enacts is her knowledge of her separateness (the knowledge that, beyond any withholding or manifestation of her private thoughts, and beyond any isolation imposed or invaded by others, she remains rooted in her finitude), and her knowledge of the inescapable transience of the present moment (the knowledge that each moment is to be mourned, to be appreciated as what it is but also as something that must be allowed to pass away, from which one must move on).

This is a photographic manifestation of human finitude and transience, and of Garbo as an individual possessed of and capable of bearing that knowledge; but Cavell goes on from this to think of the privacy of the women in these melodramas as something more specific, or more personal—as their (knowledge of their) individuality as well as of their separateness. He sees Bette Davis in *Now Voyager* as a prime exponent of this:

Bette Davis' command and deployment of [the] capacity for somatic compliance, for the theatricalization of desire and of its refiguration or retracking that, so it seems to me, made her one of the most impersonated of Hollywood stars ... impersonated not alone by men and women who did vaudeville impersonations ... but most taken on by female impersonators. This ... testifies to a sense that an essential dimension of Bette Davis' power is its invitation to, and representation of camp; an arrogation of the rights of banality and affectation and display, of the dangerous wish for perfect personal expressiveness. The wish, in the great stars ... is a function not of their beauty, such as that may be, but of their power of privacy, of a knowing unknownness. It is a democratic claim for personal freedom. (UDFB 227–8)

Where Garbo's privacy emblematizes the ability to mourn, the sense of one's own (as well as the world's) separateness and transience, Davis's privacy is more a matter of idiosyncrasy—of a desire and a capacity to accept, rework, or reject the forms of expressive human behaviour made available to her by her culture, and to do so in accord with her specific sense of (an unattained but attainable future) self; it is a declaration of her distinctness and freedom from the present state of the world, a world that is attempting to strangle her attempts at self-transcendence. Accordingly, her self-reliance necessarily functions as a standing rebuke to her present world, and to the people who make it up and maintain it—people whose existence takes the form of conformity to that world, people who do not attempt to enact their own existence, who repress their idiosyncrasy and so do not exist as individuals. Just as her envisioned future self functions as that which attracts her from conformity with her present fixated self, so her enactment of this doubled self-reliance functions as that which attracts her fellow citizens towards their own self-reliance. Cavell's model of acknowledgement or redemptive reading can thus be seen not only as a paradigm for achieving personal self-reliance, but also as a blueprint for averting public or political conformity.

The entitlement to idiosyncrasy is the way Mill encapsulates the thought that, in an imperfect democracy, protection of idiosyncrasy becomes as important to democracy as liberty itself; so those who maintain and enact their idiosyncratic selves perform a crucial social function—their consent to society seems to be something that that society cannot afford to do without. But of course, in the case of these unknown women, the personal costs of giving that consent are very high—unending irony, enforced transcendence, suffering their unknownness; and the real existence and depth of that consent beneath such covers of irony and privacy cannot easily be known by their society. Moreover, if the self-reliance of these women functions as a standing rebuke, as an emblem of the fact that there is a better state of society to be envisioned and then achieved, then even their enacted consent can at best show that their present society is good enough to merit radical reproof rather than outright rejection.

All in all, then, the existence of unknown women is a very uncomfortable matter for a democratic society to acknowledge. As Cavell puts it when discussing the status of the Bette Davis character in *Now Voyager*:

the legitimacy of the social order in which she is to participate is determined (to the extent that it can be determined) by her consent, by whether she, in her state of freedom, finds that she wants the balance of renunciation and security the present constitution of society affords her . . . That Charlotte consents in the moments we conclude with—and for her own reasons—is clear enough. That she would consent under altered conditions is unknowable. A good enough or just enough society—one that recognizes her say in it—will recognize this fact of, this threat in, or measure by, the woman's unknownness. (UDFB 246–7)

It is to this issue—to the way in which self-reliance as it is enacted through the feminine side of the human character underwrites or undermines society's sense of itself as good enough—that Cavell's most recent work on the constitution of Emersonian perfectionism is devoted, and to which we must turn in the following chapters of this book.

PART IV
Philosophy, Perfectionism, and Religion

10

Thoreau: Writing, Mourning, Neighbouring

The figure of the unknown woman marks the point at which Cavell's recent preoccupation with aesthetic and psychoanalytic representations of gender meets up with, and inspires a revision or recounting of, his earlier interest in issues which occupy the borderline between art, morality, and politics. In the first part of this book, we saw that Cavell identified a structural resemblance between these three fields of discourse: aesthetic judgements combine a subjective grounding with a claim to universal validity, moral debate allows individuals to discover a personal stance or set of commitments within parameters that defined an intersubjective space of moral reason, and modern political theory represents society as founded upon a contract and so upon the consent of the individuals which make it up. In all of these domains, therefore, the issue of how the individual must understand her relationship with others—the ways in which her need for those others and the resources they provide might be balanced against her need to establish perspective upon the constraints they impose—is central; and this is precisely the issue that is pivotal to the melodramas and the comedies we examined in the previous chapter.

However, Cavell's most recent and most detailed treatment of this issue has appeared in the form of his readings of the work of Thoreau and (more particularly) Emerson; and his understanding of this tradition of American Romanticism—a tradition that he wishes to reclaim for and as philosophy in America—makes its spiritual thrust immediately political in its consequences. This emerges most explicitly in the 1988 Carus Lectures (in *CHU*), but its roots lie in Cavell's much earlier reading of Thoreau's *Walden* (in *SW*); accordingly, in this chapter I shall concentrate upon Thoreau, before examining Emerson in the context of the Carus Lectures in Chapter II. But it is important to bear in mind throughout these chapters that what is under examination is an *American* tradition—something which in part accounts for the fact that spiritual issues (soon to be labelled 'perfectionist') are presented as having immediately political consequences. In other words, where Parts II and III of this book broadened the cultural horizons of our analysis, revealing the way in which Cavell understands the tradition of ordinary language philosophy within the wider problematic of modernity, Part IV might be thought of as working on a narrower front, highlighting the ways in which these broader themes are appropriated and refracted in the philosophical tradition of one (albeit distinctively, perhaps uniquely, modern) country. Exploring this material thus adds to our portrait of Cavell's distinctive philosophical perspective by underlining the sense in which he conceives of his identity as an American citizen as internal to his philosophy: the notion of Americanness is now one of its central preoccupations. Since, however, he plainly thinks of (his) Americanness as in part characterized by the desire to inherit both from Britain and from the rest of Europe, and so conceives of (his) American philosophy as essentially Anglo-Continental, this narrowing of focus is in fact less culturally introverted—and so less idiosyncratic and exclusionary—than it may seem.

Looking back at *The Senses of Walden* in the light of Cavell's later writings on Romanticism makes it clear that the central themes we identified in Chapter 6 were already at work in that text. Thoreau is seen by Cavell as prophetically diagnosing a state of sceptical despair in his fellow Americans: he claims that the majority lead lives of quiet desperation, ones which mock their own potential and constitute a parody of the promise of renewal upon which their nation was founded. As Cavell summarizes it:

Everyone is saying, and anyone can hear, that this is the new world; that we are the new men; that the earth is to be born again; that the past is to be cast off like a skin; that we must learn from children to see again; that every day is the first day of the world; that America is Eden. So how can a word get through whose burden is that we do not understand a word of all this? Or rather, that the way in which we understand it is insane, and we are trying again to buy and bully our way into heaven; that we have failed; that the present is a task and a discovery, not a period of America's privileged history; that we are not free, not whole, and not new, and we know this and are on a downward path of despair because of it; and that for the child to grow he requires family and familiarity, but that for a grownup to grow he requires strangeness and transformation, i.e., birth? (*SW* 59–60)

Such a passage makes it clear how deeply Cavell's interpretation of Romanticism permeates his understanding of the American Constitution and so of what it is to be American (and particularly an American philosopher); his country's founding hopes of a new human being in a new political community in a new world are read as interrelated aspects of the same promise of renewal, and that renewal is read as part of the post-Enlightenment struggle to overcome scepticism. Philosophy, politics, and mysticism meet at the place we call America.

But Cavell does not simply understand Thoreau to be writing in the face of this despair and in hope of this renewal; he more specifically understands Thoreau's writing to be itself the medium and manifestation of renewal. Language is placed at the heart of the relations between individual Americans, their fellows, and their world; it is part of what ties them together (criteria functioning to align speakers with one another and with the world), and the nature of the tie between individuals and their words emblematizes the nature of their ties to one another and to nature ('to imagine a language is to imagine a form of life'). Cavell's Thoreau is thus primarily a writer: his specific mode of employing language in writing *Walden* is seen as designed to highlight and overcome the present poverty of our relation to words, in just the way that his depicted mode of inhabiting Walden is standardly interpreted as a practical admonishment of the lives of his fellow townsmen. Accordingly, if we wish to understand the nature of the general renewal that Cavell's Thoreau advocates, we must examine more closely the nature of the specific renewal of language that his advocacy instantiates.

In the terms that we have used to understand scepticism throughout this book, overcoming sceptical despair is a matter of overcoming failures or denials of acknowledgement; so the sceptical attitude to language which Thoreau confronts will be one in which the specific nature of language is denied or repressed, and his attempts to overcome that denial must take the form of acknowledging it.

Writing—heroic writing, the writing of a nation's scripture—must assume the conditions of language as such; re-experience, as it were, the fact that there is such a thing as language at all and assume responsibility for it—find a way to acknowledge it—until the nation is capable of serious speech again. Writing must assume responsibility, in particular, for three of the features of the language it lives upon: (1) that every mark of a language means something in the language, one thing rather than another; that a language is totally, systematically meaningful; (2) that words and their orderings are meant by human beings, that they contain (or conceal) their beliefs, express (or deny) their convictions; and (3) that the saying of something when and as it is said is as significant as the meaning and ordering of the words said. (*SW* 33–4)

Two essential aspects of language are given prominence here: the specificity of the meaning of every word and sentence, and the fact that they are always and everywhere deployed by people, by specific individuals. Prose that is intended to acknowledge these facts is therefore primarily burdened with the need to acknowledge the specificity of utterance and utterer simultaneously—to show the full range of a word's denotations and connotations by producing sentences which collectively compute the multiplicity of their possible meanings whilst individually giving precise expression to particular beliefs, and to ensure that each meaningful mark also confirms the individuality of the person who made it. This amounts to writing in a way which acknowledges the relative autonomy of both language and its individual speakers, their simultaneous dependence upon and independence of each other. For although individuals can choose their words, they cannot choose the meanings of those words; and language, which depends upon communities of speakers for its own existence, none the less exists prior to any individual speaker and provides the essential pre-condition for individuals to attain full humanity.

The connections between this conception of writing and the philosophical practice of recounting criteria that was outlined in Chapter 6 should be obvious. Thoreau is portrayed as attempting to acknowledge the full specificity of the meanings of words, and thus as recounting both the criteria of every word he uses *and* the criteria of the words 'word' and 'language'; and the alignments that words establish both between speakers and between a speaker and her world ensure that acknowledging their specificity contributes to a revivification of the (speech) community and of its appreciation of the natural world within which its members live and to which they relate. Moreover, Thoreau's enacted faithfulness to the conditions of the enterprise of linguistic discourse emblematizes the change of attitude that is required in relation to any and all human practical activities if our lives of quiet desperation are to be transcended; it spells out what enacting the existence of any individual creature whose form of life is language must amount to.

And just as the practice of recounting criteria gives pride of place to a certain conception of reading, so Thoreau's own picture of his writing enterprise centrally invokes an analogous concept. In the first place, if acknowledging that words have a relative autonomy involves allowing them to remind us of their criteria rather than ignoring or distorting their pre-existing significance, then his writing must be thought of as the product of allowing himself to be read by words—allowing them to remind him of the true nature and scope of the language (and so the form of life) that he inherits and inhabits, or fails to. Second, if criteria align Thoreau with the world, then his being read by words can be thought of as both an aspect and an emblem of being read by nature— of his allowing each pond and bird and tree to remind him of the specific nature of its relatively autonomous existence. And third, if he is to acknowledge the conditions of language as such, and if one condition of writing is that it is to be read, then his prose must create or establish or accommodate not only his own but also his reader's presence to his words.

The reader's position [is] specified as that of the stranger. To write to him is to acknowledge that he is outside the words, at a bent arm's length, and alone with the book; that his presence to these words is perfectly contingent, and the choice to stay with them continuously his own; that they are his points of departure and origin. (*SW* 62–3)

Thoreau's specification of the reader's position brings out the fact that reading is a practical activity just like writing or farming or building, and so that it should be undertaken in the appropriate spirit if it is to help overcome rather than confirm our quiet desperation. In particular, we readers must be brought to see that our taking up and continuing to read a book is a decision, a choice we keep on making and so for which we must bear the responsibility, rather than an obligation or a necessity imposed upon us; so writing which attempts to teach this lesson must divest itself of the usual attempts to elicit the continued investment of its reader's interest.

Nothing *holds* my interest, no suspense of plot or development of character; the words seem continuously at an end ... This becomes a mood of our act of reading altogether: it is an accident, utterly contingent, that we should be present at these words at all. We feel this as the writer's withdrawal from the words on which he had staked his presence; and we feel this as the words' indifference to us, their disinterest in whether we choose to stay with them or not. Every new clarity makes the writer's existence obscurer to us—that is, his willingness to remain obscure. How can he apparently so completely not care, or have made up his mind, that we may not understand? This feeling may begin our almost unbearable sense of his isolation. Did he not feel lonesome? We are asking now. And then we find ourselves, perhaps, alone with a book in our hands, words on a page, at a distance. (*SW* 49–50)

Since Thoreau thinks of his fellow citizens as lost to scepticism, he must picture his reader as similarly lost—as having withdrawn her interest from what she is doing, as haunting her own existence, isolated from others and distanced from the world; so the first thing he must do is get her to see this fact about herself, and in particular to see this fact about her attitude to what she is now doing, i.e. reading. So he writes in a way which reveals to her that she does not not know why she is reading his text, and why she is not reading something else or doing something else; he writes to show her that she is disoriented. Her reorientation requires that she read in a way which takes up the burden of acknowledging the true nature and scope of the task of reading, which means (in terms earlier specified) that she must acknowledge the specificity and relative autonomy of the words before her and of the individual who placed them in just this order to bring out just these inflexions of their meaning. But since Thoreau also wants this reorientation to encourage her to regain an interest in herself, in her own specificity and autonomy, he cannot write in a way which allows her to become solely or wrongly interested in *him*, as if the particular way he orders words in their succession and permanence has some unique authority; he must encourage her not to take *his* word for anything, but rather to see that he and she are similarly placed with respect to learning what words can teach. What he must teach, and she must learn, is how to read in the *spirit* in which he writes, which means not accepting but assessing his computations of the surfaces and depths of words, testing his expressions against her convictions, proving his derivations to her own satisfaction.

Cavell specifies some of Thoreau's strategies of writing in which this spirit is most clearly manifest—procedures meant to enforce our simultaneous distance from and presence to our words. First, there is his emphasis upon what we call something, or what something is said by us to be—for example, '"By a seeming fate, commonly called necessity" (*Walden*, ch. 1, para. 5)', or '"The cost of a thing is the amount of what I will call life which is required to be exchanged for it" (ch. 1, para. 45)', or '"The religion and civilization which are barbaric and heathenish build splendid temples; but what you might call Christianity does not" (ch. 1, para. 78)'. Cavell comments: 'The point is to get us to withhold a word, to hold ourselves before it, so that we may assess our allegiance to it, to the criteria in terms of which we apply it. Our faithlessness to our language repeats our faithlessness to all our shared commitments' (*SW* 66). A second strategy is the construction of sentences whose meaning, in context, requires an emphasis other than, or in addition to, the one their surface grammar suggests—for example (and with the unusual emphasis stressed), '"In eternity there is indeed *something* true and sublime" (ch. 2, para. 21)', or '"I would fain say something concerning you who are said to *live* in New England" (ch. 1, para. 15)', or '"The *present* was my next experiment of this kind" (ch. 1, para. 15)'. The fact that these different emphases are available, and yet eclipse one another, shows our hand in, and so our responsibility for, what we choose to say; and the point of displaying such controlled ambiguity is to get us to assess our orientation or position towards what we say. Finally, Cavell stresses Thoreau's constant use and extraordinary placements of the word 'interest' for example, '"a young man tried for a fortnight to live on hard, raw corn on the ear ... The human race is interested in these experiments" (ch. 1, para. 87)', or '"How much more interesting an event is that man's supper who has just been forth in the snow to hunt, nay, you might say, steal, the fuel to cook it with!" (ch. 13, para. 12)'. As Cavell remarks: 'It would be a fair summary of the book's motive to say that it invites us to take an interest in our lives, and teaches us how' (*SW* 67). Examples of these writing strategies might be further multiplied, but their overall goal is clear. They teach that Thoreau's own withdrawal and his text's disinterest are designed to deliver an essentially impersonal rebuke to his reader, one which specifies her autonomy as lost but recoverable; the aim is to free her to see for herself that the meanings of our common words rebuke all our lives by showing how impoverished our possession of them has hitherto been and how rich an inheritance they bequeath.

It should be clear that the psychoanalytic model of reading which was outlined in Chapter 8 can be seen to find an analogue here. Cavell's Thoreau has therapeutic designs on his readers: just as he conceives of his own readings (of nature, of words) as a matter of allowing himself to be read, so his text is intended to subject its readers to interpretation; his writing contains a particular image of them and their needs (they are lost, lacking interest in their own lives), and involves presenting himself in such a way as to elicit his readers' transferences and to encourage them to interpret those transferences (e.g. 'He is so isolated, but then so am I'); from which activity his readers are supposed to learn how they might recover themselves whilst maintaining their freedom from the person of the author.

But the concepts of transference and counter-transference do not exhaust this parallel. The concepts of desire and seduction also play a role: Thoreau conceives of his readers' lostness as a matter of their having lost touch with their own investments of interest, and he conceives of his texts as arrangements of words whose very stillness and refusal of seduction are intended to attract his readers towards a reorientation and reinvestment of desire in language, the world, and other people. Moreover, as we saw in the previous chapter, such a conception of reorientation—one in which recovery is a matter of realizing one's loss and one's lostness, of releasing one's frozen or distorted investments of desire in past states of the world and of oneself in order to reinvest them in the future—is one for which Freudian conceptions of mourning are an appropriate paradigm.

This last point is particularly significant, for invoking the concept of mourning serves to foreground the fact that Thoreau thinks of his reader's recovery from sceptical despair as a matter of a recovery of the self—or more precisely, as a progress towards a new state of the self. According to Cavell, this accounts for the centrality of the images of moulting, dawning, and awakening in Thoreau's book: making progress amounts to discarding or moving on from the present state of our selves and allowing our selves to take on a new state, one in which we are more capable of faithfulness to the real possibilities of our words and our world. And, as these images suggest, Thoreau's vision of recovery depends upon a view of the self as doubled or as containing a double. He expresses this view in *Walden* in the following passage:

With thinking we may be beside ourselves in a sane sense ... I only know myself as a human entity; the scene, so to speak, of thoughts or affections; and am sensible of a certain doubleness by which I can stand as remote from myself as from another. However intense my experience, I am conscious of the presence and criticism of a part of me, which, as it were, is not a part of me, but a spectator, sharing no experience, but taking note of it, and that is no more I than it is you.[1]

This talk of doubleness forms part of Thoreau's more general conception of the self and its self-consciousness; for he thinks that my self is something towards which I can stand in a variety of relations—ones that are named by the same terms with which we name our relations to other selves, e.g. love, hate, disgust, acceptance, knowledge, ignorance, shame.[2] Such a conception of the self presupposes an essential doubleness within it; so the double of which Thoreau talks in the above

[1] *Walden*, ch. 5, para. II.

[2] A version of this thought is something to which Cavell is committed, as we saw in Ch. 5; and, as I emphasized there, the point here for Thoreau is not to claim that such terms have the same meaning in both of their uses, but rather to claim that each use can be thought of as an inflexion of the other.

passage is in effect one version or mode of the self's necessary relationship to itself. To talk of this double as impersonal accordingly signifies
not only that each and every self possesses such a double, but also that
its stance is essentially impartial or detached; it constitutes a distanced
mode of the self's interest in itself, one which reveals the true lineaments
of that self's present state and so provides the opportunity for the self
to move beyond it.

So the other element of this doubled self is not merely a subject of
observation but also a scene of thought and action, what Thoreau calls
an unconscious workman or indweller; and it is the combination of
these two elements which permits us to grow and change, the one
continually revealing our present state and positing (or failing to posit)
a further state of the self, the other attempting (or failing) to attain it.
This vision of self-transformation constitutes an edifying interpretation
of our experience of self-consciousness as something that may begin by
increasing our shame, but which attempts to make us ashamed of that
shame and so holds the promise of rebirth. Cavell summarizes it as
follows:

> We are to reinterpret our sense of doubleness as a relation between ourselves
> in the aspect of indweller, unconsciously building, and in the aspect of
> spectator, impartially observing. Unity between these aspects is viewed not as a
> mutual absorption, but as a perpetual nextness, an act of neighbouring or
> befriending ... *Walden*'s underlying notion, in its account of doubleness—as
> opposed, say, to Plato's notion of the harmony of the soul—is one of integrity
> conceived as an activity. (*SW* 108–9)

This notion of nextness is one which Thoreau employs to specify the
attitude towards nature which he takes to be central in the overcoming
of scepticism; it is an idea of a relation which respects otherness, which
acknowledges autonomy without denying connection. Applying it to
the self therefore internalizes the experience of otherness. It also
implies that this otherness is not to be overcome, that the nextness of
the self to itself is perpetual: there is no single final state of the self
upon accession to which our doubleness will vanish. Moreover, as the
concept of activity implies, there is no guarantee that the self will
achieve or maintain integrity; it may rather lapse into frozen passivity.
Integrity is thus something that must be worked for, something that
requires both constancy and change—a capacity to maintain that which
is worthy of maintenance, and a capacity to attain a new state of the self
by expending the very resources that have been so carefully husbanded.

And it seems clear that if we fail to neighbour ourselves, we will be incapable of neighbouring the world.

> Our first resolve should be towards the nextness of the self to the self; it is the capacity not to deny either of its positions or attitudes—that it is the watchman or guardian of itself, and hence demands of itself transparence, settling, clearing, constancy; and that it is the workman, whose eye cannot see to the end of its labours, but whose answerability is endless for the constructions in which it houses itself. The answerability of the self to itself is its possibility of awakening. (*SW* 109)

This conception of the doubled self can be thought of as the heart of Thoreau's understanding of his redemptive project, as his way of understanding not only the structure or nature of the self but also the relation in which he stands to his readers and fellow citizens. For the double, the spectating aspect of the self, possesses the very impersonality and detachment which characterize Thoreau's presentation of himself to his readers in his text. It is as if he sees his prophetic and therapeutic task as pivoting upon his ability to provide an external exemplification or instantiation of the inner double that he pictures each self as possessing; by so doing, he might return his despairing and disoriented reader to a renewed acquaintance with her own internal spectator and the possibilities of recovery for which it alone can be the source. This is another way of understanding his claim that the writing he offers can be accepted in a way which is free of the personality of the author, and so preserves the autonomy of his readers.

In addition, Thoreau's vision of the endless nextness of the self to itself can be seen as one early root of Cavell's later conception of the unknown woman. The impartial spectator represents the passive rather than the active side of human character, a side that is repressed or denied in sceptical despair, and its function is to deliver an impersonal rebuke about the present state of the self in the name of an unknown but not unknowable future state of that self. Moreover, in so far as Thoreau's own conception of himself as a redemptive writer casts him in the role of enacting a provisional, external version of that spectator, his relation to his readers and fellow citizens constitutes a preliminary sketch of Cavell's later understanding of the social role of the unknown woman.

And this returns us to the theme that was broached at the outset of our discussion of Thoreau—its political dimension. For, as we saw at the end of the previous chapter, Cavell regards the figure of the unknown woman as emblematic of a crucially important dimension of moral evaluation in a modern liberal democratic society, as a defender of idiosyncrasy against the fixations of conformity. This issue is the central concern of Cavell's most recent presentation of Emersonian perfectionism; so we can conclude our examination of the ways in which this reading of Thoreau prepares the way for his later work on Emerson by spelling out more explicitly the political dimension of Thoreau's writings.

His general vision of the state of his political community is one that I outlined in Chapter 3 when discussing Cavell's reading of Rousseau. Thoreau, too, is primarily concerned with forcing his fellow citizens to appreciate that, after the death of God and the overthrow of kings, society must be thought of in terms of the myth of the social contract, i.e. as a construction inhabited by its architects and builders, as something for which each and every citizen bears responsibility. The ills and injustices which pervade society cannot therefore be dismissed as necessities to which all must accede; they could not exist if individuals did not actively choose to remain passive, refuse to exercise their freedom to acknowledge and ameliorate such wrongs. In such a situation, conformity leads to suffering for others and, for those sufficiently fortunate or well-off not to face the reality of slavery or poverty, self-enslavement—subjecting our freedom to bonds with our fellows which (since they are not forged among ourselves as citizens acting openly on behalf of the polis) must be the result of partial, private, and secret agreements or conspiracies.

The question raised by this understanding of modern political society is how an individual citizen might protest about such matters; it is, in short, the question of civil disobedience, to which Thoreau's name is famously linked. He finds the present state of his society to be disgraceful, and so regards his own continued association with it as disgracing him; but he sees no clear way of withdrawing his consent from it. Here, we encounter one of the standing mysteries of the myth of the social contract—the question of how any citizen can be shown to have consented to membership of her polis; but if that question remains unanswered, the correlative question of how any citizen might go about declaring or effecting a withdrawal of consent must be equally mysterious. For Thoreau, this mystery means that he must recognize himself as still a member of his polis:

Apparently, as things stand, one cannot but choose to serve the state; so he will 'serve the state with [his conscience] also, and so necessarily resist it for the

most part' ('Civil Disobedience', para. 5). This is not a call to revolution, because
that depends, as Locke had said, on supposing that your fellow-citizens, in
conscience, will also find that the time for it has come; and Thoreau recognises
that 'almost all say that such is not the case now' ('Civil Disobedience', para. 8).
(*SW* 84)

   If revolution is not a possible option, civil disobedience is; and this is
the route Thoreau chooses. On his own understanding of that route,
any act of civil disobedience must force the state to recognize your
opposition to it, enter an appeal to the people (from God and from
themselves), and thereby identify and educate those amongst your
fellow citizens who have voluntarily chosen to be agents of the state.
Thoreau's night in Concord jail does not measure up well to such
standards—it fails to meet the second condition altogether; but this is to
ignore a point that Cavell takes to be crucial to Thoreau's understanding
of his deed. For he did not merely perform that act of civil disobedience,
he also engaged in the activity of depicting that act in the essay 'Civil
Disobedience'; and that second deed can be seen as the culmination or
completion of the first.
   In other words, the function of writing once again takes centre-stage;
its redemptive function extends to the domain of politics, or—more
precisely—Thoreau's conception of its function makes all of his writing
an enactment of civil disobedience, a refusal to conform to his society.
In this respect, *Walden* can be thought of as an extension or continuation
of the business of the essay 'Civil Disobedience'; in fact, a crucial part
of its work is to prepare the ground for the right reception of that
earlier essay.

. . . an appeal to the people will go unheard as long as they do not know who
they are, and labor under a mistake, and cannot locate where they live and
what they live for. Nothing less than *Walden* could carry that load of information.
(*SW* 85)

In short, Thoreau's desired political awakening requires, or can at best
be attained simultaneously with the attainment of, the self's general
awakening—its acknowledgement of its own nextness to itself. Here we
see a further way of understanding Thoreau's portrayal of himself in
Walden as withdrawn and detached; he is attempting to make himself
present to and in his words in a way which constitutes a refusal of his
voice to society, a visible withdrawal from the polis rather than an
acceptance of political muteness.
   One final point about Thoreau's notion of civil disobedience ought

to be registered here. As we saw earlier, part of his understanding of what faithfulness to the general conditions of writing involves is acknowledging the position of his reader; so enacting civil disobedience through writing must involve a certain conception of those to whom his cry of political conscience is addressed. This conception emerges in his famous remark about slavery: 'I sometimes wonder that we can be so frivolous, I may almost say, as to attend to the gross but somewhat foreign form of servitude called Negro Slavery, there are so many keen and subtle masters that enslave both North and South' (*Walden*, ch. 1, para. 8). Cavell comments as follows:

This writer's primary audience is neither the 'degraded rich' nor the 'degraded poor', but those who are in '*moderate* circumstances'; what we might call the *middle* class. We are not Chinese or Sandwich Islanders; nor are we *southern* slaves ... One mystery we make for ourselves is to say that Negro Slavery is wholly foreign to us who are said to live in New England. South is for us merely a direction in which we look away from our own servitude. This is to recommend neither that we ought or ought not do something about Negro slavery; it is to ask why, if we will not attend to the matter, we attend to it—as if fascinated by something at once foreign and yet intimately familiar. (*SW* 78–9)

Thoreau is not condoning Negro slavery, but rather suggesting his fellow citizens' complicity in its continuance and identifying an analogue between their true condition and that of the Negroes—a condition of self-enslavement, of being in servitude to their own failure to exercise freedom and to the unequal results of the private conspiracies which make up the body politic. Such spiritual unfreedom will, of course, be of little interest to those enslaved by whips and chains; and it will not be the most pressing issue about which to awaken the conscience of those who wield those whips and chains. So Thoreau's message is not directed at either group, but at those of moderate means—those who are not subject to such immediate suffering and not vulnerable to accusations of immediate responsibility for it, but whose membership of a society in which such suffering occurs makes them conspirators in its continuance. Since the conditions for revolution are not met, and the conditions for withdrawal of consent are obscure, Thoreau's aim is to get his readers to see that they must work to refuse society their voice in the name of a new and better set of social arrangements, a further state of the polis, and thereby initiate their own accession to a new and better state of the self.

The notion that a message of personal and social redemption should be thought of as primarily addressed to those of moderate means in a society which is somehow good enough to deserve the continued commitment of its citizens is, as we shall see, central to Cavell's understanding of the political pertinence of Emersonian perfectionism, to an examination of which we must now turn.

11

Emerson: Perfectionism, Idiosyncrasy, Justice

Given that so much of what Cavell attributes to Thoreau is now something he wishes to find in Emerson, it is startling to recall the briskness with which, in *The Senses of Walden*, Emerson's own claims as a philosopher of redemptive reading were dismissed, and dismissed primarily because they were seen as standing in stark contrast with Thoreau's views. We are there told that Emerson's tone is too consoling, that he offers no warnings and so no hope, and that his choice of the sermon as his literary mode is a false start (*SW* 31); and his readings of philosophers (particularly Kant) are—unlike Thoreau's—taken to be misreadings (*SW* 95). However, by the time of the Expanded Edition of that early work, Cavell had changed his view, and appended to it the first two of a series of essays and lectures which attempt to reclaim Emerson as the founder of the mode of thinking which Thoreau exemplifies; and in the rest of his work, the two thinkers are now always linked together—although (perhaps partly as an act of reparation) Emerson's work is more often foregrounded.

Although it may open my own account to accusations of repeating Cavell's earlier neglect, I will spell out the central features of Emerson's general position only in brief and primarily in terms of their similarity with features of the work of Thoreau and others—in the belief that those features have been examined in some detail in relation to Thoreau in Chapter 10 and in even more detail with respect to other thinkers in previous chapters. In effect, Cavell identifies Emerson as proposing a practice of philosophical reading as a means of overcoming sceptical despair—an essentially Romantic practice in which recounting criteria forms the central part of a more general attempt to allow oneself to be read by words and the world, and thereby to restore their life in all its relative autonomy (see 'The Philosopher in American Life', in *IQO*). His essays are seen as a contribution to that enterprise, and as constituting a very particular genre of writing; they diagnose their readers as lost, frozen, and fixated, in need of rebirth—but of a rebirth which consists of a continuous progress from one state of the self to another, an endless process of mourning and transformation to which these essays (and so their author) stand as midwife, assisting in a manner which does not countermand but rather restores and conserves the autonomy of their readers (see 'Finding as Founding', in *NYUA*). So much is common to both Emerson and Thoreau; but where Emerson is perhaps most distinctive is in the intensity and range of his commitment to criticizing the philosophical tradition. Whereas Thoreau restricts himself to a limited critique of Kant (*SW* 95, 106–7), Emerson not only deepens and extends that critique ('Thinking of Emerson', in *SW*, and 'Terms as Conditions', in *IQO*) but also engages with the empiricist tradition and with Descartes ('Being Odd, Getting Even', in *IQO*). Even here, however, the differences are not great, since neither re-gards philosophical texts as more authoritative or foundational than any other, and since both therefore regard philosophy as providing only one of many possible vocabularies within which their redemptive message can be given expression. For example, Emerson's reading of the Cartesian cogito, which generates a picture of self-reliance and so of what the individual must do to enact her existence in the face of scepticism, in essence provides a new set of terms for articulating what Thoreau called the self's answerability to itself, its neighbouring of itself.

On this new understanding of Emerson, Cavell comes to think of Thoreau 'as Emerson's purest interpreter, no one more accurate, no one else so exclusive' (*NYUA* 84); and this suggests one explanation of his inability to get Emerson right from the outset, since the latter's words were bound to keep sounding 'like second-hand Thoreau' (*SW* 124). However, another explanation is equally important, and equally perti-nent to my main theme in this chapter; for in reclaiming both Thoreau and Emerson as writers worthy of founding a tradition of philosophical thought in America, Cavell is going against America's own pervasive and almost complete denial of such a claim. In effect, then, his earlier denial of Emerson's voice partially replicated a gesture to which American culture seems wedded; he was simply succumbing to the sort of intellectual pressures which ensure that Emerson and Thoreau remain unknown to their own culture. However, Cavell thinks of this denial as a failure of acknowledgement or a mode of repression, i.e. as not just wrong but excessive and so as requiring interpretation; and his interpretation is that their unknownness results from their culture's perception that they pose a threat to or impose a demand upon it.

When the point is made in this way, it becomes clear that Cavell is interpreting Emerson's and Thoreau's relation to their culture in just the terms he used to specify the relationship between the unknown women of the melodramas and the society they confront in their films and from the screen. For these men and these women both instantiate a mode of self-reliance which amounts to a visible withdrawal from their society, a refusal of its conformity which functions as a rebuke to their fellow citizens in the name of an unknown but attainable state of each individual and consequently of society as a whole. And what these terms highlight is the political dimension of self-reliance, the implication that individuals who enact a proof of their own existence and so overcome scepticism can be thought of as engaging in a species of civil disobedience, an act that democratic society should not only permit but honour. In Cavell's most recent work, this is the aspect of Emersonian thinking that he regards as most fundamental; so, rather than trace out the details of his reading of other aspects of Emerson's writings, I shall conclude this survey of Cavell's understanding and application of Emersonian thinking by examining his attempts to demonstrate the centrality of Emersonian perfectionism to the practice of democratic politics.

Emersonian perfectionism, as it comes to be specified in the Carus Lectures, embodies an idea of the individual's truth to herself or to the humanity in herself; it is an understanding of the soul as on an upward or onward journey that begins by finding oneself lost to the world and requires a refusal of society in the name of some further, more cultivated or cultured, state of society and the self. As the myth of a journey would imply, talk of perfectionism here does not entail an idea of perfectibility, as if Emerson conceives of there being any given state of the self that is final, unsurpassable rather than simply unsurpassed; it rather captures the idea that each given and attained state of the self is final, in that each constitutes a world that the self can and does desire, to which it is (and is always at risk of remaining) attached—a world that is, one might say, self-sufficient.

Cavell claims that some such vision, or recognizable inflexions of it, form part of the Western tradition of moral thinking from its inception; he explicitly cites as perfectionist thinkers—amongst a host of others—the names of Plato and Aristotle, Augustine, Kant, Nietzsche, Heidegger, and Wittgenstein. Since, however (as this blizzard of names suggests), perfectionism is best thought of as a dimension of moral thinking rather

than a set or family of specific theories, Cavell is in no position to
define its significance by reference to a set of features possessed by all
and only perfectionist writings. Instead, in a manner that is reminiscent
of his method of characterizing film genres, he offers what can be
thought of as an account of perfectionism's founding myth or vision—a
primal story that he chooses to articulate in terms provided by Plato's
Republic but which might be differently articulated in different texts.

Obvious candidate features are its ideas of a mode of conversation between
(older and younger) friends, one of whom is intellectually authoritative because
his life is somehow exemplary or representative of a life the other(s) are
attracted to, and in the attraction of which the self recognises itself as enchained,
fixated, and feels itself removed from reality, whereupon the self finds that it
can turn (convert, revolutionize itself) and a process of education is undertaken,
in part through a discussion of education, in which each self is drawn on a
journey of ascent to a further state of that self, where the higher is determined
not by natural talent but by seeking to know what you are made of and
cultivating the thing you are meant to do; it is a transformation of the self
which finds expression in the imagination of a transformation of society into
something like an aristocracy where what is best for society is a model for and
is modelled on what is best for the individual soul, a best arrived at in the view
of a new reality, a realm beyond, the true world, that of the Good, sustainer of
the good city, that of Utopia. (*CHU* 6–7)

It should be abundantly clear by this stage of our investigation that this
image of the older and younger friends is the anchor of Cavell's work in
every one of the intellectual fields we have discussed. The older friend
is Plato's version of the Wittgensteinian philosopher, the psychoanalytic
therapist, the dramatist we call Shakespeare, the men of the remarriage
comedies and the unknown women of the melodramas, the author of
Walden, and the composer of Emerson's essays; and those whom he
befriends, who are attracted to him, constitute Plato's delineation of the
sceptic, the analysand, the audience of these genres of theatre and film
and writing. They are also, therefore, portraits of Cavell (of Cavell's
image of himself as reader and as writer) and portraits of Cavell's
(imagined) readers—they are portraits of us. As if to confirm this,
Cavell's account of the Platonic perfectionist vision concludes by
according pride of place to a certain species of writing as the medium
of this befriending:

the burdens placed on writing in composing this conversation may be said to
be the achieving of an expression public enough to show its disdain for, its
refusal to participate fully in, the shameful state of current society, or rather to

participate by showing society its shame, and at the same time the achieving of a promise of expression that can attract the good stranger to enter the precincts of its city of words, and accordingly philosophical writing, say the field of prose, enters into competition with the field of poetry, not—though it feels otherwise—to banish all poetry from the just city but to claim for itself the privilege of the work poetry does in making things happen to the soul, so far as that work has its rights. (*CHU* 7)

The practice of recounting criteria, its enactment of a renewed faithfulness to the conditions of speech and the relative autonomy of language, constitutes both an emblem and an aspect of the work of perfectionism upon and in the soul of the creature whose form of life is talking.

Even granting the coherence and attractiveness of this dimension of moral or spiritual thinking, however, there remains a key question—the question to which the Carus Lectures are primarily devoted: What does this have to do with the arrangements of modern democracies? The state of my soul might be of pressing importance to me, but why should it be of any concern to the arbitrators of what one might call public or social justice, i.e. to my fellow citizens, and to myself in the role of citizen? Indeed, is not the idea of such perfectionism inherently élitist? Can a vision which embodies some notion of spiritual aristocracy even be rendered compatible with democratic aspirations? Cavell addresses these two questions by confronting Emerson with John Rawls and his *Theory of Justice*, since the latter text forms one of the most sophisticated and humane of contemporary restatements of liberal political thought, and since Rawls explicitly sets his face against the idea that perfectionist doctrines might have a role to play in modern democratic life on the grounds that they involve élitist presuppositions.

Cavell begins by examining Rawls' reasons for this accusation of élitism; and his strategy is in effect to question whether Rawls, in his interpretation of what perfectionism demands, has correctly identified an essential feature of it. In *A Theory of Justice*, perfectionism is defined as a teleological theory which might be advanced in a moderate or an extreme form. In the moderate version, it is merely one principle amongst others and directs 'society to arrange institutions and to define the duties and obligations of individuals so as to maximise the achievement of human excellence in art, science and culture' (*TJ* 325). Everything turns here on how the notion of maximization is to be understood: does it mean that society should ensure the maximal distribution of some species of achieved excellence (e.g. a social good that might be called 'high culture'), or rather that it should encourage the maximum number of individuals to attempt to excel themselves (e.g. go beyond their attained to their unattained self)? Emersonian perfectionism, of course, is focussed upon the latter notion: committed as it is to turning away from the present state of society, it is hardly likely to be interested in extending the distribution of its present, conformity-imbued high culture; before the new state of society is attained, there is nothing—no good—to be maximized. In this sense, therefore, Emersonian perfectionism should not be regarded as a teleological theory at all.

Rawls' extreme version of perfectionism is one in which the maximization of excellence is the sole principle of social institutions; and the quotation from Nietzsche that he employs to illustrate this variant makes it clear what he deems really abhorrent about the perfectionist ideal. 'Mankind must work continually to produce individual great human beings—this and nothing else is the task ... for the question is this: how can your life, the individual life, retain the highest value, the deepest significance? ... Only by your living for the good of the rarest and most valuable specimens' (quoted in *TJ* 325 n. 51). Nietzsche's implication seems to be that there is a separate class of great men for whose good the rest of society is to live—a clearly anti-democratic notion. Cavell wishes to deny that Emersonian perfectionism requires such a principle; and, because he takes Nietzsche's thought here to be a virtual transcription of Emerson's, he also wishes to claim that Rawls is wrong to read Nietzsche as being committed to any such principle. Since the parallel between Nietzsche and Emerson is not our primary interest here, I shall concentrate upon Cavell's second claim only in so far as it illuminates his first.[1]

The question Cavell raises is how we should understand the nature and role of the 'specimens' to which Nietzsche refers. The original German term is *Exemplare*: translated as 'specimens', the term acquires biological connotations, suggesting that the grounds for identifying someone as a member of the class are specifiable independently of the instance in view and any effect it might have upon the classifier, as if such individuals are merely samples of a genus or species. However, translated as 'exemplars', the word precisely focusses upon the relationship between classifier and classified: 'the acceptance of an exemplar, as access to another realm ... is not grounded in the relation between the

---

[1] The second issue has been examined in illuminating detail by James Conant in an unpublished paper entitled 'Nietzsche's Perfectionism: A Reading of "Schopenhauer as Educator"'.

instance and a class of instances it stands for but in the relation between the instance and the individual other—for example, myself—for whom it does the standing, for whom it is a sign, upon whom I delegate something' (*CHU* 50–1).

Cavell is clearly taking Nietzsche's *Exemplare* to be instances of the older friend we encountered in the Platonic perfectionist myth, someone who does not utilize the person who accepts him as exemplary in order to further his own spiritual growth but rather reveals that person's own further, unattained self and attracts her to attain it. The 'something higher and more human' in question is thus a further or eventual state of the person who accepts the exemplar rather than of the exemplar himself; to think otherwise, to consecrate one's own person to the good of the exemplary individual, is precisely to fail to achieve freedom from the person of the exemplar, and thus to replicate the conformity of which Emersonian self-reliance is the aversion.

Cavell spells out the complex sense in which the young friend must rely upon and yet remain detached from the older friend, in which she must see herself in that friend and his words but must not see herself as or sacrifice herself to him, in relation to the reader of an Emersonian essay.

Think of it this way: if the thoughts of a text such as Emerson's . . . are yours, then you do not need them. If its thoughts are not yours, they will not do you good. The problem is that the text's thoughts are neither exactly mine nor not mine. In their sublimity as my rejected—say repressed—thoughts, they represent my further, next, unattained but attainable self. To think otherwise, to attribute the origin of my thoughts simply to the other, thoughts which are then, as it were, implanted in me—some would say caused—by let us say some Emerson, is idolatry. (*CHU* 57)

The risk of succumbing to idolatry must, however, be run—the reader needs a particular other, an older friend, to initiate her further spiritual progress—because of a possibility to which Emerson's conception of the self specifies every individual as open. For his particular version of the notion of a doubled or twofold self that we met with in Thoreau holds out the hope of change, but it also holds out the fear of fixity, of being attracted by the attained rather than the attainable self.

That the self is always attained, as well as *to be* attained, creates the problem in Emerson's concept of self-reliance—he insists on it, though not in the following terms exactly—that unless you manage the reliance of the attained on the unattained/attainable (that is, unless you side that way), you are left in precisely the negation of the position he calls for, left in conformity. That one way or the other a side of the self is in negation—either the attainable negates the attained or vice versa—is the implication I drew earlier in saying that *each* state of the self is final, one we have desired, in this sense perfect, kept, however painful, in perfect place by us. (*CHU* 12)

What the Emersonian Exemplar does is to stand for the attainable self in each reader—to free the reader's ear to hear its voice; and this means revealing the reader's present reliance upon her attained self. On such a conception of the Exemplar's task, however, the reader is drawn to perceive that the present balance of her soul is her own responsibility, something she maintains, and so that the possibility of shifting that balance is within her own grasp; in short, both the diagnosis of her dissatisfaction and its cure emphasizes the self's endless answerability for itself, and thus does not negate but rather attempts to resuscitate her autonomy. So Emersonian Exemplars are indeed representative, but representative of something that is present in and available to each and every individual, representative of a possibility to which each has access in herself; at once attracted and repelled by them, our relation to them figures our necessary relation to the further state of our selves.

Emersonian perfectionism is thus the reverse of élitist; it neither privileges nor requires any unequally distributed resources (which might have contravened Rawlsian principles of justice). Certainly, what has been said so far should make it clear that it does not presuppose inequalities of talent or of social goods; and although its focus is upon individual autonomy and so upon the good of liberty (to the allocation of which Rawlsian principles do address themselves), it does not conceive of it as the focus of distributive questions. 'Where a reforming society is characterized by enough goods and enough similarity of need and of vulnerability so that what Rawls names "the circumstances of justice" . . . are realized, liberty has no economy; I mean it is not subject to the questions of scarcity, productiveness, fair distribution, and so forth, that goods are' (*CHU* 26–7). To be sure, we can argue that one person's liberty ought to be limited by the liberty of others, but this simply means that liberty is not to be limited by such factors as taste or opinion; and if this form of words encourages the idea that there is a stock of liberty available to my social group such that, if I draw upon it, I deprive others of their fair share, then it is purely and simply misleading. According to Cavell, when liberty is the issue in politics, what matters is not rationing it but exercising it; my individual liberty may be limited by the conditions needed to establish and maintain the social order, but it should itself be exercised in determining the content of that order. Here, Cavell is reiterating the classical Rousseauian perception (examined in Chapter 3) that the realm of politics should be an extension of the realm of individual liberty: since the modern political community is understood to be the construction of its members, its laws (being determined by those members) are not heteronomous impositions upon individual citizens but are rather norms which each citizen gives to herself, and so constitute a further expression of individual autonomy. However, the uplifting force of this perception of politics depends upon its being the case that each citizen has a real voice in determining the constitution of the social order. It is to this question—the question of the reality and pertinence of my voice in arguments over the form of my society, the question of my consent to society—that Emersonian perfectionism is addressed; and Cavell's suspicion is that Rawls' theory of justice cannot accommodate but is rather committed to denying Emerson's claims at this vital point.

This suspicion will seem ill-founded to those aware of the basic structure of Rawls' theory of justice; for it involves constructing a hypothetical location within which deliberation about the founding principles of social justice might take place (the original position) which is explicitly designed to give each citizen an equal voice—this is the Rawlsian reinterpretation of the myth of the social contract. Cavell recognizes this obvious truth, and is happy to honour the emphasis Rawls places upon a notion of free and equal discourse about justice—what Cavell labels 'the conversation of justice'; but he argues that Rawls may not have distinguished sufficiently clearly between two different phases or types of such discourse.

In the Rawlsian picture, something that we might call the conversation of justice occurs at two points: there is the conversation eventual citizens must have about the justice or fairness of the original position in which the principles of justice are chosen, and there is also the conversation actual citizens must have in settling judgements about the degree of embodiment of those principles in the actual society, or system of institutions, of which they are part. For Rawls, then, the main purpose of the first, founding conversation is to establish the fairness of the principles that actual citizens will employ in the second; those principles are intended to provide a standard with which they can measure the degree to which existing social institutions diverge from ideal justice. But how are we to imagine the ways in which these two types of conversation are to be conducted?

Rawls imagines the first, founding type of conversation to be aiming at, and to be capable of attaining, reflective equilibrium: in this process, our initial intuitions or judgements about justice are used to test our initial formulations of certain principles of justice (to see whether the principles match those of our judgements in which we have great confidence), and then they are themselves adjusted by the duly refined principles (so that the principles can correct our initial intuitions about cases in which we are not certain of our rectitude, providing an answer which we can affirm upon reflection), until the two are brought into harmonious balance. Rawls attempts to demonstrate—successfully, in Cavell's view—that in the original position one particular set of principles will receive optimal agreement. But he discusses the course and possible outcomes of the second, more practical type of conversation in far less detail. What he does say is that 'The measure of departures from the ideal is left importantly to intuition' (*TJ* 246) but is ultimately to be understood as a matter of the degree of society's compliance with 'the principles that characterize a well-ordered society under favorable circumstances' (*TJ* 245), and that 'Those who express resentment [towards the existing state of society] must be prepared to show why certain institutions are unjust or how others have injured them' (*TJ* 533). These remarks seem to imply that the second, more practical conversation of justice also involves a matching of intuitions and principles, and that the matching process follows (at least one aspect of) the pattern sketched out with respect to the first, that is, that if an initial judgement that an injustice is being perpetrated cannot ultimately be backed up by reference to (or articulated in terms of) a principle of justice, then it must be rejected; and those of us to whom the accusation was voiced can think of ourselves and 'our conduct [a]s above reproach' (*TJ* 422).

It is this assumption—that even in the second type of conversation about justice, intuition must be checked, and can only be legitimized, by being brought into stable alignment with principles—that Cavell regards as problematic; for it omits or misrepresents what he takes to be (at the very least) a fundamental dimension of such conversations. It imposes a restricted conception of how we go about assessing the claims that might be made upon us in the name of justice when the degree of society's compliance with its ideals is in question (because it presupposes a restricted conception of the true nature of such claims); and it thereby encourages us to think that we are beyond reproach when we are not. Cavell labels this missing dimension or species of assessment 'reflective judgement', and contrasts it with the process of assessment as specified in Rawls' picture of reflective equilibrium in the following way.

In arriving at reflective equilibrium the picture is that judgement finds its derivation in a principle, something more universal, rational, objective, say a standard, from which it achieves justification or grounding (though the principle will typically undergo challenge and modification by the intuitive force of judgement in order to fit itself for this role). In reflective judgement, rather, the idea is of the expression of a conviction whose grounding remains subjective—say myself—but which expects or claims justification from the (universal) concurrence of other subjectivities, on reflection; call this the acknowledgement of matching ... In the former case, intuition is left behind; in the latter case, intuition is left in place ... (*CHU*, p. xxvi)

Cavell is not, of course, contesting Rawls' general methodological invocation of reflective equilibrium, or his demonstration of the existence of a single optimal set of principles upon which it is rational to agree in the original position; and he need not even deny that some questions concerning society's compliance with its ideals may best be approached in the terms suggested by the reflective equilibrium model (although he points out that Rawls has not provided any analogous demonstration that there will be an optimal resolution to this second type of conversation). His claim is that such acknowledgements need not and should not compromise the moral necessity of the demand for and exposure to the matching of one's judgement by the judgement of others in measuring our departure from the ideal of justice. The model of reflective judgement here invoked (as its Kantian label suggests) harks back to the material we examined in the first part of this book. In the fields of aesthetics, morality, and politics, Cavell identified a dimension or species of judgement that was grounded in nothing other than the self of the one judging, but which claimed to be giving expression to a conviction that those to whom the judgement was addressed shared (or should share). With respect to aesthetic judgement, Kant thinks of it as the claim to be speaking with a universal voice; with respect to morality, we might also think of the analogous phenomenon in Kantian terms, as the claim to be listening to the universal voice (of the moral law, which commands respect from all rational beings); and Cavell's claim is that the field of politics manifests something similar when an individual gives expression to a personal conviction of intolerable inequality or discrimination and claims to be speaking in the name of (to be giving voice to a real but unacknowledged conviction shared by) those she is addressing.

Since, however, the person making the claim is expressing a conviction about social injustice in a modern democracy of which both she and her interlocutor are members, a further implication of her claim is that both are somehow implicated in that injustice—that they must hold themselves and each other responsible for it. Thus, the self-grounded criticism that is being articulated is also self-directed: the critic claims to speak not only in the name of some unacknowledged conviction on the part of her interlocutor, but also in the name of an unacknowledged self-rebuke. This universal political voice is thus founded upon the idea that measuring the degree of one's society's distance from strict compliance with the principles of justice is a function of taking the measure of one's sense of compromise with injustice (or at least with imperfect justice) in one's daily life within those institutions. Cavell specifies the concepts of the self and of society that the idea of this universal voice requires as follows:

> [The] idea of the self must be such that it can contain, let us say, an intuition of partial compliance with its idea of itself, hence of distance from itself, space for consciousness of itself or of consciousness denied. The companion concept of society is such that partial compliance with its principles of justice is not necessarily a distancing of oneself from it, but may present itself as a sense of compromise by it or conspiracy with it. (*CHU* 31)

We might think of this sense of conspiracy or compromise with society as an aspect of our sense of having always already consented to society, and so to the present state of society. And Cavell's intuition of his difference with Rawls can then be articulated in the following way: for Cavell, the modern political notion of consent essentially embodies or articulates this sense of compromise or implication, and so is not such as to be constrained by principles.

The point is that Rawls' reinterpretation of the myth of the social contract places so much emphasis on principles that they come to define the very substance and range of our consent, and thereby implies that our consent to society can be precisely proportioned to the degree to which it diverges from those principles.

> The idea of directing consent to the principles on which society is based rather than, as it were, to society as such, seems to be or to lead to an effort to imagine confining or proportioning the consent I give my society—to imagine that the social contract not only states in effect that I may withdraw my consent from society when the public institutions of justice lapse in favour of which I have forgone certain natural rights (of judgement and redress), but that the contract might, in principle, specify how far I may reduce my consent (in scope or degree) as justice is reduced (legislatively or judicially). But my intuition is that

my consent is not thus modifiable or proportionable (psychological exile is not exile): I cannot keep consent focussed on the successes or graces of society; it reaches into every corner of society's failure or ugliness. (*CHU* 107–8)

The claim Cavell is making here is, in effect, that Rawls' reinterpretation of the social contract is too contractual; it captures the ideas of freedom and equality that this myth's emphasis upon agreement foregrounds, but it misses the full reach of the idea of implication in or identification with society that is also part of its attraction. For Cavell, when an intuition of our society's divergence from the ideals of justice is articulated by another and acknowledged by us, this does not always demonstrate the degree to which society (since it has departed from the principles for the sake of which I agreed to sacrifice certain natural rights) has distanced itself from me and forfeited my consent, but can rather sometimes reveal the degree to which (given that I know that I have not withdrawn from membership of society) I have given my consent to injustice. Rawls' contractual picture of consent misses the idea that the full reach of our consent is not determinable in advance by means of our explicit agreement to specific principles, but rather is experienced as or felt to reach beyond anything that a prior agreement might have fixed, to implicate us in the specific array of public circumstances in which we find ourselves. Faced with these circumstances, with their specific inequalities of liberty and of social goods, their uncertain measures of injustice and reforms whose delays are not inevitable, we need to *discover* how far our consent reaches, for what it makes us responsible, and to what we are prepared to continue to consent; the content of our consent is not settled in advance of such practical instances of the conversation of justice but is rather one of their central topics, part of what must be determined by them.

The full force of Cavell's point here may emerge if we recall once again some of the material encountered in the first part of this book—in this case, with respect to morality. There, Cavell was seen to argue that moral discourse should be thought of as an arena within which any given individual comes to adopt her own position with respect to a given moral issue, a position which—whilst respecting the procedures and canons of relevance which maintain the rationality of moral argument—is not itself determined by those procedures, and which another may competently oppose; and any ensuing moral argument between the two is equally incapable of resolution by reference to those canons and procedures alone.[2] The picture is thus one in which moral agents must make a judgement of finality concerning where they will stand and how they will regard the different stances of others, but in which such judgements cannot themselves be derived from or justified in terms of rules or principles. But Rawls' assumption about the second type of conversation of justice is that we can continue to think of our lives as beyond reproach if those who seek to criticize us on the basis of their conviction of present injustice cannot ground that conviction in a violated principle accepted by all. This assumption interprets those who respond to such criticisms with the assertion 'My life is beyond reproach' as making a judgement which is determined for them by an impersonal or intersubjective rule, as if the conversation had brought itself to a definitive end solely in accordance with its own agreed procedures; whereas, from Cavell's perspective, such an assertion would manifest one party's decision to end that conversation by refusing further debate. Such a decision is not an illegitimate or incompetent response, but it is one for which the individual concerned must bear responsibility, one through which a personal stance is defined; and in so far as Rawls' theory fails to acknowledge this, it not only misrepresents the nature of moral debate, but also itself amounts to a refusal to bear that responsibility.

For precisely the same reasons, of course, the person entering a complaint has a responsibility to do so competently (if she is claiming to speak in a universal voice, her utterance must not be traceable to envy or malice), and for deciding how to respond to the various ways in which her interlocutor might himself decide to respond. But for Cavell, the crucial point is that the fact that her complaint is grounded in a subjective conviction which is not subsumable under principles is not a reason for rejecting it but for honouring it; and honouring it amounts to allowing her judgement to challenge our own. The nature of such complaints is best illustrated by a concrete example; and the one Cavell employs in the Carus Lectures is that of Nora in *A Doll's House*. The manifest content of her explicit moral argument with her husband (the issue of whether she should have borrowed money in secret to help her husband and protect her father, and then have repaid the interest on the loan by skimping on household expenses) would fit very neatly into a Rawlsian emphasis on principles; but her climactic charges against Thorvald seem to apply to the social order as such (ranging over such

---

[2] Indeed, even in this relatively early material, Cavell was concerned to define his own position by contrast with that of Rawls; see *CR*, ch. II.

matters as marriage, happiness, honour, education) and culminate in her
conviction of outrage and dishonour, her claim that 'I could tear myself
to pieces'. According to Rawls, Nora must, in order to legitimize her
conviction of injustice, specify which institutions and individuals have
treated her unjustly; but Thorvald points out, and she is happy to agree,
that none of the reasons she might offer will be acceptable to those (like
himself) who represent the way the world is and thinks—indeed, this
very awareness that nothing she might say would make sense, and that
countless things (not all of them self-serving or morally obtuse) might
be said in defence of the world she criticizes, is a vital part of her sense
of outrage and violation. She is violated by every word that comes from
the mouths of her society's representatives; she and they do not speak
the same language. In other words, Nora's sense of society's distance
from ideal compliance takes a form which makes it inevitable that no
argument of right and wrong could or should assess it; what is required
is rather radical personal and social transformation, symbolized in the
play as a departure from her previous self and from her society.

I am taking Nora's enactments of change and departure to exemplify that over
the field on which moral justifications come to an end, and justice, as it stands,
has done what it can, specific wrong may not be claimable; yet the misery is
such that, on the other side, right is not assertible; instead something must be
shown. This is the field of moral perfectionism, with its peculiar economy of
power and impotence. (*CHU* 112)

We can think of this moral encounter as one in which a complaint is
directed to someone who, in this context, represents society, and
entered by someone claiming to be victimized by that society; and the
complaint is not dismissible as incompetent or uncaused. Then society's
representative *may* simply assert 'This is simply how it is, this is the
way things are: this is what we do'—in which case he would, in the face
of radical misery, simply be reasserting his and society's rectitude; or he
may find himself dissatisfied with what we do, with what he consents to,
find it somehow unnatural to him and yet not changeable by him
alone—in which case, as his reasons run out, he finds himself left in a
state of impersonal (and yet highly personal) shame.

Then if, as is overwhelmingly likely, I continue to consent to the way things
are, what must be shown, acknowledged, is that my consent, say my promise,
compromises me; that that was something I always knew to be possible; that I
know change is called for, and to be striven for, beginning with myself. But then
I must also show, on pain of self-corruption worse than compromise, that I

continue to consent to the way things are, without reason, with only my
intuition that our collective distance from perfect justice is, though at certain
moments painful to the point of intolerable, still habitable, even necessary as a
stage for continued change. (*CHU* 112)

In such an encounter, the voice of society's victim is the voice of the
next or further self of society's representative, and so of the next or
further state of society; and the hope is that the mode of character
formed under such a voiced invitation to one's next self is one capable
of withstanding the inevitable compromises of democracy without
cynicism. It is a way of reaffirming one's consent to society by reaffirming that this idea of consent is one of responsiveness to society; and it
thereby extends that founding consent. By showing responsiveness, and
thus showing consent, we attest our belief in society as a site for the
public pursuit of happiness in the presence of unexplained misery; thus
acknowledged, that misery compromises our happiness but it does not
falsify it.

Our acknowledgement succeeds in establishing this relationship to
the victim's misery because that misery flows from the way in which
the present state of our society has effectively deprived her of a voice
in the conduct of its affairs and the arrangements of its institutions. She
has not been victimized by being deprived of certain goods; she has
been deprived of freedom, of having a say in the constitution of her
society. As a result, that society does not give expression to a further
reach of her autonomous personality but rather cripples and distorts it,
forcing her into conformity with the voices of others, depriving her of a
part in the conversation of justice and so depriving her of her own real,
enacted existence as a citizen. Accordingly, by listening to her complaint
and refraining from reiterating our rights, we effectively give her voice
a hearing—we do not speak across or over it; and our silent renewal of
our consent in the name of a future state of society and ourselves does
not force her to renew hers, but rather offers her the chance (and a
reason) to do so.

... the demand of one's human nature for expression demands the granting of
this human demand to others ... [the granting] of their voice in choosing the
principles, or say ideas, of their lives ... every word urged from one in the
state of conformity causes chagrin, violates the expression of our nature by
pressing upon us an empty voice, hence would deprive us of participation in
the conversation of justice ... When Rawls says 'Those who express resentment
must be prepared to show why certain institutions are unjust or how others
have injured them' ... he seems to be denying precisely the competence of

expressions claiming a suffering that is (in Marx's words, but without Marx's differentiations of classes) 'the object of no particular injustice but of injustice in general', or of expressions attesting (in Mill's idea, but without Mill's indifference to classes or say social 'positions') that the mass of individual members of society have been deprived of a voice in their histories. (*CHU*, pp. xxxvi–xxxviii)

What is at stake when a cry of outrage such as Nora's is given voice is a particular individual's realization that she has been chained to her attained self—that the balance within her soul has been maintained (by her society, and so by her fellow citizens *and* by herself) against the voice of her attainable self, the voice with which she now expresses her conviction of present injustice and her call for future change. One way of thinking of that attained state of her soul, a way which gives a specific Wittgensteinian inflexion to the idea of her having been deprived of her own voice, is as one in which her own self is no longer intelligible to her. According to Cavell, this interpretation makes it clear why Emersonian perfectionism should be thought of, not as a particular and competing moral theory, but rather as emphasizing a dimension of the moral life which any theory (including that of Rawls) should wish to accommodate. For, as we saw in Part I, in Cavell's eyes any moral theory must regard the moral creature as one that demands and recognizes the intelligibility of others to herself, and of herself to others; this is a way of claiming that moral conduct is based on reason—that moral conduct is subject to questions whose answers take the form of giving reasons.

Moral Perfectionism's contribution to thinking about the moral necessity of making oneself intelligible ... is, I think it can be said, its emphasis before all upon becoming intelligible to oneself, as if the threat to one's moral coherence comes most insistently from that quarter, from one's sense of obscurity to oneself, as if we are subject to demands we cannot formulate, leaving us unjustified, as if our lives condemn us. Perfectionism's emphasis on culture or cultivation is, to my mind, to be understood in connection with this search for intelligibility, or say this search for direction in what seems a scene of moral chaos, the scene of the dark place in which one has lost one's way. (*CHU*, pp. xxxi–xxxii)

The point to be stressed here is that this search for direction is initiated by the friend or Exemplar; and in such cases as that of Nora, both accuser and accused are able to play that role for each other. The victim functions as her interlocutor's friend by rebuking him, by expressing her outrage to him and so expressing her conviction in his moral intelligibility—thereby attracting him towards the task of discovering it, finding words and deeds in which to give it expression; and her interlocutor can also function as her friend, by acknowledging her rebuke and his own compromised position, and yet showing his continued consent to their society as a site at which the necessary personal and public transformations may take place—a demonstration which rebukes any tendency on her part towards exile and attracts her to express and extend her consent to her present society as none the less good enough.

Such a process of conversation and demonstration, of saying and showing, is, therefore, an instantiation of the Emersonian picture of how and why the self is endlessly answerable to and by itself, yet none the less in need of a friend; and, according to Cavell, it is essential to the democratic enterprise. This is not because such perfectionism subsumes or is more important than the need to enact the principles of justice upon which Rawls focusses, or the need to fight economic or political victimization; these are vital issues in their own right, and they must be addressed by any modern democracy that is worthy of political allegiance (for example, by encouraging the inculcation of Rawls' difference principle—which licenses inequality only if it is to the benefit of the relatively disadvantaged, the worst-off)—and it has to be conceded that they are not matters that perfectionism directly addresses. But it does address them indirectly: for part of the moral perfectionist's claim is that if the self's duties to itself are neglected, if each individual's endless pursuit of her next, unattained self is repressed or otherwise brought to a halt, then this may cripple the capacity to formulate and recognize one's duties to others.

The idea is that it is only by cultivating a sensitivity to the claims that one's unattained self make upon one that one develops a responsiveness to the genuine needs of others. After all, if we think of the matter in Kantian terms, the essentially other-directed moral law is something that must not only be followed but internalized; actions done in conformity with it will count as genuinely moral only in so far as an inner respect for that law is the agent's reason for so acting—in other words, only if that law is addressed to the self by the self, only if it has become an element or expression of the agent's autonomy. But it then follows that the moral law can only be properly enacted if the individuals concerned are autonomous, if they have a living, genuine self from which and to which that law is delivered; and since perfectionism's concern with the cultivation of the self is precisely a concern with the establishment and maintenance of genuine selfhood or individuality, it can be argued that ignoring the dimension of the moral life with which perfectionism is concerned makes it impossible for genuinely moral (autonomous rather than heteronomous) actions to occur. In this sense, accommodating the demands of perfectionism is a pre-condition for avoiding the mere conformity with moral principles (the purely external acknowledgement of moral obligations) that in Kant's eyes constitutes an absence of genuine concern for others. Indeed, we might think of Cavell's presentation of the limitations he finds in Rawls' theory of justice as an attempt to illustrate just the lack of responsiveness, the lack of sensitivity to the genuine needs of others, that he takes to be the result of failing to honour perfectionist concerns. For as we have seen, he interprets Rawls' insistence that any genuine claim of actual injustice must be underwritten by an impersonal principle as an avoidance of the fact that bringing such conversations to an end is a personal choice, the fixing of a position rather than the result of applying an objective decision procedure. It thus amounts to a failure to respond to the specific individual and her specific cry, an invocation of general rules and principles which obliterates the possibility that this may be the expression of a genuine need. Rawls' model thus presupposes an unduly narrow conception of the needs of others; and in so far as these others and their claims stand for the needs of their interlocutor's unattained self, Rawls is also thereby failing to heed a duty he owes to himself. Seen against this background, his general rejection of perfectionism for embodying an inadequate degree of concern for others may come to appear not as a reclamation but rather as a moralization of morality—an invocation of duties to others that excuses a failure of one's duties to oneself.

Even if we set aside these indirect reasons for honouring perfectionist demands, however, Cavell wishes to argue that the dimension of social justice that perfectionism highlights possesses an independent significance whose acknowledgement is essential to the well-being of liberal polities. He is happy to admit that, in this respect, it focusses upon a form of victimization that primarily affects those who are in what Thoreau would have called the middle classes and what Rawls might call the relatively advantaged, and thereby reveals an aspect or dimension of social justice which may seem less vital than the more immediate and extreme forms of victimization that are addressed by the Rawlsian difference principle. But this appearance is, he claims, deceptive, and for two main reasons. First, because the loss of one's self is an absolute injustice whose importance modern democracy should be the first to realize; if a central part of the distinctively modern conceptualization of politics is the idea that it provides an arena within which the self might realize itself, develop a further aspect of its autonomy, then the possibility that society has systematically prevented some of its so-called citizens from participating in these opportunities constitutes a danger that must be identified and guarded against with unending vigilance. And second, because in the absence of the sort of character perfectionism cultivates, the failures of democracy will become intolerable.

That we will be disappointed in democracy, in its failure by the light of its own principles of justice, is implied in Rawls' concept of the original position in which those principles are accepted, a perspective from which we know that justice, in actual societies, will be departed from, and that the distance of any actual society from justice is a matter for each of us to access for ourselves. I . . . speak of this as our being compromised by the democratic demand for consent, so that the human individual meant to be created and preserved in democracy is apt to be undone by it . . . I understand the training and character and friendship Emerson requires for democracy as preparations to withstand not its rigours but its failures, character to keep the democratic hope alive in the face of disappointment with it . . . (*CHU* 57, 56)

Against this background, we might think of Emersonian representativeness as the condition of democratic morality: holding oneself open to the further state of one's self and one's society, requiring oneself to become intelligible as a member of that further realm and expecting others to be similarly intelligible, constitutes that dimension of the representativeness of democracy which cannot be delegated.

12

'Philosophy Cannot Say Sin'

The interpretation given in the preceding chapters of Cavell's under-standing of, as well as his willingness to identify himself with, the tradition of perfectionist thinking founded by Emerson brings us abreast of his most recent work and almost to the end of this survey of the main themes or foci of his philosophy. It also brings us to the point at which a serious critique of his overall project is at last feasible. The reader will hardly have failed to notice that my account of Cavell's work thus far has been primarily exegetical rather than critical: apart from certain limited attempts to locate his position in relation to alternative interpre-tations of the various traditions, fields, and texts in and upon which he has worked, my efforts have largely been devoted to identifying and developing its inner logic and resources. There are several reasons for this. First, there is the obvious general point that no penetrating or profound criticism of an intellectual project possessed of this degree of complexity and richness is likely to emerge from a partial or inadequate understanding of its target; in this sense, until we have been brought to see precisely what Cavell is up to, and how that project might be thought of as a species of perfectionism, we are in no position to set about criticizing it. And in fact, the exegetical account so far provided has already revealed the standard lines of criticism of Cavell's work to be either essentially irrelevant or insufficiently thought through. For example, much of the criticism hitherto directed at his work has focussed on his interests in Romanticism, psychoanalysis, and the theory and criticism of literature and film, taking them to be an indication that, whatever value his project may have, it can have nothing to do with philosophy. By demonstrating that his work in those supposedly non-philosophical areas is in fact a carefully worked-out consequence of recognizably philosophical concerns, my exegetical account as a whole is intended to constitute a definitive rebuttal of this type of criticism. The other standard line of criticism focusses upon Cavell's style: his use of parentheses and qualification, his idiosyncratic modes of punctuation, his reliance upon complex, allusive, and endlessly

The title of this chapter comes from *IQO* 26.

reflexive rhetorical strategies, his constant foregrounding of essentially personal or biographical matters—all of these seemingly self-indulgent features of his writing are taken to derogate from his claim to be engaging in philosophically rigorous work. My account thus far has, in effect, attempted to provide an implicit rebuttal of this type of criticism in two ways. First, by examining a large number of specific passages in enough detail to demonstrate that these stylistic idiosyncrasies in fact make an essential contribution to the meaning of these passages, and are deployed in a tightly controlled way which actually heightens the rigour of Cavell's work; it may be a species of rigour that analytical philosophers are not accustomed to, but it is no less admirable for that. Second, by demonstrating that many of the worries raised by Cavell's style are in fact responses to aspects of his project that can be given a powerful justification from within the perspective of his overall project: for example, the widespread accusations of self-indulgence and un-seemly self-display correctly identify the projection and enactment of self as a central feature of Cavell's work, but ignore the fact that it is one of which he is perfectly aware and which he justifies as an inevitable part of attempting to write philosophy in a way which takes on the problematic of modernism and attempts to affirm modernity, to overcome sceptical abdications or distortions of true individuality in a manner which holds out the possibility of an uncoerced community.

None the less, to claim that the standard lines of criticism fail to provide good reasons for rejecting Cavell's project is not to claim that this project is beyond criticism. On the contrary: it is only now, when the general shape of that project has been clearly set out and misleading objections to it have been dismissed, that we have any chance of developing a truly penetrating and productive critique. The most appropriate ground for such a critique can best be identified by pointing out that our explorations up to this point have left two main aspects of Cavell's project unaddressed. To begin with, certain questions concerning the political dimension of Emersonian perfectionism remain. In particular, I utilized the preceding chapter to lay out the clearest possible case for accepting Cavell's claim that contemporary liberal democratic thought—in the person of John Rawls—was bound not only to acknowledge but to honour the claims of Emersonian perfectionism, but without paying much attention to the possible ways in which Rawls and his followers might attempt to rebut that specific charge and to question the liberal democratic credentials of the Emersonian tradition more generally. Moreover, one thread in the complex intellectual tapestry of Cavell's work has so far been completely omitted from this account: that of religion, and, more specifically, the question of the relation between Cavell's philosophical practice and the writings of certain pivotal figures in modern Christianity (especially Kierkegaard). Although this issue is detectable in the background at every prior stage of the development of Cavell's work, the present stage of our investigation seems the best point at which to address it explicitly; for it can thereby be treated in conjunction with the question of Cavell's perfectionism and with that of possible liberal responses to Cavell's Emersonian critique of Rawls—and this conjunction is appropriate because the very same elements in Cavell's mode of thinking that make it characterizable as a species of perfectionism also provide the most important grounds for suspecting that it is intimately bound up with recognizably religious preoccupations, and so give the best reasons for doubting whether it is genuinely compatible with secular liberal individualism.

As this last point suggests, it could well be argued that the question of Cavell's understanding of his relationship with religion is not merely one element amongst others in his work, but the most fundamental and so the most revealing of his preoccupations. Indeed, there is one remark in his recent writings which virtually declares as much; but in order to see that this is (part of) its meaning we must recall a specific implication of Cavell's general identification with the tradition of Emersonian thinking. The relevant feature or property of writing in that tradition is in fact spelt out by Cavell himself in a recent essay: 'Emerson's "Experience" announces and provides the conditions under which an Emerson essay can be experienced—the conditions of its own possibility. Thus to announce and provide conditions for itself is what makes an essay Emersonian' (*NYUA* 103). Given Cavell's claim to be working in this tradition, and given his therapeutic conception of reading as a process of managing transference and counter-transference (in which the reader is understood to recognize her own rejected thoughts returning with a certain alienated majesty, to recognize the writer as representing her unattained but attainable self), the conclusion seems unavoidable that this particular characterization of the Emersonian genre should also be regarded as a self-characterization—as the specification of an ideal to which Cavell's own prose aspires. Any reader of Cavell is accordingly directed to look for such reflexivity in Cavell's descriptions of the work of any and all of the authors upon which his own writings have focussed—to see his accounts of their self-understandings as attempts to announce and provide the conditions under which his own essays are to be understood. And seen in this light the following pair of sentences from a late essay on Shakespeare, in which Cavell outlines his understanding of the sense in which the final scene in *The Winter's Tale* is a translated moment of religious resurrection, take on an extra dimension of significance.

> I look for it in a sense of this theater as in competition with religion, as if declaring itself religion's successor ... the reason a reader like Santayana claimed to find everything in Shakespeare but religion was that religion is Shakespeare's pervasive, hence invisible, business. (*DK* 218)

The reflexive application of this remark is not, of course, exact. Certainly, the pervasiveness of religion as a point of reference in Cavell's writings is undeniable: his awareness of it is registered at every stage of his work, from the strikingly sympathetic essay on Kierkegaard in *Must We Mean What We Say?* to the citation of St Matthew's Gospel, St Augustine's *Confessions*, and Pascal's *Pensées* in the list of perfectionist texts which introduces his Carus Lectures. But its invisibility is not solely due to its omnipresence. For between that early essay and those very recent lectures, Cavell's engagement with religion is much less concentrated and explicit, emerging primarily in a widely scattered set of isolated and glancing remarks—as if being overlooked was the condition to which they aspired; so that, in largely ignoring these remarks, Cavell's readers have maintained them in an obscurity that they seem to seek. Any attempt to dissipate that obscurity cannot therefore avoid asking why Cavell has for so long manifested his sensitivity to the pressure of religious themes in a way which courts unknownness, and why he now seems less concerned to do so. It is to be hoped that the answers to these questions, taken together with the shift to which the latter question is a response and with (both the fact and the content of) Cavell's own recent work on the unknown woman, justify the dangerous assumption to which this chapter is unavoidably committed— that one does not best acknowledge unknownness by maintaining it.

Cavell contra *Christianity*

Cavell's study of Kierkegaard's book on Magister Adler[1] fitted very neatly into the general vision of modern culture that is articulated in his first volume of essays and the roughly contemporaneous material on

---

[1] 'Kierkegaard's *On Authority and Revelation*', in *MWM*.

ethics and the social contract developed from his doctoral dissertation, and that we examined in the first part of this book: for it argued that structural analogues of the practice of ordinary language philosophy could be discerned not only in the domain of politics, morality, and modern art but also in the methods of a particular defender and critic of post-Reformation religion. Since Kierkegaard diagnosed the central ill of contemporary Christianity as a form of amnesia about its own concepts, a failure to remember and enact the true significance of the Christian form of life, it is not surprising that both this diagnosis and the consequent curative strategy—presenting reminders of the grammar of those concepts through narratives of lives in which they are either embodied or tellingly absent—should seem to Cavell to manifest a family resemblance to his own philosophical practice of recounting criteria. None the less, at this early stage, Kierkegaard seemed primarily to provide a philosophically congenial mode of access to a specific aspect or inflexion of ordinary language and ordinary life; the more radical possibility that his religious perspective might contain within it the terms of an autonomous critical understanding of modernity, and so of Cavell's own project, is at once indirectly registered and effectively dismissed only in two brief steps taken at the essay's close.

The first amounts to a critical comparison of Kierkegaard's excoriation of the press and the public with Marx's more dialectical respect for the progressive possibilities they might embody. Here, perhaps, we have an early expression of Cavell's sense that religion is somehow badly placed to acknowledge the claims of the democratic impulse (a matter to which we shall return later in this chapter); but his choice of Marx as a figure of comparison at least implies a sensitivity to the real scope and the potential power of Kierkegaard's vision.[2] The second step seems less assured; for it involves the startling suggestion that Kierkegaard's category of apostleship sets out criteria by means of which we might fruitfully understand the condition of the modern artist. Cavell is emphatic that this does not amount to the crass idea that the modern artist *is* an apostle, 'because the concept of an apostle is, as (because) the concept of revelation is, forgotten, inapplicable. So, almost, is the concept of art' (*MWM* 178). His point is rather that categories which were originally developed within the religious realm are now applicable

[2] A sensitivity that is even more apparent in Cavell's presentation of Christianity as the angel with which Becket's characters wrestle, in his essay on *Endgame* ('Ending the Waiting Game: A Reading of Beckett's *Endgame*', in *MWM*; particularly in its penultimate paragraph).

(if they are applicable at all) to the realm of aesthetic production and reception. But this picture of conceptual migration takes it for granted that the original home of these concepts has somehow been lost; in the terms emphasized by the quotation, it presupposes that, whereas the concept of art has not *quite* been forgotten or rendered inapplicable, our amnesia with respect to the concept of an apostle is total. Cavell's second step thus appears to be based, not on the obvious truth that Kierkegaard's categories are a historically specific and historically conditioned way of articulating a religious form of life, but on the tendentious and unargued assumption that they articulate a form of life that is historically outmoded; he is, in short, assuming that religion is no longer a live human possibility. If the assumption is granted, employing religious categories as a resource for clarifying our present conception of the aesthetic realm may seem insightful; but if it is not, it will seem myopic— and the conclusion that Cavell's real concern to acknowledge the specificity of religious belief was in the last analysis less strong than his desire to underline the present claims of art will appear unavoidable.

Cavell's attachment to this assumption remains evident throughout his work: for example, in *Disowning Knowledge* (a collection of his essays on Shakespeare spanning a period of twenty years), he tells us that detailed dependence on God of the sort espoused by Descartes 'is no longer natural to the human spiritual repertory' (*DK* 198), that 'satisfaction [of our increased sense of subjectivity] is no longer imaginable within what we understand as religion' (*DK* 27), and that 'Respectable further theologizing of the world has, I gather, ceased' (*DK* 36 n). These claims are, of course, tactfully presented as registrations of his personal impressions, but those impressions are of a cultural shift which renders religious belief no longer intellectually respectable or spiritually feasible; and as they stand, with no obvious argumentative support, they are unhappily reminiscent of the sort of sociological question-begging which underpins Richard Rorty's suggestion to his fellow liberals that they ignore or mock the outlook of anti-liberal intellectuals.[3] Happily, however, they form only one thread in a much more complicated weave of intellectual response.

Another important thread is woven into part 4 of *The Claim of Reason*, and relates at first sight to what Cavell takes to be the Christian attitude towards the body, towards the fact that human beings are flesh

---

[3] Cf. R. Rorty, *Contingency, Irony and Solidarity* (Cambridge, 1989). For a defence of the view that Rorty's position depends upon sociological question-begging, see S. Mulhall and A. Swift, *Liberals and Communitarians* (Oxford, 1992), ch. 7.

and blood. As Cavell rightly points out, this aspect of human nature, the fact of our physicality or embodiment, has been interpreted by Christianity as 'requiring mortification' (*CR* 471); but he fails to stress that such a requirement is ambiguous. It can be read as the expression of a wholesale disgust for the physical, a rule designed merely to repress any and all bodily demands—which amounts to reading St Paul's advocacy of the demands of the spirit over those of the flesh as expressive of a conviction that the needs of the soul oppose, and must triumph over, those of the body. Or it can be read as part of a spiritual discipline whose end is the reordering or transformation of our present nature, and which accordingly contains within it a vision of a further state or stage in which our physicality and our spirituality properly inform one another; this would amount to interpreting the Pauline dichotomy between spirit and flesh as not synonymous with, but rather as cutting across, the dichotomy between soul and body.[4] Some calling themselves Christians have adopted the first reading, thereby producing a perversion or parody of the framework they claim to inhabit—and one to which it is peculiarly vulnerable. But the obvious truth that there can be Christian denials of human nature does not entail that Christianity itself is a denial of human nature; and those commentators on Christianity who conflate the two claims are in no position to elucidate its real depths.

On occasion, Cavell leans towards the externality and reductionism implicit in such interpretations. At one stage, he presents Christianity as purely and simply a libel against the body, a libel which de Sade criticizes by literally enacting its dictates (*CR* 471); and in the final paragraphs of the book, he asserts: 'there are those for whom the denial of the human *is* the human. Call this the Christian view' (*CR* 493). But the core of his criticisms seek a level on which he avoids these lapses, and can be seen to centre around the issues crystallized in the following set of sentences.

Can a human being be free of human nature? (The doctrine of Original Sin can be taken as a reminder that, with one or rather with two exceptions humankind cannot be thus free. Yet St. Paul asks us to put off our (old) nature. What is repellent in Christianity is the *way* it seems to imagine both our necessary bondage to human nature and our possible freedom from it. In this Nietzsche seems to me right, even less crazy than Christianity . . .). (*CR* 416)

[4] A similar ambiguity attends Kant's vision of morality: does the Categorical Imperative embody a flat denial of the claims of phenomenal desire in favour of that of reason or a way of rationally ordering (and so of acknowledging) them?

Christianity appears in Nietzsche not so much as the reverse of the truth as the truth in foul disguise. In particular, the problem seems to be that human action is everywhere disguised as human suffering: this is what acceptance of the Will to Power is to overcome. (*CR* 352)

On this account, St Paul's Christian denial is of our *old* nature, and so is indeed in service of the attainment or acquisition of a new nature; what is repellent is the Christian conception of that transformation. And the aspect of this conception which befouls the truth is its emphasis upon suffering—but not (or not solely) suffering in the sense of guilt and self-punishment, rather suffering understood as passion, as the negation of action. The doctrine of Original Sin encapsulates this emphasis, for it registers the Christian sense that our bondage to our old nature is such that release from it cannot be achieved by human resources alone, that this transformation is ultimately something that happens to us rather than something that we can make happen—something that is and must be done for us. In short, it crystallizes an idea of human inadequacy and dependence upon the grace of God, and so amounts in Cavell's eyes to a denial of human self-sufficiency. The true Christian libel is thus not against the body—or rather, the Christian tendency to libel the body, understood as a resentful denial of finitude, figures a much more radical libel against human integrity and autonomy, that of (Original) sinfulness (see *CR* 455).

In his writings after *The Claim of Reason*, Cavell develops several variants of this criticism of Christianity. In a comment on Heidegger's careful maintenance of the distinction between philosophy and religion, Cavell states that 'philosophy cannot acknowledge religion as letting— the way religion works to let—truth happen, say by authority or revelation' (*NYUA* 3). When accounting for the openness of his list of perfectionist texts, he says that 'none is safe because sacred' (*CHU* 6); and when discussing the endless answerability of Emerson's prose to itself, its 'commitment to subject every word of itself to criticism', he points out that 'it is not a commitment that religion may make, sometimes to its credit, sometimes not' (*CHU* 137). These issues converge upon the figure of Christ: Cavell cites with approval Emerson's Divinity School Address, in which Christianity's focus on the person of Jesus is described as a 'noxious exaggeration', commenting that this is the 'originating case of our ... attributing our potentialities to the actualities of others ... Evidently, Emerson is treating this form of worship and consecration, even if in the name of the highest spirituality, as idolatry' (*CHU* 54). All of these remarks reflect different facets of a single perception: religion claims to have discerned truths to which it solicits the consent of all human beings, but its modes of justifying or validating those truths—by authority or revelation, by citations of sacred texts or references to the life of one particular, more than merely human, person—are not themselves fully open to human questioning; individuals have no capacity and no right to make an independent critical assessment of them, and to this degree their autonomy is denied. We can express the point in the terms definitive of modernity, according to which affirming human autonomy amounts to treating persons as free and equal. For by rejecting the responsibility of ensuring that their discourse is fully and endlessly answerable to those from whom they seek conformity with its demands, religious believers bar the free exercise of critical reflection; and by giving unique status to one historical individual, they controvert any idea of the equality of all individuals in the realm of the spirit—they deny that, in Emerson's words, 'the soul knows no persons'. From the perspective of religion, truth cannot be derived from or ultimately underwritten by merely human resources; it is authorized by someone or something radically other than those over whom it none the less has authority. And in this respect, religion sets its face against modern liberal democratic concep- tions of the individual.

On this reading of the essence of Christianity, it is not surprising that Cavell should feel unable to honour, let alone to engage with or to employ, a religious perspective;[5] for in more than one respect, his work constitutes an affirmation of just the conception of human autonomy that religion fails to honour. In particular, religion's unwillingness or inability to be fully self-critical, the fundamentally constrained relation in which this body of thought stands to itself, 'is not what one demands of a work of philosophy, certainly not what the *Investigations* expects of its relation to itself, its incessant turnings upon itself' (*NYUA* 40). And such an intellectual framework will seem doubly alien to a philosopher who is also an American, and so a citizen of a political community whose founding text is a paradigm of modern liberal democratic think- ing: 'inheriting, by interpreting in some way, the texts of ... Kierkegaard ... will not, so far as I can see, suggest one's credibility as a present philosophical voice, not for an American writer' (*NYUA* 82). Against this background, Cavell's tendency to assume that Christianity

---

[5] Although of course, he *is* able to honour congenial elements of such a framework— see *CHU* 131.

is historically outmoded becomes more than understandable; indeed, what becomes puzzling is exactly what he might mean by maintaining that religion's inability to be fully self-critical might ever be to its credit.

Between Christianity and Liberalism

If, however, we are right to see Cavell's hostility to Christianity as being rooted in a perception of its distance from the founding assumptions of modernity, what are we to make of the following claim?

> [There is] a perception shared by Marx and Emerson and Nietzsche, that 'the criticism of religion is the presupposition of all criticism.' When Marx used those words he prefaced them by claiming that in Germany the criticism of religion is essentially complete, while Nietzsche a generation later will show it to be still beginning, as Emerson had, in effect, shown him. (*CHU* iii)

Applying our reflexivity principle, we must interpret this remark as indicating that Cavell understands the reopening or the keeping open of this critical enterprise to be fundamental to his own present business, a vital part of the task of inheriting Emerson in and for contemporary America. But assigning it such priority implies that Christian thinking not only stands in fundamental contrast with American philosophy but also poses an immediate and radical threat to it, and so suggests (contrary to Cavell's own insistence that Christian presuppositions are alien to American culture) a sense of its uncanny intimacy with that which it threatens. Against this background, Cavell's increasing concern to emphasize his aversion to Christianity asks to be read as betraying a growing sense of its intellectual proximity to the presuppositions of his own philosophical practice.

This interpretation gains in credibility if we note that the quoted assertion about the importance of criticizing religion appears in the Carus Lectures, which provide a detailed account of Cavell's own philosophical practice in terms which locate it firmly within a perfectionist tradition in which such texts as St Matthew's Gospel and Kierkegaard's *Repetition* are also at home; and if we look more closely at those terms, we can see just how intimate is the connection between Cavell's practice and the very elements of a Christian perspective that he wishes to reject. In Christian thought, our unending sequence of particular sinful acts reveals that human beings are possessed of a nature which disposes them to sin and prevents them from escaping their bondage by using their own resources; what they need to attain their new nature is a fully acknowledged relationship with a particular person—one through whose words divine grace is made accessible, one who exemplifies the further, unattained but attainable human state to which God wishes to attract every individual whilst respecting her freedom to deny its attractions and spurn his grace. In Cavellian thought, the unending sequence of specific manifestations of scepticism in modernity reveals that human beings are possessed of a nature in which the sceptical impulse is ineradicably inscribed; what is needed if it is to be combated is a fully acknowledged relationship with a particular human other—one whose words have the power to make us ashamed of our present frozen and fixated state, one who, by exemplifying a further attainable state of the self, attracts us to it whilst respecting our autonomy. When the two bodies of thought are juxtaposed in this way, it becomes clear that Cavell's philosophical practice is not hostile to Christianity simply because Christianity is hostile to a fundamental value that Cavell wishes to honour; it is hostile to Christianity because the twists and turns of Christian thought at once track and travesty the truth.

Cavell's general charge in the fourth part of *The Claim of Reason* that Christianity disguises human action as suffering exemplifies this intimacy. For, as we have seen, that part of the book is precisely where he begins to develop his own intuition that a reconceptualization of human action under the aspect of passivity is essential to overcoming a sceptical understanding of human relationships with others and with the world; and this passive inflexion of the key concepts of 'acknowledgement' and 'acceptance' forms the root of his later model of philosophical thinking as essentially receptive—as a matter of reading by being read. What this suggests is that his growing reliance upon one particular version of the notion of passive activity brought to the forefront of his attention a corresponding reliance upon a different version of the same notion in Christianity, and so made inescapable a new perception of Christianity as a *rival* perspective—not something that was historically outmoded or essentially engaged with issues beyond Cavell's philosophical horizons, but a viewpoint on human life with which his own is in intimate competition at almost every point. In short, Cavell's later work on Emersonian perfectionism merely confirms his much earlier remark that one ought to 'find the *words* of the Christian to be the right words. It is the way that he means them that is empty or enfeebling' (*CR* 352).

If, however, we acknowledge the truth of this remark—if we see Cavell as wishing, and so presumably needing, to employ Christian words in essentially unchristian ways—and if we put it together with his perception of the cultural impertinence of Christianity to America, then it becomes clear that Cavell's own practice runs the risk of being culturally impertinent to his fellow Americans. For if his position is characterized by its need to employ words whose original grammar articulates a perspective that is both distant from and hostile to the modern, liberal democratic conception of individual autonomy, how can he know that he avoids that estrangement? That this worry is at present a guiding one for him is, I think, evident throughout the Carus Lectures, which he structures in such a way that their primary (although not exclusive) preoccupation is an attempt to juxtapose his perspective with that of John Rawls—a scholar who could happily stand as the contemporary Exemplar of American liberalism. Cavell thus invites his audience to regard them as an attempt to demonstrate the pertinence of his Emersonian perfectionist practice to the living present of democratic politics in the Western world. Revealingly, however, the call of collegiality puts Cavell in a position to report the reaction of Rawls himself to this putative juxtaposition. 'In the two long and full conversations we devoted to them, the topic that most interested both of us was whether *A Theory of Justice* denies anything I say, whether it doesn't leave room for the emphases I place on things' (*CHU*, p. xxii). The context makes it clear that Rawls sees his theory as leaving room for Emersonian perfectionism not because the latter embodies claims about social justice with which a liberal should or must agree, but rather because the issues with which this perfectionism is preoccupied (with the self's coming to its next self) are ones which on the face of it are 'not ... of any particular interest to the rule of justice' (*CHU*' p. xxii). Now, of course, first impressions may require revision—and I attempted to present the best available case for such revisions in the preceding chapter; but those impressions do take the form of questioning the pertinence of Cavell's concerns rather than their accuracy or validity, and so oblige Cavell to spend most of his time in the relevant parts of the lectures struggling with this particular possibility.

Moreover, these worries are not just ones posed by outsiders or others ill-versed in Cavell's work; their voice clearly haunts Cavell himself. He repeatedly presents himself as doubtful about his own view that his concerns are pertinent to those of Rawls: he talks of that view as merely a surmise or as raising a question, acknowledges that even if it is valid it may be 'marginal enough' (*CHU*, p. xv) not to require any modification of Rawls' theory, and describes his endeavour as expressing and proposing reservations about certain passages which may never 'arrive at anything other than local supplementations or extensions of those passages [or] uncover a disagreement with that work whose line of resolution is not clear' (*CHU*, p. xxvii). And the idea that such remarks are merely introductory (rhetorical or real) expressions of uncertainty about having mastered the intricacies of Rawlsian thinking loses its initial plausibility once it is noted that the perturbation which they register can be felt in the structure of the lectures as a whole.

It will, I believe, be agreed by those familiar with the rest of Cavell's work that the text of the Carus Lectures presents problems of accessibility which outstrip those raised by any other of his writings. From the outset, his books have worked to let truth happen through complex patterns of resonance and mutual implication between relatively discrete essays, and have typically been prefaced by material whose import with respect to the main body of the writing went far beyond the introductory. Even by these standards, however, the reader of the Carus Lectures faces an entirely new degree of difficulty. Presented with a set of three lectures to which a preface, an introduction, and two appendices are attached, and attempting to read them in printed order, she will find that not only the preface (within which a brief warning to this effect is buried) but also the introduction provide substantial clarifications and elaborations of the central pillars of Cavell's position which make little sense before the main lectures are read. But on turning to begin with the lectures themselves, she will find that they remain deeply obscure on certain basic points in the absence of the 'preliminary' material. There is, in short, no right place to begin reading: light will dawn, if at all, only over the whole and as a result of frequent and often bewildering oscillations between disparate and chronologically distinct stretches of prose. The text is experienced as one whose meaning crystallizes, not in particular passages or sequences or lectures, but in the spaces between them; and this makes it almost impossible to attain a real conviction that that meaning has been correctly grasped. But of course, in so far as his readers remain uncertain whether they have grasped the true nature of Cavell's perfectionism, they can never deliver the final judgement that that perfectionism is not really pertinent to them. In other words, hypothesizing an anxiety about pertinence makes good sense of the otherwise puzzling fact that, in these lectures, Cavell's most fundamental desire seems to be that the perfectionist character of his thinking be made known whilst remaining unknown.

However, compiling evidence for thinking that Cavell is subject to

this anxiety leaves unaddressed the important question whether he—
and we—should conclude that his position really is impertinent to
American culture; anyone attempting to develop a position which
employs Christian words whilst maintaining an affinity with modern
liberal democratic ideals is engaged on a task that is fraught with
difficulty, but not one that can be seen to be impossible from the outset.
The next question that must therefore be addressed is whether his
declared affinity with the liberal conception of the individual is real, or
rather a defensive denial of his real distance from it.

At first glance, it may seem that the liberal can have no real reason
for anxiety here: after all, has not Cavell explicitly rejected any reliance
upon God in his practice of thinking, and declared the Christian sense
that human nature stands in need of supernatural aid a calumny against
human self-sufficiency? But, as we have already seen when noting the
structural analogies between Cavellian and Christian thought, rejecting
a God-centred account of human beings is not equivalent to accepting
an orthodox liberal account; what, for example, is a wholly secularized
liberal to make of Cavell's attempt to recover the significance of
Romanticism for philosophy, his use of such notions as the death and
resurrection of world and self? The mere absence of a capital letter or
two in his deployments of these terms will not assuage such a liberal's
discomfort over Cavell's interest in ways in which an old story of
human redemption may be recounted. This type of objection, however,
is one that Cavell has already met head-on in other contexts; for,
example, responding to the accusation that his talk of self-creation or
self-re-creation is mystical or metaphysical, he makes the following
point:

> what is discredited in the romantic's knowledge about self-authoring is only a
> partial picture of authoring or creation, a picture of human creation as a
> literalized anthropomorphism of God's creation—as if to create myself I were
> required to begin with the dust of the ground and magic breath, rather than
> with, say, an uncreated human being and the power of thinking. (*IQO* iii)

In short, although Cavell's use of such terms as resurrection and
redemption is not careless or merely rhetorical, they can be thought of
as evoking pictures—and so as in need of elucidation; and this means
that their value depends on the value of that elucidation, in our sense of
their precision and comprehension when the specific application that
Cavell wishes to give them has been spelt out. Accordingly, if the
liberal wishes to justify her discomfort, she must locate difficulties in

the conception of the human individual which emerges from Cavell's elucidation of his pictures of redemption.

Moving to this deeper level of debate, we can see at least two reasons for liberal discomfort with Cavell's conception of the self. First, Cavell's subject is essentially dependent: when he summarizes his reclamation of the Christian vocabulary by saying that 'the other now bears the weight of God' (*CR* 470), he rejects Descartes's way of interpreting a human intuition of dependence without rejecting the intuition itself—he simply reinterprets that dependence (and so reclaims and preserves it) as relating to something other than God. In particular, he makes central the idea of our dependence upon other human beings, or more precisely upon one human other (variously described as the Wittgensteinian philosopher, the best case of knowledge of other minds, the Platonic older friend, or the Emersonian Exemplar), without whom our redemption from particular sceptical onslaughts is not easily imaginable; and he also pictures us as dependent upon language, which provides the essential resource for the redemptive philosophical practice of recounting criteria, constitutes the defining characteristic of the human animal, and is encountered as something always already in place—something over which the individual could never conceivably attain fully transparent mastery.

It is striking that both species of dependence are themes central to the recent communitarian critique of liberalism—a critique which centres around the suspicion that political theories such as that of John Rawls are founded upon a conception of the person that is incapable of acknowledging the constitutive importance of social and linguistic matrices in the life of the human individual. However, Rawls' most recent writings have attempted to map out a reading of his own work in terms of which his liberal emphasis upon the rights of the individual is not only rendered largely compatible with such communitarian claims, but is also characterized in such a way that its pursuit is inseparable from a commitment to the construction of a certain type of community (one in which, roughly speaking, the maintenance of individual rights is understood to be a communal good);[6] and this suggests that, in so far as Cavell's position resembles that of the communitarians, the Rawlsian liberal is not likely to be discomfited by it.

Of course, questions might be (and have been) raised about whether such a communitarian reading of Rawls is, in the end, justifiable; but

---

[6] Both the original communitarian critique and Rawls' more recent response to it are discussed in some detail in Mulhall and Swift, *Liberals and Communitarians*.

298 Philosophy, Perfectionism, and Religion

from Cavell's perspective, such a strategy would miss the key point of difference between Rawls and himself, for that lies not so much in the absence of the concept of community in Rawls' thinking but in its inadequacy. Here, we must recall the central point of conflict that emerged in Cavell's Emersonian critique of the *Theory of Justice* in the previous chapter, namely, the idea that Rawlsian liberalism is founded on an unduly contractual conception of the social contract. On this reading, Rawls' tendency to dismiss the Emersonian perspective as irrelevant to questions of social justice stemmed from his inclination to assume that the question of how far actual societies diverge from ideal justice must be settled by the invocation of impersonal and objective principles; and this in turn was said to depend upon the assumption that those principles define the very substance and range of citizens' consent to that society, so that consent was pictured as being precisely proportionate to the degree to which those principles are implemented. But on Cavell's view the myth of the social contract is precisely not such as to specify that and how the scope or degree of my consent is modifiable; on the contrary, it captures an intuition that I cannot keep my consent focussed upon the successes or graces of my society, but rather find that it reaches into every corner of society's failures or uglinesses. In other words, where Rawls is inclined to picture our membership of society as being determined by a prior agreement to certain rules or principles, Cavell characterizes it as something we feel to reach beyond anything that a prior agreement might fix or a set of rules delimit: for Cavell, society is something in which we are always already implicated, and with which we always already identify. Invoking the concept of rules or principles as an interpretation of the myth of the social contract (no less than doing so as an interpretation of morality[7]) is, according to Cavell, to distance the individual from society in a way which fails adequately to capture the intimacy and depth of our dependence upon it.

In short, even if Rawlsian liberalism is given a communitarian reading, Cavell's inflexion of communitarian themes of dependence is such as to conflict with that liberalism at a particularly sensitive point; and if one of the most sophisticated theoretical exponents of liberalism is likely to find this aspect of Cavell's conception of the individual and society fundamentally alien, then that conception will seem even more distant from the values and assumptions of contemporary American culture more generally. But Cavell also emphasizes that he conceives of

[7] As I mentioned in the previous chapter, this is a strategy for which Cavell roundly criticizes Rawls in *CR*, ch. II.

the subject as essentially divided as well as dependent. His understanding of the role of scepticism in modern Western culture has always made him prone to situate the sceptical impulse as the modern inflexion of an ineradicable element in human nature, and so to think of the drive to deny the human as itself internal to the human; he thereby offers a picture of human beings as language animals essentially riven by a desire to deny their essence in just the way that the reviled doctrine of Original Sin imputes a necessarily non-integral human nature. But in his most recent work, this perception of rivenness has achieved a new formulation and renewed centrality; for Emersonian perfectionism is predicated upon a conception of every individual as inherently doubled or duplex, and so as always already riven. This is an inevitable presupposition of any theory that pictures having a self as a process of becoming or failing to become—of being committed to one's attained self and thereby blind to the attractions of one's further or unattained self, or of being committed to one's next self and so avoiding conformity with one's present self.

> ... being drawn by the standard of another, like being impelled by the imperative of a law, is the prerogative of the mixed or split being we call the human. But for Emerson we are divided not alone between intellect and sense, for we can say that each of these halves is itself split. We are halved not only horizontally but vertically ... (*CHU* 59)

Such multiple splittings of the self may hold few terrors for someone whose work has always honoured the work of Freud, but they will seem unattractive to liberals such as Rawls who, even whilst wishing to locate themselves in a Kantian tradition, wish to dissociate themselves from the single internal split that it envisaged.[8]

The difficulty of mapping Cavell's dependent and divided subject on to what I am crudely calling 'the' modern liberal conception of the individual is, I believe, mirrored in the difficulty Cavell finds in mapping his perfectionism on to the contours of the cultural terrain as liberalism defines them. As Alasdair MacIntyre has recently reminded us,[9] liberalism traditionally divides cultural life into a series of compartments or spheres, each with its own self-sufficient standards and goods: science, sport, politics, morality, art, and so on. One might say that its respect for the autonomy of the individual and its respect for the

---

[8] See J. Rawls, 'Kantian Constructivism in Moral Theory', *Journal of Philosophy*, 77/9 (1980), 515–72.

[9] A. MacIntyre, *Whose Justice? Which Rationality?* (London, 1988), 337.

autonomy of these cultural spheres hang together. Cavell's Wittgensteinian method is hardly uncongenial to the acknowledgement of differences
between language games and aspects of our form of life; but from his
earliest work, as we have seen, it has been harnessed to a project which
depends crucially upon uncovering connections between these spheres.
In Cavell's first volume of essays, this was manifest in his repeated
discoveries of structural analogies between modern art, morality, and
politics and modern philosophy; and in his more recent lectures,
Romanticism, Freudian psychoanalysis, and certain genres of film are
seen to offer converging models of redemption. The tensions generated
by these competing instincts emerge in the Carus Lectures when Cavell
asks whether Emersonian perfectionism should be characterized as a
specifically moral or a political or even an aesthetic matter (see *CHU*,
pp. xxii-xxxii). He sees good reasons for relating it to all three spheres,
and no good reasons for relating it primarily to any one of them; but
even if he is right to think that the confusion of categories his
perspective thereby produces suggests that the orthodox liberal conception of the integrity and autonomy of those categories must be re-
thought, that is likely to involve a corresponding revision of the liberal
conception of the integral, autonomous individual which hangs together
with it.

   I am inclined to summarize the problem by saying that, whereas
liberalism typically begins by assuming the existence of autonomous,
integral individuals and proceeds to establish and defend their possession and exercise of particular rights, Cavell regards such autonomy
and integrity as a qualified and always provisional or threatened
achievement, and so concerns himself with establishing and maintaining
the individual's more basic right to the genuine possession and exercise
of a self (or to the possession and exercise of a genuine—a becoming
rather than a becalmed—self). 'Emersonian Perfectionism is not primarily a claim as to the right to goods (let alone the right to more
goods than others) but primarily as to the claim, or good, of freedom ...
[It is] the paradoxical task of secularizing the question of the profit in
gaining the whole world and losing one's soul' (*CHU* 26). It may be the
case that these stark differences should best be thought of as differences
with liberal individualism rather than with liberalism—that Cavell's
vision of a divided and dependent self, one capable both of losing itself
and of being drawn to find itself, in reality conflicts only with certain
outmoded liberal conceptions of individual integrity and autonomy, but
none the less maintains a focus upon the individual that secures an

affinity with liberal thinking more generally. But it may rather be the case that even a secularized version of finding and losing one's soul must enforce alterations to liberal conceptions of individuality or selfhood which take them beyond the point of intellectual integrity. The choice between these two conclusions cannot definitively be made here; but as they stand at present, Cavell's arguments to show that Rawlsian liberalism fails to acknowledge a perfectionist demand that any genuinely liberal democracy must honour—based as they are upon extremely limited textual citations and so upon a large degree of speculative extrapolation—display a tentativeness and so suggest a fragility which makes the first conclusion less than compelling.

Christianity contra *Cavell*

However, in concentrating on the liberal's worries about the stability of Cavell's chosen intellectual and spiritual location somewhere between liberalism and religion, we have thus far overlooked the question whether the Christian might have anything to contribute to this debate. The structural analogies between the Christian and the Cavellian stories of redemption—the substitution of a drive towards scepticism for Original Sin, of ordinary language for the Word, of an Emersonian Exemplar for the Divine Archetype—would alone be enough to tempt two very different responses: first, to regard such employments of Christian concepts as empty and enfeebling, as the truth in foul disguise, and accordingly strive to prevent their abuse; and second, to infer from this need to employ Christian terms an ultimate dependence upon the spiritual and moral resources of the wider Christian framework of thought, and accordingly to encourage their use.

   The second of these strategies is doubtless the less obvious of the two, so it may be worth examining it in some detail by exploring its deployment (although not, of course, with specific reference to Cavell) in Charles Taylor's recent work *Sources of the Self*.[10] As part of his general attempt to provide a genealogy of the modern notion of the self, Taylor claims that one important element in that notion is the sense that the self not only possesses a first-person viewpoint on its world but also has a rich and inexhaustible inner nature which stands in need of exploration and articulation if it is to be realized—and only if it

[10] (Cambridge, 1989), esp. part 3.

is realized can the self's full individuality be achieved. This notion of the self's inner nature is clearly consolidated most explicitly in Romanticism, but according to Taylor it is but one aspect of a more general phenomenon whose roots he traces back to the time of the Reformation and which he labels the affirmation of ordinary life. By 'ordinary life', he means the domain of work and of family life, of production and reproduction; and by its affirmation, he means that Western culture began to recover a sense that the activities prosecuted in those domains constituted an important element of human flourishing. In part, this revaluation had a social and political dimension, since it involved a shift away from activities (such as contemplation of the good or achieving honour in battle) that had been open only to certain social classes and towards more democratically accessible ones; but most importantly for Taylor, it also had a religious inflexion—since on his view, the Protestant Reformation centrally involved a challenge to prevalent (if theologically inaccurate) Catholic conceptions of the sacred, rejecting the idea that God's power could be more intensely present or easily accessible in certain times and places (e.g. sacraments) or through certain modes of life (i.e. those of monk, nun, and priest), and arguing instead that the supposedly profane life of work and the family was just as much interpenetrated by and responsible to the divine.

In effect, productive and reproductive fruitfulness became seen as part of man's role as steward of God's creation, as the human contribution to the maintenance and development of God's purposes as embodied in the natural order. Monkish asceticism scorned God's gifts, but complete absorption in earthly pleasures would be equally reprehensible, since it involved loving creation rather than its Creator. Stewardship was thus a matter of cultivating the world whilst remaining detached from it: in work, that meant unremitting labour devoted to the greater glory of God; in marriage, it meant cultivating a sense of the sanctity of love for one's spouse and children without such love being centred on itself. Protestantism thus precipitated a renewed sense of nature as a providential order, a system of beings with interlocking purposes set by God. This underwrote the new Baconian science and its task of discerning and utilizing the natural order; and when later developments (epitomized in Locke and Shaftesbury) diminished the Reformation emphasis on Original Sin, an awareness of human beings as part of this order led to wider ranges of human desires and needs being seen as divinely implanted (and therefore ultimately valid) impulses. In particular, it meant that the human instinct to seek pleasure and avoid pain became seen as a sign that God's purpose would be served by the maximization of overall human well-being; and the new centrality of benevolence in the scheme of the virtues flowed from this.

According to Taylor, these are the roots of deistic affirmations of the ordinary such as Hutcheson's. God is to be praised as the author of a world in which the purposes of all beings interlock harmoniously, so that each in seeking her good will also serve the good of others. Here, God's goodness consists in his bringing about our good; and that good is defined in purely creaturely terms as happiness—even the rewards of the next life seemingly being more intense but qualitatively identical to those available here below. There is no sense of God's purposes, and so our own most fundamental purpose as his creatures, being inscrutable from a human viewpoint—no sense of religion as embodying a super-natural telos, as taking human beings beyond (as well as incorporating) natural morality. To know how to live, we need only read off God's intention from the design of nature, ourselves included; we live well by furthering that design, which means acting in accord with our normal instincts towards benevolence. Our reason may be needed to demon-strate that those instincts are good; but only acting in accord with them will allow us to participate in God's purposes. In short, we encounter nature as a moral source in experiencing the right inner impulse.

On Taylor's view, Rousseau pushes this sense of nature as norm from an inner tendency to an inner voice: conscience speaks to us in the language of nature, and regaining contact with that voice would mean transforming our motivation, having a wholly different quality of will. This way of affirming nature's goodness suggests that attention to our desires, feelings, and sentiments need not be just one mode of access to the good but rather definitive of it; the spirit of nature in me *is* the good. Rousseau thereby provided the terms in which Romantic expressiv-ism would later develop an idea of the autonomous moral competence of the voice of nature within us. The normativity of nature thus generates a sense of the normativity of our sentiments, and a correspond-ing imperative to explore nature as a moral source by exploring and articulating the impulses and feelings through which it speaks in us; we find ourselves with a conception of each individual as possessed of an inner voice.

It is important to see that, for Taylor, the account that I have just summarized is not intended as a scholarly exercise in historical explana-tion. It is not an excessively idealist analysis of how one element of the complex and multi-faceted modern notion of the self came about; it is rather designed to elucidate the appeal of that element by means of an analysis of the discourse of its most articulate advocates at the time of its emergence and crystallization, and to show how each alteration in its conceptualization can be seen to improve on or to impoverish available conceptions of the human good. In short, Taylor wants to highlight both the attractions of and the logical connections between aspects of our prevailing self-conception. For example, a key lesson that he wishes us to draw from the development of his narrative is a development or modulation that he sees as inherent in the concept of the ordinary itself: introduced as denoting one particular set of activities in contrast with others, by the time of Hutchesonian deism, the range of activities and feelings deemed 'ordinary' has expanded to the point at which it is evident that what matters is not the activity engaged in but the attitude adopted towards it. But for Taylor, this was already adumbrated in the Reformation: for when the Puritans affirmed the profane, they did not wish merely to invert a fixed hierarchy of activities but to subvert it entirely; by denying that Holy Orders brought one closer to God, they did not mean to affirm this of family life instead, but rather to argue that what determined one's closeness to God was not the nature of one's activity at all but the (worshipful) spirit in which one did it—as their sermons had it, God loveth adverbs. And this emphasis upon attitudes rather than activities is itself a distinctively modern turn, according to Taylor, since it exemplifies a new sense that both self-examination and self-transformation are essential to the achievement and maintenance of human goods. The simple recognition of an objective order of goodness in the world is no longer enough; the world's being good is no longer independent of our seeing and showing it as good.

And a crucial part of the relevance of Taylor's account for my purposes lies precisely in its claim to have anatomized essential elements of the culture of modernity. For it thereby provides a framework of cultural analysis within which the distinctive features of Cavell's Emersonian philosophical practice can be seen to fit very happily: not only does that practice clearly constitute a philosophical inflexion of the general theme of affirming ordinary life, its central elements as we have outlined them (a concern with the ordinary understood as the domestic and the profane, an interest in marriage and in threats to marriage, a reliance upon self-knowledge and self-exploration as a fundamental mode of self-realization, and a participation in Romantic themes of renewing the intermingled life of self and nature through an alteration in attitudes towards the ordinary) correspond in startlingly precise detail with the pivotal stages and key elements of Taylor's own account. In this respect, the form and trajectory of Cavell's Wittgenstein-ian practice of recounting criteria serves simultaneously to confirm the accuracy and perceptiveness of Taylor's analysis of modernity, and to place Cavell in the mainstream of modern culture rather than on its periphery; we might say that Taylor's work provides independent confirmation of Cavell's own view that his philosophical perspective is committed to the affirmation of values that are central to modernity.

However, the other main respect in which Taylor's account is relevant for my purposes derives from the fact that he employs it as a means of prosecuting an additional aim or project: for, as we have seen, it is structured so as to lay great emphasis on the religious roots of the distinctively modern affirmation of the ordinary. On Taylor's view, every element of that affirmation can be seen not only to have a counterpart in the Christian religious tradition, but also to have origi-nated in that tradition (or more precisely, in a quarrel internal to that tradition). With respect to the first point, Cavell himself acknowledges that there are religious inflexions of this affirmation of the ordinary, e.g. Kierkegaard's vision of the Knight of Faith expressing 'the sublime in the pedestrian' (see *NYUA* 39); but what Cavell does not address, and what Taylor is particularly interested in raising, is the issue of whether an affirmation that is historically rooted in religious understandings of self and world may not also be spiritually rooted in such a framework. For that historical rootedness at least raises the question of whether the intellectual underpinnings of such secular affirmations can be estab-lished, and whether the extensive and intensive spiritual demands they make can be borne, without falling back upon the resources of a theistic framework.

In the work he has so far published, Taylor has done no more than raise this question; and it is indeed difficult to specify how one might establish a clear answer to it. But one way of attempting to show that Cavell's perspective may not have fully uncoupled itself from the religious tradition in which some of its elements originate and find their counterpart is to question whether his own practice avoids the criticisms he levels at religious thought. Is it, for example, really possible for idolatry to be avoided in the relationship with an Emersonian Exemplar, for such a person's words to be treated as fully open to revision and rejection; or is it rather the case that, with respect to the key figures to which Cavell has related his own reading practice (e.g. Wittgenstein,

Emerson, Shakespeare), there is a clear point at which criticism is no longer allowed a purchase and the Exemplar's words are in effect treated as safe and so sacred? Again, is the central Cavellian idea of an ineradicable human impulse to deny the human, an impulse whose modern inflexion is scepticism, any less offensive to modern conceptions of individual autonomy and integrity than the doctrine of Original Sin? Another way of approaching the issue would be to suggest that, in the face of all the obstacles and threats (both inner and outer) to the achievement of an enacted individual existence, a genuine human community and a recovered world that Cavell himself notes—in the face of the self-deceptions and self-punishments tracked by psychoanalysis, the conformities imposed by society, and the ravages of the natural world—no individual could conceive of those goals as attainable by drawing upon purely human resources. Are such doubts about human self-sufficiency, such worries that the notion of a supernatural source of aid (i.e. of grace) may after all be indispensable to redemptive visions of this kind, really open to dismissal as a further expression of human self-denigration? Or is Cavell's conviction that ordinary humans in community possess the resources with which to overcome these obstacles itself closer to naïve optimism than to an earned and cheering realism?

Unfortunately, I can at present do no more than suggest the form in which such questions might be posed and prosecuted. I can, however, make a little more progress in the direction of imagining possible ways of applying the first strategy mentioned at the beginning of this section—that of asking what a Christian might say about Cavell's depiction of Christianity and about the attractions of Cavell's own position. With respect to the first of these issues, she must acknowledge the truth of Cavell's claim to have detected elements in religious thought which controvert any conception of human beings as fully self-sufficient beings; the workings of grace and of arguments from authority and revelation are essential to Christianity. But of course, religion does not absolutely exclude or deny the importance of human individuality. On the contrary: we should recall, as does Cavell himself, 'Hegel's interpretation of Christianity as the new form of civilization that gives expression to the infinite right of subjective freeedom, "the right of the subject's particularity, his right to be satisfied"' (*DK* 27). The centrality of free will, and of the infinite and equal importance of every human soul, in the Christian framework means that its conception of the subject is certainly not wholly alien to modernity. It would be better to say, with Wittgenstein, that 'the attitude that's in question is that of taking a certain matter seriously and then, beyond a certain point, no longer regarding it as serious, but maintaining that something else is even more important'.[11] But what is this 'something else'?

In the Carus Lectures, Cavell gives expression to religion's failure to attach ultimate importance to the individual in terms which relate it to, and so distinguish it from, Emersonian perfectionism:

the [religious] idea would be that the end of all attainable selves is the absence of self, of partiality. Emerson variously denies this possibility ('Around every circle another can be drawn', from 'Circles'), but it seems that all he is entitled (philosophically) to deny is that such a state can be *attained* (by a self, whose next attainment is always a self). Presumably a religious perfectionism may find that things can happen otherwise. (*CHU*, p. xxxiv)

In other words, against Cavell's Emersonian emphasis upon endlessly reasserting the attainability and attractions of every next state of the self, Christian thinking would posit the goal of the self's endless journey as that of selflessness—some mode of absence of the self; and, as long as the Christian avoids imagining that such a state is attainable on earth (a view that would clearly be a religious as well as a philosophical error), Emerson has no ground for denying its coherence. How, then, might we evaluate the merits of these rival visions of the self's sublunary orientation?

Certain Christian writers have offered uncompromising pictures of this striving to attain selflessness:

We possess nothing in the world—a mere chance can strip us of everything—except the power to say 'I'. That is what we have to give to God—that is, to destroy ... the chief use of suffering is to teach me that I am nothing ... I must love being nothing. How horrible it would be if I were something! I must love my nothingness, love being a nothingness. (*GG* 23, 101)

Simone Weil's call for the destruction of the 'I' can easily read like an avocation of spiritual masochism or suicide; and as such, it seems to offer little more than 'an excuse for our passiveness, or self-punishment, our fear of autonomy, hence ... a cover for our vengefulness' (*IQO* 38). But this ignores a crucial connection these passages make between the destruction of the self and the presence of God. According to Weil, destroying the self means giving the self up to God, allowing God to manifest Himself in the self's place: where ego was, there God shall be.

---

[11] L. Wittgenstein, *Culture and Value*, ed. G. H. von Wright, trans. P. Winch (Oxford, 1980), 85.

And since the Christian God is the God of love (since love is not what He does but what He is), then aiming at self-annihilation amounts to aiming at that particular orientation of the self through which it exists in love. What Weil's talk of self-destruction brings out is that this love, of which Christ's salvific action is the pattern, is essentially self-sacrificial, a matter of self-abnegation.

So, the nothingnesss to which we must freely tend is not a simple absence; it is a practice of dying to the self. As Kierkegaard spells out in *Works of Love*, it constitutes a form of love in which the believer loses herself in the object of love, which in the Christian case is the whole of creation but most particularly the neighbour. The neighbour is every human being, and the Christian loves her neighbour not because of any particular relationship in which the two stand (as relatives, lovers, friends), but simply because the neighbour stands there; she is loved not because of who she is but because she is, because of her sheer contingent existence. In so loving her, the Christian renounces herself in that she does not press those claims that human beings normally and legitimately advance even in the context of a loving relationship with others—she places no limits on her responses to her neighbour's claims on her, she does not expect reciprocation or consideration from her, she does not resent ingratitude, deceit, or betrayal. In short, her love is independent of the way things go, unchanging and immune from defeat; and in so far as she achieves this, she participates in the love of God, losing herself in God by dying to the claims of the self.

However, Simone Weil also presses the theme of dying to the self into contexts in which it does not result in any direct gain for others.

The principal claim we think we have on the universe is that our personality should continue. This claim implies all the others. The instinct of self-preservation makes us feel this continuation to be a necessity, and we believe that a necessity is a right. We are like the beggar who said to Talleyrand: 'Sir, I must live', and to whom Talleyrand replied: 'I do not see the necessity for that.' Our personality is entirely dependent on external circumstances which have unlimited power to crush it. But we would die rather than admit this. (*SWR* 498)

When we make an effort and it bears no fruit, we feel a sense of false balance and emptiness—as if we have been cheated; and when difficulties or suffering engulf and wound us without any visible gain or purpose, we live in the expectation of recompense and feel resentful when it is not forthcoming. This feeling goes very deep in us—it seems to be part of what it means to have an ego; but it shows a fundamental unwillingness to grasp the fact that we have absolutely no rights to claim against the universe, that it is not a system of checks and balances centring around our well-being. So, religion does dwell upon the wounds of human suffering, but not because it offers a supernatural remedy for them; rather, because it has a supernatural use for them. And their use is not to make us good (worthy of pardon) or powerful (worthy of praise):[12] the marks of *these* wounds signify neither expiation nor commendation, but a threat to the very integrity of the self, and so they can teach us what is the hardest lesson of all—the contingency and gratuitousness of our existence. Religion's most fundamental goal is to get us to accept that truth, and to be happy that this is the way things are; and it invokes the action of grace at precisely this point because it sees that living this truth is beyond the unaided human reach.

Is this lesson one that it is possible for thinkers in the tradition of Emersonian perfectionism to acknowledge? Certainly, it is not a teaching that Emerson himself seems to have absorbed. In his essay 'Compensation', he rejects the idea that compensation will be meted out in the next life for the misery of good and the triumph of evil here below; but he rejects it on the ground that such compensation is instantly and automatically meted out in this life. Of course, this is not an expression of his ignorance of or failure to acknowledge present injustice and suffering; the detail of his arguments shows rather that he is persuasively developing a grammar within which such phenomena take on a different aspect. He points out, for example, that the swindler who counterfeits a task swindles herself, since she does not and cannot gain the knowledge of material and moral nature which the honest labourer attains by doing the task itself; and he takes this to verify 'The absolute balance of Give and Take, the doctrine that everything has its price—and if that price is not paid, not that thing but something else is obtained' (*CW* 67). But for the Christian, this doctrine amounts to an attempt to confer a consoling meaning upon fundamentally comfortless facts, thereby satisfying the ego's need for compensation; and it comes as no surprise that, according to Emerson, the doctrine's deepest import lies in its underwriting of the reality and significance of the existence of the individual soul: 'In a virtuous action, I properly *am*; in a virtuous act I add to the world ... the soul refuses limits' (*CW* 71).

And what of Cavell? As we saw in Part II of this book, Cavell's Emersonian practice of redemptive reading has its roots in the central

---

[12] *Pace* Cavell's gloss on certain Nietzschean criticisms of religion in 'Ending the Waiting Game', 151.

place he accords the concept of acknowledgement in his understanding of the nature and the possibilities of human relationships; and that concept crystallizes a logic of reciprocation, a quasi-Hegelian vision of the ways in which the words and deeds of others react upon, determine, and are required by one's own states and attitudes (as well as vice versa)—a sense of the depth and the profundity of the human need for acknowledgement from others. But, of course, Kierkegaard takes the refusal or transcendence of that need for acknowledgement to be a defining feature of Christian love, and so identifies a point at which the demands of Christianity explicitly sever one of the vital nerves of Cavell's thought.

Moreover, the centrality of the concept of acknowledgement in Cavell's work is simply one manifestation of a much more general tendency to place the demands of the self at centre-stage. Indeed, the element of his thought which stubbornly links it with liberalism is precisely its overriding concern with the enactment and realization of human individuality. Cavell's awareness of the individual's dependence upon communal and linguistic matrices does not so much qualify that concern as sharpen his perception of the essential pre-conditions and the underlying form of individual self-realization; and his unusual sensitivity to the obstacles that can be placed in its way may have resulted in a more sober assessment of the chances of successful self-realization, but certainly has not led to an abandonment of it as a goal—indeed, such sensitivity might be seen as an inevitable consequence of the heightened clarity with which one examines any matter close to one's heart. And of course, given the reflexivity of so much of Cavell's work, self-realization is not merely the central theme of his thought but also the central goal of his reading and writing: the fact that a myriad of reflections of his own thoughts—variously inflected and reformulated—return to him (and so to us) with alienated majesty from the surfaces and depths of the various texts with which he has engaged may not be dismissible in advance as an effect of narcissism; but when his readers wrestle with that suspicion, the Christian may well feel that they are responding to an undeniable dimension of self-assertion or self-enactment, to a ubiquity of self, that stands in essential conflict with any vision of dying to the self.

The issue is crystallized in Cavell's most recent work in his guiding concern for the unknown woman, for the citizen whose voice is suppressed by a society whose arrangements chain her to her attained self. The Christian can honour Cavell's desire to penetrate deeper than the Rawlsian conception of a charter of specific rights for persons whose essential integrity and real existence is taken for granted; for liberal thought is thereby forced to confront the prior question of the life (and hence the death) of the self, the presence (and hence the absence) of the ego. But, having opened up this level of investigation, the liberal point of origin of Cavell's thought inclines him towards life and presence rather than death and absence; he acknowledges the reality of certain threats to the integrity of the self in society, but only as an injustice to be overcome in the name of the individual's right to her own life, her right to enact her existence—and for the Christian, such a rallying-cry occludes the fundamental lesson that our experience of the world's capacity to wound the human personality can teach. It is not that Nora's cry of rage in *A Doll's House* ought to be ignored: understood as a call for help from another human being, such cries demand our unstinting response; and the Christian should have no desire to discourage persons from seeking the conditions for a meaningful existence. But by leaving incompletely assessed the attitudes that can find their expression in such cries, by not raising the possibility that such rage may be fuelled by a hallucinated claim on society and the universe that the personality should continue, Cavell fails fully to interrogate the ego's maddened and maddening desire to believe itself at the centre of things, and so fails fully to acknowledge either the world's independence of the self or the uttermost depths of the self's finitude. In leaving the final layer of the self's self-deceptions unquestioned, his philosophy contributes to their maintenance.

It may be that this limitation is inherent in philosophy rather than in Cavell's philosophy alone; for, as the Christian will acknowledge, the idea that such a deep-rooted need for compensation is a deception is not something that reason can demonstrate. The image and reality of the crucified Christ not only knots together the Christian concepts of love, self-sacrifice, and suffering, but symbolizes the crucifixion of the understanding; as St Paul emphasizes, it is, and must be, an offence to reason. It may therefore be the case that philosophy, reborn in an era which has deified reason, cannot, according to its own conception of itself, say 'sin'—although we should not forget the truth in Cavell's remark that 'a criticism of philosophy, moving in close enough to matter to philosophy, becomes philosophy', so that 'the philosophical here includes the religious mind' (UDFB 289). Regardless of our final adjudication of these boundaries, however, particular philosophers might find that meditation on the strange fruit of the cross will draw them from their deep commitment to the substantiality of the self and towards a further state of themselves and their society in which that substance dissolves into air. It cannot be known that such a state neighbours our present one; but, as Cavell points out, 'Christianity is something that in its very presence is to be expected, that exists only in expectation, say faith. Then the absence or refusal of Christianity is a constant offer of its possibility or presence' (*DK* 21).

Postscript

Philosophy's Closet

Looking back over this extended and dense account of the trajectory of Cavell's philosophical project, what none the less strikes me most forcibly is how much of that project has been left unexamined. In particular, I have made no attempt to assess in any detail the nature of Cavell's relationship to the early and late work of Heidegger, or to the recent efflorescence of French Post-Structuralist thought (both psychoanalytic and deconstructive). These matters are, I think, important to Cavell's self-understanding. Heidegger's early work illuminates Cavell's perception of the truth in scepticism and his later work explores one powerful conception of the active passivity of philosophical thinking (thinking as thanking); and Lacan's and Derrida's reconceptualizations of the subject and of writing (amongst a variety of other topics) provide a useful point of comparison with Cavell's own, and one which might make clearer the degree of Cavell's attachment to, as well as the power of his defence of, the central values of modernity. However, quite apart from limitations of space, Cavell's engagement with the work of all three seems to me to be as yet so fragmentary and occasional as to resist the type of exegetical techniques to which my work is committed, and accordingly to stand beyond this book's present scope.[1]

Another aspect or dimension of Cavell's work cannot so easily be passed over, however. It is a problematic of which Cavell has been aware for a reasonably long period of time, and so has already surfaced—at least implicitly—in previous chapters of this book; but I wish to conclude my account by examining it in a little more detail. Cavell himself has touched obliquely upon this theme in a number of places: for example, in the preface to *Disowning Knowledge*, he acknowledges that the stylistic revisions to which he has, in that reprinting, subjected the prose of his early essay on *King Lear* primarily concern its period-piece, male-centred use of pronouns; and in so doing, he specifies

---

[1] Some essential preliminary work on the task of relating Cavell's project to that of Derrida has been effected by Michael Fischer in *Stanley Cavell and Literary Skepticism* (Chicago, 1989).

two reasons that weighed heavily against the rephrasing to which he eventually committed himself.

First, I am in fact there often concentrating on the male inflection of the world, Lear's and ours, one in which, from which, I felt I suffered as much as I profited, my expression of which will eventually have to enter into the balance of whatever credit may be mine for whatever feminism was mine early, forever. Second, the male inflection cannot be undone, needless to say, by altering a few pronouns, and the essay has meant too much to me to dismiss, without more care than I can exercise now, the possibilities that the inflection was the condition both of worse things, and perhaps of some better things, say more progressive, than show up at a glance. Yet I could not after all let the pronouns, all of them, stand. The effect of tone was sometimes simply too grating, so I have accordingly here and there rephrased. That feminism is in these years a movement of such depth that its pressure on, say, pronouns poses a continuous stylistic pressure not to be answered with the use of certain set formulas but to be decided in each case does not surprise me. But I was I guess surprised, reading over the essay with this particular question in mind, by the experience I called grating. For a political experience to have moved back out from the mind and onto the skin and into the senses means that in these twenty years something like a new set of natural reactions has formed, which means a new turn of history. (*DK*, p. x)

The note of optimism, of Emersonian cheer, struck in the final sentence of this passage may, of course, itself be found grating by some feminists; but assessing the array of intuitions articulated in the preceding sentences is of more moment if we wish to understand the true nature of Cavell's relation to feminism. For they carry two implications: first, that Cavell, as a man, feels able to identify himself not only as (at least in part) capable of participating in feminism but also as a victim of (at least some of) the sufferings against which feminism sets itself; and second, that in the fight against these forms of oppression (even at the level of style) he rejects the use of abstract generalizations in favour of a consideration of particular cases. Of course, these two implications are aspects of a single underlying intuition: for as we have already seen in previous chapters, Cavell's view is that male and female perspectives, the identification, interrogation, and revision of which is the essential business of any feminist thought, are not the exclusive prerogative of men and women respectively (a claim which might be thought to license a refusal to attend to, and to test the true value of, the words and deeds of particular men and particular women), but are rather modes or inflexions of thought and practice to which any individual may be subject and from which she may be detached.

Inevitably, this intuition brings him into profound conflict with some of those who identify themselves as feminists—particularly when (as we have also seen) he develops from it the tuition that the contrast between male and female perspectives is to be thought of in terms of the contrast between activity and passivity; and the tendency of his recent work to foreground the figure of the unknown woman and to relocate his central preoccupation with scepticism and its overcoming in terms suggested by that figure has intensified the conflict by leading him to present his work as an attempt to relocate and deploy her repressed voice. To those less convinced than he of the specific nature (let alone the universal accessibility) of male and female inflexions of human thought and practice, and to those profoundly sensitive to the opportunities for reinforcing female oppression that are opened up by men's claims to be speaking for women, the present formation and orientation of Cavell's work is undeniably provocative; and some have already responded heatedly to that provocation.[2] It should, however, be noted that Cavell's conception of provocation is underwritten by Emerson's remark (deployed as an epigraph to *The Claim of Reason*) that 'Truly speaking, it is not instruction, but provocation, that I can receive from another soul'—a remark which suggests that a Cavellian provocation is designed to initiate a specific form of human intercourse or conversation, one from which true learning might arise, and so inevitably constitutes a revisionary challenge to rather than a reiteration of received wisdom. If we wish to think through that challenge, then—given Cavell's refusal of abstract oppositions in favour of attention to the concrete, and given his conception of thought as reading and being read—we should examine the confrontation that he has recently staged between his own perspective and that of an exemplary literary critic and theorist of gender with respect to a specific literary text: a Henry James short story entitled 'The Beast in the Jungle'.[3] As we shall see, this conflict not only illuminates the issues at stake in Cavell's relation to feminist theory, but also draws together the main strands of his present understanding of the philosophical enterprise in a way which offers both a surview of its development to date and a prospectus of his future work.

[2] Consider, for example, Tania Modleski's brief but biting response to Cavell's essay on *Now Voyager*, published (together with a reply from Cavell) in *Critical Inquiry*, 16 (1990), 237–8; and her more expansive but equally hostile references to Cavell's project in her recent book *Feminism without Women* (London, 1991), 8–13.

[3] In *The Complete Tales of Henry James*, ed. L. Edel (London, 1964).

Patriarchy, Homophobia, and Male Homosexual Panic

The conflict I have in mind is the main business of the essay-length postscript Cavell attached to his reading of *Now Voyager* upon its first publication. Entitled 'To Whom It May Concern', it constitutes an attempt to relate and codify his sense of the pertinence of Eve Kosofsky Sedgwick's 'The Beast in the Closet: James and the Writing of Homosexual Panic' to his work on film melodrama (and, as it turns out, to a great deal of his other work). If we are to attain a real grasp of the thrust of Sedgwick's essay, however, we must begin by sketching in the wider theoretical framework into which it fits—a framework outlined and developed in her two book-length studies of literature from the mid-eighteenth to the late nineteenth and early twentieth centuries.[4]

Sedgwick's first book, *Between Men*, focusses upon literature in the context of a wider cultural analysis, one in which she claims that a fruitful approach to an understanding of the functioning of modern patriarchal Western culture can be attained from close attention to that aspect of it which she labels 'male homosocial desire'. As used in such disciplines as history and the social sciences, 'homosocial' typically describes social bonds between persons of the same sex; but, although clearly a neologism formed on the model of 'homosexual', it is equally clearly designed to pick out forms of behaviour that are usually contrasted with sexual ones. Given her interest in understanding patriarchy, it is unsurprising that Sedgwick focusses upon *male* homosocial bonds—in patriarchal contexts, they are likely to form a key medium of social power and a central determinant of gender inequality; but by linking them with the concept of 'desire', she is in effect implying that there is rather a continuum between male homosocial and male homosexual behaviour, that the forms of male bonding which the former term picks out are in fact within the orbit of the potentially erotic.

Sedgwick offers many reasons for seeing this reconceptualization as anything but startling. To begin with, she claims that within the world of women the idea of a continuum between homosexuality and homosociality—between lesbians and women who teach, nurture, march for, give jobs to, or otherwise attend to and promote the interests of other women—is much less controversial and at least intelligible; and

---

[4] The books are *Between Men* (New York, 1985) and *Epistemology of the Closet* (London, 1990). Her essay on James (originally published in R. Yeazell (ed.), *Sex, Politics and Science in the Nineteenth-Century Novel* (Baltimore, Md., 1986)) is reprinted in the latter, and my references to that essay will be keyed to its pages.

within the world of men at certain other historical periods (that of classical Greece, for example) the continuum also seems to have been—and to have been acknowledged to have been—quite seamless. Even in the modern male world, moreover, many of the most sanctioned forms of homosocial bonding—the celebrations of soccer players, the camaraderie of the locker-room and the army camp—can look quite startlingly 'homosexual' with only a slight shift of focus. And yet, in this modern male world, homosocial/homosexual discontinuity is not only insisted upon but is in fact typically founded upon homophobic views and practices—so that both gay men and heterosexual men who are engaged in promoting the interests of other men tend to reject with disgust the idea that their two types of same-sex bonding are in any way congruent. Since the earlier example of classical Greece suggests that patriarchy is quite capable of maintaining itself without either perceiving or laying stress upon that divide, and without any settled reliance upon homophobia, the question why a homophobically founded stress on this division should be so central in modern Western patriarchy remains.

Sedgwick's answer is that such homophobia constitutes a mechanism by means of which the form and the limits of male homosocial desire might be described and proscribed, and thus provides a means of control over a fundamental conduit of social power in patriarchal cultures. In other words, such homophobia simultaneously denies and exploits the continuity between homosociality and homosexuality: in so far as the point at which highly valued male bonding turns into highly disvalued homosexual bonding is difficult to locate, any systematic form of oppression that is immediately directed at those who explicitly adopt and affirm homosexual behaviour and identity simultaneously functions as a means of controlling those whose homosocial activities inevitably stray close to the blurred and shifting borderline with homosexuality. As Sedgwick puts it:

It is crucial to every aspect of social structure within the [patriarchal] framework that heavily freighted bonds between men exist, as the backbone of social form or forms. At the same time, a consequence of this structure is that any ideological purchase on the male homosocial spectrum—a (perhaps necessarily arbitrary) set of discriminations for defining, controlling and manipulating these male bonds—will be a disproportionately powerful instrument of social control. The importance—an importance—of the category 'homosexual', I am suggesting, comes not necessarily from its regulatory relation to a nascent or already-constituted minority of homosexual people or desires, but from its potential for giving whoever wields it a structuring definitional leverage over the whole range of male bonds that shape the social constitution. (*BM* 86)

In *Between Men*, Sedgwick pursues her analysis of male homosocial desire under homophobic pressure in two main directions. First, she claims to identify as one effect of this pressure a phenomenon she calls 'male homosexual panic', which she defines as the most private, psychologized form in which many twentieth-century Western men experience their vulnerability to the social pressure of homophobic blackmail; this constellation of self-directed anxieties concerning sexual identity is seen as resulting not just in expressions of extreme homophobia, but also in specific (de)formations of the blackmail victim's homosocial and heterosexual bonds. This last point is picked up in much more detail to form the second main theme of Sedgwick's analysis, namely, an investigation of the role of women as it comes to be defined in, and presented in the literature of, modern Western patriarchal societies. In particular, she offers a reinterpretation of Lévi-Strauss's insight that relations between men and women can be understood as conduits for relations between men and other men, arguing not only that women are in effect objects of exchange between men rather than subjects relating to other subjects, but also that male–female relations (and so conceptions of female identity) are in effect structured as detours in the manifestation and control of male homosocial desire. Both of these themes will be relevant when we turn to her reading of the James short story.

But before we do so, it is worth stressing that the whole of her analysis depends upon one crucial presupposition: that the break between homosociality and homosexuality is genuinely indeterminate— or more precisely, that it is essentially subject to the threat of unpredictable and arbitrary redefinition. For homophobia can function as a disproportionately powerful mechanism of social control in a patriarchal context only if it is not possible for those men existing outside a clearly defined homosexual minority culture to ascertain that they are not (that their homosocial bonds are not) homosexual; only thus can a relatively small exertion of physical or legal compulsion—directed at distinctly homosexual behaviour and life-styles—potentially influence far greater reaches of male behaviour and filiation. In other words, on Sedgwick's analysis, it is (and can be) no coincidence that the bonding behaviour of sportsmen and soldiers looks startlingly similar to the very forms of homosexual bonding which are most intensely proscribed in just those social arenas; on the contrary, it crystallizes what she sees as the nature of a general male double-bind—namely, that, for a man, to be a man's man is separated only by an invisible, carefully blurred, always-already-crossed line from being 'interested in men'.

However, this pivotal claim that the concept of male homosexual (and so heterosexual) identity is subject to a fundamental epistemological unclarity is buttressed and developed only in her second book, *Epistemology of the Closet*. There, she details various ways in which questions of knowledge and ignorance concerning male sexual identity are heightened in intensity and rendered structurally unsettlable by the way in which the concept of homosexual identity is constructed in modern homophobic culture; and she takes the image of the closet to summarize these epistemological tensions. Most immediately, of course, this notion of the closet conjures up a private space within which a gay man can (and often must) hide his sexual identity, and thus implies that he has an important degree of control over the dissemination of this knowledge; but in reality, Sedgwick points out, it is not always clear to such a man how many of the people with whom he deals on an everyday basis have already penetrated his privacy in this respect—and it is equally unclear how he might ensure that he has definitively come out of the closet, when every encounter with a new set of colleagues and acquaintances in effect closes him within it again. Moreover, in legal terms, American judicial decisions impose contradictory requirements on such men, since they simultaneously punish those who do declare their sexual identity (by depriving them of certain possibilities of employment) and those who do not (for depriving their employers of information deemed relevant to their employment); in this sense, gay men live in an environment which renders nugatory their control of this information by simultaneously demanding and forbidding its disclosure. Most important of all, however, it is by no means clear that they have privileged access to knowledge about their sexual identity at all: for the question what it is to be a homosexual man is highly contested.

According to Sedgwick, prevalent understandings of the nature of homosexuality are structured in two main dimensions, and both dimensions are themselves structured in terms of two competing conceptions. The first dimension concerns the nature of same-sex desire, and here the conflict is between minoritizing views (i.e. those which define homosexuals as a discrete species of human being) and universalizing views (i.e. those which identify every human creature as potentially bisexual and therefore subject to same-sex desires). The second dimension relates same-sex bonding to gender identity, and here the conflict is between theories of gender inversion (i.e. those which conceive of homosexual desire as indicative of a woman's soul trapped in a man's body and vice versa, and thereby preserve a conception of the essential heterosexuality of sexual desire) and theories of gender separatism (i.e. those which conceive of sexual desire as most naturally directed at those of the same gender, thereby affirming an essential continuity between homosocial and homosexual desire). Sedgwick's own theoretical desire is not to settle these disputes; her claim is rather that the conflict on both dimensions has had no resolution and is not likely to achieve one, and that as a result, the question of homosexual identity is an essentially porous and mutable one. Of course, this has crucial effects upon homosexuals: for example, it undermines gay men's authority over the definition of their own sexuality, permitting those to whom a gay man attempts to come out of the closet to respond by questioning the accuracy of his self-identification. But it also has significant conse-quences for those men who do not identify themselves as homosexuals, since any intractable unclarity about the definition of homosexual identity makes the matter of heterosexual identity equally undecidable; so the field of highly structured discursive incoherence that Sedgwick claims to identify at this crucial node of social organization in effect underwrites her earlier claim that the homosocial and heterosexual relations of non-homosexual males are open to social control because of their essential vulnerability to homophobic blackmail and so to homo-sexual panic.

It is against this wider analytical background that Sedgwick organizes her reading of James's short story 'The Beast in the Jungle'. The narrative focusses upon John Marcher and his decades-long intimacy with May Bartram: this is a relationship which is standardly held to be structured around Marcher's failure to desire Bartram—not because he desires some other woman but because he fails to desire at all, and is indeed unaware either of the absence of desire from his life or of the possibility that May Bartram desires him until after she has died from his obtuseness. Marcher's culminating dawning of awareness at Bartram's grave is, in other words, held to have an unproblematically heterosexual content, namely, that May Bartram desired him and that he should have desired her. Sedgwick is prepared to acknowledge that certain aspects of James's handling of the final scene support that assumption, but she is primarily concerned to highlight aspects of the narrative which go against this (heterosexist?) reading of those unacknowledged desires.

After citing the ambiguities of James's own sexual identity, she focusses upon the theme which James places at the centre of Marcher's sense of himself and which forms the basis of his intimacy with Bartram. He has a secret, a destiny, something unknown in his future; and this sense of being kept for something rare and strange, possibly prodigious and terrible, that is sooner or later to happen is a conviction that he confides only to Bartram. Sedgwick's claim is that this secret, in so far as it has a content, is homosexual; and she takes this to be confirmed by the very feature of James's presentation that seems to undermine it— namely, Marcher's revelation in the final scene that he 'had been the man of his time, the man, to whom nothing on earth was to have happened'. At first sight, this would seem to deny that Marcher's secret has a content at all—and given the circumstances in which it is received, it implies if anything that that missing content was hetero- sexual, i.e. that the nothing that is now to happen to him is the result of his having missed (his having failed to desire) May Bartram. Sedgwick begins to counter this interpretation by pointing out that James's attribution of nothingness or absence to Marcher's secret in fact falls in with a traditional rhetorical technique for identifying male same-sex desire, that of preterition: seen in that light, asserting that the content of the secret is precisely a lack is just one more way of using space- clearing negatives to simultaneously refer to and erase the homosexual possibility—the unspeakable, the unmentionable sin, the love that dare not speak its name.

Having raised this possibility, Sedgwick then goes on to point out that Marcher's secret is in fact (at least) two secrets: 'Marcher feels that he knows, but has never told anyone but May Bartram, (secret number one) that he is reserved for some very particular, uniquely rending fate in the future, whose nature is (secret number two) unknown to himself' (*EC* 204–5). Sedgwick reads the unknownness of Marcher's second, future secret as, in effect, his articulated denial of its articulability, and so as indicative of his sense of it as including the possibility of something importantly homosexual; and she reads the reifying, totaliz- ing, blinding effect of it upon him (his articulation of it as 'a cataclysm', 'a catastrophe', 'horrors', 'all the loss and all the shame that are thinkable') as indicative of his being unable to exclude that possibility whilst having accepted the prevailing homophobic interpretation of it (the interpretation which knows it to be unspeakable rather than understanding it to be unknowable because arbitrarily and self-contradic- torily defined). He is, in short, a paradigmatic victim of male homosexual

panic: and it is this panic that leads to the construction of his outer
secret (the secret of having a secret), which functions in his life
precisely as the closet. Not, of course, a closet in which there is a
homosexual man, since Marcher is not a homosexual man; rather, it is
the closet of the homosexual secret, the closet of imagining a homosexual secret, of imagining the homosexual possibility monolithically
and negatively, as linked with discovery, scandal, shame, and annihilation.

According to Sedgwick, Marcher's angle on daily existence and
intercourse is that of the closeted person, not just in the sense that the
whole of his behaviour with others is one long dissimulation, but more
precisely in the sense that his relationship with May Bartram contributes
to a play-acting of heterosexuality; to this degree, her admission into
the closet of his outer secret does not so much diminish as consolidate
and fortify it. But May Bartram's own perspective on the matter is not
to be thought of either as essentially unwitting of or as dimly compliant
with Marcher's strategies; Sedgwick's claim is that, whilst it is true that
she feels desire for him, her involvement is originally motivated by an
identification of his panic and a desire to dissolve the closet it con-
structs.

May Bartram from the first sees, correctly, that the possibility of Marcher's
achieving a genuine ability to attend to a woman—sexually or in any other
way—depends as an absolute precondition on the dispersion of his totalizing,
basilisk fascination with and terror of homosexual possibility. It is only through
his coming out of the closet—whether as *a homosexual man* or as a man with a
less exclusively defined sexuality that nevertheless admits the possibility of
desires for other men—that Marcher could even begin to perceive the attention
of a woman as anything other than a terrifying demand or a devaluing
complicity. (*EC* 206–7)

In other words, May Bartram understands that the leverage of homophobic blackmail in patriarchal societies victimizes not only homosexual
men but also heterosexual men, and thereby victimizes women in their
relations (whether sexual or otherwise) with those men. But what the
ending of the story then signifies is not the success but the final and
complete failure of her liberating project. First, because—as the details
of that final scene make clear—Marcher's acknowledgement of her
comes about only when she is dead, and only after a striking encounter
with another grieving man in the graveyard moves him to identify
himself with that man and his mourning for a dead woman; in other
words, the acknowledgement is essentially mediated by a homosocial

(and, according to Sedgwick, potentially homosexual) relationship, and it is an acknowledgement of a woman safely dead. And second, because Marcher's achieved conviction that his escape would have been to love her is not the liberation for which May Bartram worked; for it amounts to a *compulsory* heterosexuality, one in which his homosexual possibilities are not acknowledged but denied, a move from a vexed and gaping self-ignorance around those possibilities to a completed and rationalized and wholly accepted one. Rather than attaining a self-knowledge that would have freed him to find and enjoy whatever sexuality emerged, he becomes irredeemably self-ignorant: the homophobic heterosexual imperatives of his culture cease to coerce him, but only because he has completely internalized them.

Philosophy, Scepticism, and the Repression of the Female Voice

The relevance of Sedgwick's reading of 'The Beast in the Jungle' to Cavell's purposes derives in part from the fact that he has cited the story in two of his accounts of films in the the genre he labelled 'Melodramas of the Unknown Woman',[5] and so has aligned it with a field of concepts and concerns which might seem to contest (and so be contested by) Sedgwick's interpretation. But to think of the matter as a dispute within Jamesian literary studies makes it seem too marginal to have produced a response as detailed and as urgent as Cavell's 1989 postscript turns out to be; and indeed, it soon becomes clear that both the detailed imagery and the key analytical components of Sedgwick's account press upon virtually every central theme of Cavell's work to date. Without pretending to provide an exhaustive dissection of these points of contact, I want to trace out some of the main threads of agreement and disagreement.

As we have seen, according to Sedgwick, Marcher's homosexual panic is manifest in the way his life takes on the aspect of a closeted person under the pressure of his double secret—his privileged knowledge of his unknown, inarticulable fate, where that fate is held to include a homosexual possibility understood in a monolithic, reifying, homophobic way. On one level, Cavell writes his postscript in order to express his grateful sense that the figure of the closet, thus specified, is

[5] The story is referred to at the end of 'Psychoanalysis and Cinema: The Melodrama of the Unknown Woman' (in *IIS*), and at crucial points in UDFB.

one that provides him with a way of re-presenting or recounting a number of thoughts, speculations, and diagnoses that he had previously found himself driven to propose concerning the nature of scepticism in philosophy. This is particularly evident if we recall Cavell's explorations of scepticism concerning other minds—an area in which all will admit that our thinking is shot through with pictures of Inner and Outer. According to Cavell's Wittgensteinian account, the sceptic is driven to interpret human separateness and privacy as consisting in each individual's privileged knowledge of or certainty about something within himself to which no other has access—as if privacy were a matter of secrecy, and the maintenance of one's humanity a matter of defending that secrecy. This sceptical interpretation amounted, in Cavell's eyes, to a vision of the mind as hidden within or by the body—closeted by it, we might now say.

But the sceptic's understanding of his relation to the realm of the Inner does not merely reproduce both the structure and the air of privileged arrogance which we saw to go along with Marcher's outer secret, his privileged knowledge; it reflects the nature of his inner secret as well. For, in the first place, the sceptic's understanding of the nature of the closeted mental realm is as monolithic and reified as Marcher's understanding of his homosexual possibility: it is a realm of thoughts, sensations, and emotions one and all construed on the model of outer objects—a construal that emerges most starkly when the sceptic defends the reality of his pain by claiming that *something* is accompanying his cry of pain (to which Wittgenstein replies that pain is neither a something nor a nothing—in other words, that the grammar of object and designation invoked here must be rejected). Second, just as the object of Marcher's privileged knowledge—his future fate—is understood by him to be unknown or more precisely inarticulable, so the object of the sceptic's knowledge is seen as untellable, indescribable, incommunicable. This, at least, is the conclusion Cavell draws from Wittgenstein's perception that sceptical fantasies of the Inner might be released by constructing the idea of a private language—an idea whose coherence is regarded by the sceptic as an indispensable implication of the reality of the Inner, a belief which commits him to thinking of the Inner as necessarily incommunicable. And third, the deeper roots of this fantasy of privacy lead to an interpretation of the relations between Inner and Outer, of the security of the mind's hiddenness in the body, that matches the conflicting pressures of life in the closet as Sedgwick has mapped it. For Cavell has argued that the fantasy of a private language is the manifestation of a fantasy of necessary inexpressiveness (according to which I am powerless to make myself known—perhaps even to myself) and/or of a fantasy of necessary expressiveness (according to which I am powerless to prevent myself from being known). Here, the sceptic's fluctuations between a nightmare of suffocating privacy and one of public betrayal are strikingly homologous with those of the closeted person.

If, however, Sedgwick's image of the closet can serve as a way of summarizing the sceptical vision of the relation between mind and body as Cavell understands it, it is equally appropriate as a way of crystallizing his interpretation of the nature of scepticism more generally. To begin with, both the note of privileged knowledge encapsulated in Marcher's outer secret and the note of apocalyptic horror encapsulated in his understanding of his inner secret are integral to any philosophical stance which claims to know that we do not know what we think we know—that claims, in effect, privileged insight into our true, world-deprived or solipsistic state. Of course, from Cavell's perspective, this state of affairs is one that scepticism produces, not one it discovers; and his diagnosis of how it is produced also matches the double-secret structure of Marcher's closet. For the recession of the world from the sceptic is due to his refusal of our common criteria; and that refusal at once expresses his desire to transcend the human (i.e. of a craving to be exceptional, to arrogate privilege) and reduces him to an insistence on empty or nonsensical statements (i.e. renders his putative discovery inarticulate). And Cavell underwrites this more general connection between scepticism and the closet by drawing our attention to the startling (but purely literary?) fact that some of the most famous of philosophical sceptics find themselves driven to employ the figure of the closet in describing the genesis and the impact of their sceptical discoveries.

Both Hume and Descartes depict themselves as meditating in a private chamber; and within those walls, Descartes is forced to consider and work through hypotheses which he declares would, if taken seriously, threaten his sanity, whilst Hume equally famously specifies his closet as the place of a disorienting and paralysing sceptical panic from which he escapes with joyful elation only by rejoining the public world of merry, backgammon-playing (homosocializing?) men. It is, of course, important to acknowledge that both philosophers are in a sense devoted to disclosing the secrets upon which they have stumbled in their chambers—we are, after all, reading their accounts of them; but it should also be noted that Hume, for example, depicts his life outside the closet as one in which he has no inclination to communicate his sceptical discoveries to his friends but rather dissimulates and uses them to distract himself from those discoveries. In other words, Hume's image of the closet seems to embody a notion of secrecy, of unshared and privileged knowledge, together with a sense of division or dichotomy—between inside and outside, the public and the private, the ordinary and something which sides against it; and in these respects, his own depiction of ordinary life as transformed by sceptical discoveries into a theatre of distraction seems very much akin to that of the closeted person as Sedgwick depicts it and Marcher enacts it.

This set of analogies between Cavell's Wittgensteinian understanding of scepticism and Sedgwick's understanding of the closet is more than enough for him to conclude that the one somehow answers to the other—in other words, that the sceptical impulse has an inherent tendency to throw up that particular figure, as if finding its satisfaction in just such an image of divided epistemological space. But then Cavell must face the most important implication of that connection: for of course, according to Sedgwick's analysis, the figure of the closet as it finds expression in the story of John Marcher's life is a manifestation of male homosexual panic. Does it then follow that scepticism must also be thought of in these terms? It is to this question that Cavell's postscript is primarily devoted.

In general, accommodating the idea of a connection or equation between the field of scepticism and that of sexuality or gender poses few difficulties for Cavell, since his own work has made much of just such a link since his pivotal essay on *The Winter's Tale*. But Sedgwick's analysis suggests a more precise connection, one between scepticism and homosexuality; and accepting this would bring an essentially new element into his calculations. None the less, Cavell is happy to suggest grounds for believing that the more precise connection might be an illuminating one. For example, in relation to the reifying tendencies of scepticism about other minds, its inclination to think of the reality and nature of the Inner in terms of a monolithically defined 'something', he comments:

The idea that there are things on the inside of us that determine our differences and our connections is, here as elsewhere, subject to the Shakespearean sexualisation of 'thing' and 'nothing'. It is, in this area where false unities and monoliths abound, notable that even so apparently unsexy a writer as Thoreau is moved to remark, in speaking of what adventurous, improvisatory life should be, in place of its present self-tortures and fixated desperations ...: 'We should live quite laxly and undefined in front.' He means, whatever else—I might say that his words say—that we should not take a thing in front, say on the outside of us, to define the essence of our sexual differences and connections. (PS 255)

However, even if we are prepared to consider accepting this connection between certain expressions of the sceptical impulse and certain homo-phobic assumptions as indicative of a thematic convergence, we should recall that this talk of somethings and nothings is an articulation of scepticism deriving from Wittgenstein's text—an attempt on his part to find words for the sceptic; from which it would seem to follow that, by highlighting this connection, Cavell is simultaneously attempting to pose the question of whether the thematic convergence is one that Wittgenstein himself might have wished to imply or indicate. And granted the truth of the widespread assumption that Wittgenstein's sexual orientation is to be identified in relation to homosexuality, posing such a question would be tantamount to asking whether this identification is the business of philosophy—in short, whether Wittgen-stein's writing is also internally related to that orientation.

Noting (as Cavell does) that the general thought of such an internal relation between philosophy and homosexuality is difficult to ignore when one recalls that the discipline originated (in ancient Greece) in an environment of homosexual intimacy is not likely to defuse its out-rageousness in this particular context. But before dismissing it as a tasteless piece of impertinent speculation which would reduce the question of a major intellectual achievement of the century to a personal concern, it is worth being clear exactly what claim Cavell takes himself to be making here.

... what [my question] asks is how certain human beings can take their private torments (for example, by intimacies scandalously greeted as scandalous) as the means of providing humanity with a further perspective on itself (for example, with its wish to escape itself, to become inhuman in order not to be a scandal to itself) ... Would it make the claim more credible if one thinks of this as a historical or human scandal exemplifying itself in a mind of extreme expressive-ness? (PS 256)

In other words, Cavell takes his question to be licensed by a feature of the Wittgensteinian philosophical method that has always been central to his own work—the startling (scandalous?) fact that by speaking for oneself one can speak for others, that philosophy can be done by tapping the depths of one's self-knowledge in giving voice both to temptations and to the means for their overcoming, so that others can come to find their deepest reserves of seemingly private knowledge, speculation, and fantasy in these proffered words, and thereby have a chance of assessing their real weight. To claim that Wittgenstein was prepared to take such a perspective on his most private torments—that he saw, and was prepared to declare, that the infliction of such torments was an exemplary expression of a human desire to transcend the human—would then amount to the claim that he was prepared to extend the scope of his method to its furthest extent, and would thus presume an unparalleled willingness for self-exposure on his part; but it would none the less be entirely consonant with that method, and its extremity might even be regarded as confirming the depth of therapeutic significance that Wittgenstein attached to his philosophical project (something that his often-mentioned tone of spiritual fervour independently suggests).

However, even as Cavell makes the best attempt he can to distinguish the answer he wishes to canvass to his own question from other, more biographically impertinent ones, he stresses the fact that what he primarily wishes to do at this point is to ask the question rather than to answer it. More precisely, he takes himself to be asking the question in order to raise a possibility and open up a field for further thought rather than as a way of implying that he has the definitive answer to it or even that it necessarily has a definite (let alone a definitive) answer. Indeed, he prefaces his whole discussion by wondering whether it is even possible to pose such a question seriously enough, in the face of the currently interlocked views that Wittgenstein's sexuality is obviously impertinent and that it is obviously pertinent to his philosophizing. None the less, he clearly thinks that, if that difficult task can be executed, it should be; after all, if one of the central impulses of the ordinary language approach to philosophy is that of attempting to take seriously the fact that the meanings of words are in part a function of the context of their use and the identity of the person using them, then it would go entirely against the grain of Cavell's work to proscribe even the idea of a connection between Wittgenstein's words and the personal circumstances of their utterance. Accordingly, he takes it as one of the central virtues of Sedgwick's analysis from his perspective that it provides a potentially productive means of opening up the question of that connection.

None the less, the relations between philosophy, scepticism, and homosexuality hypothesized above would not accommodate the centrality of the idea of male homosexual panic in Sedgwick's account of Marcher's closet. For those relations seem to amount to a claim that certain homophobic interpretations of homosexuality are expressive of the same underlying human impulse to deny the human that is at the root of scepticism, and thus commits us to understanding the pressures of fear and fantasy that produce the figure of the closet as ultimately rooted in drives that cannot be restricted to a specific class of person— namely, those men who are not consciously and self acceptingly homosexual, and so can be thought of as vulnerable to homophobic blackmail in general and homosexual panic in particular. In other words, on Wittgenstein's understanding of the closet, both the perspective which produces it (by producing distorted, dichotomous interpretations of inner and outer, public and private) and the perspective which seeks perspective on its production (by refusing the voice of sceptical temptation, and so refusing to occupy either side of the dichotomies it produces) are open to all human beings; so Cavell's philosophy must contest Sedgwick's understanding of the reach and the genesis of the panic or anxiety that finds expression in the figure of the closet. More precisely, because it finds its reach to be less restricted, it must offer an alternative understanding of its genesis; and Cavell devotes the remainder of his postscript to providing such an alternative understanding.

In effect, Cavell commits himself to a more orthodox psychoanalytic reading of the panic which produces the figure of the closet in Marcher's life: he interprets it as castration anxiety, that is, as an anxiety produced by the castration complex which itself lies at the heart of the Oedipus complex. This is in fact an alternative that Sedgwick herself notes as pertinent to her concerns, and the degree of structural congruence between it and the notion of homosexual panic is indeed striking. For castration anxiety is tied to masturbation, a phenomenon which is typically itself understood, in a monolithic and reified way, as necessarily generating the very sequence of yielding, discovery, scandal, and shame that Marcher specifies as his ineluctable fate—the crucial difference being that the masturbation scenario ends not with annihilation but with castration. Furthermore, just as with homosexual panic, anxiety relating to masturbation generates a sense of one's unknownness to oneself—producing questions about one's sexual identity (Will I be a different sex if I am castrated? What sex is my mother?) and a sense of theatre in dissimulating how one's desires are satisfied. And in addition, the concepts of homosexuality and masturbation are both historically tied to disputes concerning morbidity.

If these points of similarity and difference are enough to justify the claim that the notion of castration anxiety is at least pertinent to Marcher's panic, it then becomes vital for Cavell to note that Freud's own account of that notion contains a significant emphasis.

When Freud introduces the threat of castration he notes at once that 'usually it is from the woman that the threat emanates' . . . and he goes on to specify the medium of that threat (as well as of the symbolic mitigation of the threat (substituting the hand for the original member that 'is to be removed') as the work of the woman's voice: it is the woman who *says* what 'the father or the doctor' will do, and who *says* how the punishment may be mitigated; her overwhelming threat, accordingly, is *to tell.* However this division of legal labour—between telling and executing—gets encoded, it emerges that the one responsible for maintaining and affirming the child's existence is the one whose voice can negate it, mar it, give it away. Then the key to one's (male) preservation is to control the woman's voice, contradictorily to stop it from speaking (from reporting) and to make it speak (to promise a further mitigation or intercession). Some control. (PS 276)

This is how Cavell wishes to understand the vital role of May Bartram in Marcher's life. He takes the latter's closeted existence, his maintenance of a dissimulated or distorted heterosexual relationship with his one true friend, to amount to the maintenance of a place that he cannot let the woman leave, the space of what he simultaneously wants and does not want her to say. In this respect, the concept of castration anxiety provides a different way of accounting for what Sedgwick correctly identifies as Marcher's compulsive heterosexuality, his compulsion to love women; the claim is that Marcher identifies her both as the source of the ratification of his existence and as the central threat to it, and so resorts to seduction and suggestibility as the only possible way to satisfy his contradictory need to preserve her confidence and her silence. In short, Cavell accepts Sedgwick's identification of the element of victimization in Bartram's role in Marcher's life; but he proffers a different understanding of its causes and nature.

But this leaves a seemingly insuperable obstacle in the way of transferring this reading of Marcher's closet to the matter of the sceptical closet in philosophy; for all too obviously, there is no woman closeted with the philosophical sceptic. Cavell's response is to cite one further element of a Freudian understanding of human sexual identity, namely, the notion of the essential bisexuality of human desire—of an oscillation between the male and the female components of desire (linked by Freud with sadism and masochism respectively). Cavell comments:

Anyone with civilization enough to be reading Freud has all but inescapably been amply prepared for what Freud suavely phrases as the 'possibility' that our male and female desires will *not* be thus satisfied ('on the same object'). What Freud evidently imagines will do us good is to think, to prepare ourselves to discover, or rediscover, the experience, the 'possibility', that they *can* be satisfied on the same object, which is to say, the same body; perhaps even that 'normally' they are. (PS 281)

If both male and female desires may occupy and be satisfied upon the same body, then the same may be true of the male and the female voice; and if so, then it may be uncivilized simply to assume that the philosophical closet can only be thought of as a construct designed to control the female voice if it can be shown to contain a woman. As Cavell puts it:

the feminine voice the philosopher is (has been) bound not to let out ... is the man's own, his to own, one of its tones, his voice of response and of satisfaction, as opposed to his voice of debts (accounts, consequences) and of orders (demands, compulsions). Does someone imagine that one set of tones is confined to one sex or gender? Or that tones may not be modified in moving from sex to sex or gender to gender? (PS 285)

Here we see the reiteration of a central theme in Cavell's Shakespearean sexualization of scepticism and so of philosophy—a shift that was initiated in his study of *The Winter's Tale*, that has been developed through his work on psychoanalysis, cinema, and American Romanticism, and that now seeks confirmation and reinforcement in his recounting of Sedgwick's figure of the closet. For that figure's yoking of epistemology and sexuality is in effect being used to underwrite the centrality and the interconnectedness of the familiar Cavellian figures of the unknown woman and the Emersonian Exemplar—a point that becomes obvious if we note how this vision of competing voices within each man and each woman informs Cavell's interpretation of Marcher's unknown woman, May Bartram. Like Sedgwick, Cavell accords her a degree of independence from the dictates of Marcher's tortured compulsions—not in order to deny that he sacrifices her in order to sacrifice a part of himself, but in order to deny that she was a being as if bred for this sort of sacrificial fate, to deny that his perception of her is one that she has absorbed and by which she has come to define herself. On Cavell's account, this independence or unknownness amounts to her functioning as an Emersonian Exemplar, a friend whose goal is to exemplify the repressed feminine register of Marcher's voice in the

hope of attracting him to attain that next or further state of his self in
which those tones might be listened to and articulated, and in which its
satisfactions might be sought as easily on a female body as well as on a
male.

To this degree, of course, nothing in Cavell's specification of May
Bartram's overall role contradicts the account Sedgwick has offered,
since on her interpretation the idea of helping to alleviate Marcher's
self-punishing and other-victimizing panic or anxiety is central to
Bartram's self-understanding: thus far, both readings attribute the necessary knowledge of the nature of Marcher's frozen, fixated state to the
suffering, unknown woman in his life. Moreover, under the pressure of
Segwick's invocation of the concept of homosexual identity, Cavell is
driven to find a further layer of significance in one of the most famous
characteristics of the female stars who play the unknown women in the
films about which he has written, namely, their capacity to place gender
boundaries under question. This is evident in such familiar matters as
Dietrich's and Garbo's cross-dressing, and Bette Davis's invitation to
and representation of camp: and Cavell is thereby brought to return to
their characters in these films in order to raise and pursue the question
whether, in contexts in which the specific figure of these women's
mothers and the general 'world of women' (both repressed in the
comedies) is strongly emphasized, we should understand them to be
contemplating (even if only to refuse) a homosexual possibility.

On the other hand, Cavell stresses that such cross-dressing and camp
could equally be read as signifying these women's access to both male
and female desire within themselves, and so as expressive of their
demand to find the satisfaction of both tracks of their desire upon a
single male body as well as of their desire to provide that satisfaction
for the man—a reading that accords more with his specification of the
content of the knowledge that these women have about what is causing
the frozenness and fixation of the men in their lives. And in so far as
Cavell's specification links May Bartram to his model of Emersonian
perfectionism, it allows him open up a less pessimistic reading of the
final scene of the story than that propounded by Sedgwick. Whilst not
denying the possibility of taking Marcher's culminating revelation as a
final reinforcement of his monolithic, reified thinking about his own
identity (invoking the Emersonian project carries no inbuilt guarantee
of its success, if only because its aim forbids forcing change upon the
one in need of it), Cavell at least wishes to point out that Marcher's
culminating insight ('she was what he had missed') and his correspond-

ing invocation of a heterosexual possibility in his relations with May Bartram may be read not as an expression of compulsive or compulsory heterosexuality but as a sign that that his Exemplar had finally (posthumously) succeeded in attracting him to release his feminine voice and to acknowledge the (missed) possibility of its satisfaction on the body of a female.

Provoking Conversation

We are now in a position to encapsulate the dispute between Sedgwick and Cavell in the following way: does Cavell's invocation of castration anxiety or Sedgwick's specification of male homosexual panic provide the better account of the figure of the closet that now seems to Cavell to be integral to any understanding of the philosophical conflict between Wittgenstein and scepticism? If anyone were to wish to question Cavell's line of interpretation, then two sensitive points immediately stand out, both of which flow from the depth of Cavell's reliance on Freudian psychoanalytic conceptualizations. As we have seen, his account is founded on Freud's interpretations of the Oedipus complex and of the inherent bisexuality of human desire—the former specified in relation to the threat of castration, and the latter in a way which presupposes a fairly clear distinction between male desire (identified with sadism, and so more broadly with activity) and female desire (identified with masochism, and so more broadly with passivity). From Sedgwick's particular analytical viewpoint, therefore, Cavell's Freudian interpretation is questionable because it presupposes the truth of one particular universalizing theory of human desire (i.e. one asserting its inherent bisexuality) rather than appreciating that any such theory has no more claim to validity than any of the species of minoritizing theories with which it stands in conflict; in short, Cavell has committed himself to one side of a conflict which is not only irresoluble but whose irresolubility is a crucial factor in generating the seemingly permanent and socially charged unknownness of homosexual (and so of heterosexual) identity. At the same time, from the more general viewpoint of feminism, Cavell's Freudian interpretation falls under suspicion because it invokes a psychoanalytic vision that employs concepts (e.g. castration anxiety) or understands gender differences in terms (e.g. maleness as sadistic and active, femaleness as masochistic and passive) that appear to have an inherent male bias; in other words, Cavell stands accused of reiterating Freud's distorted conceptions of sex and gender.

Taking the criticism from a Sedgwickian point of view first, Cavell's room for manœuvre here seems far from limited. For Sedgwick's basic assumption that the concepts of homosexuality and heterosexuality are inherently conflictual seems to be backed up not by any a priori logical demonstration but rather by reference to the facts of recent social history. Admittedly, those facts are sometimes assigned an influence that almost amounts to a logical or theoretical impasse: for example, when discussing the two main dimensions of conceptual conflict in the field of gender and sexual identity, a note of real pessimism is struck. 'I have no optimism at all about the availability of a standpoint of thought from which either question could be intelligibly, never mind efficaciously, adjudicated, given that the same yoking of contradictions has presided over all thought on the subject, and all its violent and pregnant modern history, that has gone to form our own thought' (*EC* 90). The tenor of this passage seems very much to be that no resolution of the theoretical impasse can reasonably be hoped for; but in other passages, a rather different perspective seems to be articulated. For example, with reference to the conflict between minoritizing and universalizing views of sexual definition, she writes:

It has been the project of many, many writers and thinkers of many different kinds to adjudicate between [these] views ... and to resolve this conceptual incoherence. With whatever success, on their own terms, they have accomplished the project, none of them has budged in one direction or another the absolute hold of this yoking of contradictory views on modern discourse ... and this incoherence has prevailed for at least three-quarters of a century. (*EC* 86)

Such a passage suggests that Sedgwick is not committing herself to the view that the incoherences she has identified are necessarily irresoluble in themselves; a theoretical resolution of the logical tensions is here regarded as not only not impossible, but as achievable and perhaps already achieved. The crucial point for her is that no such resolution has succeeded in affecting the social situation, and that no future resolution is likely to fare any better; on her view, this social incoherence will continue precisely because it makes possible the construction and maintenance of vitally significant levers of social power, and it therefore becomes theoretically interesting to examine the significance of this prevailing social dispensation in more detail.

But this suggests that Cavell's position is not one which need come into serious conflict with Sedgwick's own. It is of course clear that Cavell is placing himself within the field of force of the Freudian universalizing mode of discourse on homo-/heterosexuality, and thus in effect committing himself to the belief that this side of one central theoretical conflict in the domain of sexual identity can prove itself superior to (rather than remain locked in undecidable conflict with) its competitors. It follows from this that Cavell must live up to his commitment in the theoretical realm, but Sedgwick has provided no specific reason for thinking that he cannot conceivably do so; and in so far as Sedgwick's real concern is with the cultural impact of prevailing conflictual and homophobic social norms, whereas Cavell's focus is on working out the vicissitudes of the sceptical impulse in terms of a model which does not embody the conceptual incoherences Sedgwick has identified, we might conclude that no real conflict exists between their two perspectives and projects.

On this general level, then, what matters is the degree to which Cavell's version of the Freudian discourse can show itself to have overcome its theoretical rivals and to offer a richer and more compelling articulation of human experience.[6] But more specific doubts might be raised about this discourse, and in fact Sedgwick does precisely that when offering a brief comment on the status of Freudian theory from the perspective of her own theory of social formation:

It was in the period of the so-called 'invention of the homosexual' that Freud gave psychological texture and credibility to a countervalent, universalizing mapping of this territory, based on the supposedly protean mobility of sexual desire and the potential bisexuality of every human creature; a mapping that implies no presumption that one's sexual penchant will always incline towards persons of a single gender, and that offers, additionally, a richly denaturalizing description of the psychological motives and mechanisms of male paranoid, projective homophobic definition and enforcement. Freud's antiminoritizing account only gained, moreover, in influence by being articulated through a developmental narrative in which heterosexist and masculinist ethical sanctions found ready camouflage. If the new common wisdom that hotly overt homophobes are men who are 'insecure about their masculinity' supplements the implausible, necessary illusion that there could be a *secure* version of masculinity ... and a stable, intelligent way for men to feel about other men in modern heterosexual capitalist patriarchy, what tighter turn could there be to the screw of an already off-centre, always at fault, endlessly blackmailable male identity ready to be manipulated into any labor of channelled violence? (*EC* 84)

Here, the claim seems to be that Freudian theory has had an oppressive

---

[6] Such a criterion seems in fact to be one that Sedgwick makes central to her own assessments of the worth of conceptualizations in this area: see *EC* 83.

as well as a liberating impact, but only as a result of the social uses to which that theory was and is put. The heterosexist consequences she specifies follow only if the Freudian developmental narrative is supplemented by the notion of a secure or stable masculine identity; and even if she is right to suppose that modern Western social formations supply such a supplementation, we have as yet no reason to suppose that Cavell's precise reading of Freud introduces anything corresponding to it. None the less, her reference to the masculinism of Freud's developmental narrative highlights precisely those aspects of Cavell's Freudian inheritance upon which certain feminists are likely to look with great suspicion; so the question arises whether the account Cavell offers in competition with Sedgwick—centring as it does around the notion of castration anxiety and a highly controversial reading of the nature of male and female desire—in fact embodies a masculinist bias.

The general point that can be made in Cavell's defence here is that such questions can all too easily make use of a simplistic model of the relation between Cavell's texts and Freud's—or more precisely, that they imagine Cavell's reliance upon Freud to be simplistic. In other words, even if we accept that charges of sexism and misogyny might successfully be made against Freud's texts, to assume that they can simply be transferred to Cavell's presupposes that his texts simply reiterate Freud's. But reiteration is the model of thinking and reading against which the Emersonian tradition as Cavell understands it sets its face, a mode of conformity entirely opposed to the aversive, transferential model of reading by being read which Cavell deems to be at the heart of his philosophical practice. It would therefore be surprising, to say the least, if his use of Freudian texts in close conjunction with a set of other texts—cinematic, philosophical, literary—were not designed as much to allow Freud's words to be questioned by those companion, competing words as to put them in question. And that in turn suggests that we should expect the Freudian concepts of which Cavell makes such central use to be themselves subject to revision or recounting.

Let us take the case of castration anxiety. One reason for regarding Cavell's reliance upon this concept as embodying a male bias arises from noting the obvious fact that castration anxiety refers to an aspect of the castration complex (itself closely linked to the Oedipus complex) which is specific to men. Laplanche and Pontalis summarize matters as follows:

[The Castration complex centres] on the phantasy of castration which is produced in response to the child's puzzlement over the anatomical difference between the sexes . . .: the child attributes this difference to the fact of the girl's penis having been cut off.

The structure and consequences of the castration complex are different in the boy and in the girl. The boy fears castration, which he sees as the carrying out of a paternal *threat* made in reply to his sexual activities; the result for him is an intense *castration anxiety*. In the girl, the absence of a penis is experienced as a wrong suffered which she attempts to deny, to compensate for or to remedy. (*LP 56*)

Given that Cavell is attempting to offer an interpetation of the relationship between scepticism and gender which can accommodate his sense of the universal accessibility of sceptical doubts, interpreting those doubts in terms of castration anxiety hardly seems to guarantee their accessibility to women. Here, however, we must recall that the postcript which assigns such centrality to castration anxiety is structured around a reading of 'The Beast in the Jungle', which itself is centred upon the anxieties of John Marcher, i.e. upon an anxious male. It is hardly surprising—and certainly not masculinist—that Cavell should attempt to interpret Marcher's frozen, fixated state in terms specifically developed to fit the male experience of the castration complex; and, although the matter is not perhaps as clearly signposted as one might wish, it is evident in the text that when Cavell shifts to discussing women whom he wishes to claim are facing the same difficulties that Marcher confronts, he analyses their behaviour in terms of their attempts to deny, compensate for, or remedy a loss suffered. The best example of this is his interpretation of Lisa in *Letter from an Unknown Woman.* Cavell attributes to her a compulsion to be desired by Stefan (a version of an idea of the fanaticism of love that he thinks of as the female counterpart of the violence of male doubt, and one which precisely inverts rather than replicates the Sedgwickian idea of Marcher's compulsion to desire), together with a desire to punish him by withholding the knowledge of his son's death—all of which can be understood as a Freudian interpretation of the female experience of the castration complex.

In other words, we must understand that it is the castration complex rather than castration anxiety that is central to Cavell's attempt to link scepticism and gender through psychoanalysis. Even then, however, the worry about an inherent male bias emerges—not because Cavell is universalizing Freudian concepts that are developed specifically to apply to male experience, but because the centrality of the notion of

castration to Freud's (and so to Cavell's) understanding of the universal
experience of the Oedipus complex might itself embody a skewing of
that theory towards the male perspective. After all, a girl could hardly
experience as serious a threat to deprive her of what she has not got.
This, however, is a problem with the Freudian perspective that has
generated a series of responses within psychoanalysis; and Laplanche
and Pontalis specify one of the more important of these revisions:

It is possible to put castration anxiety in the context of a series of traumatic
experiences which are also characterized by an element of loss of or separation
from an object: the loss of the breast in the routine of feeding; weaning;
defecation. The validity of this assimilation is confirmed by the symbolic
equivalences which psychoanalysis has brought out between the various part-
objects from which the subject is separated in this way: penis, breast, faeces, and
even the infant in childbirth. (*LP* 57)

It is clear from the text of the postscript that Cavell has very much
absorbed this revision: for a central theme of his discussion of the
castration complex is given by the concept of mourning and so of loss;
and of course, his own understanding of that concept is importantly
inflected by its place in the work of Thoreau and Emerson as we
specified it in earlier chapters. The general model of Emersonian
perfectionism, with its conception of the self as inherently divided
between its attained and attainable states and in need of an Exemplar to
help it to manage the shift from the former to the latter, in effect places
the process of mourning at the centre of human existence; for spiritual
orientation is thereby presented as an endless process of unpicking the
strands of fear, fantasy, and love that attach the self to its present
situation and allowing it to reattach itself to its next, attainable state,
which is understood in turn as a matter of gaining access at once to
individual and to intersubjective flourishing—to a living rather than a
dead self, to a true acknowledgement of the significance and the
separateness of others and to a sufficiently just rather than a suffocatingly
conforming society. Some of these familiar connections emerge when,
in a discussion of Marcher's climactic graveyard revelation, Cavell cites
the question to which he (Marcher) is prompted by his encounter with
the other male mourner:

'What had the man *had* to make him, by the loss of it, so bleed and yet live?'
The implied answer is that the question misses something. The question is not
as to what, but as to how the capacity for mourning ... comes, let us say the
capacity to let yourself matter to another, one you have found for yourself. The

positive answer, that mourning comes with the dissolution of the Oedipus complex, with the threat of the appointment or happening of castration, is going around in circles. If the necessity to mourn implies an incapacity to challenge pain, to live it, it at least shows the capacity to let pain terminate, if it will, not interminably to kill time—yours and others—by humouring it; wry sadness is not mourning. (PS 277)

Perceiving the centrality of mourning to Cavell's understanding of the castration complex and its dissolution has two important consequences. First, it constitutes an instance of the degree to which, and the manner in which, Cavell's use of Freud involves a revision of his work. Of course, the general idea of this connection is present in some of Freud's own work, and many of its more sophisticated extrapolations are perfectly familiar within the field of psychoanalytic discourse; but it does none the less constitute a repetition which is more than a simple reiteration, and it is a repetition which is in large part generated in Cavell's work by subjecting the original Freudian framework to an Emersonian critique or reclamation. And second, it is a recounting of Freud which preserves a sense of the universal accessibility of the complex, and so of the sceptical anxieties with which Cavell wishes to connect it; for, as is suggested in the passages by Cixous and Lacan that Cavell cites when discussing Modleski's alternative readings of some of the melodramas, experiences of loss (whether in relation to the penis or to other part-objects) are both accessible to and yet differently inscribed in male and female experience. Such a nuanced and open-ended revision of the concept of the castration complex is not obviously marked by sexism or misogyny.

A similar complexity attends any serious evaluation of Cavell's Freudian conception of the essential bisexuality of human character, and of the charge that this conception is itself sexist. The main difference lies in the fact that the feminist case against this central component of his analysis is one that Cavell addresses directly.

The value of the idea that masculine/feminine oscillation may be studied by mapping it onto active/passive oscillation is of course a function of how good a map you have of the active and the passive. (PS 281)

The point here, I take it, is that the assertion that such a mapping exists should neither be accepted nor dismissed—since it cannot be understood at all—in the absence of an understanding of how the concepts invoked are being employed. Taken in isolation, what such an assertion gives us is a picture; and the significance and fruitfulness of any picture depends

340

upon the value of the elucidations of it that its proponents are in a
position to proffer. And in Cavell's case, it is vital to see that his varied
and detailed analyses of the ways in which ideas of activity and
passivity are deployed and scrutinized in the texts of Emerson, Thoreau,
Wittgenstein, and his favoured comedies and melodramas are meant to
constitute his elucidation of the picture. Of course, Freud's texts make
their contribution to this elucidation, but those other texts no more
replicate Freud's own understanding of the dichotomy than his replicates theirs; rather, the fields of force and implication set up by their
interaction—some of the dimensions of which we have traced in the
preceding pages—are what constitutes Cavell's map of the active and
the passive.

For example, when Cavell associates the female inflexion of human
thought and speech with passivity, he thereby invokes not a simple
picture of masochism (crystallized in the joke, cited by Freud, about the
peasant woman who interprets her husband's failure to beat her as a
sign of diminishing love) but rather the convergent Emersonian, Heideggerian and Wittgensteinian attempts to replace a conception of thought
as a matter of grasping, ordering, and forging connections between
elements of experience with a conception of thinking as receptive, as a
process of allowing oneself to be drawn to and read by one's experience.
Moreover, the picture of thought as grasping or clutching is understood
to be a mode of activity that is essentially destructive or negating,
associated as it is with the sceptical annihilation of world and self
(dramatized in Leontes' need to negate time and its—including his
own—issue in *The Winter's Tale*), and so to be itself masochistic;
whereas the picture of thought as receptive or accepting is presented as
a strenuously active sort of passivity, a mode of powerful self-engage-
ment and self-mastery akin to the capacity for conversion as studied by
psychoanalysis in its first female patients and as recorded in the
somatograms of the cinema's most famous female stars. And at a more
general level, Cavell plainly regards orthodox Anglo-American philosophy's attempts to deny the existence of any real relationship between it
and 'low culture' (as represented for example by Hollywood films),
between it and literature, even between it and work done in the
Continental tradition or the tradition of ordinary language philosophy,
as further expressions of a destructive and masochistic mode of thinking,
further manifestations of philosophy's anxious (male) desire to secure
itself by repressing certain (female) tones of the human voice and of
human experience—tones that might be thought of as reverberations of

the ordinary within philosophy. Cavell could therefore argue that associating his vision of thinking as thanking with femaleness does not so much reiterate the rigidified and constraining cultural stereotype of passive femininity as reactivate elements of it whose value has been repressed and requires reclamation and reveal the presence of analogous rigidities and constraints in the prevailing stereotype of active masculinity. We therefore cannot dismiss his picture of male and female on the grounds that invokes a potentially reductive and oppressive binary opposition; we must rather show the precise points—if any—at which the complex, provisional, and open-ended elucidation of that opposition which emerges across the full range of his work is reductive or oppressive.

What this really means is that any genuinely illuminating critique of Cavell's work will emerge, if it does at all, only through the initiation of a detailed conversation about the fine grain of his readings of specific texts. When, for example, Cavell raises his question about the identity or location of those who suggest that the male and female tones of the human voice are restricted to one sex or gender, he pursues his answer to it by offering a detailed reading of the concluding scene from *Adam's Rib*, in which Spencer Tracy discusses the differences between men and women with Katharine Hepburn; and he implies that he would take his answer to that question to have been validated just in so far as he can bring his readers to acknowledge the accuracy and depth of his characterization of Tracy in terms which apply primarily to what he has identified as female inflexions of the human voice and of human desire. Similarly, when articulating his general theoretical disagreements with Modleski and Sedgwick, Cavell puts them to the test by expounding his alternative views of certain films and short stories upon which his interlocutors have already commented. In other words, Cavell is staking his authority as a thinker upon nothing more and nothing less than his capacity to produce readings of the fine grain of his (literary) experience which earn the acknowledgement of his readers. It is, of course, a form of authority which is inherently open to revision and repudiation, since it cannot guarantee that a better, competing interpretation will not appear on the scene: as Cavell notes, it is characteristic of the sorts of film (and other texts) he studies 'to invite competing interpretations (and of course of interpretation itself)' (PS 268). On the other hand, it is a form of authority that can only be overturned in specific ways—not by invoking a theory of social formation or of sexual identity, or rather, only by demonstrating that such a general theory can provide a richer

and more compelling reading of specific texts. Thus, the form of
Cavell's engagement with these two theorists of feminism and gender
specifies the stringent but essentially democratic terms upon which a
conversation between him and them might be pursued and the real
worth of a feminist critique of his work thereby assessed.

None the less, the pressure under which Sedgwick and Modleski's
readings place Cavell's own interpretations has at least served to
underline the founding importance of Freudian psychoanalysis in
Cavell's approach. Indeed, the very excitement and urgency with which
he attempts to appropriate the figure of the closet for his understanding
of scepticism and philosophy shows that—however much he subjects
the Freudian texts to searching revision—the sexualization of his work
that Shakespeare helped to initiate has now reached the stage at which
its intimacy with psychoanalytic conceptualizations has passed beyond
the point of intellectual divorce. In an earlier chapter, I argued that
psychoanalysis played a threefold role in Cavell's project, providing
him with interpretative tools, a model of reading and a further identifiable phase or mode in the history of the modern cultural battle against
the sceptical impulse. However, the text of the postscript is saturated
with psychoanalytic terminology and modes of analysis to a degree
which strongly suggests a gradual but inexorable commitment on
Cavell's part to the psychoanalytic framework as one within which
further work must be done; it is as if, having highlighted the contribution
psychoanalysis can make to the overcoming of scepticism, he has now
decided that his own work must itself form part of that contribution.[7]
This does not entail that this work will not include significant revisions
to that framework; but it does entail that Cavell will not be able to
regard that framework as simply one competing perspective. And as a
result, he will not be able to ignore criticisms of that perspective as a
matter that is impertinent to his own project. He will not, for example,
be able simply to note that 'psychoanalysis has not surmounted the
obscurities of the philosophical problematic it inherits of representation
and reality ... [continuing] to shrink before the derivative question, for
example, of whether the stories of its patients are fantasy merely or
(also?) of reality, and [continuing] to waver between regarding the
question as irrelevant to its work and as of the essence of it', and to
suggest that 'The matter is to express the intuition that fantasy shadows
anything we can understand reality to be' (*IIS* 28); he must rather

[7] This is a shift which might retrospectively be seen as signalled by a passage in *IIS*
22–3.

attempt to penetrate these obscurities and find helpful words with which to express and explore such critical intuitions. And in particular, he must acknowledge that a conversation with feminist critics of Freudianism is no longer a matter of manners or tactics; it is a necessity.

BIBLIOGRAPHY

AUSTIN, J. L., *Philosophical Papers*, ed. J. O. Urmson and G. J. Warnock, 3rd edn. (Oxford University Press: Oxford, 1979).

BUDICK, S., and ISER, W. (eds.), *Languages of the Unsayable: The Play of Negativity in Literature and Literary Theory* (Columbia University Press: New York, 1989).

CAVELL, S., *Must We Mean What We Say?* (Cambridge University Press: Cambridge, 1969).

—— *The World Viewed: Enlarged Edition* (Harvard University Press: Cambridge Mass., 1979).

—— *The Claim of Reason* (Oxford University Press: Oxford, 1979).

—— *The Senses of Walden: An Expanded Edition* (North Point Press: San Francisco, 1981).

—— *Pursuits of Happiness: The Hollywood Comedy of Remarriage* (Harvard University Press: Cambridge, Mass., 1981).

—— *Themes Out of School: Effects and Causes* (North Point Press: San Francisco, 1984).

—— 'The Division of Talent', *Critical Inquiry*, 11 (June 1985), 519–38.

—— 'What Photography Calls Thinking', *Raritan*, 4 (1985), 1–21.

—— *Disowning Knowledge: In Six Plays of Shakespeare* (Cambridge University Press: Cambridge, 1987).

—— 'Psychoanalysis and Cinema: The Melodrama of the Unknown Woman', in Smith and Kerrigan (eds.), *Images in Our Souls*. A short extract from this article, with additional footnotes, was published in Meltzer (ed.), *The Trial(s) of Psychoanalysis*.

—— *In Quest of the Ordinary: Lines of Scepticism and Romanticism* (University of Chicago Press: Chicago, 1988).

—— 'Naughty Orators: Negation of Voice in Gaslight', in Budick and Iser (eds.), *Languages of the Unsayable*.

—— *This New Yet Unapproachable America: Lectures after Emerson after Wittgenstein* (Living Batch Press: Albuquerque, N. Mex., 1989).

—— 'Who Disappoints Whom?', *Critical Inquiry*, 15 (Spring 1989), 606–10.

—— *Conditions Handsome and Unhandsome: The Constitution of Emersonian Perfectionism* (University of Chicago Press: Chicago, 1990).

—— 'Postscript: To Whom It May Concern', *Critical Inquiry*, 16 (1990), 248–89.

—— 'Reply to Modleski', Critical Inquiry, 16 (1990), 238–44.

—— 'Ugly Duckling, Funny Butterfly: Bette Davis and *Now Voyager*', *Critical Inquiry*, 16 (1990), 213–47.

—— 'In the Meantime', *The Yale Journal of Criticism*, 5/2 (1992), 229–37.

—— 'Macbeth Appalled' (unpublished).

CONANT, J., 'Nietzsche's Perfectionism: A Reading of "Schopenhauer as Educator"' (unpublished).

Bibliography

DESCARTES, R., *Meditations* (Dent: London, 1912).

EMERSON, R.W., *The Collected Works of Ralph Waldo Emerson*, ii, ed. A. R. Ferguson and J. Ferguson Carr (Harvard University Press: Cambridge, Mass., 1979).

—— *Selected Essays*, ed. L. Ziff (Penguin: London, 1982).

FISCHER, M., *Stanley Cavell and Literary Skepticism* (University of Chicago Press: Chicago, 1989).

FLEMING, R., and PAYNE, M. (eds.), *The Senses of Stanley Cavell* (Bucknell University Press: Lewisburg, Pa., 1989).

FREUD, S., *The Standard Edition of the Complete Psychological Works of Sigmund Freud*, ed. L. Strachey (Hogarth Press: London, 1953-74).

GRICE, P., *Studies in the Way of Words* (Harvard University Press: Cambridge, Mass., 1989).

HANSEN, K., 'Being Doubted, Being Assured', in Smith and Kerrigan (eds.), *Images in Our Souls*.

HEIDEGGER, M., *Being and Time*, trans. J. Macquarrie and E. Robinson (Blackwell: Oxford, 1962).

JAMES, H., *The Complete Tales*, ed. L. Edel (Rupert Hart-Davis: London, 1964).

KANT, I., *Critique of Pure Reason*, trans. N. Kemp Smith (Macmillan: London, 1929).

—— *Prolegomena to Any Future Metaphysics*, trans. L. Beck (Bobbs-Merrill: Indianapolis, 1950).

—— *Critique of Judgement*, trans. J. C. Meredith (Oxford University Press: Oxford, 1952).

KIERKEGAARD, S., *Works of Love*, ed. H. V. and E. H. Hong (Collins: London, 1962).

—— *Fear and Trembling* (together with *Repetition*), ed. and trans. H. V. and E. H. Hong (Princeton University Press: Princeton, NJ, 1983).

LAPLANCHE, J., and PONTALIS, J. B., *The Language of Psychoanalysis* (Karnac Books: London, 1988).

MacINTYRE, A., *Whose Justice, Which Rationality?* (Duckworth: London, 1988).

MALCOLM, N., *Thought and Knowledge* (Cornell University Press: Ithaca, NY, 1977).

MELTZER, F. (ed.), *The Trial(s) of Psychoanalysis* (University of Chicago Press: Chicago, 1988).

MODLESKI, T., 'Reply to Cavell', *Critical Inquiry*, 16 (1990), 237-8.

—— *Feminism without Women* (Routledge: London, 1991).

MULHALL, S., *On Being in the World: Wittgenstein and Heidegger on Seeing Aspects* (Routledge: London, 1990).

—— and SWIFT, A., *Liberals and Communitarians* (Blackwell: Oxford, 1992).

RAWLS, J., *A Theory of Justice* (Harvard University Press: Cambridge, Mass., 1971).

—— 'Kantian Constructivism in Moral Theory', *Journal of Philosophy*, 77/9 (1980), 515-72.

RORTY, R., *Contingency, Irony and Solidarity* (Cambridge University Press: Cambridge, 1989).

SEDGWICK, E., *Between Men: English Literature and Male Homosocial Desire* (Columbia University Press: New York, 1985).

—— 'The Beast in the Closet: James and the Writing of Homosexual Panic', in Yeazell (ed.), *Sex, Politics and Science in the Nineteenth-Century Novel*; repr. in Sedgwick, *Epistemology of the Closet*.

—— *Epistemology of the Closet* (Harvester Wheatsheaf: London, 1990).

SHAKESPEARE, W., *The Complete Works*, ed. S. Wells and G. Taylor (Oxford University Press: Oxford, 1986).

SMITH, J. H., and KERRIGAN, W. (eds.), *Images in Our Souls: Cavell, Psychoanalysis and Cinema* (Johns Hopkins University Press: Baltimore, Md., 1987).

TAYLOR, C., *Sources of the Self: The Making of the Modern Identity* (Cambridge University Press: Cambridge, 1989).

THOREAU, H., 'Civil Disobedience', in *The Portable Thoreau*, rev. edn., ed. C. Bode (Penguin: London, 1964).

—— *Walden*, in *The Portable Thoreau*, rev. edn., ed. C. Bode (Penguin: London, 1964).

WEIL, S., *Gravity and Grace* (Routledge: London, 1952).

—— *The Simone Weil Reader*, ed. G. A. Panichas (David McKay: New York, 1977).

WISDOM, J., *Other Minds* (Blackwell: Oxford, 1952).

WITTGENSTEIN, L., *Philosophical Investigations*, trans. G. E. M. Anscombe, (Blackwell: Oxford, 1953).

—— *Culture and Value*, ed. G. H. von Wright, trans. P. Winch (Blackwell: Oxford, 1980).

YEAZELL, R. (ed.), *Sex, Politics and Science in the Nineteenth-Century Novel* (Johns Hopkins University Press: Baltimore, Md., 1986).

INDEX